PASCALE ARGOD

The Art of Sketching

400 years of travel diaries

promopress

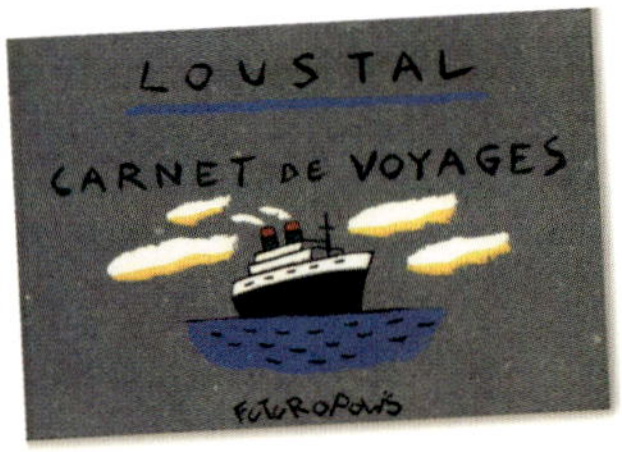

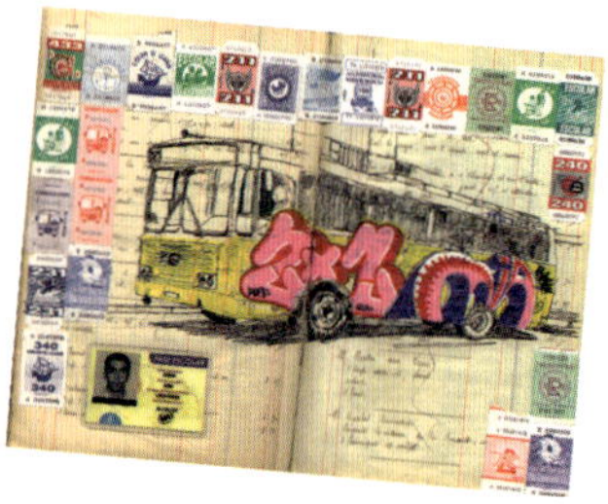

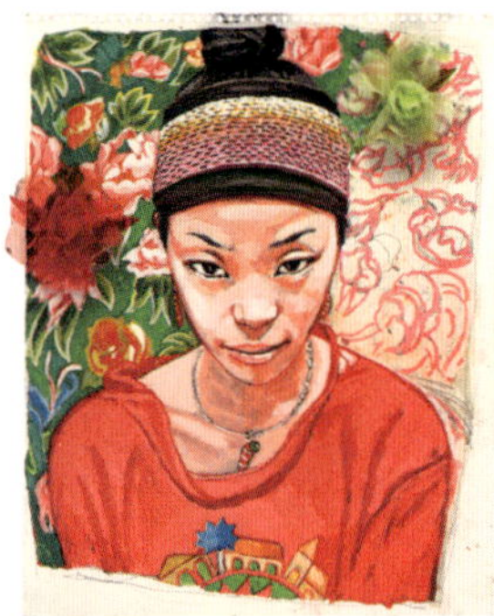

• *From top to bottom: Loustal (*Carnet de voyages, *Futuropolis, 1990), Julien "Seth" Malland (*Globe-painter, *Alternatives, 2007) and Titouan Lamazou (*Zoé Zoé femmes du monde, *Gallimard, 2007).*

• *Right-hand page, from top to bottom: Emmanuel Michel (*Cuba New York: peinture, sculpture, *Elytis, 2013), Fabrice Moireau (Japan diary) and Stéphanie Ledoux (Istanbul diary).*

Contents

4 INTRODUCTION

A GENRE THROUGH HISTORY

8 **THE MEETING OF THE ARTS AND THE HUMAN SCIENCES**

9 **FORMATIVE TRAVELS** – THE HUMANIST'S TRAINING – THE TRIP TO ITALY – THE *VEDUTA*, MEMENTO OF AN ITALIAN JOURNEY

12 **DISCOVERING THE WORLD AND THE NATURAL SCIENCES** – THE JOURNEY TO THE AMERICAS – BOTANISTS' AND NATURALISTS' CIRCUMNAVIGATIONS – GEOGRAPHERS' SCIENTIFIC EXPEDITIONS – THE EVOLUTION OF THE SPECIES – LA SOCIÉTÉ DE GÉOGRAPHIE AND LA SOCIÉTÉ DES EXPLORATEURS FRANÇAIS

15 **OUTDOOR PAINTING** – THE "PICTURESQUE" AESTHETIC – ENGLISH WATERCOLOUR, TOPOGRAPHICAL DRAWING AND ARCHITECTURAL DETAIL – FROM ROMANTICISM TO IMPRESSIONISM

18 **THE CALL OF THE EAST** – THE TASTE FOR EXOTICISM AND EGYPTOLOGY – THE GRAND TOUR SKETCHED BY WRITER-ARTISTS – ORIENTALIST PAINTERS' TRAVEL DIARIES – EUGÈNE DELACROIX'S DIARIES – NAVAL PAINTERS AND THEIR JOURNEY DIARIES – THE TOURIST CRAZE

22 **THE ART OF REPORTAGE** – THE BIRTH OF VISUAL AND TRAVEL REPORTAGE – FROM PRESS CARTOONS TO THE RISE OF THE COMIC STRIP – THE DRAWN TRAVEL REPORTAGE BOOK – PICTURESQUE PUBLICATIONS AND THE BIRTH OF ETHNOLOGY AND ANTHROPOLOGY

25 **FROM ETHNOGRAPHY TO THE ESTABLISHMENT OF THE HUMAN SCIENCES** – THE ETHNOLOGIST-ANTHROPOLOGIST'S DIARY – FROM ETHNOGRAPHIC ALBUM TO ETHNOGRAPHIC CINEMA – ART MEETS ETHNOGRAPHY: THE WORKS OF PAUL GAUGUIN

HYBRIDITY IN THE TWENTIETH AND TWENTY-FIRST CENTURIES

30 **FROM ARTISTS' BOOKS TO INTERARTISTIC WORKS**

32 **LEGACIES FROM ARTISTIC MOVEMENTS** – THE ARTIST'S BOOK – COLLAGE ART, CUBISM AND THE DADA MOVEMENT – POP ART AND THE JUXTAPOSITION OF HETEROGENEOUS IMAGES – MAIL ART AND THE FLUXUS MOVEMENT

36 **INSPIRATION FROM CONTEMPORARY ARTISTS** – MATHURIN MÉHEUT (1822–1958): POLYMORPHIC AND ETHNOGRAPHIC DIARIES – LE CORBUSIER (1887–1965): ARCHITECTURE DIARIES – JEAN DUBUFFET (1901–1985): ABSTRACT NOTES AND DIARIES – ZAO WOU-KI (1921–2013): DIARIES AND MIXES – PETER BEARD (BORN 1938): DIARIES AND COLLAGES – CLAUDE LAGOUTTE (1935–1990): JOURNEY FRAGMENTS – MAX PAM (BORN 1949): SCRAPBOOKS – MIQUEL BARCELÓ (BORN 1957): DIARIES AND NOMADIC INSTALLATIONS – HERVÉ DI ROSA (BORN 1959): DIARIES OF THE ARTS MODESTES – TONY SOULIÉ (BORN 1955): PHOTO-PAINTING DIARIES – JEAN PATTOU (BORN 1940): DIARIES OF URBAN PAINTINGS – JULIEN "SETH" MALLAND (BORN 1972): STREET ART DIARIES

42 **ARTISTIC AND LITERARY GENRES** – TRAVEL LITERATURE AND TRAVELLING WRITERS – "DRAWN" OR "GRAPHIC" LITERATURE – PHOTOGRAPHERS ON THE ROAD – THE EMERGENCE OF A PUBLISHING GENRE IN FRANCE – TRAVEL GUIDES AND ILLUSTRATION

48 **CONTEMPORARY TRENDS** – TOWARDS THE ARTIST'S TRAVEL BOOK – TOWARDS DRAWN REPORTAGE – TOWARDS THE ILLUSTRATED TRAVEL GUIDE – TOWARDS MEDIA CIRCULATION AND COMBINING ARTS – TOWARDS DIGITAL AND TRANSMEDIA

ARTISTIC TECHNIQUES

56 **TRAVELLING AND LOOKING: THE ARTIST AS EYEWITNESS AND TRAVELLER**

57 **CHARACTERISTICS** – REPORTING AND WITNESSING – THE TEXT-IMAGE LINK OR THE ICONOTEXTUAL – NARRATION THROUGH IMAGES IN DIARIES – THE ITINERARY AND THE MENTAL MAP

60 **TECHNIQUES** – ADAPTING GRAPHIC ARTS TO TRAVEL – AWAKENING THE SENSES – PORTRAIT ART

64 **TRAVEL TIME AND CREATION TIME** – GRAPHIC REPORTAGE AND SKETCHING – IN THE FIELD AND IN THE STUDIO – THE CONCEPTUAL APPROACH – FROM THE PALIMPSEST TO THE FUTURE WORK

66 **ARTISTIC INNOVATION AND CREATIVITY** – THE MIXING OF GRAPHIC ARTS AND FREE EXPRESSION – THE PATCHWORK AESTHETIC AND COLLAGE – THE LIVRE-OBJET AND DIARY FORMS – COMBINING MEDIA

TYPES OF TRAVEL DIARY

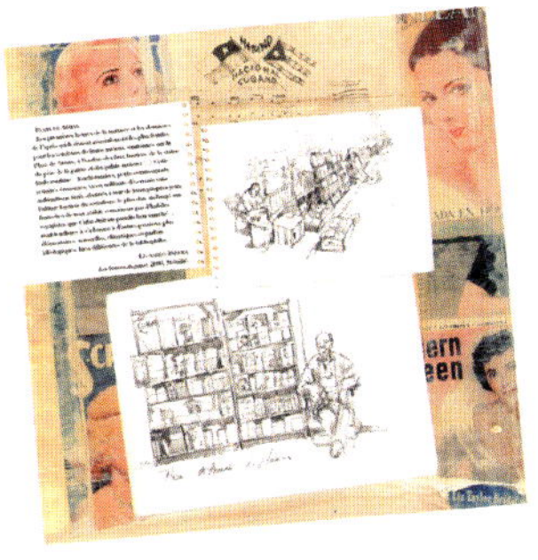

72 **A GENRE OF ARTS, WRITING AND TRAVEL**

74 **REPORTAGE DIARIES** – REPORTAGE DIARIES AND "CARNETS DU MONDE" – ILLUSTRATED COURT DIARIES – DIARIES ON SOCIETY – DIARIES FOR ENCOUNTERS AND PORTRAITS – HUMANITARIAN DIARIES – WAR DIARIES – DIARIES OF CULTURAL AND GEOPOLITICAL DIVERSITY – SEAFARERS' LOGBOOKS – SCIENTIFIC EXPEDITION DIARIES – GEOGRAPHERS' DIARIES – PERFORMANCE DIARIES

90 **HERITAGE DIARIES** – REGIONAL HERITAGE DIARIES – ARCHITECTURE DIARIES – MEMORY DIARIES – ETHNOGRAPHIC DIARIES – INTERCULTURAL DIARIES – CULTURAL EXPEDITION DIARIES – ITINERARY DIARIES – URBAN DIARIES – ARCHAEOLOGY DIARIES – GEOLOGY DIARIES – NATURALIST DIARIES – DIARIES ON FOODS AND FLAVOURS

106 **INTERMEDIA DIARIES** – EXHIBITION AND INSTALLATION TRAVEL DIARIES – TRAVEL DIARIES ON STAGE – AURAL TRAVEL DIARIES – AUDIOVISUAL TRAVEL DIARIES – MULTIMEDIA DIARIES – DIGITAL AND ANIMATED TRAVEL DIARIES – WEB DIARIES

TRAVEL DIARY ARTISTS

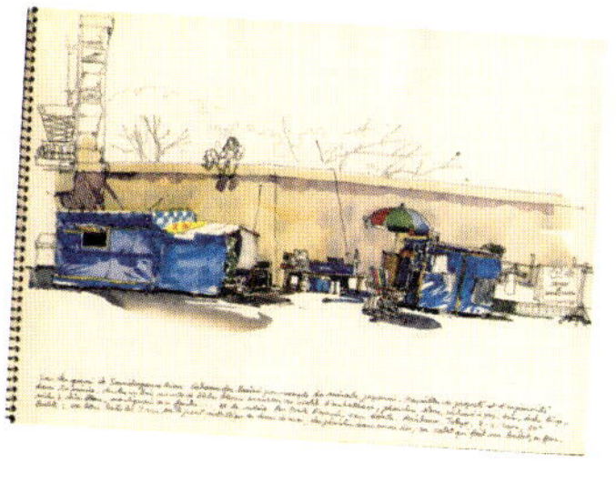

114 BRUNO PILORGET — BERTRAND DE MIOLLIS — CATHY BEAUVALLET — ELSIE HERBERSTEIN — DAMIEN CHAVANAT — NOËLLE HERRENSCHMIDT — DENIS CLAVREUL — ALAN JOHNSTON — ARNAUD D'AUNAY — PHILIPPE DELORD — GIANCARLO ILIPRANDI — EMMANUEL MICHEL — CLAIRE AND RENO MARCA — TITOUAN LAMAZOU — VINCENT DESPLANCHE — URBAN SKETCHERS — SIMON — LES CARNETTISTES TRIBULANTS — STEFANO FARAVELLI — FABRICE MOIREAU — LIZZIE NAPOLI — DAMIEN ROUDEAU — FRANÇOISE CAILLETTE-DENEUBOURG — STÉPHANIE LEDOUX — GWENAËLLE TROLEZ — CATHERINE LEGRAND — PATRICK CHAPPATTE — BASTIEN DUBOIS — KAREN GUILLOREL — DAVID LOPEZ — JULIE SARPERI — EMMANUELLE TROY — EDMOND BAUDOUIN — TROUB'S — CHARLES BERBERIAN — JACQUES FERRANDEZ — LOUSTAL — MARC P.G. BERTHIER — OFFICIAL PAINTERS OF THE ARMED FORCES — MICHEL MONTIGNÉ — ALAIN BOULDOUYRE — NICOLAS VANIER

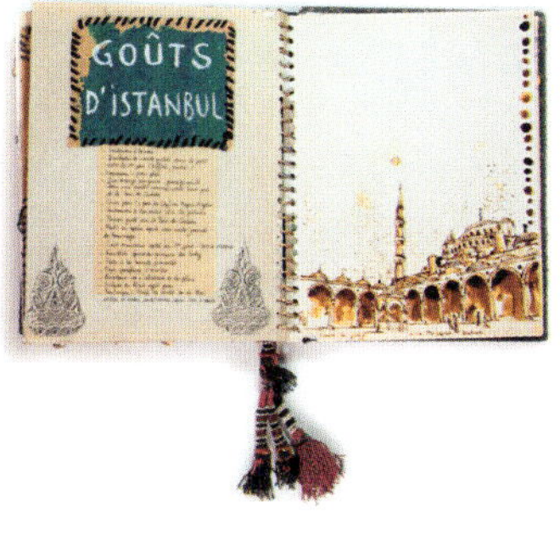

156 CLERMONT-FERRAND'S RENDEZ-VOUS DU CARNET DE VOYAGE

158 BIBLIOGRAPHY – ACKNOWLEDGEMENTS – PHOTO CREDITS

Introduction

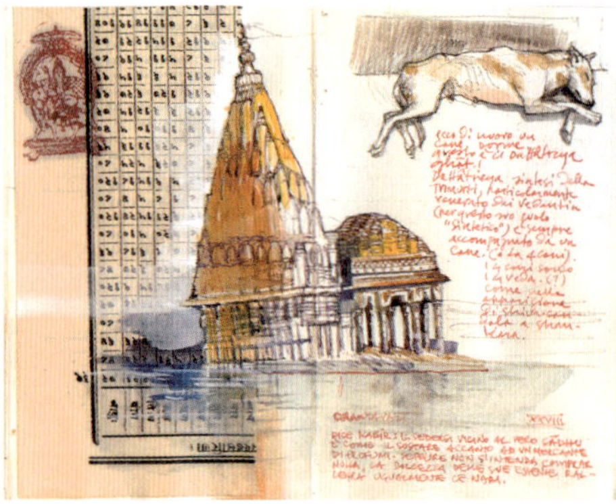

• *Ci-dessus : Stefano Faravelli*
*(*India, per vedere l'elefante*, EDT, 2007).*

• *Ci-contre, en haut : Denis Clavreul*
*(*Les Jardins ouvriers*, Gallimard, 2006).*
Ci-contre, en bas : Bruno Pilorget
*(*Bao Nguyen, artiste vietnamien*, 2005).*

A HYBRID WORK OF ART

A study visit to Italy with the Académie de France of Rome, English watercolours or one of nascent romanticism's picturesque tours: all have represented artistic journeys into new horizons and sources of artistic renewal for painters—whether Orientalists or official naval artists—since the nineteenth century. Illustration, which serves the purpose of "enlightening the text" and which was thriving in 1830, blossomed with the spread of pictorial publications. Lithography, meanwhile, paved the way for the publishing of art books, a form of dialogue between poets and painters. Caught between illustrated reportage and Orientalists' exotic illustrations—and also between travel guides and artists' books—the travel diary has swung between a journalistic documentary style and visual expression. The genre therefore seems to lie at the heart of the conundrum of graphic arts and the art of illustration. The artistic movements of the twentieth century introduced the juxtaposition of composite, mixed and heterogeneous images, elements that give the contemporary travel diary, which falls between artist's book and personal travel account, its originality. But does the travel diary fit in more within the tradition of the artist's book or that of the album?

Between text and images, the travel diary borrows as much from travel literature as it does from the visual arts, including photography. Its illustrations and the reporting function of its text put the travel diary in a genre that is both artistic and literary—one that is conducive to a reflection on the mixing of disciplines and that maintains a duality between autobiography and reportage, between artistic and documentary production, and between a personal view and an engaged or journalistic one. Writer-travellers, sketch artists and illustrators (in particular American ones) of drawn or graphic literature and road photographers with their photo albums: all contributed to the emergence of a new genre of publishing from the 1980s that involves artists' and travel books, sketched reportage, illustrated travel guides and multimedia and interartistic works.

Through its artistic hybridity, the travel diary has inspired, following on from Mathurin Méheut, contemporary artists of all shapes and sizes, from illustrators and architects to creators of **arts modestes** and street artists. Arnaud d'Aunay, Stefano Faravelli, Titouan Lamazou, Emmanuel Michel, Simon and Patrick Singh are all as well known for their travel diaries as they are for their pictorial works. Over the course of the different movements of the nineteenth and twentieth centuries, travel diaries have been shaped by the techniques used within them, by an interplay between time spent travelling and time spent creating, and by an innovative creativity, all of which have transformed this simple format into a work of art and also caused its definition to evolve continually.

Nowadays, the travel diary is a unique publishing speciality. It is a typically French phenomenon that can be explained by the development of the human sciences (and, in particular, of anthropology and geography), by the importance of former colonies and the French-speaking world, by Orientalist trends and the sort of outdoor painting that was dear to the impressionists, and probably also by a type of education that is grounded in discovering the world and in personal expression and a curiosity about the Other. Whether he or she is an adventurer or just a tourist, in a society based on communication and information that encourages media exposure, the digital and blogging, every traveller wants to share his or her personal experience. Various media draw on the travel diary: reportage cartoons, TV shows on exotic destinations, graphic reportage in the press and audio diaries on the radio. The new generation of travel diary makers, while still illustrators, painters and visual artists, have become digital authors and producers by working with both paper and digital formats.

NARRATING THROUGH IMAGES AND GRAPHICAL REPORTAGE

The travel diary is a literary and artistic genre that is composite and plural, heterogeneous and subjective. It is a legacy of the sketchbooks of Turner, Delacroix and Gauguin and of anthropologists' research journals. Engaging in an art of experimentation, which fosters a sensitive outlook on the Other, allows identity to be expressed through a quest for authenticity, turning it into a personal tool for research and creative inspiration for painters and photographers, but also into a medium for reflection on cultural differences and curiosities for exploring ethnographers and anthropologists, combining images, narration, styles and genres. The narration is carried out primarily through images—rough sketches taken on the spot—that give an account of the journey in an almost cinematographic way, following the example of Delacroix's *Album du Maroc*, in which a multitude of drawings and viewpoints transcribe wanderings through a medina without using text. This travel diary is also a milestone in the history of the genre; it is a work of art in its own right that seems to be an intersection of artist's book, graphic novel and storyboard.

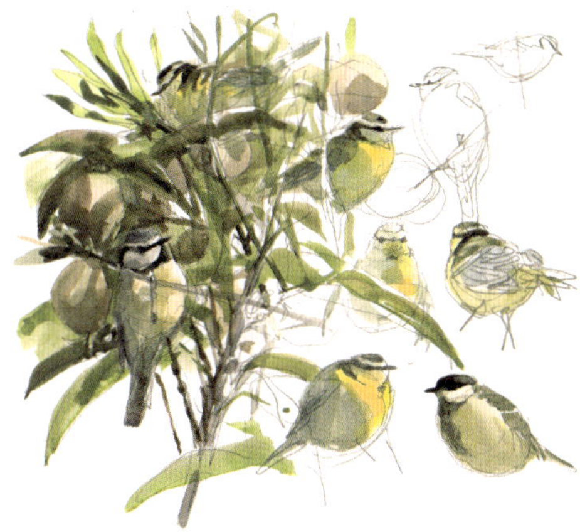

Artist's book

A legacy of the dialogue between poet and painter, the travel diary is both an illustrated book that provides full freedom of expression and an artist's book, a work of art "whose only author is an artist who has chosen to work with the form of the modern book."[1] Travel diaries are often at first glance artists' books about travelling, which can then become publishing projects in the form of classic albums that are sometimes formatted by the publisher to fit into a collection and are far removed from the original artisanal version.

Graphic novel

The geographical path and the layout of the travel diary seem to have certain similarities with the graphic novel, as is shown, for example, by *La Ballade de la mer salée* and *Mû, la cité perdue* by Hugo Pratt and *Big City* by Will Eisner. This type of production is based around double-page spreads that do not use boxes or a predefined layout, with each page providing a perspective device that varies based on a change of location, a movement, or even a journey. Moreover, visual creativity often takes precedence over the text, which is usually reduced to a legend that conveys the feeling of the author or clarifies things that can only be communicated by writing, a vector for the autobiographical aspect.

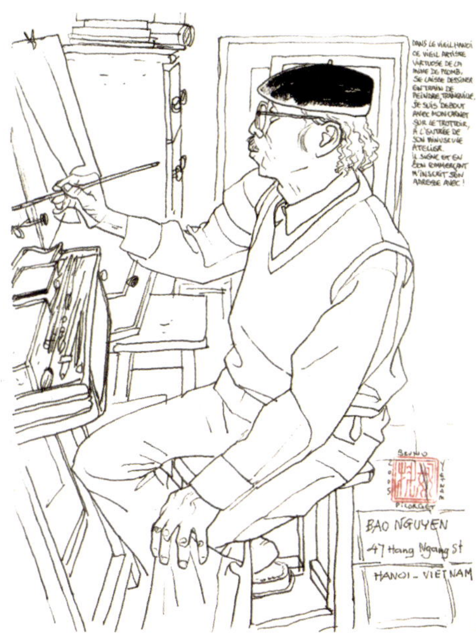

Storyboard

Storyboards, which give a visual version of the editing of a film sequence, appear to have connections to travel diaries. The narration of the camera's spatial movement that is sketched could be compared with the travel diary maker's own narrative. He or she transcribes his or her journey, encounters and experiences and translates space and movements through an image composition and a layout produced through sketches. The juxtaposition of images and a fragmentary or synthetic representation are signs of a form of visual thinking that the graphic arts and cinema have in common.[2] Moreover, the first published travel diaries drew on them: *L'Étoile oubliée de Laurie Bloom – Los Angeles, 1984* by Enki Bilal and Pierre Christin, a panoramic "road-movie album," and *L'Autre-là, carnet de voyage* by Jacques Faton and Christian Coppin (L'Atelier d'édition, 1996), which recounts the shooting of animation films in refugee camps in the former Yugoslavia.

1. Anne Moeglin-Delcroix, *Esthétique du livre d'artiste - 1960-1980 : une introduction à l'art contemporain*, Le mot et le reste/Bibliothèque nationale, 2012.
2. Eisenstein, *Le Film, sa forme, son sens*, Bourgeois, 1976.

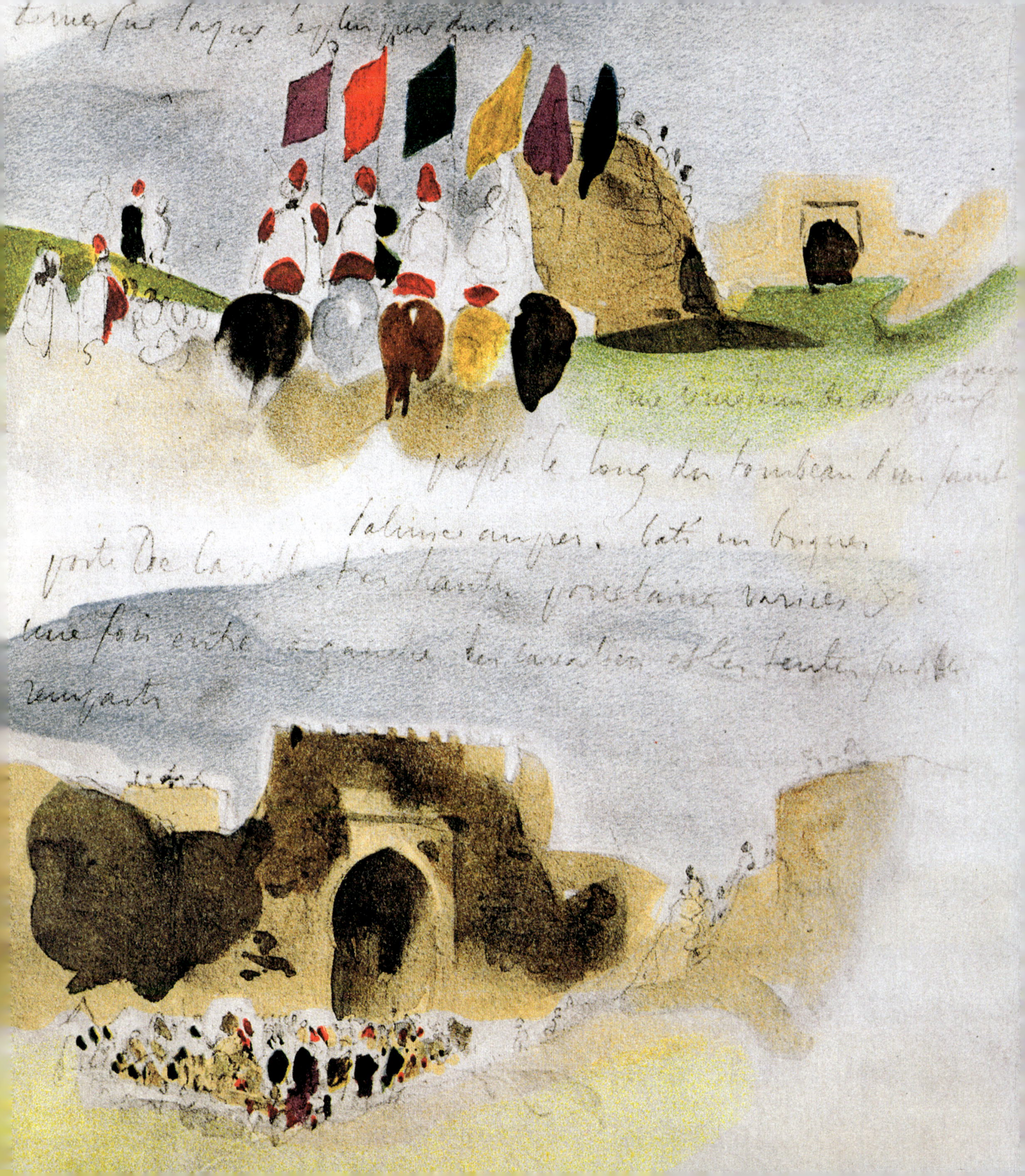
passé le long du tombeau d'un saint
porte de la ville très haute
porcelaines variées
remparts

A genre through history

The meeting of the arts and the human sciences

The journey that a travel diary focuses on is the pivot of its iconographic narration. The desire of the explorer to share his or her discoveries engenders the writing of the story, the compiling of fragments and the representation of the things seen. Illustrated reports disseminate knowledge of *terrae incognitae*, popularize natural and geographical discoveries and bear witness to the horizons and the world beyond the seas and physical and mental borders. Representing the unknown and the invisible means going beyond boundaries, something that is reflected in a polymorphous publishing genre that is at the fringes of others. The travel diary, a crucible for science and the arts, puts graphical art in the service of the sciences and their dissemination. The representation of the foreign, fed by legends, exoticism and a quest for the truth, is ambiguous, as Plato's myth of the cave demonstrates. Scientific iconography's rigorous representation merges with the sense of artistic and literary wonder of the traveller or explorer, who projects a fantasized vision onto the lived reality. During the Enlightenment, ethnographic inquiries had the objective of alleviating these metamorphoses of the image and working towards scientific goals. Accounts from the time show us that, in his relationship with the Other, man constructed a world of images that made the unknown intelligible. The illustrated works from which contemporary travel diaries stem took various forms. During the nineteenth century, diaries and travel journals, tools that went hand in hand and that allowed the exotic vision of other places to be objectivized, would henceforth be used to record ethnographic observations.

However, between the "tour of Italy" of Renaissance artists and until the Orientalists, graphic art tended to dissociate itself from its object of study to acquire its own artistic recognition, doing so through drawing and sketching, the peak of which came through English watercolour during the romantic era. The travel diary is thus part of the lineage of artistic endeavour—a source for creating pictures and for picturesque inspiration. Depending on the artistic technique used (drawing, watercolour or photography), the medium has accompanied the travelling artist's exploration in different ways, fluctuating between an artistic approach and an ethnographic one. The "academic travel diary"[1] style has tended to move towards freer forms of expression. From the Renaissance, the forces of education and the discovering the world motivated travel, especially to Italy, which was recorded in various forms of books, such as collections, journals and codices. In the eighteenth century, the human sciences and outdoor painting saw watercolour as the technique that was best suited to reproducing reality and detailing natural specimens or the topography of landscapes while travelling. Trips to the Americas, the circumnavigations of botanists and naturalists, the scientific expeditions of geographers and the research of zoologists ushered in the apogee of the natural sciences and geography through the creation of the Société de géographie de Paris and the Société des explorateurs français. The call of the East stimulated appetites for the exotic, encouraging writers and painters seeking artistic inspiration to discover new places, sites and subjects. Picturesque publications, guides and travel mementos all contributed to the growth of tourism. From the nineteenth century, works on travel became more ethnographic than picturesque, taking a turn towards reportage and the human sciences. Three approaches that characterize contemporary travel diary trends emerged: the ethnographic orientation of Delacroix and Gauguin, the reportage of Guys and Régamey, and the comedy of manners of Doré and Töpffer.

---

1. Farid Abdelouahab, *Ces merveilleux carnets de voyage*, Sélection du Reader's Digest, 2004.

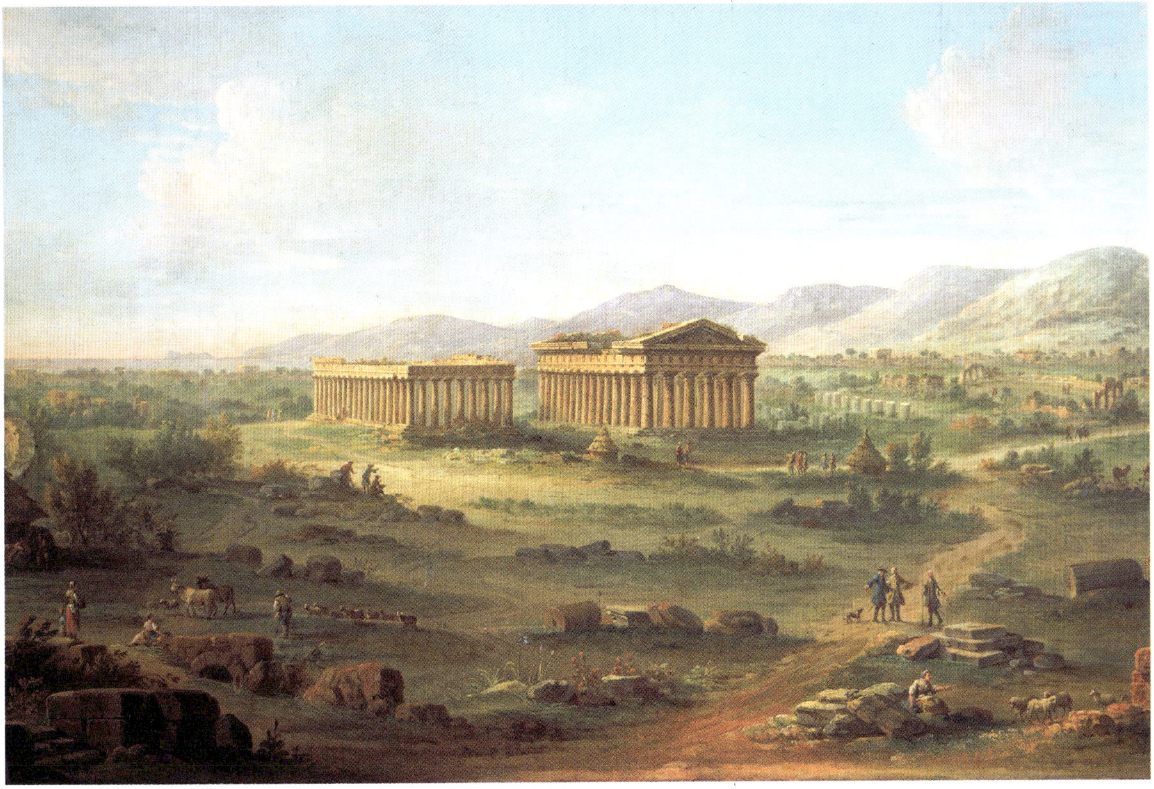

• *Italy (Paestum), an obligatory destination for artists in training from the Renaissance, as seen by John Robert Cozens (1752–1797).*

1. Formative travels

THE HUMANIST'S TRAINING

Guides and accounts by writers are a distant part of the origins of the travelogue. There is, for example, the *Mirabilia*, which refer to the seven mandatory stations of the pilgrim and which suggested, during the sixteenth century, visiting ancient Rome according to the *Topographia antiquae Romae* of Marliani; the *creanciale* (credential), the book of the Camino de Santiago pilgrim, a sort of "passport" containing a summarized itinerary; or *Le Guide des chemins de France*, which was published in 1552 by Charles Estienne and republished a dozen times, even though it was devoid of maps and travelling was indissociable from pilgrimages at the time.

Trips to Italy, born during the Renaissance under the impetus of writers—for example Rabelais, Magny, Du Bellay and Montaigne—looking for ancient culture, initiated the earliest reporting and stimulated a taste for observation. For example, in his *Journal de voyage*, Montaigne traces the habits and customs of Germany, Switzerland and Italy, countries he visited in 1580 and 1581, and advocates travel as a way of opening the mind to humanism. Some artists are known for their curious wanderings: Dürer and Bruegel travelled to Italy in 1552, and then to the Tyrol and Switzerland the following year. And Savery spent time in Prague between 1605 and 1610. Dürer travelled to northern Italy from 1494, especially to Venice, and perhaps to Padua and Mantua, where a decisive meeting with Jacopo de Barbari shaped his aesthetic. Sensitive to the landscape he crossed on the way back, he produced watercolours that reveal a great art of observation. Between 1505 and 1507, he travelled in Italy once more, staying in Venice. He then went to Switzerland (1519) and the Netherlands (1520), where he wrote a journal that was enriched by his studying of the Flemish masters and his exchanges with the humanist Erasmus and many painters. In the journal, he notes the discoveries of explorers (animals and treasures from the New World) and Luther's theses that reflect sixteenth-century humanism. Twenty years later, he followed the waterways of the Main, Rhine and Meuse. During these travels, he would put his name to more than two thousand sketches or drawings of various sorts, including portraits, religious or secular scenes, animals, landscapes, plants, architecture and decorations. His repertoire of models provided him with a reservoir of inspiration. Leonardo da Vinci made the link between scientific diaries and diaries for artistic inspiration by defining the diary above all as a "research diary," in which drawings provide a way to experiment and demonstrate. Under his instigation, graphic art came to serve science for the first time and demonstrated linkages between research disciplines.

In the sixteenth and seventeenth centuries, students who set off to Germany and the Netherlands to spend time at the universities (*peregrinatio academica*) and meet the learned did so under the initiative of the first book aimed at facilitating student mobility, the *Album amicorum*. This practice spread to France (Paris, Montpellier and Poitiers) and then to Italy (Bologna, Padua, Pisa and Rome), the must-see destination for men of letters and nobles during the eighteenth century. A young aristocrat's recounting of his journey from Florence to Rome facilitated his entry into cultured society and the elite. The Grand Tour, born around 1695, confirmed the ideas expressed by Locke in *Some Thoughts Concerning Education* (1693), and it caused the aristocratic youth to converge on Italy. During the Enlightenment, Lalande's *Le Voyage d'un François en Italie fait dans les années 1765 et 1766* marked the advent of the travel journal, which most often took the form of correspondence or reports. The private journal, which would announce the arrival of romanticism, then appeared, as did the philosophical journey instigated by Voltaire and Rousseau, who in *Émile ou de l'éducation* expresses his anger at the superficial nature of the aristocracy's travels.

• *In his* Album amicorum *during the seventeenth century, the student Michael van Meer described an ancient form of land sailing, which he witnessed on a beach in Holland.*

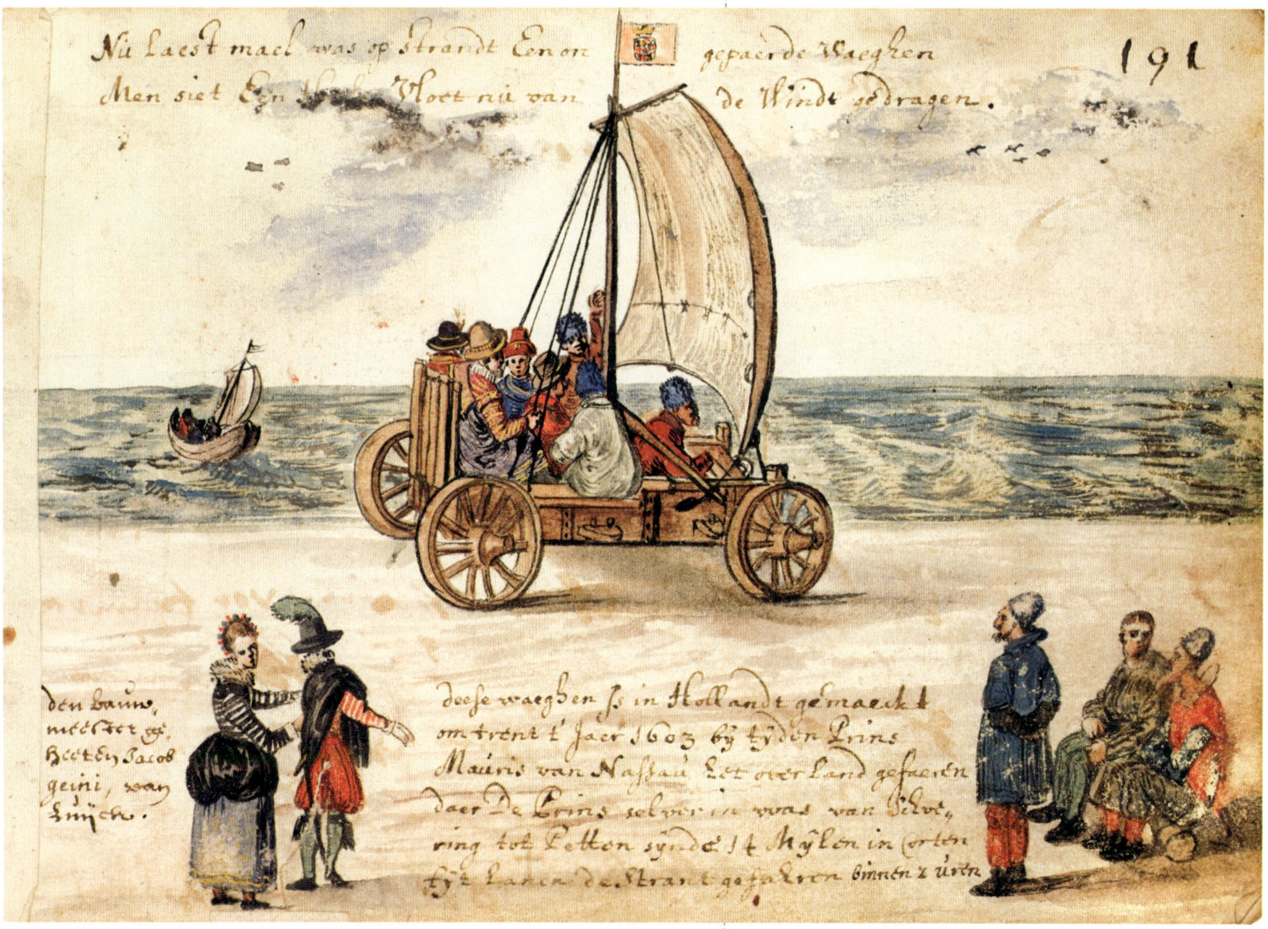

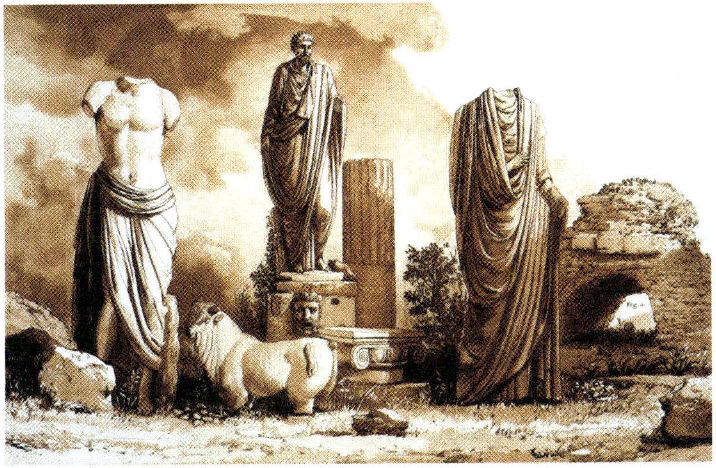

• *A realist painter, Jean-Pierre Havers (1735–1813) studied Italy's Greco-Roman ruins using gouache or ink and pencil.*

THE TRIP TO ITALY

After 1666, the year the Académie de France in Rome and the Prix de Rome were founded by Colbert, the practice of copying became compulsory and, following the discovery of the remains of Herculaneum in 1738 and of Pompeii in 1848, it made a trip to Rome and then Naples essential. Fragonard, the president of the Académie de France in Rome in 1756, fell in love with Rome's ruins, and in 1776 Houel travelled to Sicily and Malta. From 1821, the Académie des Beaux-Arts's architecture training demanded, at the end of three years of study, a tour of Italy to compete for the Académie de France's Prix de Rome, which required the production of works inspired by antiquity. With Greece off limits to the French but not to German and English architects, the French were confined to studying Rome's ancient monuments, until the military and scientific expeditions to Morea (1829–1831) and Algeria (1839–1845). In 1829, Abel Blouet became the first architect who was authorized to complete a trip to Greece to draw up a topographic map and organize the excavations of the Peloponnese. His plans suggest a restoration based on a process of graphic reconstruction, and they facilitated the development of archaeology. In 1846, the École française d'Athènes was created to encourage members of the Académie de France in Rome to focus on Greek ruins. Algeria was also opened up to research into Roman remains, with Rome remaining a reference point up until the reforms to the École des beaux-arts in 1863. Accordingly, between 1840 and 1842, Amable Ravoisié made in his capacity as an architect accurate drawings of ancient monuments for the archaeological mission, which wanted to avoid sketch artists and painters who were too taken with the picturesque. Thanks to new processes such as daguerreotype, drawing became a means of conserving and cataloguing heritage. Ancient Rome was brought to life mainly through a selection of Roman monuments from around Constantine's era. Based on seven hundred drawings and fifty daguerreotypes, in 1846 Ravoisié published *Exploration scientifique de l'Algérie pendant les années 1840, 1841, 1842* in three volumes of one hundred and ninety plates. The tour of Italy established the practice of on-the-spot sketches and drawing, and it would be followed by many architects, including Debret (1777–1850), Lesueur (1794–1883), Bouet (1795–1853), Denuelle (1818–1880), Lebas (1782–1867), Garrez (1802–1852) and Garnier (1825–1898). The travel diary has therefore been essential to the evolution of artistic disciplines—architecture and archaeology—and reflects the evolution of the role of artists and scholars.

THE *VEDUTA*, MEMENTO OF AN ITALIAN JOURNEY

A *veduta* is a very detailed painting of a cityscape or of a panorama. It emerged among the Flemish in the sixteenth century with Paul Bril. It partly shaped Flemish painting in the next century, as Vermeer's *View of Delft* shows. During the eighteenth century, Venice—an unmissable stage on the Grand Tour for artists in Italy—was recognized as the capital of the vedutisti. The *veduta* recorded the "poetry of cities" through the painting of "views," which satisfied foreigners who were eager to keep a souvenir of the city of the doges, and also of Rome and Naples. After Canaletto and Bellotto, Giovanni Pannini was the main painter to focus on painting ruins. In the nineteenth century, photography, which provided the topographic details demanded, replaced the *veduta*, which also declined with the end of the Grand Tour. This pictorial style, with its connections to describing landscapes, travelling through Italy, romanticism and the picturesque aesthetic, ushered in the English watercolour, in which painters sought topographical and architectural detail.

2. Discovering the world and the natural sciences

THE JOURNEY TO THE AMERICAS

In *Histoire d'un voyage faict en la terre du Brésil* (1578), Jean de Léry (1536-1613), the first ethnologist traveller, attempts to provide a scrupulous and systematic presentation of the country and traditions of the Tupinambá Indians. He devotes six chapters to describing the local beliefs and customs. De Léry, a Protestant pastor, demonstrated a concern for observation, characteristic of the beginnings of a science defined as "seeing and experience," but also for an ethnographic way of seeing that places its object at a distance: "My intention and my subject will be in this story, only to say what I did, saw, heard, observed... this is science: seeing and experience." This book, illustrated in the 1580 edition with engraved plates that seem to foreshadow the sketches of the future travel diary, was reprinted five times until 1611—proof of its success—and it influenced some of Montaigne's reflections on cannibals in his *Essais* and contributed to the subsequent development of the myth of the noble savage.

The first illustrated ethnographic descriptions, which like the travel diary included observation and iconography, date from the mid-sixteenth century and relate to the Americas. For example, in 1562 the bookseller Theodor de Bry (1528–1598) published a book of engravings on the Indians of Florida entitled *Indorum Floridam proviciam inhabitantium eicones* by J. Le Moyne. Similarly, in the chronicle *El Primer Nueva Crónica y Buen Gobierno* by Felipe Guamán Poma de Ayala, which describes the pre-Hispanic and colonial Andes in 1615, each plate illustration relates to a text. John White's diary, kept during the conquest of North Carolina (1585–1590), makes use of watercolour for portraits of the Secotans and of the Algonquin tribes and their customs and traditions. Zacharias Wagner, a mapmaker who joined the general staff of Governor Johann Moritz von Nassau in Brazil in 1634, devoted his efforts to producing a treatise on animals, the *Zoobiolion*, which compiled one hundred and eleven watercolours (naturalistic works, portraits of Indians and views of sites).

BOTANISTS' AND NATURALISTS' CIRCUMNAVIGATIONS

Botanists were great travellers. They criss-crossed lands and seas between 1640 and 1789 as they hunted for plants to develop the herbarium of the "Jardin du Roi" (1635), the future Muséum national d'histoire naturelle. Lamarck (1744–1829), author of the first botanical encyclopaedia in 1778 and then professor of invertebrate zoology at the museum in 1793, and the Jussieu brothers headed for Spain and Portugal. Commerson (1727–1773) and the "Bougainville" expedition set their sights on Brazil, the Philippines and Madagascar, while Poivre (1719–1786) followed the spice route and sailed to the Bourbon Islands. Some of the great names associated with the kind of encyclopaedic knowledge that characterized the Enlightenment kept diaries of their travels. Tournefort (1656–1708), precursor of the works of Linnaeus with a first classification of plants based on the nature of their flowers, recounted his journey to the Levant in Asia Minor; Joseph de Jussieu recorded his discoveries in Ecuador and Peru; Linnaeus (1707–1778), the creator of so-called "binomial" nomenclature, published his *Iter lapponicum*; and Humboldt (1769–1859) and Bonpland (1773–1858), figures who were behind the synthesis of the natural disciplines, brought back studies and sketches of their Amazonian escapades. Four types of illustrated works—the culmination of a process of inventorying nature—were made by naturalist scholars: herbaria, harvest books, books of models and entomology works.

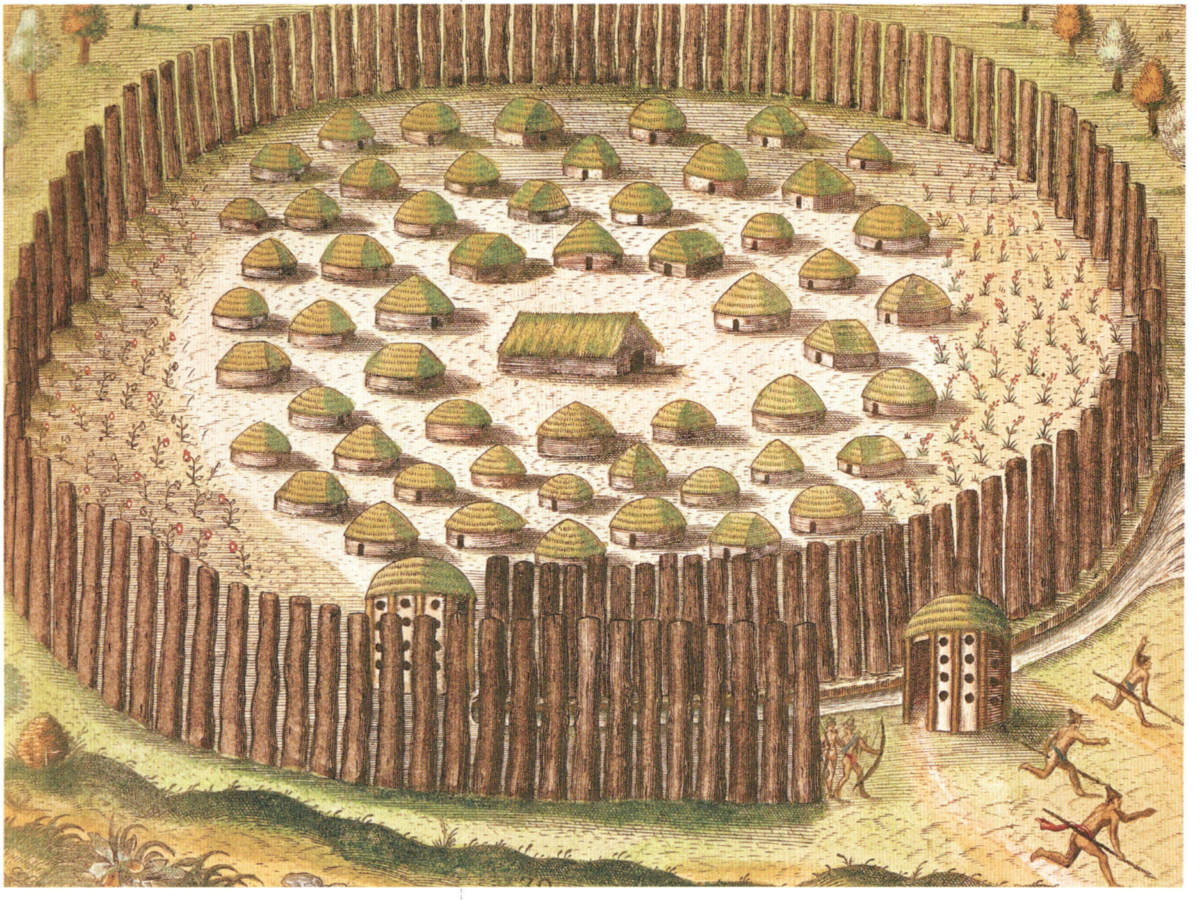

• *In 1562, Le Moyne's engravings describing the habits of the Florida Indians questioned the values of Western society.*

GEOGRAPHERS' SCIENTIFIC EXPEDITIONS

The great French explorers of the eighteenth century were seafaring geographers who mapped the kingdom's new lands. They kept logbooks, in which they provided all the information necessary for sailing purposes, including latitude and longitude, maps, weather data, navigation instruments and discoveries—all in all, evidence of their journey and their story. Bougainville's and La Pérouse's logbooks provide discoveries of *terrae incognitae*. In addition to geography and cartography, physical sciences were essential to any maritime explorer: Francis Drake (West Indies, 1577–1580), Duplessis (Brazil, 1701) and Cook (Australia, New Zealand, Tahiti, Easter Island, 1768–1773) are perfect examples of this.

The discovery of Venezuela by Alexander von Humboldt and Jacques Goujaud (known as Aimé Bonpland), whose expedition went up the Orinoco River, was, on the eve of the nineteenth century, the peak of natural science and botany. It marked the birth of biogeography, a convergence of new disciplines: the geography of plants, studies into terrestrial magnetism, physical oceanography and climatology. If *Essai sur la géographie des plantes accompagné d'un tableau physique des régions équinoxiales* (1807) was an openly scientific work, another book by Humboldt and Bonpland, *Voyages aux régions équinoxiales de 1807 à 1834,* denounced slavery and argued for the reinstatement of the aboriginal peoples, an innovative perspective on Spanish America on the eve of its independence.

During the nineteenth century, two botanists achieved a certain level of renown. The Englishman Hooker (1817–1911) became an expert in exotic environments following the release of *Journal of a Tour in Marocco and the Great Atlas* and his multiple trips, especially in India, which were the subject of publications. The French naturalist d'Orbigny (1802–1857) specialized in palaeontology and geology during expeditions to Latin America (Brazil, Uruguay, Argentina, Chile, Peru and Bolivia). The founder of micropaleontology, of the study of fossils and of geological stages, he illustrated numerous plates of foraminifera.

THE EVOLUTION OF THE SPECIES

Naturalists who were zoologists with drawing skills also led many expeditions around the world: Lesueur (1778–1846), Buffon (1707–1788) and Audubon (1785–1851) recorded their findings in the form of illustrated plates and travel diaries. During the first Napoleonic expedition by Nicolas Baudin to the southern lands of the Australian coast (1800–1804), Lesueur produced nine hundred and sixty drawings of zoological findings, which amounted to one hundred thousand samples and more than two thousand five hundred species of animals. He produced the atlas that accompanied *Voyage de découvertes aux terres australes* (1807). Driven by the encyclopaedist's ambition, Buffon planned to paint, over the course of ten years, all of nature, collected in a large thirty-six-volume bestiary, *Histoire naturelle générale et particulière* (1749–1789). An artist, ornithologist and pioneer of ecology, Audubon emigrated to Ohio in 1807 to describe, over a period of thirty years, all the birds of North America. In 1839, he completed a work entitled *The Birds of America*, which included four hundred and thirty-five plates in total.

In 1831, Darwin (1809–1882) sailed as a naturalist on the *HMS Beagle* for a five-year trip around the world to South America via Cape Horn and the Cape of Good Hope. He surveyed rocks, fossils, flora and fauna, natural phenomena and societies in his *Journal of Researches into the Geology and Natural History of the various countries visited by H.M.S. Beagle*, which included contributions from other zoologists. With the release of *The Origin of the Species* in 1859, modern evolutionary theory was up and running, taking precedence over Lamarck's transformism, which was outlined in *Philosophie zoologique* (1809).

LA SOCIÉTÉ DE GÉOGRAPHIE AND LA SOCIÉTÉ DES EXPLORATEURS FRANÇAIS

The Société de géographie, founded in 1821, is one of the oldest learned societies and probably the oldest one with a focus on geography. It was proposed in 1785 by Jean-Nicolas Buache, Louis XVI's first cartographer. Other geography societies have spread around the world, but at an international level they are always overseen by the French society. Most of the scholars who went on the expedition to Egypt (1778) became members, and renowned members have followed in their footsteps, such as Chateaubriand (as president), Élisée Reclus, Jules Verne, Anatole France and Jean Charcot, as well as around a dozen European sovereigns. The headquarters of the society, built in 1878, have become a Mecca of French and world geography, and they are famed for their heritage collections.[2]

2. The diaries of French explorers in Latin America (1886–1887) are kept in the collections of the Société de géographie in the Bibliothèque nationale de France.

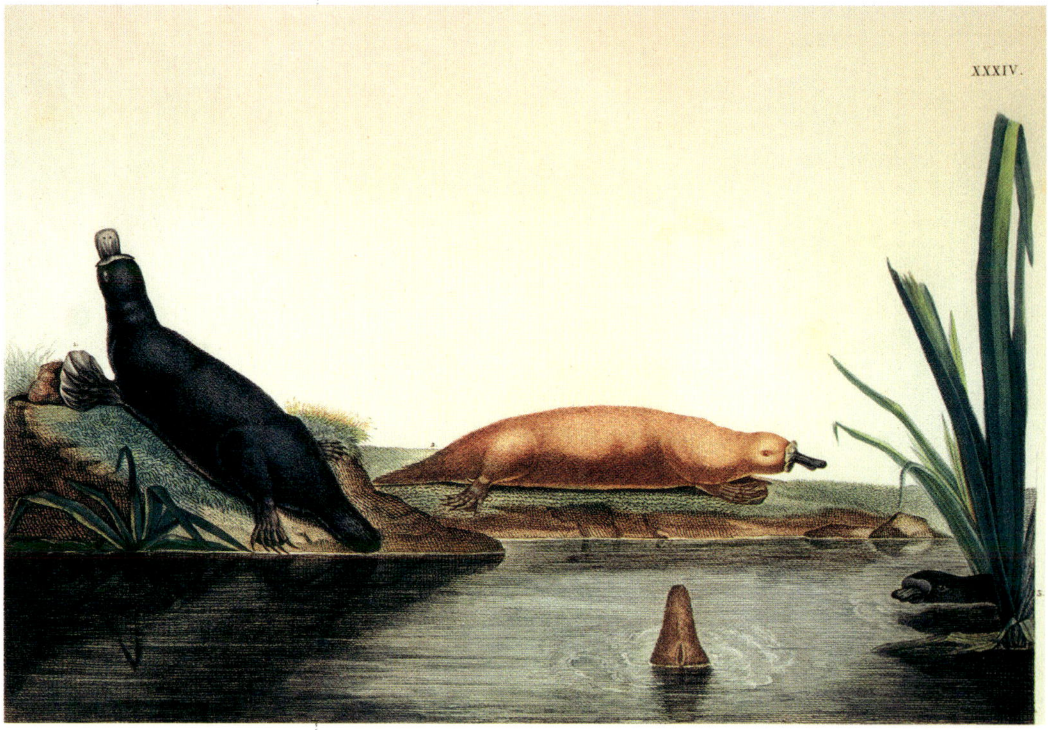

• *On board of the* Géographe *as it sailed towards southern lands, the naturalist Lesueur was promoted to the position of artist. His studies of animals in the natural environment attracted the admiration of the scientific world.*

During the International Polar Year of 1879, numerous scientific expeditions were organized to study the geodesy of the poles, such as that led by the explorer Jean Charcot (1867–1936) on board the *Pourquoi-Pas?*, and that led by the zoologist and botanist Louis Gain (1883–1963). These expeditions were the subject of travel diaries. The explorer and ethnologist Paul-Émile Victor (1907–1995) brought back more than three thousand objects and two hundred and fifty masks from his many expeditions. His "field diary" is full of pencil-sketched portraits of Inuit and notes on the bone-, stone-, metal- and wood-working techniques he observed during his wintering in Ammassalik. He also recorded descriptions of kayaks and hunting and fishing tools. All of this would give rise to the book *La Civilisation du phoque* in 1989. His "journey logs" demonstrate his drawing talents.[3]
The Société des explorateurs français, also known by the name of "Club des explorateurs," was founded in 1937 by young explorers—the doctor Robert Gessain, the filmmaker Fred Matter, and the ethnologists Michel Pérez and Paul-Émile Victor—after their return from the first crossing of Greenland. The explorer Bertrand Flornoy and the geologist Louis Liotard, meanwhile, had respectively been on missions to the Peruvian Amazon and eastern Tibet. The team received the support of such colleagues as Louis Audouin-Dubreuil (known for the *Croisière jaune* of 1931), Jean de Guébriant (Upper Amazon), Théodore Monod and Henri Lhote (Sahara). The society was open to explorers, adventurers, scientists, writers and filmmakers provided that they pursued original research in regions that were still not well known and that they communicated the results of their missions, including through lectures. Among recent expeditions, three that were the subject of accounts and travel diaries are especially worthy of mention: the "Clipperton" expedition of 2005, led and organized by Jean-Louis Étienne; "La Boudeuse autour du monde" by Patrice Franceschi; and "Ultima Cordillera," (2006) which was devoted to the discovery of the Darwin Cordillera, a mountain range located on a Tierra del Fuego peninsula.

3. Farid Abedelouahab, *L'Aventure des pôles: carnets de voyages de grands explorateurs*, Sélection du Reader Digest, 2006.

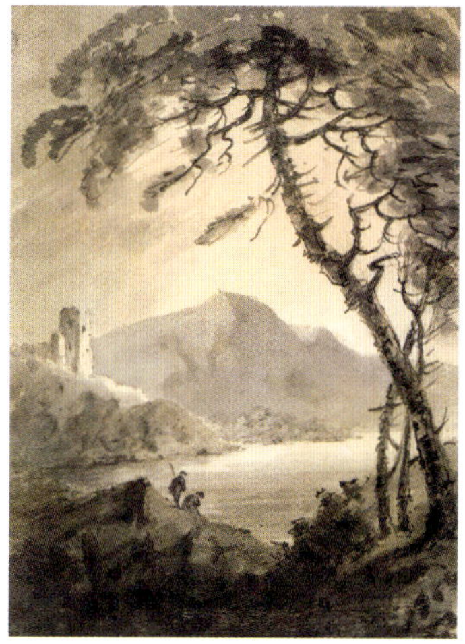

• Made with charcoal, ink and aquatint, this landscape dominated by the ruins of a castle is characteristic of the work of Gilpin, inventor of the "picturesque."

3. Outdoor painting

THE "PICTURESQUE" AESTHETIC

The term "picturesque" evokes both publications decorated with prints and a particular technique of graphic reproduction characterized in three different phases: the creation of views by artists that show the landscape from the ground; the production of lithograph copies; and the creation of everyday scenes by artists specializing in figures. The craze for the picturesque trip corresponded with the birth of romanticism and was popularized between 1770 and 1855: then there was an interest in the "unusual effects of landscapes and striking features of beings" and, consequently, in the folklore of the French regions and the exoticism of the Orient. The term "picturesque" effectively means "an appropriate subject for painting"—*alla pictoresca*, in the manner of painters. This notion touches on Delacroix's diary on Morocco, *Album d'Afrique du Nord et d'Espagne*, which consists of preparatory sketches for the creation of pictorial works. In 1708, the word appeared in France in its Italian meaning, *pittoresco*, describing "a composition that has a great impact when looked at," before being defined in 1726 by the *Encyclopédie* as "a striking and singular choice of the impact of nature"—a special way of relating to nature, in sum, and one that was included into the Académie in 1732. From 1730 to 1790, the term was used to describe British landscape art that highlighted unusual natural features. The Grand Tour pushed the young British aristocracy to the continent's historical and religious sites and called for the painting of ruins, an exercise that combined the picturesque,

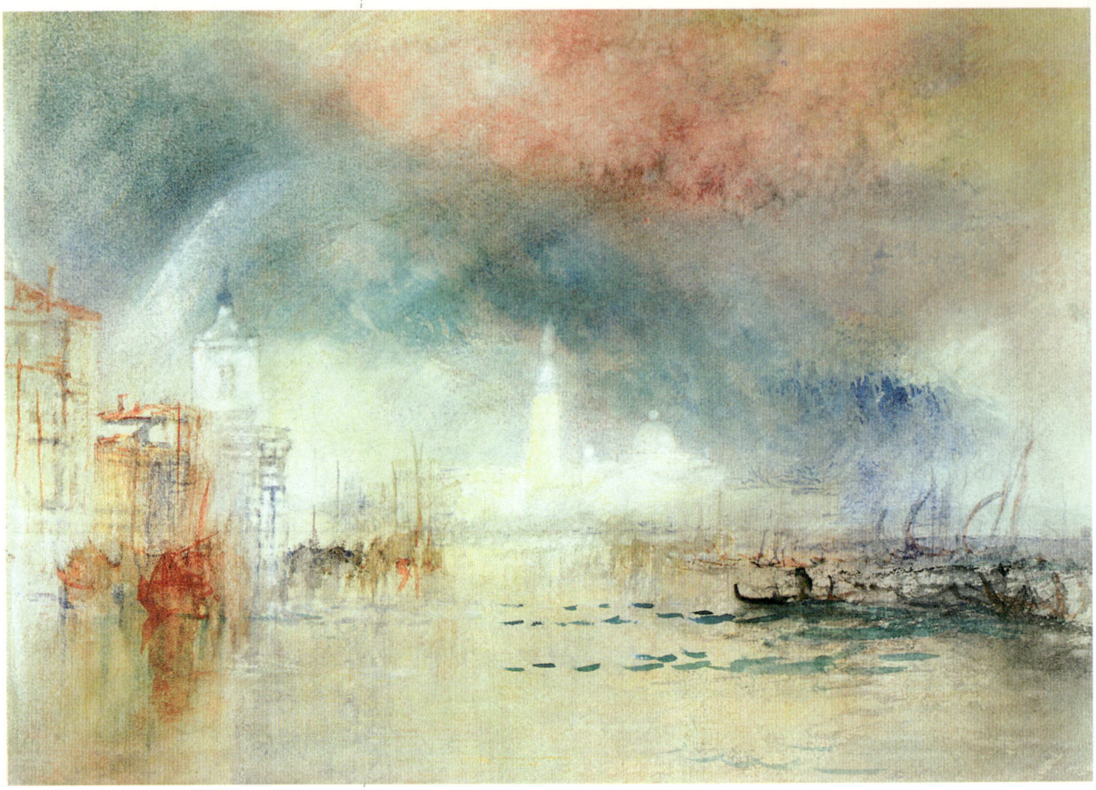

• *Under the emerging influence of romanticism, Turner produced this watercolour,* Venice from the Giudecca, *in which he strives to reproduce the fiery sun in the mist.*

the poetic and the romantic, that promoted contemplation and that spoke to the mind and touched one's sensitivity. The scene reproduced by the artist reflected the feelings experienced on the spot, producing a so-called "picturesque" view. This aesthetic was defined by William Gilpin (1724–1804) in *Observations Relative Chiefly to Picturesque Beauty, in Several Parts of Great Britain, 1782-1809*: the idea was to move the viewer through representations of ruins, waterfalls or rocks. The watercolourists, who were pioneers in the field of colour, tried to apply the Newton's research into optics through playing with shadow and light over the course of the day. Cozens (1752–1797) used colour to create a poetic atmosphere or an affective tone and turn the landscape into a vector for feelings. His *A New Method of Assisting the Invention in Drawing Original Compositions of Landscape* (1786) allowed, according to him, a sense of the strange and the unusual to be created from the imaginings generated by the watercolour.

ENGLISH WATERCOLOUR, TOPOGRAPHICAL DRAWING AND ARCHITECTURAL DETAIL

The golden age of watercolour in England took place between the end of the eighteenth and the mid-nineteenth centuries, between Cozens's first voyage to Italy in 1776 and Turner's death in 1851. The national memory sites—abbeys, cathedrals, castles and monuments—inspired realistic works with an incredible accuracy of details, such as those of the surveyor Paul Sandby (1730–1809). In addition, this technique was connected with the development of art being published as a result of engraving. Early tourists, the English of the eighteenth century were fond of travel mementos, and artists such as William Pars (1742–1782) turned their efforts to reproducing the famous sites visited on the Grand Tour. Watercolour, which was used in illustrating a number of travel diaries, reached its apogee in 1804, the date of the foundation of the Royal Watercolour Society in London. The topographical artists Thomas Girtin (1775–1802) and William Turner (1773–1851) became virtuoso watercolourists. Girtin introduced the concept of the picturesque tour, a journey to sites that were worthy of being visited, and he underscored the complexity of the urban landscape in *Durham Cathedral* (1799).

And Turner put to use the extensive work (*colour beginnings*) that he completed during his wanderings on the transparency of colours. Between 1794 and 1799, he made his first trips to Wales and Kent in search of picturesque landscapes, which would be engraved and published in 1825 (*Picturesque Views in England and Wales*). He then went to Greece in 1799 with Lord Elgin to produce topographic drawings. After that he went to Paris in 1802, and then he went on a tour of Italy between 1819 and 1820 (Turin, Milan, Venice, Bologna, Rome, Naples, Pompeii and Paestum). These trips were rounded off in 1828 and 1829 by a visit to Genoa, Florence, Rome, Ancona and Turin. His sketches reflect his impressions, though he left notes on the paper that were inspired by Poussin's and Claude Le Lorrain's paintings. In 1821, Turner travelled along the Seine from Rouen to Paris and also along the Loire, before staying in the Alps. From 1825 to 1841, he crossed Belgium, the Rhineland, the Netherlands, the Baltic, Prague, Vienna, Switzerland, Venice and Bavaria, filling his diaries with sketches, drawings and watercolours—the foundations of his landscape work—as he did so. He became one of the masters of the "topographical" watercolour, intended for engraving printed works and regular instalments. After Turner, watercolour became a minor art, but his art became popular across society.

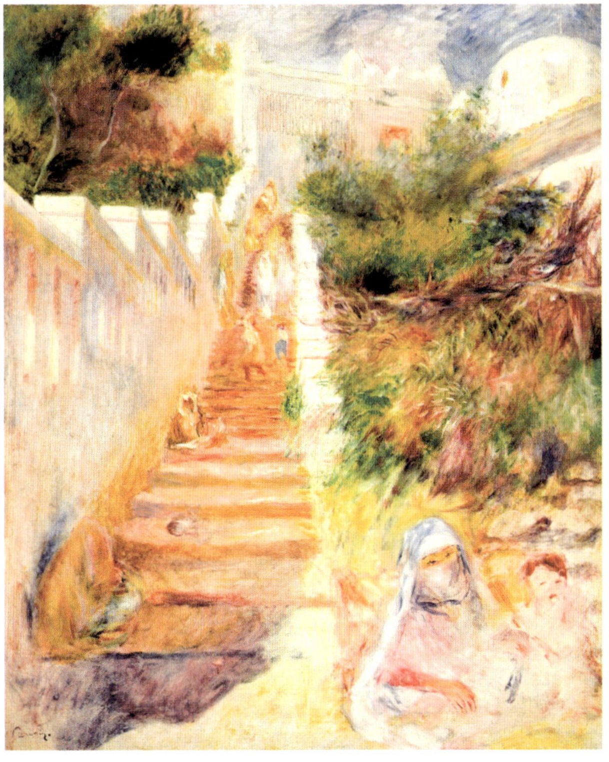

• The second trip by Renoir—a supporter of colonization and an occasional Orientalist—to Algeria provided him with the inspiration for Marches d'Alger *(1882).*

FROM ROMANTICISM TO IMPRESSIONISM

Romanticism and then modern art asserted the absence of any borders between the different means of artistic expression. Moreover, impressionist painters became known through their illustrating of poets' works: this was the case of Pierre Bonnard (1867–1947), who was inspired by Verlaine, and Gauguin (1848–1903), who was inspired by Charles Morice. Manet (1832–1883) put his name to eight etchings to accompany Charles Cros's compendium of poems, *Le Fleuve* (1874), and he then made illustrations for the French version of Edgar Allan Poe's *The Raven*. The impressionists' great innovation may have been outdoor painting, but it was actually in following on from the English watercolourists that motifs in nature became a practice for oil painters. Constable (1776–1837) in England, then Courbet (1819–1877) and Corot (1796–1875) in France diverted painting's objective: they evolved from narration towards a description of reality. Following the exhibition of Constable's works at the Salon de Paris in 1824, which showed rural scenes freed from any academicism and were produced by drawing on nature, the Barbizon and Crozan schools met in 1848 to paint nature itself—Millet (1814–1875) focused his works on simple peasant life (*Les Glaneuses*, 1857)—paving the way from around 1860 for an impressionism characterized by a bright style produced by the use of light tones. Painting the fleeting impression of the instant, of nature in movement and of the atmosphere was the order of the day for followers of the movement, with lighting effects, colours, blurred shapes and colourful vibrations made by the juxtaposition of primary colours. The impressionists—Boudin, Monet, Pissaro, Renoir and Sisley—travelled through the countryside, to riverbanks and to the seaside coasts, canvas and brushes in hand. Some produced sketchbooks of drawings, for example Renoir (1841–1919) during his trip to Italy and Algeria (1881–1882).

4. The call of the East

THE TASTE FOR EXOTICISM AND EGYPTOLOGY

The concept of exoticism appeared as early as 1548 in Rabelais. It took clearer shape through archaeological missions in the East (1630–1640), and then came to greater prominence through the publication in 1697 of *La Bibliothèque orientale*, an encyclopaedic work on Eastern peoples. It arose alongside accounts of trips to Istanbul between 1680 and 1700, which were extensively illustrated in the case of *Voyage du chevalier Chardin en Perse et autres lieux de l'Orient* (1686) by Jean Chardin, a precious-stones merchant who then became a representative of the English East India Company. The turquerie vogue then excited artists' enthusiasms. In July 1798, Napoleon landed in Egypt, having been dispatched there by the Directory. He arrived with forty thousand soldiers and ten thousand scientists and sailors, including 21 mathematicians, 3 astronomers, 17 civil engineers, 13 naturalists and mining engineers, 4 architects, 8 draftsmen, 10 men of letters, 22 printers, and personalities such as Monge, Berthollet, Geoffroy Saint-Hilaire, the archaeologist Jomard, the Orientalist Jaubert, Vivant Denon, Conté and the poet Parseval-Grandmaison. Over a period of thirty months, the expedition catalogued the region's archaeological heritage and prepared a report on the state of the country. On imperial orders, the Imprimerie nationale published the *Description de l'Égypte*. Two hundred artists were involved in its illustration: 907 plates with more than 300 drawings of architecture, zoology, botany, picturesque views, crafts and everyday objects. The archaeological excavations at Thebes, Luxor and Karnak, the discovery of the Rosetta Stone and the sketches taken by Vivant Denon's team demonstrate a keen interest in this lost civilization. The expedition became part of the tradition of eighteenth-century scientific voyages and gave birth to Egyptology, which until then had just been a branch of Orientalism.

THE GRAND TOUR SKETCHED BY WRITER-ARTISTS

The East attracted the nineteenth century's writers. Chateaubriand, Stendhal, the Goncourt brothers and Dumas, the first French reporter, recounted travelling through Italy. Chateaubriand, Nerval, Gauthier and Lamartine evoked the East through their Grand Tour. The ideal route—Alexandria, Palestine, Lebanon, Syria, Istanbul and Italy—was plotted in 1849 and 1850 by Flaubert and Maxime du Camp. Orientalist literature, full of artifice and seduction, turned the Eastern world into genre painting. Reality was dramatized and fragmented into a series of close-ups that were framed, according to a pictorial code, in several picturesque places, such as cafés, baths and markets. And we find these features in travel diaries. Sensitive to the romantic transgression of the boundaries between the arts, some writers—the brothers Jules (1830–1870) and Edmond Goncourt (1822–1896), Hugo, Lamartine and Pierre Loti, for example—translated their wanderings using a paintbrush. Hugo travelled across western France (1834–1836), including Brittany, and spent time on the banks of the Rhine in 1839, producing pen-and-ink sketches of landscapes and architecture. His dreamlike brown ink and wash drawings were a "visionary" graphic work, made in the image of his poetry's quest for the supernatural, invisible and strange. His travels in Europe (the Basque Country, Belgium, Holland and the Rhine Valley) are described in *Récits et croquis de voyage*. The Goncourt brothers—Jules with watercolour and Edmond with ink—offered their vision of Italy in *Notes sur l'Italie* in 1870.

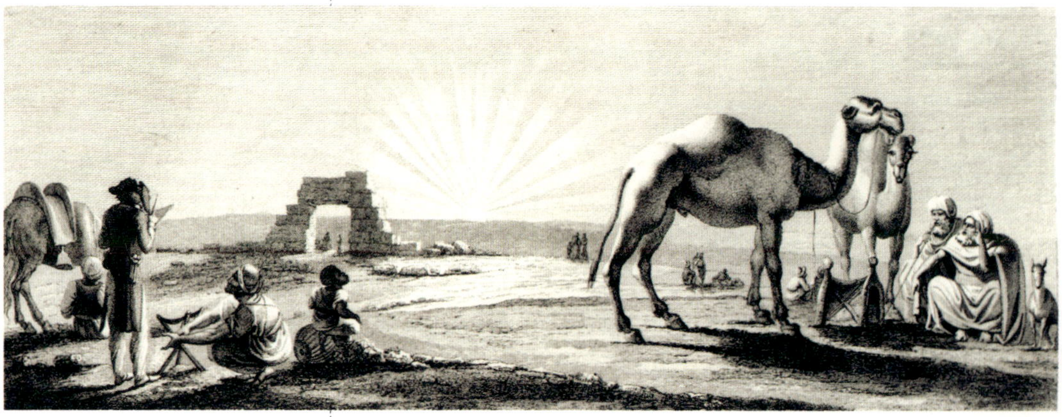

• Baron Denon (1747–1825) accompanied Napoleon to Egypt and provided an accurate overview of the daily lives of the artists who documented the treasures of this ancient civilization.

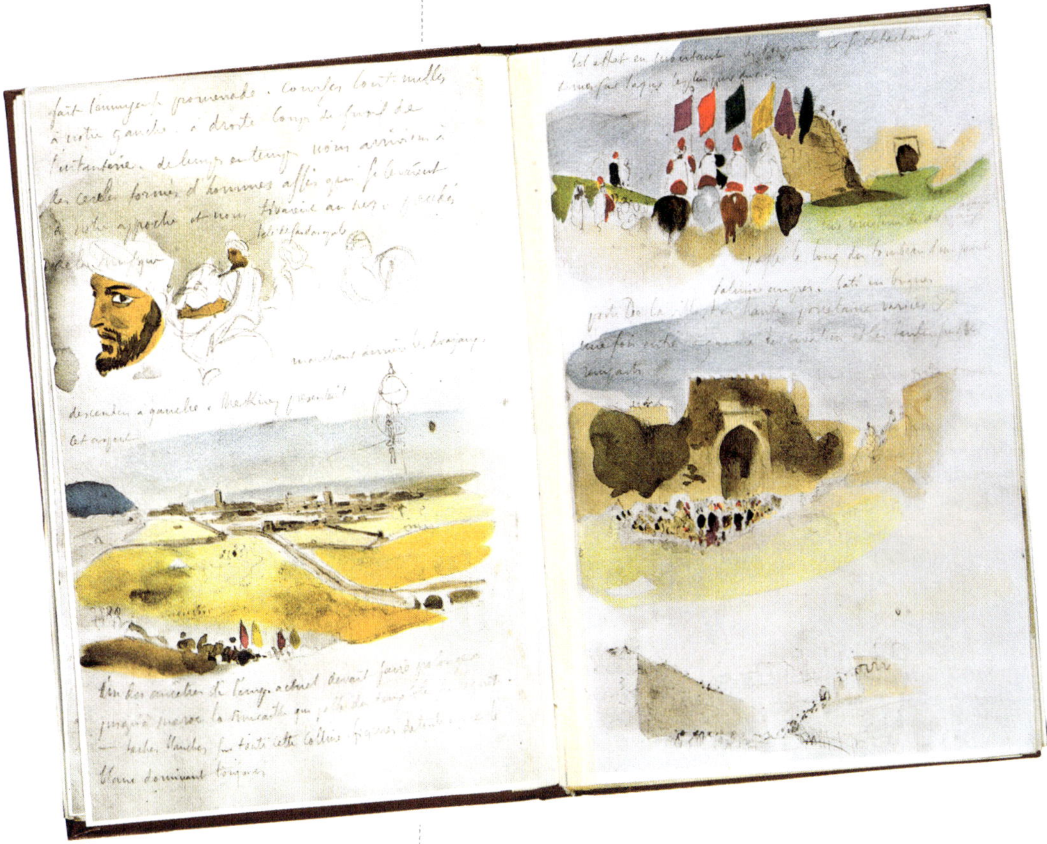

• *Delacroix recorded memories and impressions of his trip to Morocco (1831–1832) in seven albums of sketches and an album of watercolours; these were a source of inspiration for his future masterpieces.*

ORIENTALIST PAINTERS' TRAVEL DIARIES

Delacroix filled three travel diaries: the first, *Album d'Angleterre,* produced during his trip to England in 1825, is a collection of seventeen pages. The second, *Album du Maroc* (1832), includes fifty-three pages illustrated with pencil, pastel and watercolour sketches that are accompanied by notes. The third, *Album d'Afrique du Nord et d'Espagne,* is a collection of ninety-seven pages of pencil, pen and brown-ink illustrations, many of which are enhanced with watercolour and annotated. His journey to Morocco provided material for his future paintings, including *Femmes d'Alger dans leur appartement* (1834), *L'Entrée des Croisés à Istanbul* (1840), *La Noce juive au Maroc* (1841), and *Le Sultan du Maroc* (1845).

In the nineteenth century, Eastern countries (for example, Egypt, Palestine and Syria) attracted many artists. Roberts (1796–1864), a painter of architecture, reached Alexandria in 1838 to undertake a fabulous trip, on Turner's advice, around Egypt, Nubia and the Holy Land. He would return with turn two hundred and seventy-two lithographs, which were reproduced between 1842 and 1849 by the engraver Louis Haghe. Eugène Fromentin (1820–1876), a writer and Orientalist painter, went to Algeria three times, in 1846, 1847–1848 and 1852. The desert was the central theme of his travel diary *Un été dans le Sahara*, and his various trips inspired his future pictorial and literary works. Promoted to officer in 1859, he was present in Egypt for the opening of the Suez Canal, an experience he recounts in *Notes d'un voyage en Égypte*, which was published posthumously in 1881. He ended his career as an art critic, specializing in Dutch painting following a trip to Holland (1875).

EUGÈNE DELACROIX'S DIARIES

Four of Eugène Delacroix's seven diaries[4] have survived until the present day, among them *Album de Charente* (1822), *Album d'Afrique du Nord et d'Espagne* (1832) and *Album de Croze* (1855). Appointed official painter to Charles de Mornay's diplomatic delegation, Delacroix headed to Morocco and Algeria in 1832, where he engaged in a veritable ethnographic study, as his diaries show. The cities he visited—Tangier, Meknes, Oran, Algiers, Marrakesh—inspired *La Mariée juive de Tanger* and then *Femmes d'Alger dans leur appartement.*

4. Three are kept at the Louvre, and one at the Condé Museum in Chantilly.

Two page spreads in *Album d'Afrique du Nord et d'Espagne*, depicting a "crowd of Moroccans at a busy gate, court and prison, Jewish gate, horse and Arabs in front of a fountain" in one case and a "landscape with a mosque in the background and people" in the other, merit further analysis. Notes, sketches, people, plans and details are juxtaposed in an original composition, giving the impression of depth and suggesting a particular reading of the image. The first double-page is divided into three successive views, taking us from the exterior to wandering towards the interior of the medina. The second is more confusing in its organization; it offers two main views, greater details and more limited angles. Just like a filmmaker, the artists' movement of his brush is the outcome of his careful viewing. He moves forward, stops on some feature or other, recedes, watches and wanders. These sketches are visual notes—sketch-form studies of frames, compositions, and elements that would later will be brought together in a pictorial work produced in the studio.
The diary seems to announce the storyboard technique, such is the importance of the notion of movement and angles, in a way that sometimes comes very close to tracking. Recording wanderings and ethnographic approaches in the form of drawings, the travel diary reflects here a journey and an exotic experience filled with encounters. Everyday scenes are transcribed in great detail: objects, utensils, decorative elements, costumes, jewellery, and so on. The diary contains numerous watercolour studies produced by Delacroix prior to *Les Femmes d'Alger*, these are accompanied by captions indicating the colours and materials that could not go into a simple sketch. On some pages, for example "Arab horsemen, clump of trees and sea in the background," the manuscript text is incorporated into the drawing, overlapping and mixing with and entering the composition. Delacroix's work therefore appears as an accomplished version of the "travel diary" genre, in which neither the image nor the text takes precedence, combining instead in an ambulatory journey within space and time and at the very heart of the page. Delacroix may have been the creator of the travel diary, which he breathed life into with a frenzy of discoveries, research and visual studies that were stimulated by the Orientalist quest for impressions, sensations and emotions through an ethnographic approach.

NAVAL PAINTERS AND THEIR JOURNEY DIARIES

The mission diaries by the armed forces' official painters stand out within the genre for their pictorial qualities. Heirs to the painters of the Dépôt de la guerre (war repository) created by Louvois in 1688, they have recorded the greatest military achievements of the Royal, Imperial and Republican forces and exalted the scale and scope of France overseas. A 1981 decree restructured and updated the status of the painters of the land, sea and air branches of the armed forces, so that they, in a contingent of twenty painters by force, are appointed and approved for a renewable term of three years by the defence minister. The official naval painters have provided their artistic, cultural and patrimonial takes on the events experienced and the peoples encountered during exploration voyages.
Two years after his appointment as a naval painter, Félix Ziem (1821–1911), an architect by training, set off in 1842 to Rome and Venice. He fell for the city of the doges, representing it in a style comparable to that of Turner. He continually travelled until 1860. He went to the Midi, Italy, Greece, Russia and Istanbul in 1844; the latter inspired him as much as Venice had. He then went to Belgium in 1850, England in 1852, the East and the Danube in 1856, Algiers in 1858 and Holland in 1860. A decorated painter, not to mention a productive one (he produced four thousand works), he was a precursor of impressionism through his work on light, as his four albums show. These were: *Album de Russie et d'Italie* (1843–1844), which included one hundred and six pages illustrated with sketches and fifty-five pasted drawings; *Album d'Italie* (1847-1848), fifty-eight pages; *Album de Turquie* (1856); and *Album de Provence* (1862, 1863, 1872, 1883, 1885), sixty-three pages accompanied by notes.
Pierre Loti (1850–1923), a sailor before he became a naval painter, made numerous trips around the world, and his diaries were the source for his literary work. Between 1872 and 1913, he travelled to Easter Island, Tahiti, San Francisco, Montevideo, Rio de Janeiro, Piraeus, Salonika, Algeria, the Adriatic, Saigon, Hong Kong, China, Nagasaki, Bucharest, Palestine, Syria, the Lebanon, Turkey, India, Rangoon, Muscat, Persia, Nagasaki, Angkor, New York and Edirne. The ink works he produced on Tahiti and Easter Island, collected in *L'Île de Pâques: journal d'un aspirant de La Flore*, reflect his interest in ethnology and are still a reference for specialists. Portraits of women suggest his romance with the odalisque Aziyadé, which motivated his seven stays in Istanbul between 1876 and 1915 and is the subject of his first novel, published in 1879. His *Journal, volume 1, 1868–1878,* traces the ten years he spent travelling around the world and learning the ropes of life as a sailor, while his personal diary (1890) tells the story of his discovery of Tétouan and the Fez court, to which he was led by an 1889 diplomatic mission.

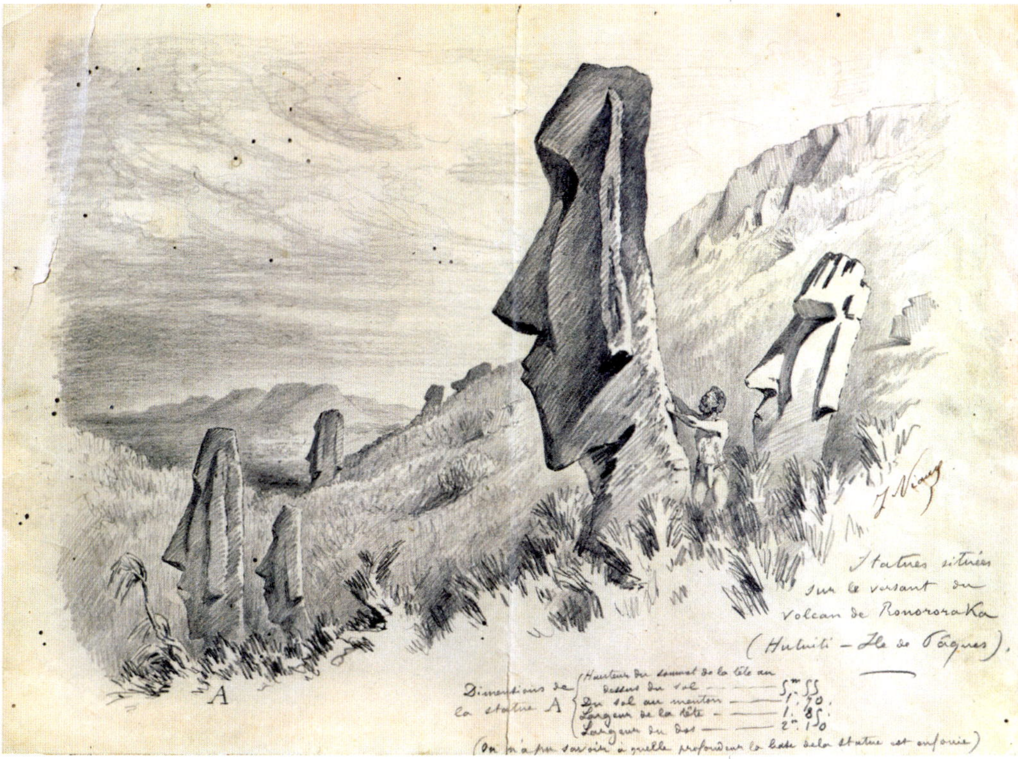

• *Four days spent sketching on Easter Island provided Pierre Loti with material for an article for* L'Illustration *that would give this "mysterious and isolated" land a mythical dimension.*

THE TOURIST CRAZE

On the back of the Grand Tour, the British aristocrats of the eighteenth century set the tone for leisure sites, practices and periods—that is, the tourist spots and seasons that were "linked to a counterculture of idleness that set them apart from the rich entrepreneurs."[5] Examples of such places and trends included the thermal season in Bath, the taste for the countryside, wintering in the Midi and, from 1763, the discovery of the coast, the glaciers of Chamonix and the mountains. The tourist was primarily a wealthy Briton who visited the things that needed to be seen—the places identified in his guide. The pleasure trip was born with the tourist, "who travels out of curiosity and idleness," spreading the literary clichés on this or that country: the intriguing Italy of Stendhal, the passionate Spain of Mérimée, and so forth. Works such as Vivant Denon's *Voyage pittoresque de Naples et de Sicile* (1788) were accompanied by travel guides illustrated with maps, plans and itineraries. The first such book may have been *Le Guide des voyageurs en Europe* by the German Heinrich August Ottokar Reichard, published in 1784 and translated into French in 1793. Mme de Genlis's *Le Manuel du voyageur* paints a portrait of the "tourist," an English term that was Gallicized in 1816 and redeployed by Stendhal in 1837 in his *Mémoires d'un touriste*.

In 1841, Thomas Cook launched his "organized trip" by offering for the first time a journey from Leicester to Loughborough for a group of five hundred people (he negotiated the price of railway tickets based on a promise of an occupancy rate for the train). He then organized other trips of the same kind: a visit to the first world's fair in London (1851), and then to that of Paris (1855); a tour of the North of Europe, from Brussels to Paris via Cologne, Heidelberg, Baden-Baden and Strasbourg; and a Nile cruise through Egypt (1869). In 1868, he created the first discount coupons for hostelry and then, in 1874, the traveller's cheque, which ensured the success of the company until 1928. The travel souvenir and postcard, born with the use of German *Korrespondenzkarten* during the Franco-Prussian War of 1870, spread with the growth of tourism. Lidonis's engraving of the Eiffel Tower, published by *Le Figaro* in 1899 to mark the structure's inauguration, marks the birth of the illustrated postcard in France. Millions of cards were printed for the 1900 Exposition universelle, including the series "Paris vécu," which offered an ethnographic vision of daily life on the city's streets.

5. Marc Boyer, "Comment étudier le tourisme?" in *Ethnologie française*, vol. 32, 2002–2003.

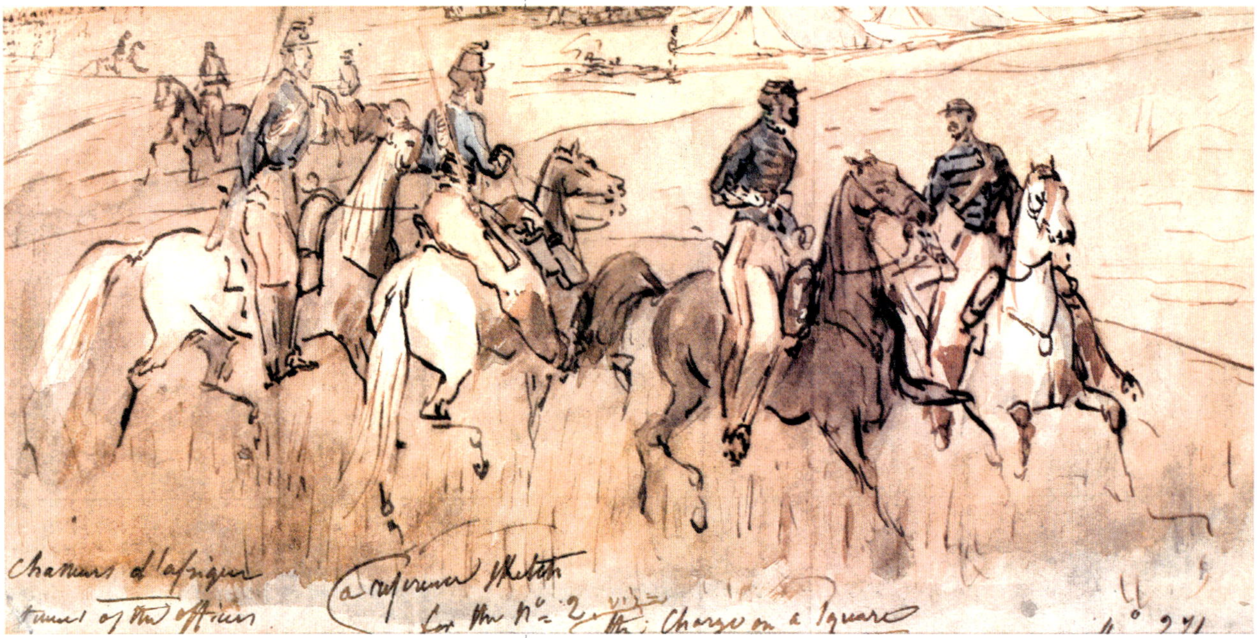

5. The art of reportage

THE BIRTH OF VISUAL AND TRAVEL REPORTAGE

The beginnings of periodicals focused on travel reportage came about through two events: the birth of *Annales de géographie* in 1808 and the publication of the Société de géographie's *Bulletin* in 1822. The success of this type of journalism in the 1830s facilitated the dissemination of newspapers illustrated with woodcuts: *Le Magasin pittoresque* (1833), *L'illustration* (1843) and *Le Tour du monde* (1860). The last of these featured illustrations from Librairie Hachette's wood-engraving workshop between 1860 and 1914, helping to make it a success. Between 1863 and 1905, Jules Verne published *Voyages extraordinaires à travers les mondes connus et inconnus*—a total of sixty-five novels. Between 1877 and 1914, this type of publication became specialized, following the example of *Journal des voyages et des aventures de terre et de mer*.

The Crimean War (1854-1856) marked the beginnings of both drawn reportage and the reporter, a figure glorified in *Michel Strogoff* in 1876. The conflict resulted in a large-scale production of images that were replicated using various techniques (for example, lithography, photography and engraving) and in a variety of media (for example, illustrated press, books and loose-leaf sheets). The drawings were translated into engravings for printing, and from lithographs of current events drawn reportage was born. Lithography facilitated a European media coverage of the conflict through several magazines that were published simultaneously: *Illustrated London News* (1842), *L'Illustration* and *Illustrierte Zeitung* (1845). Editors sent correspondents to the scene to provide accounts of the "Eastern war": Constantin Guys (1802–1892) for the *Illustrated London News*, and Colonel Langlois, who produced a panorama of the siege of Sevastopol (November 1855 to May 1856) through combining photography with pictorial work.

FROM PRESS CARTOONS TO THE RISE OF THE COMIC STRIP

In the tradition of the great caricaturists (Hogarth, Rowlandson), and well before the birth of the magazine *Le Charivari* in 1831, press cartoons adopted a deliberately satirical tone, exaggerating colourful features to better convey cultural difference. Thomas Rowlandson (1756–1827) was inspired by the subject of travel to publish his first album, *The tour of Doctor Syntax in Search of the Picturesque*, in the form of prints in 1812.

• *A war correspondent for the* Illustrated London News, *Constantin Guys became a sketch artist-reporter and covered the Crimean War (1854). Opposite, the Chasseurs d'Afrique, captured in watercolour.*

Gustave Doré made a derisive account of tourists through the "physiologies" of the 1830s, which marked the peak of caricature with Gavarni, Daumier, Grandville and Cham, the main illustrator of *Charivari*. Cham, who was equally adept at literary parody as he was at satirizing manners, notably published *Impressions de voyage de monsieur Boniface* in 1844. Gustave Doré (1832–1883), the illustrator of one hundred and twenty works, invented a complex graphic style to make a series of captioned drawings (vignettes) arranged in a row on the same page, influenced in this by Töpffer's "literature in prints" and "autographies." As with Épinal prints or Quantin's images, the text is separated from the visuals. Doré published his first album, *Les Travaux d'Hercule,* at the age of fourteen, before being hired as a caricaturist by *Le Journal pour rire*. In *Des-agréments d'un voyage d'agrément*, published in 1851 by Aubert, he records the travel impressions of a Genevan retiree who had worked in the trimmings industry and who sets out with his wife and his dog to conquer the Alps. Its one hundred and seventy captioned vignettes satirize the fashion of the time for mountaineering tourism. The composition of the pages is innovative, since like a cartoon it integrates a cutting of the action into vignettes of different sizes and forms, translating space, time and movement according to the future iconographic code of comics. The album's oblong format prefigured that of the contemporary travel diary, and the setting of its narrative into the drawing and the diversity of its graphic signs and image ranges make it a completely original work. Doré then developed this very personal style in *Histoire pittoresque, dramatique et caricaturale de la sainte Russie* (1854). He teamed up with Charles Davillier to publish *Voyage en Espagne* in 1862, which also appeared in 1866 in the magazine *Le Tour du Monde*, "the new travel journal." A dozen articles were published in it on a regular basis for ten years, from 1863 to 1873.

THE DRAWN TRAVEL REPORTAGE BOOK

Drawing on his predecessors, Rodolph Töpffer (1799–1846) drew "stories in prints" for his friends. These brought eccentric and caricatured figures embroiled in extravagant adventures to life: *Histoire de monsieur Jabot* (1833), *Histoire de monsieur Crépin* (1837) and *Histoire de monsieur Vieux-bois* (1893). These stories were reminiscent of the "physiologies," small and cheap illustrated books that mocked contemporary mores and the different social types. Having founded his own boarding school in Geneva, Töpffer implemented a programme of excursions with his students to the Alps, the Swiss cantons and Italy between 1825 and 1842. He recounted his walks between 1837 and 1842 in *Les Nouveaux Voyages en zigzags*, published in 1844 and engraved, for the most part, by Karl Girardet. His incongruously linked geographical "zigzags" foreshadow the travel diary. Of the forty-six books published by Töpffer, seventeen were accounts of travelling in the Alps and Italy between 1826 and 1835. As with Épinal and Quantin's images, Töpffer's text is separated from his visuals. For many theorists, he is considered the founder of modern structuralism or the precursor to visual semiotics.
Félix Régamey (1844–1907), a renowned sketch artist and teacher at the Academy Institute of Chicago, was hired by Émile Guimet, a Lyon-based industrialist and noted collector of Asian art, to conduct an extensive investigation on the religions of Japan. The two men spent two months in the field, in Tokyo, Ise, Kyoto, Osaka and Kobe. Guimet created the Guimet Museum in 1889 out of the collections of Lyon's Museum of Religions, which he had opened in 1879. His goal was to bring together the Buddhist art collections he had brought back from China, India and Japan. He branched out into Khmer art from 1890 and then to exchanges between India and China with Paul Pelliot's mission to Dunhang. Régamey illustrated the *Okoma* serial in *Le Monde illustré* between 1879 and 1883, produced around forty works for the world's fair of 1878 and wrote the article "Le Japon vu par l'artiste" in the book *Le Japon pratique*. Guimet and Regamey jointly published the story of their stay in Yokohama and Kamakura, *Les Promenades japonaises – Tokio-Nikko*, from 1878. Instigators of Japonism, they encouraged lectures on Japan that were illustrated by Régamey, and they ran the Société franco-japonaise. Following their model, other artists hit the road to the Land of the Rising Sun: Georges Ferdinand Bigot (1860–1927) stayed there for eighteen years from 1882, and Mathurin Méheut went there in 1914, thanks to Albert Kahn.

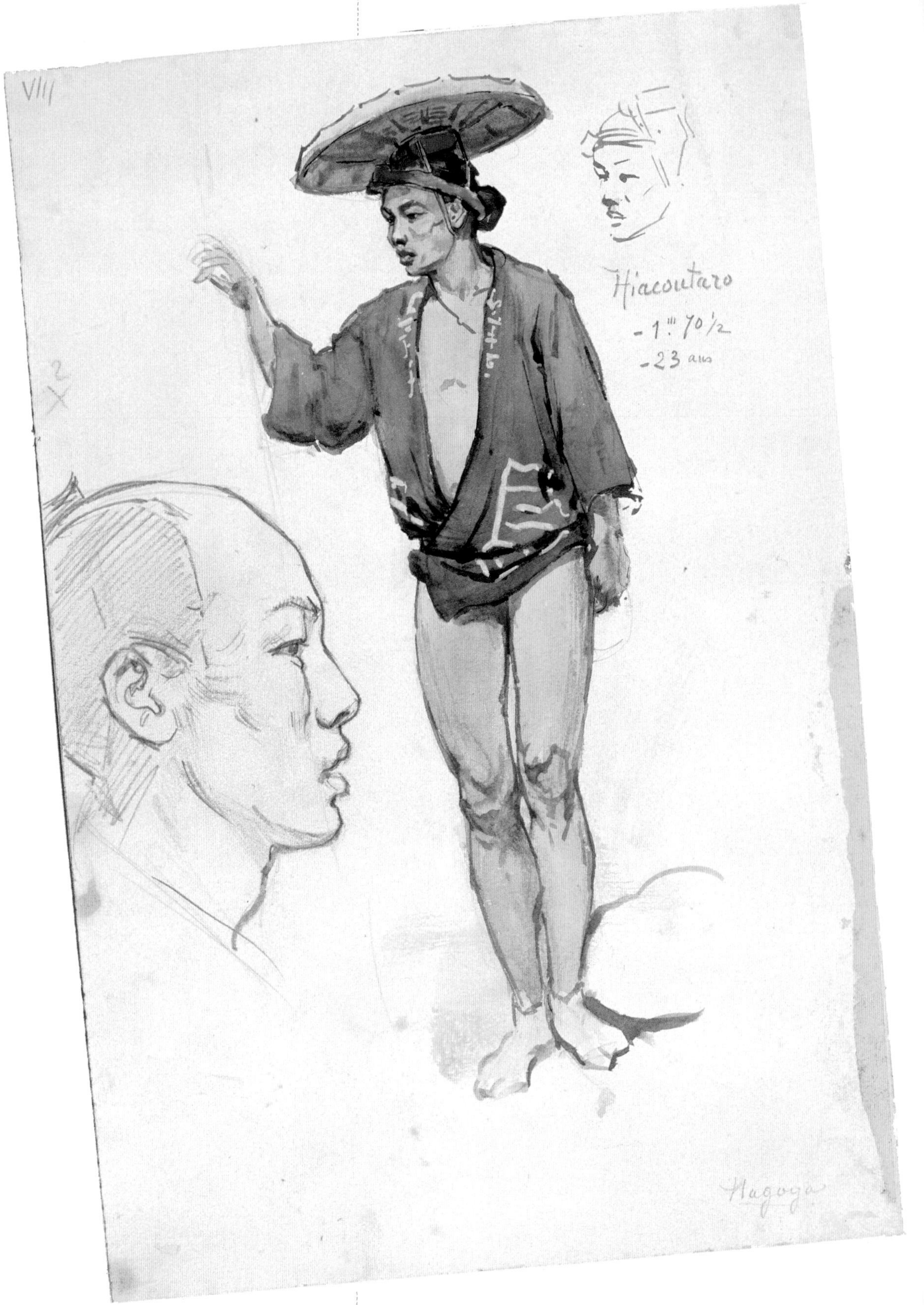
VIII
Hiacoutaro
-1m 70½
-23 ans
Nagoya

PICTURESQUE PUBLICATIONS AND THE BIRTH OF ETHNOLOGY AND ANTHROPOLOGY

From the seventeenth century, there were many travellers who, in crossing the French provinces, reported their experiences in the form of narratives or travel diaries (John Lauder, Arthur Young, Stevenson and the Cévennes, Mérimée and Corsica, and so on). Two centuries later, the genre's pedigree was recognized following the publication between 1820 and 1878 of *Voyages pittoresques et romantiques dans l'ancienne France* by Charles Nodier, Justin Taylor and Alphonse Decailleux, who presented both the architecture and the daily life of the French regions via works by a hundred artists commissioned across the country. This was followed in 1835 by Abel Hugo's *La France pittoresque*. The Académie celtique, founded in 1804, set about collecting French traditions and Celtic and Gallic heritage. Paul Sébillot (1843–1918) wrote *Folklore de France* (1904-1907), which collected the beliefs and legends of the land in eight thematic volumes. Arnold Van Gennep (1873–1957) connected folk facts and ethnological truths in *Rites de passage* (1909) and the monumental *Manuel du folklore français contemporain* (1937–1958). Until around 1850, the illustrated book owed its success to the forerunners of today's magazines: *Le Magasin pittoresque* (1833), *L'Illustration* (1843), *L'Artiste* (1831), *La Caricature* (1830), *Le Charivari* (1832) and *Le Journal des enfants* (1833).

Édouard Chardon (1807–1890), who became an honorary member of the Société de géographie in 1884, was behind a travel encyclopaedia and the three magazines *Le Magasin pittoresque*, *L'Illustration* and *Le Tour du monde*. Illustrators gained great fame through these works with their representations of the colonial empires and distant lands: Gustave Doré and Spain, Désiré Charnay and the Yucatan then Chile, Francis Garnier and Indochina, Édouard Riou, illustrator of Jules Verne and Grandsire, and Pierre Savorgnan de Brazza's expedition.

• **Portrait de Hyakutaro, tireur de pousse-pousse** ***(1876). Régamey's drawings, which have an almost ethnographic precision, were presented to the public at the World's Fair of 1878.***

6. From ethnography to the establishment of the human sciences

THE ETHNOLOGIST-ANTHROPOLOGIST'S DIARY

Keeping a travel diary is advocated in the *Instructions pour les voyages d'exploration* by Antoine d'Abbadie (1867), a member of the Société de géographie. The explorer René Caillé (1799–1838), who used illustrated notes as his vehicle for expression, was involved in the prize of the Société de Géographie in 1824, and in 1830 he published *Journal d'un voyage à Tombouctou et à Jenné, dans l'Afrique Centrale*. Théodore Monod (1902–2000) favoured a "harvesting diary"; in his 1934 diaries he revealed his surveying methodology, which combined all kinds of areas: geology, fauna, flora, study of everyday objects and vocabulary of the Tuareg language, to name but a few. His travelogue *Tais-toi et marche: journal d'exploration – El Ghallaouya-Arafane-Chingetti de 1953 à 1954* recounts his journey across Mauritania as he searched for the strategic points that determine the watercourse and nomadic life. His twenty modest quick-reference books of records, notes and sketches establish interdisciplinary links—a key element of encyclopaedic knowledge, which is based on the technical inventorying facilitated by the "harvesting diary" and scientific expertise. The travel diary, a method designed to serve "field" work and participant observation, needed to respect the principle of impartiality. Indeed, the ethnologist, committed to neutrality, was required to exercise his or her critical faculties in order to deliver quality information. Ethnography acquired a scientific scope due to Marcel Mauss (1872–1950), the founder of French anthropology, who wanted to shape ethnographers with experience in fieldwork methods. He also taught his students the rules of the ethnographic method by offering them a questionnaire that could guide them in their research. All social life, including the study of religious phenomena, is presented in such a way his *Manuel d'ethnographie*, which was published in 1947. With its illustrations, the travel diary may be the heir to visual anthropology and the ethnographic approach. But can it, as Claude Lévi-Strauss suggested, have a "distant gaze"?[6]

---

6. Claude Lévi-Strauss, *Le Regard éloigné*, Plon, 1983.

FROM ETHNOGRAPHIC ALBUM TO ETHNOGRAPHIC CINEMA

The photo album stimulated the development of ethnography and archaeology, and it replaced sketched findings from the middle of the nineteenth century. Désiré Charnay (1828–1915), Jean Chaffanjon (1854–1913) and Nadar (1856-1939) introduced this new process for reproducing images into scientific missions. A photographer and archaeologist, Charnay was considered the pioneer of overseas photographic reportage as a result of his expedition to Yucatan between 1857 and 1860; his archaeology shots of Mexican sites illustrate *Cités et ruines américaines* (1862). Chaffanjon organized expeditions from the Orinoco River to Venezuela between 1885 and 1887. In 1890, Nadar carried out a photographic journey to Turkestan via the Trans-Caspian to learn about the Turkmen people. Five years on from the country's liberation from Russian domination, it offers remarkable insights into the Central Asian Silk Road.
Following Burton Holmes's *Travelogues* (1870–1958), communicating one's passion travel became highly fashionable; the trend was accelerated by the democratization of photography and a thirst for pictures and news. Burton coined the term "travelogue" in 1904 to promote his "illustrated stories," which were projected and hand-coloured images shown on magic lanterns—presaging the audiovisual travel diary style of the "Connaissances du monde" lecture series. Having roamed the planet and taken more than 30,000 photos, he performed his "epic"—like a contemporary bard—live to his fellow Americans to open them to other worlds: Europe in 1886, Japan in 1892, then India in 1913 and 1914.
Ten years later, the banker Albert Kahn (1860–1940) followed Burton's example and financed different photographic and cinematographic ventures to create the "Archives de la Terre" between 1901 and 1931, doing so with Jean Brunhes between 1912 and 1920. His teams, who were sent across the world, used two of the Lumière brothers' inventions, the cinematograph (1895) and the autochrome (1907), to identify and preserve the heritage of peoples: habitat, art, culture, religion, daily life, economy, society, and so forth. Kahn therefore created an iconographic memory of traditional societies; he was convinced that knowledge of cultures encouraged mutual respect between peoples.

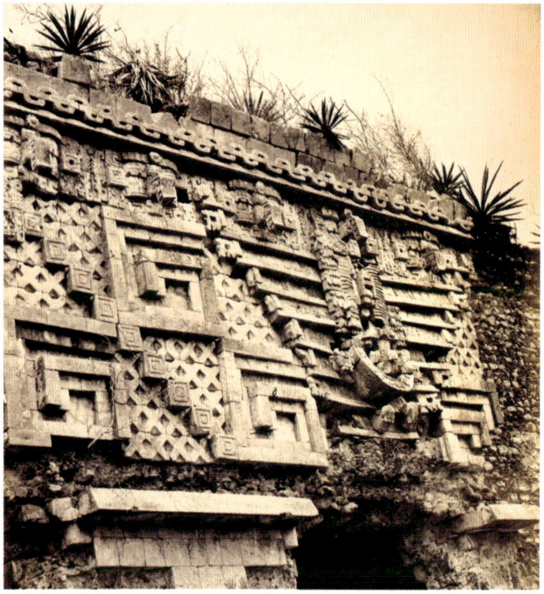

• Désiré Charnay, an explorer and archaeologist, began his world tour in Mexico (1857–1860). This shot of the palace of the governor of Uxmal appeared among the pages of the album Cités et ruines américaines *(1862).*

ART MEETS ETHNOGRAPHY: THE WORKS OF PAUL GAUGUIN

The contemporary travel diary was born out of the encounter between anthropology, ethnology and the different methods of artistic expression. The work of Gauguin, a precious alchemy of graphic art and cultural objects collected during his overseas stays, is the perfect illustration of this. Between his Peruvian childhood and his position as officer in the merchant navy, Gauguin acquired the faculty of perceiving the otherness of the things and beings he observed, whether in Pont-Aven or Tahiti. Having filled up diaries while in Brittany, and influenced by Delacroix's journal, Gauguin headed to a new East, a topos of Orientalist literature, out in the Pacific. In Tahiti from 1892, he researched the "Ancien Culte Mahorie" ("ancient Maori religion"), which had completely disappeared under the influence

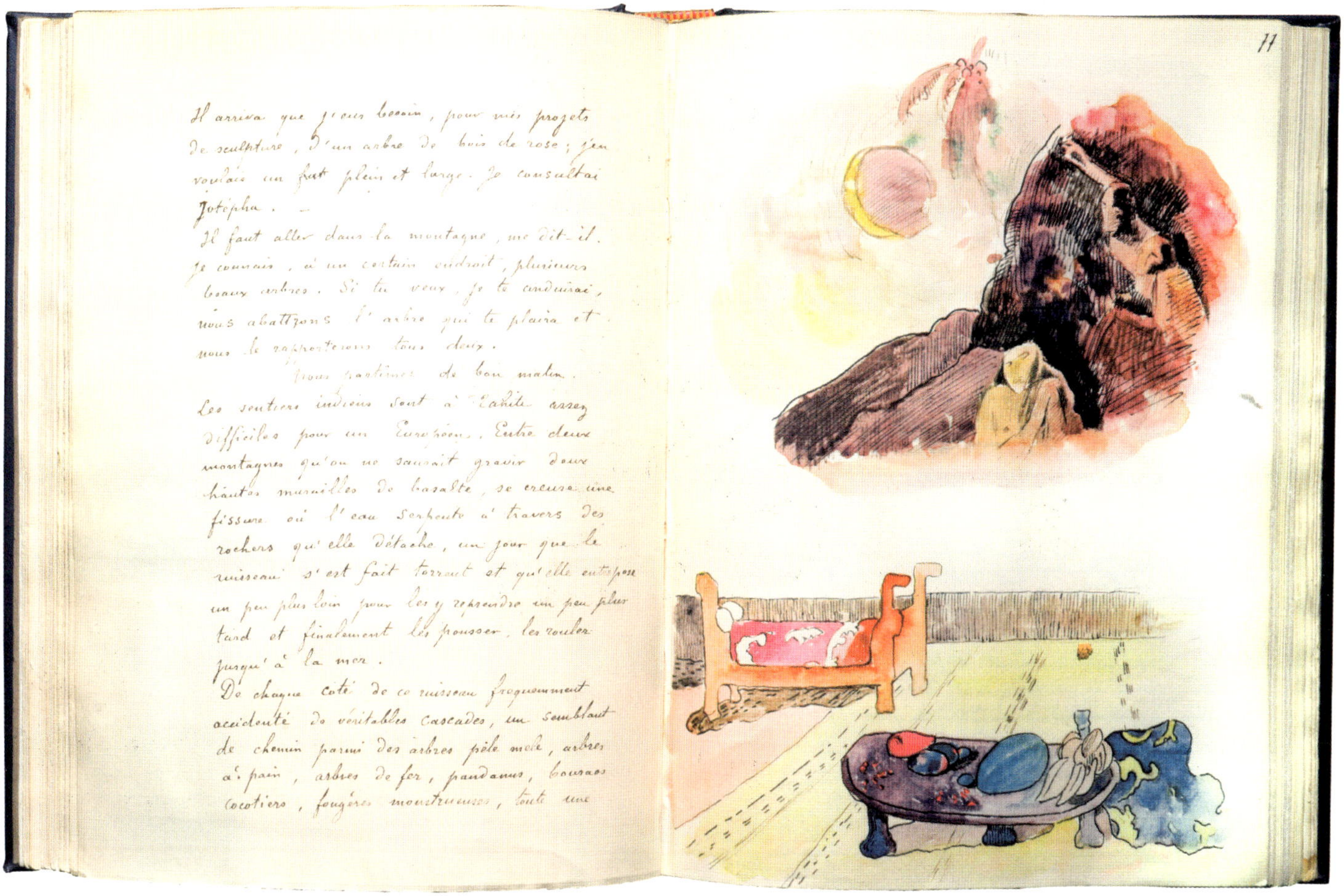

• *Describing the customs, history and landscapes of Tahiti through a very varied iconography, Paul Gauguin's* Noa Noa *would enlighten the public about works by the painter that were deemed too esoteric.*

of colonization. He did so guided by his reading of *Voyage aux îles du grand océan* (1837), by the former consul of Oceania, Jacques-Antoine Moerenhout. He used watercolour to illustrate his account of the genesis of the world according to the Maori, which he compared to Christian worship, thus revealing his passion for the comparative history of religions. Compiling sketches on native decorative arts, tiki sculptures, tattoos and motifs, Gauguin wrote several travel books, including *Noa Noa: voyage de Tahiti*, in which he describes the "new Kythira" or "island paradise." He was critical of European culture and society, and he argued in favour of Polynesian traditions, leading a fight against the bishop and the colonial administration. Appointed to a position as naval doctor, Victor Segalen (1878–1919) set off for a stay in Polynesia in 1903–1904, which inspired his "ethnographic novel" *Les Immémoriaux*, in which he attempts, like Gauguin, to adopt the point of view of the indigenous people. Segalen strove to collect the last testimonies of this civilization, particularly in his *Journal des îles*. While collecting Gauguin's belongings, he discovered *Noa Noa*, from which he took an idea for a book, "Le Maître-du-Jouir," dedicated to the artist's struggle. On the way back, he had the idea for *Essai sur l'exotisme: une esthétique du divers*, a synthesis of all his research that would be published posthumously.

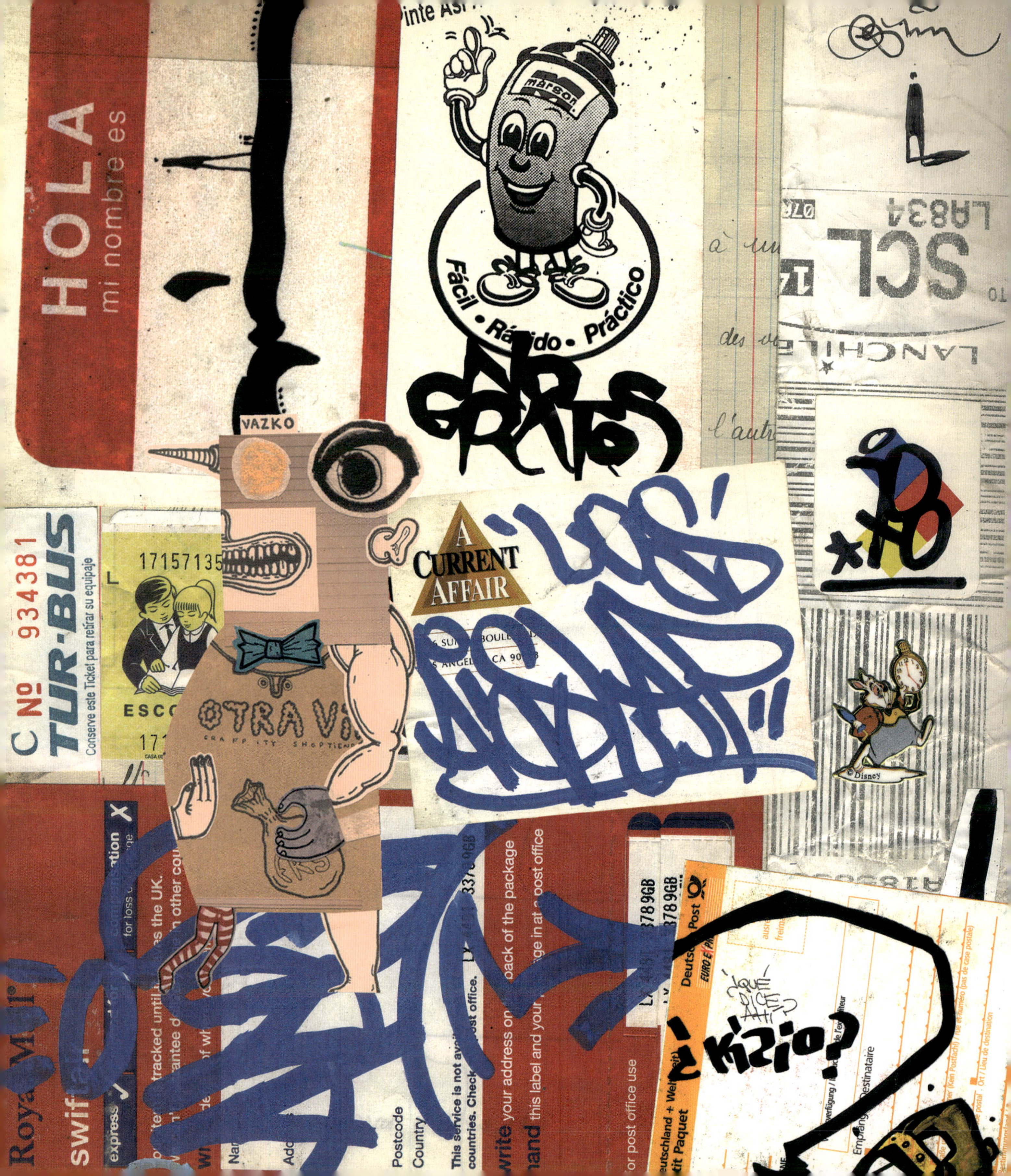
HOLA
mi nombre es
Fácil • Rápido • Práctico
VAZKO
C Nº 934381
TUR-BUS
Conserve este Ticket para retirar su equipaje
17157135
A CURRENT AFFAIR
SCL
LA834
Disney
¿KIZIO?
compensation
tracked until
write your address on
back of the package
hand this label and your
This service is not available
Postcode
Country
for post office use
Deutsche Post
Destinataire

Hybridity in the twentieth and twenty-first centuries

From artists' books to interartistic works

The travel diary veers between an artist's book and the retelling of a journey. An artist's book is a work of art that the artistic movements of the twentieth century developed based on their visual experiments, such as the Dadaist collage, the subversion of media images and the montages particular to pop art, and the mail art of the Fluxus movement. The juxtaposition of composite images that makes the contemporary travel diary original seems to have been inherited from different forms of visual expression. What, then, are the points of convergence and the similarities between artists' books and travel diaries? The artist's book evolved from a 1960s *livre-objet* to a scrapbook in the 1980s, before becoming a publishing genre. At the instigation of Mathurin Méheut, who developed the ethnographic form of the diary—in Britanny, in Japan and at the front during the First World War—a few contemporary artists (Le Corbusier, Peter Beard, Max Pam, Miquel Barceló and Tony Soulié) and painters have used this medium, while others (Zao Wou-Ki, Claude Lagoutte, Jean Pattou, Julien Malland and Hervé Di Rosa) have taken inspiration from it to open their pictorial works up to another dimension, lending a creative edge to their journeys. The result is mixed-medium diaries made with collages, fragments from the trip, photographic paintings, urban paintings, elements of art modeste—diaries made up of nomadic elements, borrowing from scrapbooking or street art. More than the published book, it is the journey that interests these artists. But the concepts of "diary" and "travel" remain at the heart of reflections on the genre. How are they combined in these contemporary variations that fluctuate between unique work of art and publishing format? And is the travel diary an artist's book or an album?

The travel narrative, the link between the diary and the journey, is in the tradition of travel literature, but it has a singular feature: narration through images. This mixing of visual arts and literature therefore has a plural and polymorphic lineage—travel literature, but also "illustrated" literature and photography taken "on the road." Travel literature invites reflection on the mixing of genres and the autobiography of reportage; the "comic" or "graphic" literature forms borrow from the definition of comic reportage and "graphic reportage." The travelogue, composed in the form of text fragments or sketches, claims a certain kinship with the travel diary's mosaics and combinations of images. From personal writing to ethnographic description, travel literature reflects the ambiguities of the diary: between inside and outside, between subjectivity and objectivity. Writers, photographers and diary makers offer an "on the road" take that was bequeathed by the Beat Generation and that evokes travel, nomadism and wandering. Photography has also faced the same issues: between a personal documentary take and an engaged journalistic one, travel photography seems to stand in contrast to the "photograph-expression." Traveller-photographers have created different forms of photographic albums, ranging from photojournalism to artistic visions.

There are many different trends in contemporary travel diaries, including the unpublished artist's book, drawn magazine reportage, the illustrated travel guide and multimedia works that follow the model of Titouan Lamazou or Karen Guillorel's form of transmedia.

• *In* Kailash, 1999 – No Hope, No Fear, *the Australian photographer and storyteller Max Pam brings us a pictorial account of the Mount Kailash pilgrimage in Tibet.*

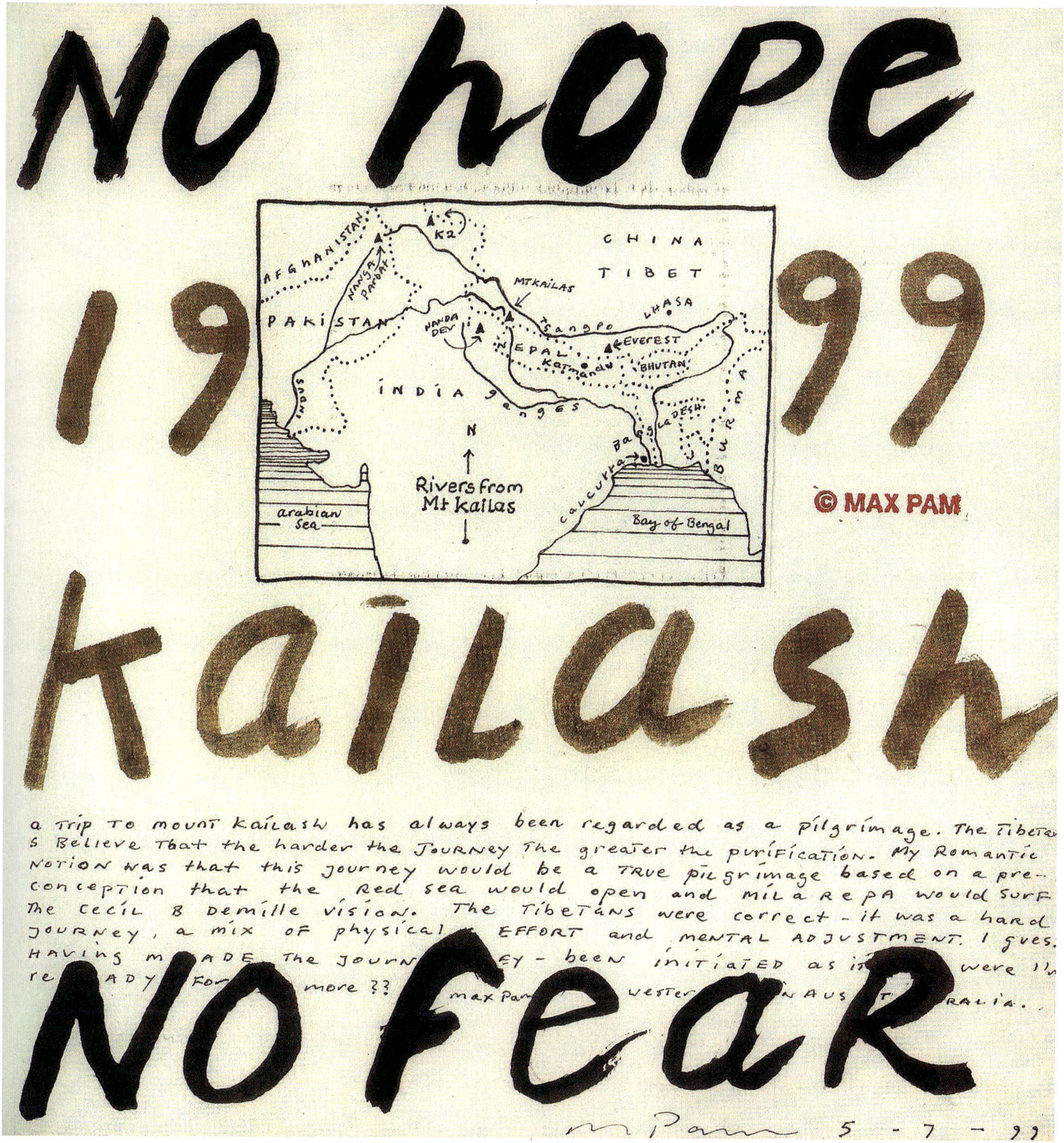

NO hope
1999
kailash
NO fear
CHINA
TIBET
AFGHANISTAN
PAKISTAN
NANGA PARBAT
K2
MT KAILAS
LHASA
Tsangpo
NANDA DEV
NEPAL
EVEREST
Katmandu
BHUTAN
INDUS
INDIA
ganges
N
Rivers from Mt Kailas
arabian Sea
Calcutta
Bangladesh
BURMA
Bay of Bengal
© MAX PAM
a trip to mount kailash has always been regarded as a pilgrimage. The Tibetans believe that the harder the journey the greater the purification. My romantic notion was that this journey would be a true pilgrimage based on a pre-conception that the red sea would open and mila repa would surf the Cecil B Demille vision. The Tibetans were correct - it was a hard journey, a mix of physical effort and mental adjustment. I gues. having made the journey - been initiated as it were I'm ready for more ??
max Pam
5 - 7 - 99

1. Legacies from artistic movements

THE ARTIST'S BOOK

Relative to illustrators dependent on the engraving industry, publishers preferred painters focused on creating the *livre de peintre*, a new art form—one superior to that of the democratized illustrated book—of which Goethe's *Faust*, painted by Delacroix in 1828, and the French version of Edgar Allen Poe's *The Raven*, painted by Manet, are perfect examples. This type of book, in which painter and poet enter into dialogue, originated in China in the thirteenth century[1] and reached its peak in the early seventeenth century with the publication in Nanking of *Shizhu Zhai shuhua*. Delacroix, author of the first travel diary, *L'Album d'Afrique du Nord et d'Espagne*, and creator of *livres de peintre*, placed the diary in the artist's-book genre. This type of work inspired the impressionists, before evolving under the creators of the simultaneity school. *Prose du Transsibérien et de la petite Jehanne de France* (1913), by Blaise Cendrars and Sonia Delaunay, is a two-metre-long folded work; it is considered to be the first simultaneous book, integrating text and image rhythmically, chromatically and melodically. It includes collages, breaks, changes in pace and juxtapositions of time and space as it seeks the ephemeral. Some makers of travel diaries have been inspired by the artist's book, producing accordion-form albums,[2] homages to Edward Ruscha's *Every Building on the Sunset Strip* (1966). From Edward Ruscha (*Twenty Six Gasoline Stations*) to Anselm Kiefer (*Les Reines de France*), the scope of artists' books is vast: with or without text, variable length, single copy or multiple copies. Anne Moeglin-Delcroix, a specialist in artists' books, defines them as a work produced under the sole responsibility of the artist, from its conception to its publication or even distribution. There is no sharing of intellectual responsibility with a writer; a single person creates the work, motivated by a sense of autonomy. This is known as "self-publishing" and "self-distribution." They are an "artist's work in terms of both the images and text on the one hand, and a work made in an unlimited number of copies using mechanical means of printing and reproduction that are specific to the current book on the other."[3] The emblematic artists of the genre include Edward Ruscha, Lawrence Weiner and Sol LeWitt from the United States, and Dieter Roth, Marcel Broodthaers, Ian Hamilton Finlay, Herman de Vries, Robert Filliou and Christian Boltanski from Europe.

1. The *Mehua Xishen pu*, published in 1261, is a xylographic work of images linked to poems.
2. The term "album" derives from the Arabic *muraqqa*, which refers to an accordion-folded sheet.

COLLAGE ART, CUBISM AND THE DADA MOVEMENT

With the advent of Cubism in 1910, the visual arts took up collage, referencing Arcimboldo's fantastical portraits. Collage, a "poetic reality"[4] or "evident poetry,"[5] became a creative mechanism for the Cubists. Typographic letters reproduced with stencil entered the composition of works inspired by the "painting-object." Picasso (1881–1973) produced the first Cubist collage by introducing a waxed canvas for his *Nature morte à la chaise cannée* (1912), a genuine evocation of a material reality. Playing on the visual force of printed paper, he cut headlines from the major newspapers to subvert their meaning and articulate his own political beliefs. This iconoclastic technique, known as *papiers collés*, gave free rein to a new poetics of material, a "subconscious of form" according to Bachelard. Braque (1883–1963), an inventor of Cubism, used sand, sawdust, iron filings and wallpaper. Towards the end of his life, Matisse (1869–1954) used a technique based on cut paper, particularly for the "blue nudes" and "cut gouaches" series. In his "Manifesto of Futurism" (1910), Marinetti announced the arrival of collage by advocating the use of "banal" materials, which "ensure an indispensable topicality for the artwork"—a theory put into practice by Umberto Boccioni (1882–1916) in *Fusion of a Head and a Window* (1911). In 1913, the founder of the Futurist movement advocated this technique both in painting and in writing, and demanded the destruction of syntax to give birth to a new poetry that would "release words." In 1921, he laid the first foundations of tactilism, a form of art intended to be enjoyed with closed eyes that was soon adopted by the Russian avant-garde (Malevich, Tatlin and the collagist Ivan Puni).

3. Anne Moeglin-Delcroix, *op. cit.*
4. Louis Aragon.
5. Jiri Kolar.

Dadaist artists (Rodchenko, Man Ray, Picabia, Miró, Duchamp and Charchoune) seized on the collage to unleash "the antiartistic subconscious" through assemblages of perishable materials and to assert temporariness of everything. In their struggle against the unique and sacred work, followers of the Dada movement invented a process that entailed diverting from their original context images or often fragmented texts that were taken from the most common sources: posters, newspapers, dictionaries, popular reference works and advertising catalogues. The art of collage was also applied to photography: based on fragments of reality, Man Ray developed photomontage and the photogram in a surrealist spirit.

• Union. Needles, California. Twentysix Gasoline Stations *(Alhambra: Cunningham, 1969) by Edward Ruscha features 26 images of functional architecture. This livre-objet is, according to this artist, "a visual material", a "sculpture" with "a volume... a thickness."*

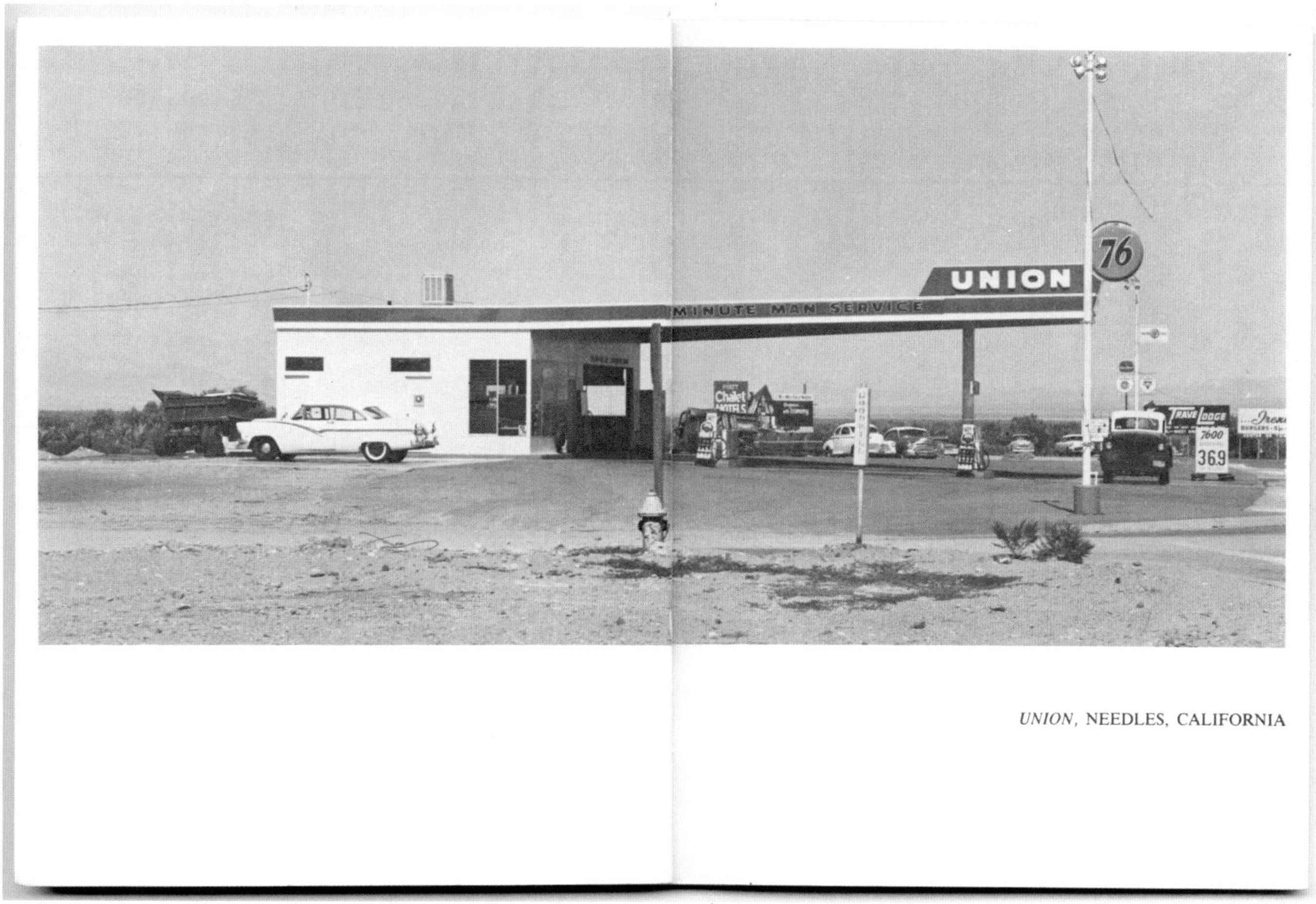

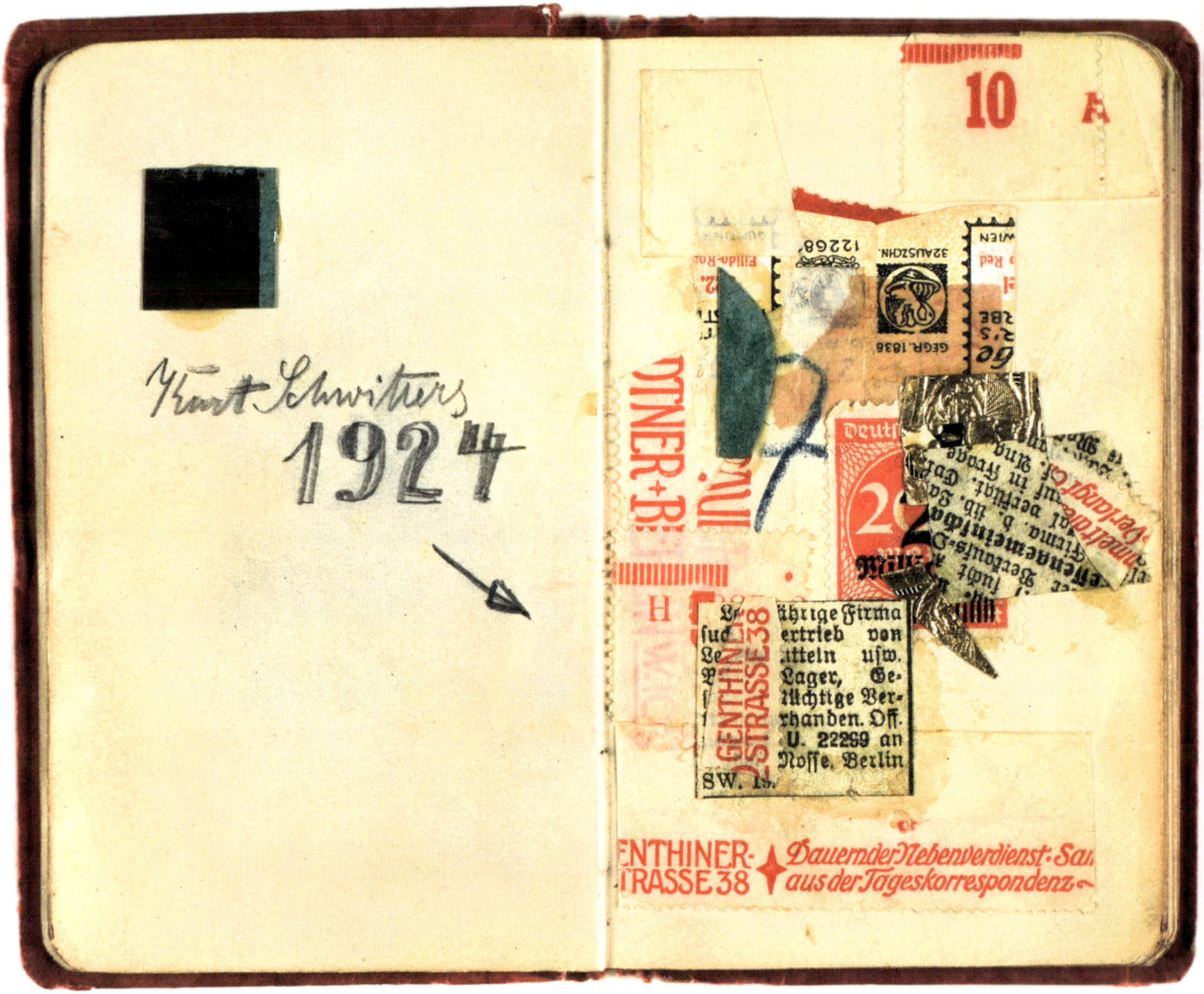

• *The Cubists and Surrealists were influenced by letters and postcards. In 1924, Schwitters assembled cut-outs and elements of correspondence on this page of Nina Kandinsky's diary.*

POP ART AND THE JUXTAPOSITION OF HETEROGENEOUS IMAGES

The travel diary is based on collage and a diversion of images, two principles of contemporary art taken up by pop art. The images produced by the consumer society, such as graphics and advertising signs or comics, were ridiculed to become an artistic initiative with a new aesthetic, that of the "patchwork," in which art and consumption are fused. Jean Dubuffet (1901–1985) reinvented the collage in the 1950s, using textures and ink-stained paper ("texturologies," 1957), plants and prints ("materiologies," 1962). "Art [needing to be] born through materials and tools," he created landscapes out of tar, rust, sand and sponge, and he glued the wings of butterflies on wrinkled papers or plates painted with oils. Arman (1928–2005) helped the collage to evolve towards being an "assemblage" and then a "collage-quotation," a mixing of all the artistic fields. In 1959, he started making "accumulations" of ordinary objects, "poubelles" made up of waste, smashed objects ("colères"), cut ones ("coupes"), burnt ones ("combustions") and ones immersed in resin ("inclusions") or embedded in concrete ("objets armés").

In taking inspiration from the Dadaist assemblages of Schwitters, Robert Rauschenberg (1925–2008) had an influence on pop art. Combining painting, images and objects, his "combine paintings" wiped out the boundaries between painting and sculpture. By including elements from everyday life, these asserted the link between reality and its artistic representation, like "silkscreens," which, by making methods of image reproduction and painting coexist through montage and collage, reduced "the gap between life and art."

MAIL ART AND THE FLUXUS MOVEMENT

Mail art emerged following the first exhibition of illustrated postcards at the third international exhibition of art in Venice in 1889. Many artists—for example Bonnard, Matisse, Apollinaire, Picasso, Duchamp and Picabia—were letter writers, but it is thanks to the Cubists that correspondence was turned into pictorial art through entering in the composition of collages: Gaston Chaissac (1910–1964) produced letter-pictures, while Paul Éluard and the surrealists created montages of postcards. The Futurist painters and writers Pannaggi and Marinetti seized on these attempts to abolish the official art network. In the 1930s, Kurt Schwitters (1887–1948) appropriated reality by composing his collages from recovered items, the founding principle of an artistic movement that he called "Merz." The Fluxus group, formed in the 1960s, rejected the traditional classification of art forms, institutions and the notion of work of art. An advocate of collage, the group gave birth, under the leadership of Ray Johnson, to mail art. "Put art in life and make life an art" was the maxim of Georges Maciuna (1931–1978), who advocated the use of humour, satire and provocation to celebrate the definitive link between art and life, and also to lead to a "nonart" defined by the nonproduction of paintings and objects and by antimusic, antipoetry and "pieces of life as raw materials."

By having allowed a new relationship between viewer and work of art, mail art might be behind the current success of the travel diary, a slice of life outside the traditional art world and institutions that focuses on the random, the ridiculous, the humorous and the vital flow of its creative process, and that engages in a playful relationship with art that foils the market system. Mail art, the link between artist's book and travel diary, acts as a mediator between the artist-traveller and the viewer. But its conceptual approach, based on the ephemeral nature of the work and on transitory and simultaneous modes, distinguishes it from the art of the published travel diary, which is connected to the book industry.

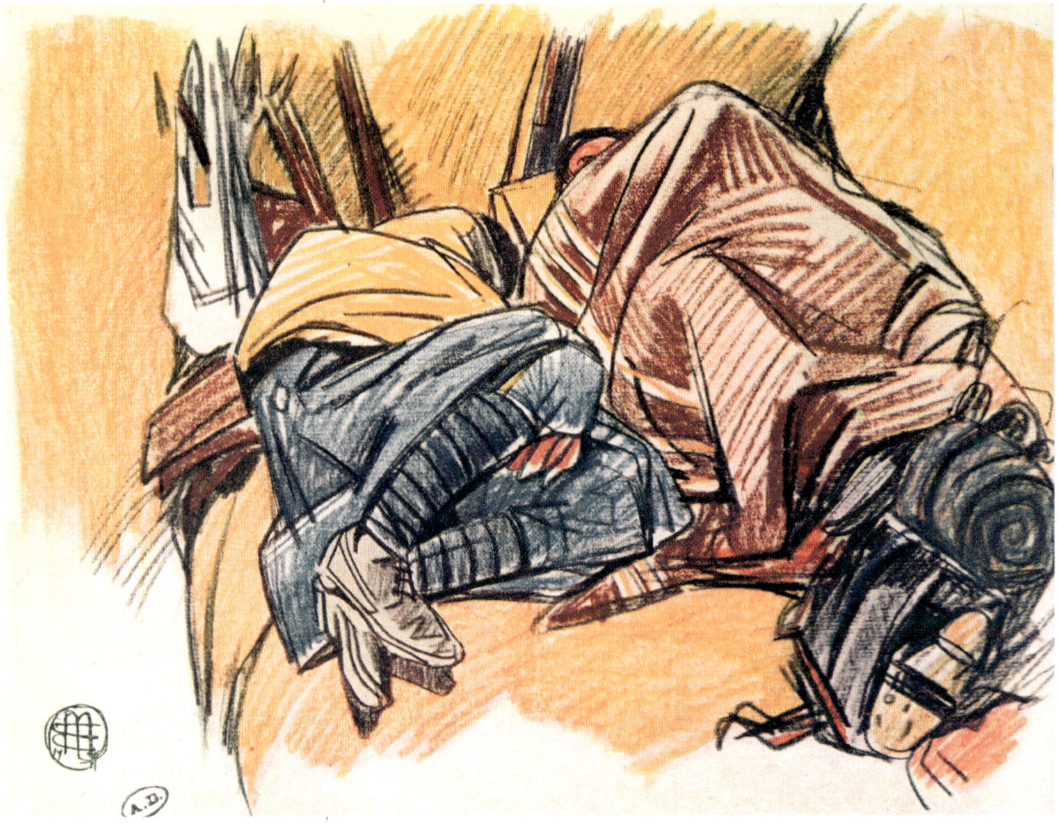

• Soldats endormis *(1915). Sent to the front in October 1914, Mathurin Méheut was involved in some of the bloodiest fighting; he drew and painted the daily life for poilus between each assault.*

2. Inspiration from contemporary artists

1. MATHURIN MÉHEUT (1882–1958): POLYMORPHIC AND ETHNOGRAPHIC DIARIES

Trained at the École des beaux-arts of Rennes, at the Arts décoratifs and then at the École normale d'enseignement du dessin, Mathurin Méheut became an artist for the prestigious magazines *Art et décoration, L'Illustration* and *La Bretagne touristique*. Following a two-year stay at Roscoff's biological station, he published naturalistic plates, including in the work *L'Étude de la mer, de la flore et faune de la Manche et de l'océan* (1913). In 1914, he spent five months in Japan[6] as part of the "Archives de la Terre" project founded by Albert Kahn in 1909. He was inspired by this country where "everything has been brought together and concentrated for the joy of the painter, architect and man of letters. One immediately thinks of Hokusai, so amazingly true and prodigiously modern; the same rigging, the same props, the same types as in his views of Fuji." His travelling was interrupted by his mobilization orders for World War One. While involved in the trench warfare, he produced a number of drawings, a true documentary labour that bore witness to the lives of his fellow soldiers.[7] Upon his return to civilian life, Méheut collaborated with writers like Genevoix and Colette, producing the illustrations for Pierre Loti's *Pêcheurs d'Islande*. He then collaborated with Roger Vercel on *Pêcheurs des quatre mers* (1957). These two books are in keeping with the tradition of maritime travel stories and reportage work created in situ. In 1941, he taught at Rennes's art school. In 1944, he painted scenes of daily life in Brittany and participated in the publication of Florian Le Roy's *Vieux métiers bretons*, illustrating the work with three hundred and fifty drawings. An official naval painter from 1921, he became an honorary artist of the army in 1951, before being received into the Académie de marine five years later.

6. This stay is now the subject of a retrospective travel diary, *Voyage d'un peintre breton au Japon: Mathurin Méheut, avril-août 1914*, which presents two perspectives that are almost a century apart: that of the painter and that of his great-granddaughters (Ouest-France, 2004).

7. Some of these drawings have been reproduced in Patrick Jude's work *Méheut et la Grande Guerre, des ennemis si proches* (Ouest-France, 2001).

2. LE CORBUSIER (1887–1965): ARCHITECTURE DIARIES

The first voyage of Charles Édouard Jeanneret (known as Le Corbusier), accompanied by his friend, the sculptor Léon Perrin, took place in 1907. Following the classical curriculum of art or architecture studies, he spent three months in Florence, and then went to Pisa, Siena, Ravenna, Bologna, Verona, Padua and Venice. Out of his discoveries, he offered to his master, Charles L'Eplattenier, five travel diaries of watercolour sketches and surveys that featured annotations in the margins. In 1910, he undertook a long trip to Germany, where he carried out a study on arts and crafts related to industrial production. This *Étude sur le mouvement d'art en Allemagne* was the basis for his major work, *L'Art décoratif d'aujourd'hui* (1925). He then spent a year in the East and in the Mediterranean, developing the habit of taking down notes and drawings in diaries,[8] which were published in *Voyage d'Orient*: "We draw in order to push the things seen inside us, into one's own story. Once things have entered through pencil work, they stay in for life. They are written; they are inscribed." Accordingly, he sketched the rural architecture of Serbia, Romania and Bulgaria; Mount Athos and the Parthenon in Athens; Turkish mosques; and villas in Naples, Rome and Florence, dazzled by the whiteness of Mediterranean architecture.

3. JEAN DUBUFFET (1901–1985): ABSTRACT NOTES AND DIARIES

Jean Dubuffet made three trips to Algeria: two between 1947 and 1948, and a third in March 1949, to El Goléa in the Sahara. The materials of the desert entered the repertoire of simple signs that the artist, a theorist of "art brut," set about developing: the moving texture of sand, footprints, ridges of palm-tree trunks, tracks, a bright geometry of forms, turbaned silhouettes, animal shapes, and so on. His book of abstract notes or embryonic forms was as much a sketch or idea book as it was a travel diary.

8. In total, he kept eight travel diaries during his life.

4. ZAO WOU-KI (1921–2013): DIARIES AND MIXES

Zao Wou-Ki, a painter and Chinese calligrapher, taught painting in Hangzhou between 1941 and 1947. In 1948, he moved to Paris to study Western painting. Influenced by Picasso and Matisse, he published his first book, which was based on texts by Henri Michaux: *Lectures par Henri Michaux de huit lithographies de Zao Wou-Ki* (1950). Between 1948 and 1952, he produced watercolours of French landscapes on the pages of travel diaries. These were executed in the Chinese style, and between print and ink, Asia and Europe, figuration and abstraction, in a similar manner to Paul Klee. In 1960, he moved towards a gestural painting after he took a trip to New York in search of movement and noise. He illustrated Malraux's essay *La Tentation de l'Occident* (1962). From 1971, he worked with India ink. In 1982, he focused his efforts on the bibliophilic works of Claude Roy, Yves Bonnefoy and François Cheng, for whom he contributed calligraphy in black and white gradations using aquatint and etching. He illustrated Lorand Gaspar's *Journaux de voyages* in 1985. Drawn to travel diaries, in 2006 he published *Carnets de voyage: 1948–1952*. A retrospective of his work was organized by the Bibliothèque nationale de France in 2007.

5. PETER BEARD (BORN 1938): DIARIES AND COLLAGES

From the age of twelve, the American Peter Beard kept diaries illustrated with memento photographs of his holidays. He took trips to Africa between 1955 and 1960, and he then returned to Kenya in 1961 after graduating from Yale University. He worked at the Tsavo National Park, through which he witnessed overpopulation and the extinction of the elephant, which he recorded in *The End of the Game* (1965), a work that is bluntly illustrated with images of corpses of animals and annotated by hand, and sometimes with blood. It recounts the relationship between man and animal, lamenting the disappearance of Africa's wildlife. From 1970, he collaborated with Andy Warhol, Andrew Wyeth, Terry Mériodinal, Francis Bacon and Truman Capote. His 1973 book *Eyelids of Morning: The Mingled Destinies of Crocodiles and Men* is a piece of natural history reportage on wildlife and an ecological wake-up call regarding endangered species. In 1975, he exhibited his diaries before initiating an artistic turn through the exhibition of his burnt private diaries and his photographs of dead elephants. The exhibition "Carnets africains" was held in Paris in 1996 and 1997, and it launched the travel diary genre in France.

6. CLAUDE LAGOUTTE (1935–1990): JOURNEY FRAGMENTS

All of Claude Lagoutte's work is related to the journeys that shaped his life from 1959, the year he was posted to Laos after his studies at the École de santé navale. This two-year stay gave him the chance to discover Bangkok and Hong Kong. India drew him in repeatedly. In 1962, while stationed in Côte d'Ivoire, he discovered African art in Abidjan. After his return to France in 1965, he continued to travel, including to Morocco, Spain and Holland. In 1971, on a trip to Bayreuth, he began his first travel diary. In 1975 and 1976, he worked on unprimed and unframed canvas that was impregnated with pigments, mud and earth brought back from his trips out into nature, a support medium that was cut into strips that were then stitched together. From 1978, his works followed the rhythm of the landscapes he crossed and had parallels with travel diaries. From 1978, he exhibited his works in New York and at the Centre Pompidou. Between 1984 and 1986, his accordion-folded book creations were inspired by his travels in India, Kashmir and Tibet and along the Ganges. They mixed collages, stitched fabrics, drawings, text and painted letters sent to his family.

7. MAX PAM (BORN 1949): SCRAPBOOKS

Max Pam, an Australian photographer and storyteller, spent twenty years travelling in India from the end of the 1960s.[9] To study film production, he drove from Calcutta to London via Afghanistan, spending five months on the hippie trail. He then embarked on fifteen different trips to India, and especially the Kerala region. In 1986, he photographed the Aboriginal communities of Australia. Between 1995 and 1997, he interrupted his design studies to go to Tibet and undertake a project on Asian body languages, which he finished in 1999 with a one-month pilgrimage. Out of this experience, *Kailash, 1999 – No Hope, No Fear* was born.[10] From 1997, he developed a passion for Africa and especially Ethiopia, where in 2000 he produced a daily travel journal, entitled *Ethiopia*. His work examines the relationship between photography and text and between photography and graphic arts. It encourages reflection on the layout and the framing of images with text.

---

9. His wanderings led to the publication of the book *Going East: Twenty Years of Asian Photographs* in 1992 (Marval).
10. *Tibet, Kailash* (Les Imaginayres, 2002).

• Kailash, 1999 – No Hope, No Fear.
Max Pam's tale of the Mount Kailash pilgrimage is told through 6 X 6 photographs that are truly composed like paintings.

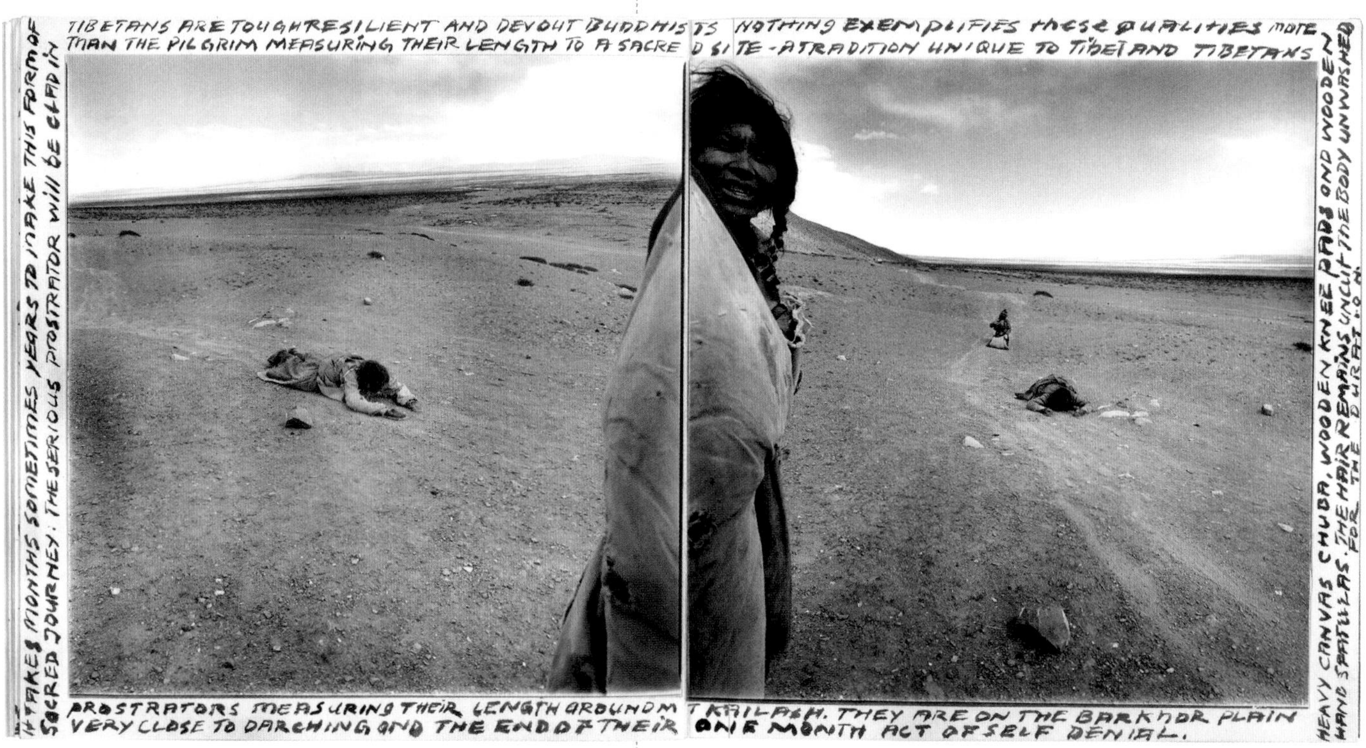

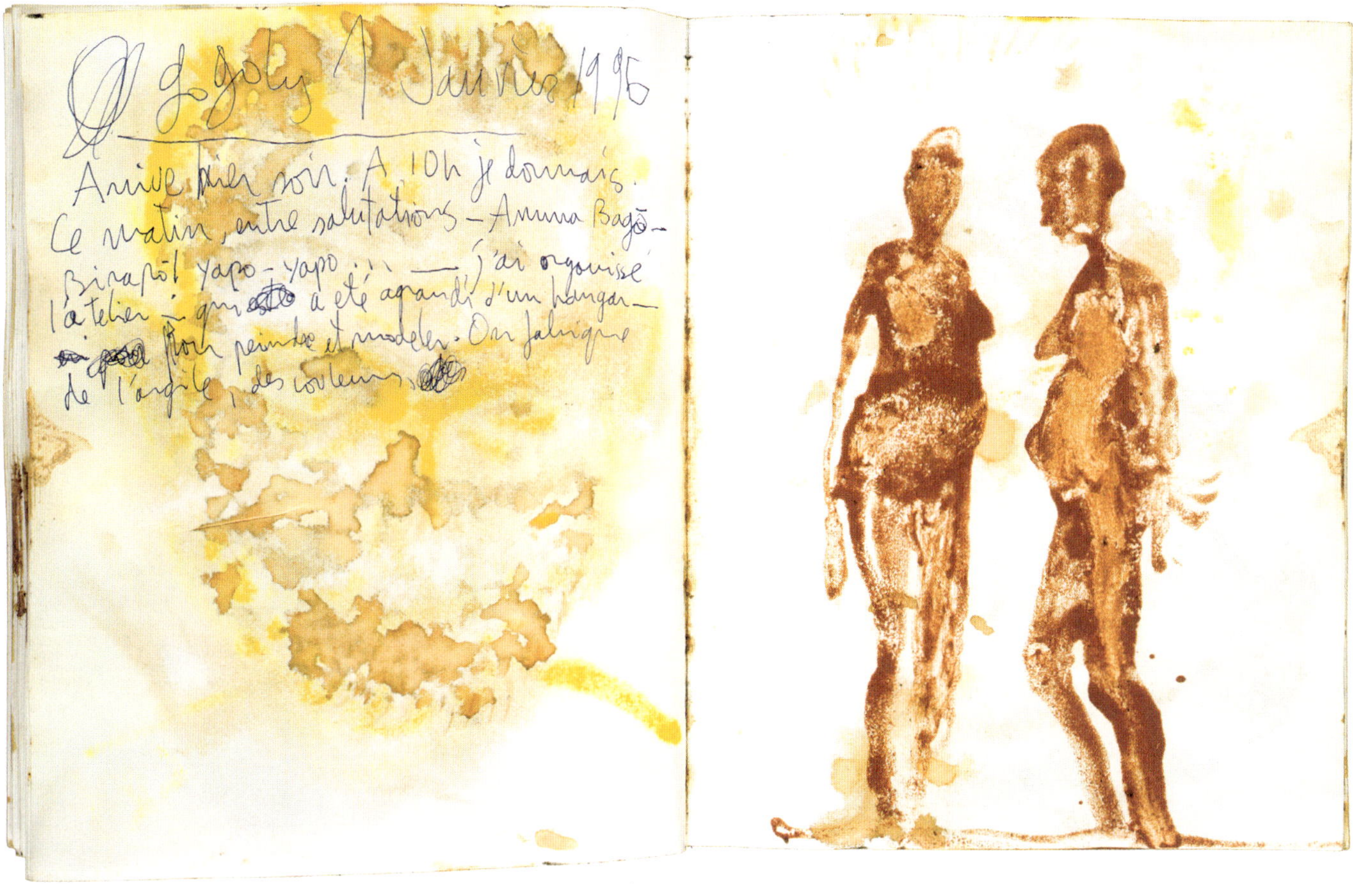

• During his trips to Africa, the Majorcan artist Miquel Barceló was prolific in filling up diaries; he made about 30 to 50 sketches per day.

8. MIQUEL BARCELÓ (BORN 1957): DIARIES AND NOMADIC INSTALLATIONS

The Majorcan artist Miquel Barceló became interested in Africa from close up, discovering it in 1988 through Mali, Senegal and Burkina Faso. During this period, he completed many sketchbooks using watercolours or natural pigments, producing thirty to fifty drawings per day. In 1991, he built a "canoe-studio" and spent two weeks on the Niger River, making a fourteen-hundred-kilometre journey northeast as far as the Bani river, accumulating diaries as he went—some of which were eaten by termites. He then went back down the river to Ségou, where he created paintings of the Dogon country from sketches. A year later, his first diaries were exhibited at the Carré d'art in Nîmes, while those from Mali were published in the Spanish newspaper *El País*. The "canoe-studio" was also the subject of an installation, giving the journey the status of work of art. In 1992, the Malian watercolours taken from his diaries illustrated Paul Bowles's fable of an artist's life in Gao in the book *La Boucle du Niger*. In 1996, the work of Barceló, whose latest creations included mixtures of rice, seaweed, flint, cigarette butts, earth, ash and meat, was the subject of two Parisian exhibitions, one at the Centre Pompidou ("Carnets de croquis africains") and then one at the Galerie nationale du Jeu de Paume ("Impressions d'Afrique").

9. HERVÉ DI ROSA (BORN 1959): DIARIES OF THE ARTS MODESTES

Hervé Di Rosa, the visual artist behind Sète's Musée international des arts modestes (2000), began a world tour in 1993, during which he undertook a series of works inspired by the cultures and modes of expression of each country he passed through. The first series, the "Di Rosaïcônes," was created in Bulgaria according to icon-making techniques. In 1994, he created paintings on panels in Ghana, in reference to the advertising signs commonly found in West Africa. In Benin, he worked with "appliqués" (fabric sewn on canvas); these were the subject of an exhibition at the Musée national des Arts d'Afrique et d'Océanie. In 1996, he painted, following an Ethiopian technique, on parchment made from zebu and lamb skins. He then stayed in Vietnam, where he made lacquerware with mother-of-pearl inlay, before heading in 1997 to Durban, South Africa, where he collaborated with Zulu craftsmen.[11] In 1998, he began publishing his travel diaries, including *Hervé Di Rosa en Corse: sixième étape autour du monde*, *Autour du monde, 10e étape: Mexique*, and *Journal modeste: dessins, extraits de cahiers*. In total, by 2007 he had produced around fifty diaries of drawings—the fruit of drawing on a daily basis since 2000—that are halfway between personal diary and travel diary.

10. TONY SOULIÉ (BORN 1955): PHOTO-PAINTING DIARIES

A globetrotter and renowned artist, Tony Soulié has participated in two hundred collective exhibitions since 1977 in Europe, the United States, Latin America and Japan. Following his first installation in 1983, he began working at different natural sites around the world. Since 2003, he has published travel diaries that he illustrates through his very personal technique of photo-painting: *Sao Tomé: le rêve africain*, *L'Œil excessif: entre Loire et océan* (2004) and *Taros* (2006), which takes the reader from Brest to Zanzibar via the Gulf of Guinea. Along with Jean-Yves Le Dorlot and Patrick Grainville, he created a book on New York, *New York 11 206* (2011), then a travelogue, *Lagos*, with Dominique Sigaud-Rouff, before publishing his first photo album, *Tony Soulié, autour du monde*.

11. These works would be exhibited in Durban and Johannesburg.

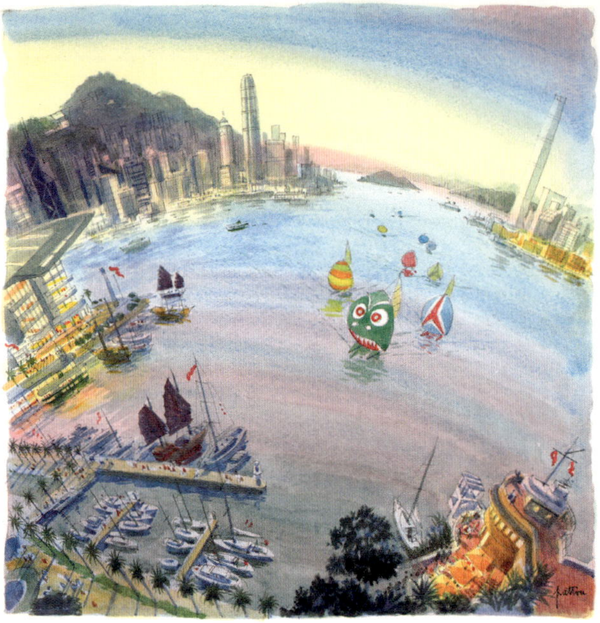

• *Inspired by the cities of the world, Jean Pattou reproduces their atmospheres in his dreamlike illustrations. Above, a preparatory watercolour sketch of the Hong Kong Yacht Club (2012).*

11. JEAN PATTOU (BORN 1940): DIARIES OF URBAN PAINTINGS

The architectural painter Jean Pattou was born in northern France in 1940 and is an architect and urban planner based in Lille. He has been exhibiting his city paintings and drawings to the world since 1980. Since 1989, he has illustrated two travel diaries with his watercolours: *Marseille sur mer* by Jean-Louis Parisis, and *Les Ponts de Paris: voyage fantastique* by Michel Cantal-Dupart. His interest in Parisian heritage gave rise to *Paris Caprices*, produced with Jacques Mullender in 1992, and to *Places de Paris*, created with Jean-Marc Léri in 1995. He has also produced some huge frescoes, such as his "Piranesian" piece (three walls of 50 x 18 m) that adorns the rough concrete walls of the metro station Lille-Europe in Lille. In this place of transit and urban interconnections, his work delivers a dreamy representation of London, Brussels, Barcelona, Athens and New York. His watercolour works *Lille Folies* (2003) and *Montmartre Délires* (2006) offer "a frenzy of incredible perspectives, a frenzy of new imaginings, a frenzy of images, a frenzy of words" and a poetic journey through the "dream towns" of Lille and Montmartre. His travel and painting diaries—*Le Pays Basque vu d'en haut* (2007), *Bordeaux, capitale inspirée* (2008) and *Saint-Jean-de-Luz, Ciboure: vue d'en face* (2013)—showcase the Southwest of France. In *Mon vieux-Lille* (2013), he invites the reader on a timeless stroll through his home town.

12. JULIEN "SETH" MALLAND (BORN 1972): STREET ART DIARIES

Alongside his studies at the École nationale supérieure des arts décoratifs, Julien "Seth" Malland worked in advertising as a sketch artist and began to paint the walls of Paris. In *Kapital: un an de graffiti à Paris* (2001), which he coauthored with Gautier Bischoff, he gives an overview of Paris's graffiti artists. For this versatile artist (he's a painter, illustrator, reporter, photographer and publisher), his immersive trips to meet people—he has explored Rio, São Paulo, Santiago, Valparaiso, Sydney, Hong Kong and Tokyo through contacts he's made on the ground—shape an artistic output that is focused on alternative ways of living and creating. *Globe-painter: 7 mois de voyages & de graffiti* (2007)[12] is a travel diary that traces his journey through countries influenced by street-art culture. His Canal+ series "Les Nouveaux Explorateurs" is an audiovisual version of the travel diary, in which he discovers countries through the prism of urban arts. After spending ten months in Brazil, in 2010 he published *Tropical Spray: voyage au cœur du graffiti brésilien*, which provides an overview of the lively street-art scenes of six Brazilian megalopolises (São Paulo, Recife, Rio de Janeiro, Brasilia, Belo Horizonte and Porto Alegre) and shows off sketches and activities that he undertook with local artists within the urban environment. *Extramuros: chroniques d'un globe-painter* (2012) follows a similar path, tracing three years of travel in eight different countries (India, China, Mexico, Chile, Indonesia, Vietnam, Senegal and Palestine).

12 Winner of the Prix spécial du jury at Clermont-Ferrand's Biennale du carnet de voyage.

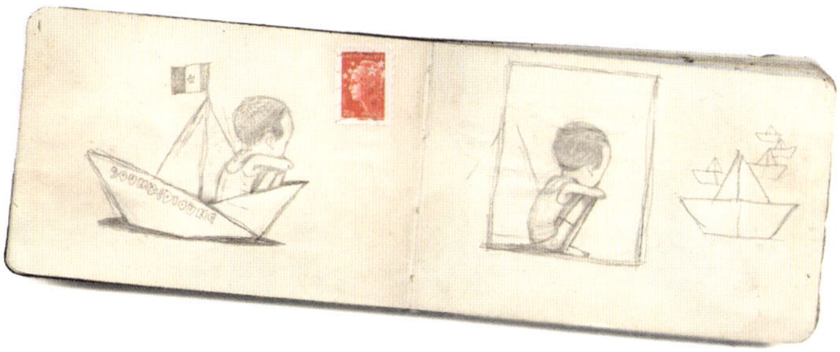

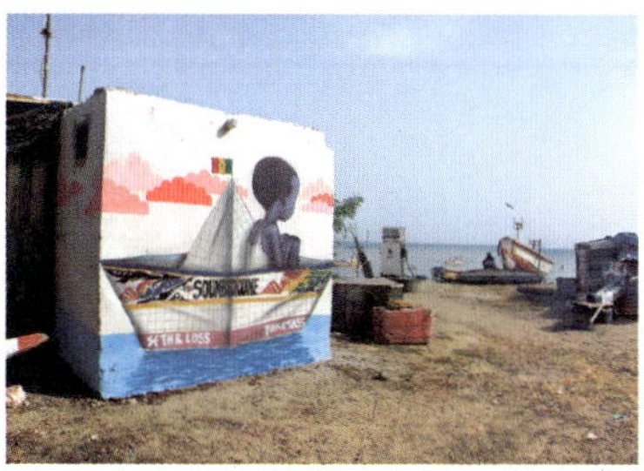

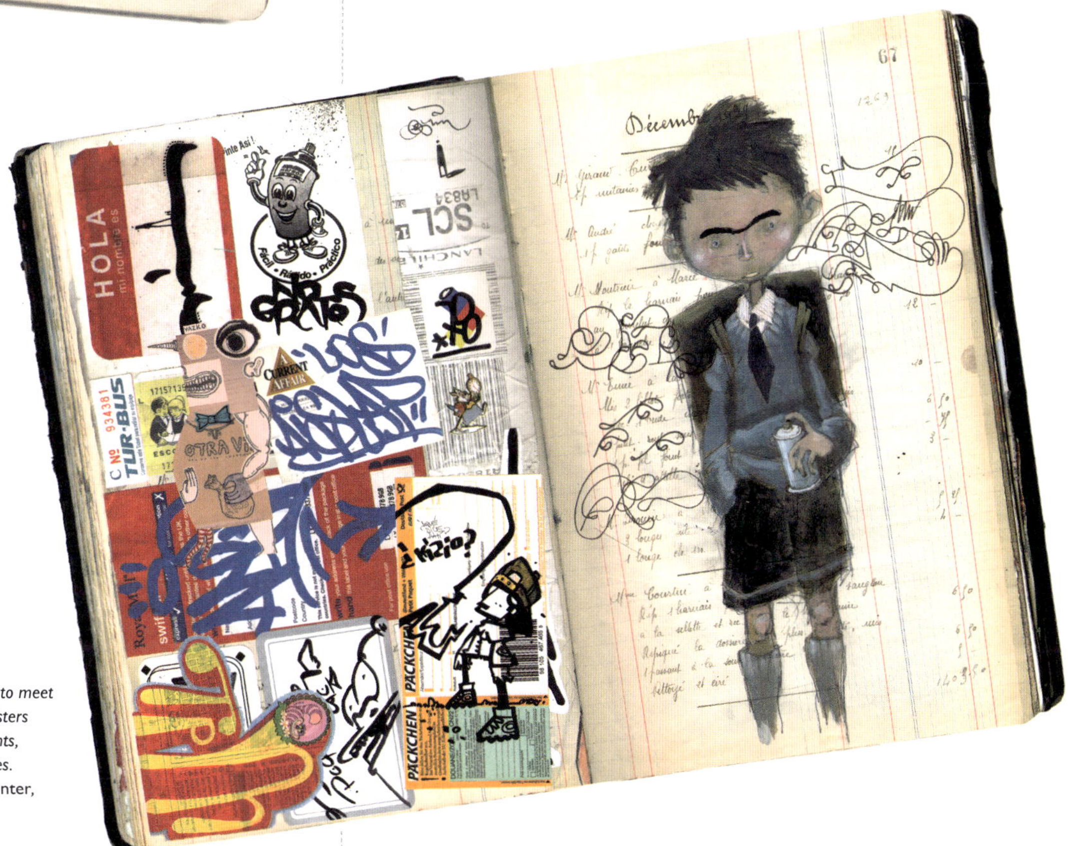

• *Julien "Seth" Malland travels the world to meet street-art communities, filling up old registers with sketches, photographs and documents, which are needed to make urban frescoes. Above,* Extramuros, *opposite,* Globe-painter, Alternatives, *2012 and 2007.*

3. Artistic and literary genres

TRAVEL LITERATURE AND TRAVELLING WRITERS

Following Victor Hugo's example, some authors have reported their wanderings with both a pen and a brush. This is the case of Henri Michaux (1899–1984), who was a writer, poet and painter. His travels fed both his literary and visual creativity. For ten years, from 1927 to 1937, he travelled around Asia, visiting India, China, Japan and Indonesia. He recounted his journey in *Un barbare en Asie*. In 1929, he discovered the Andes and then Ecuador and Brazil, which inspired his travelogue *Escuador*. Encouraged by Max Ernst and Paul Klee, his artistic explorations evolved towards the representation of signs and ideograms, and then towards calligraphy. It was only from 1936 that he exhibited his works and released, going through small publishers, books that he illustrated himself with lithographs or etchings of India ink images. From 1956, his hallucinogen-influenced drawings tended towards abstraction. The originality of his calligraphic and scriptural elements was what brought his work, which picked up an award at the 1960 Venice biennale, to the public's attention.

After travel writing characterized by journalism and the figure of the adventuring traveller, the conquest of the frontier to appropriate the new lands of the West inspired American literature. *On the Road* by Jack Kerouac (1922–1969) is a legendary work for globetrotters. In the long folk tradition of the American journey, "The road is life; it has replaced the old trail of the pioneers heading West." The manifesto of the Beat Generation, *On the Road* is based on the car trip that Kerouac made in 1949 with Neal Cassady and Anne Lu; they went from New York to San Francisco (6,200 kilometres) in three days and three nights. Kerouac took to the task of writing his novel in 1951, trying to find a natural and spontaneous flow in his writing via that famous first draft so admired by Cassady. He typed uninterruptedly for three weeks on a continuous, 40-metre-long roll to maintain an internal jazz rhythm. A first version written in French (*Sur le chemin*) appeared in 1952 in Mexico. It was then reworked once under the title *On the Road* before a final French version, *Sur la route*, was born. The Beat Generation movement celebrated the friendship between four men—Kerouac, Ginsberg, Cassady and Burroughs—in 1950s and 1960s America. It was strongly politically engaged and rejected the idea of chasing money. *On the Road* and *The Dharma Bums* by Kerouac, *Howl* by Ginsberg and *Naked Lunch* by Burroughs are its major works—symbols of freedom, a challenge to bourgeois values and a revolt against the world's greed.

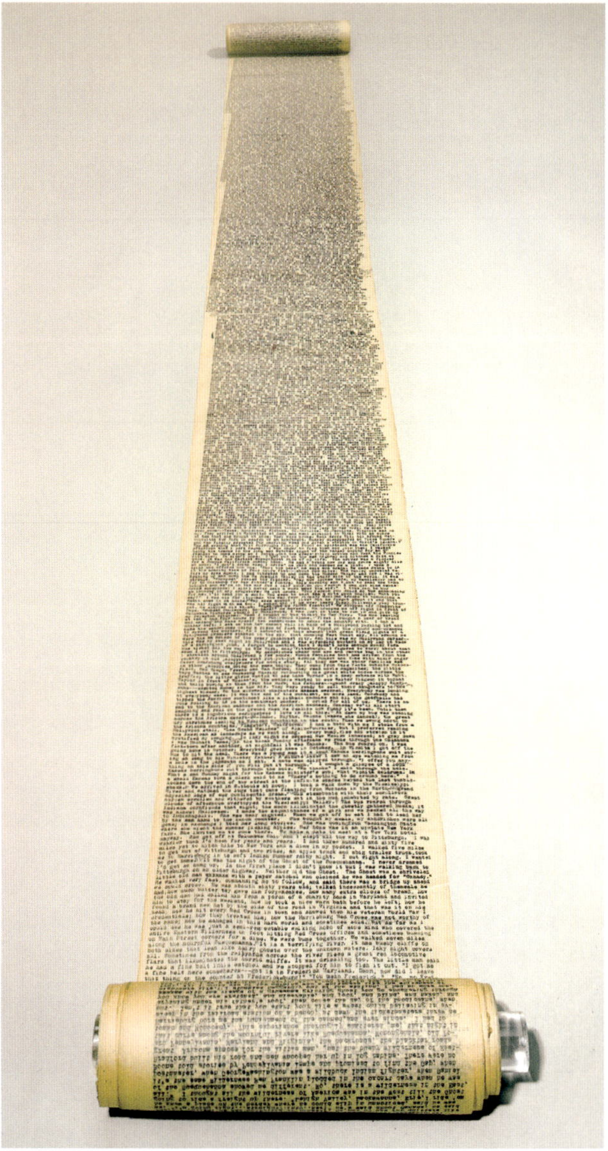

• *The scroll on which Jack Kerouac spent three weeks continuously writing the original text of the novel that became the manifesto of the Beat Generation,* On the Road *(1951).*

"DRAWN" OR "GRAPHIC" LITERATURE

From a historical point of view, American illustrators followed on in their establishment of war reporting from the French artist Constantin Guys, celebrated by Baudelaire in his essay *Le Peintre de la vie moderne*. In 1936, the cartoonist Saul Steinberg began to publish humorous drawings in a Milanese weekly, and he then became more widely known through his contributions to the *New Yorker*. He enlisted in the air force and fought in Asia in 1943 and then in Europe in 1944. The sketches he made while on duty were published the following year in *All in Line*. Will Eisner (*Last Day in Vietnam*) and Shel Silverstein became press cartoonists through their war reporting.

Steinberg subsequently took an interest in the American way of life (*Art of Living*, *Passport* and *The Discovery of America*). Robert Crumb was inspired in a similar way—he described New York's African-American neighbourhoods in 1964[13]—as was Eisner, who in 1981 published the *Big City* series on daily life in New York, as well as *The Will Eisner Sketchbook*,[14] which recounts the artist's life in the city, and 1995's *Dropsy Avenue*. These are "travel diaries" of a sort, produced through wandering around the American city, and they are also examples of graphic literature. His *A Contract with God* is an album in which text and drawings adapt freely to the needs of the story. In *Last Day in Vietnam* (Dark Horse, 2000), he freed himself from the confines of borders and text boxes and dared to produce more unexpected compositions in which captioned drawings are juxtaposed without being compartmentalized in panels. The expression "graphic novel" seems to have been born in 1964 at the instigation of Richard Kyle; the intention behind the term is to neutralize the pejorative connotations of the term "comics" (referring to the more traditional sort of cartoon) and lend nobility to this new trend in the "ninth art." This alternative type of work is unformatted and more literary; it is characterized by a more ample pagination and new, often autobiographical themes; it makes use of black and white; and it rejects iconographic language. An affirmation of this graphical style can be seen in Art Spiegelman's *Maus: A Survivor's Tale*.

PHOTOGRAPHERS ON THE ROAD

Whether it is Max Pam in India, Henri de Monfreid at the Red Sea or Henri Cartier-Bresson in Spain, Italy and Mexico, travelling photographers have captured the world with a sensitive eye. After years of sailing, the adventurer and painter Henri de Monfreid (1879–1974) turned to producing stereo photography along the Horn of Africa (Ethiopia, Harar, Djibouti and Aden) at the beginning of the twentieth century. In 1935, Ella Maillart (1903–1997), accompanied by the journalist Peter Flemming, set off to discover the isolated region of Chinese Turkestan, approaching it from India via Xinjiang and Karakoram.[15] Her travels in Central Asia and India until 1939 and then in Nepal from 1951 are recorded in over two hundred photographs. Pierre Verger (1902–1996), an ethnologist who specialized in Afro-Brazilian rituals, moved to São Salvador de Bahia, and in *Cinquante ans de photographies* he shares his research on traces of Africa's Yoruba culture (from Benin and Nigeria) in the Brazilian Northeast and in the Orixas and Voduns. Two emblematic figures of travel literature and a nomadic lifestyle, Bruce Chatwin (1940–1989) and Nicolas Bouvier (1929–1998), also used photography to convey their travels. Chatwin produced around ten observational diaries of shots from his travels around the world, including in Patagonia (*Photographies et carnets de voyage*, 1993). *L'Œil du voyageur* by Nicolas Bouvier brings together photographs of his journeys through the East between 1953 and 1958 (from Yugoslavia to India and Ceylon via Pakistan and Afghanistan), which were the focus of his *L'Usage du monde*.

Travel is a source of inspiration for photographers and provides material for their diaries—"vehicular panoramas" delivered by the road and travelling. In this context, two prolific artists have left their mark on the art of photography: Thierry Girard and Bernard Plossu. Girard, author of fourteen albums since 1982, paid tribute in 2007 to Victor Segalen through *Voyage au pays du réel* by following in the footsteps of the writer during his first stay in China (1909–1913), which was the inspiration for his poetic work *Équipée. Voyage au pays du réel*.

13. His *Sketchbook Reports* were only published in 1999, in Cornelius's "Blaise" collection.
14. A 1981 work published in French in 1989 through Comics USA.

15. A journey retraced in the 1936 work *Oasis interdites*.

• *Ella Maillart,* **Femmes et enfants kirghizes devant leur yourte de nomades: yourte en feutre,** *1935. When Maillart went to Chinese Turkestan, the region had been "forbidden" to travellers for four years.*

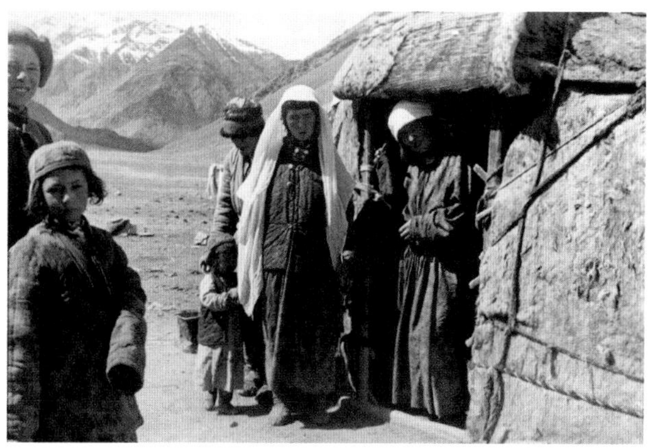

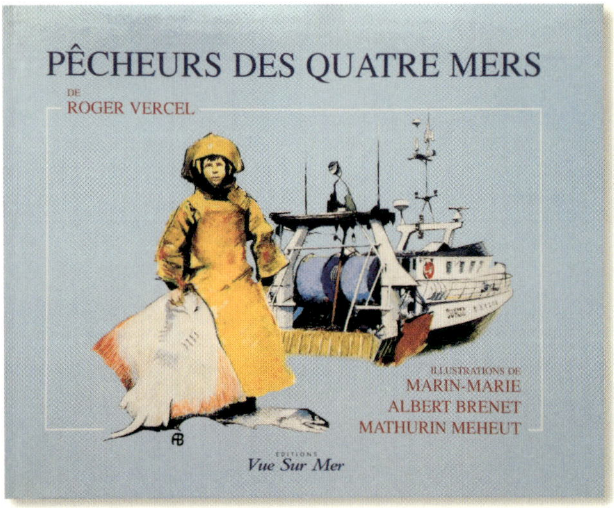

• *Written by Roger Vercel,* **Pêcheurs des quatre mers** *(Vue sur mer, 1957) was illustrated by three naval painters, including Mathurin Méheut, who produced his final work for the book in 1957.*

THE EMERGENCE OF A PUBLISHING GENRE IN FRANCE

Pioneering publishing initiatives from the 1950s to the 1980s

The two first travel diaries featuring graphic reportage date back to the 1950s. *Les Compagnons du Kon-Tiki* (1952) by Erik Hesselberg is a logbook of the expedition of the *Kon-Tiki* to the Polynesian Islands. *Pêcheurs des quatre mers* by Roger Vercel, meanwhile, published by Vue sur mer in1957, tells the story of sailors' lives. It was illustrated by the naval painters Marin-Marie, Albert Brenet and Mathurin Méheut. Gallimard's "Voiles" collection, which brings together renowned watercolourists and naval painters, published the amusing *Voyage autour du monde de la frégate l'Incomprise* by Sahib (1847–1919) in 1980. For the same publisher, Marc P.G. Berthier[16] produced *Aquarelles inédites sur l'eau et au bord de l'eau* (1988) and the travel diary *Coupe de l'América* after becoming an official naval painter in 1991. He also inaugurated the "Carnets de voyage" collection in 2000 with *Pen Duick: du croquis à l'aquarelle.* Titouan Lamazou, a member of Éric Tabarly's crew, turned his efforts to creating a travel diary in 1988 with the publication of *Sous les toits de terre: éléments d'architecture traditionnelle et décoration picturale dans l'habitat berbère des hautes vallées.* This work was followed in 1990 with *Un hiver berbère.*[17] *Antarctide, journal de bord d'un peintre dans les glaces* reveals the logbook of the polar sailboat "Antarctica," which set out on a scientific expedition conducted by Jean-Louis Étienne in southern seas between 1991 and January 1992. The following year, the young crew—aged between 12 and 16 years—of the boat *La Fleur de Lampaul*, which was used for an expedition known as "peuples de l'eau (1992–1993)," produced their first book under the title *Imraguen: les pêcheurs du désert*, published by Gallimard Jeunesse.

Sophie and Xavier Bohl Raverdy's *Maisons saisons: observation sur l'architecture vernaculaire lors d'un voyage à pied de Paris à Ankara*, was the first architecture book published by Éditions Alternatives in 1981. Six years later, Lizzie Napoli used the "travel diary" genre to highlight regional heritage through a collection with Rivages.[18] The "new generation" tourist guide is a variant of the travel diary that emphasizes excursions and visits to monuments. In 1985, the comic author Loustal made *80% d'humidité*, an artist's book in the form of a small box containing twenty-one observational drawings of the life of a small African hotel, a sort of logbook of Togo. The subsequent publication of his travel sketches was inspired by the *Escales* portfolios published by L'Atelier, to which he contributed in 1986.

Paul-Émile Victor gives an account of the life and the culture of the Ammassalik Inuit in the 1930s through the two-volume *La Civilisation du phoque*,[19] which could be considered logbooks or ethnological travel diaries.

16. Cofounder of the magazine *Voiles et voiliers* in 1971 and of the imprint Voiles-Gallimard in 1977.
17. These two books coauthored with Karin Huet have been respectively published by De Faucompret and Jeanne-Laffitte.

18. Équinoxe.
19. With Joëlle Robert-Lamblin.

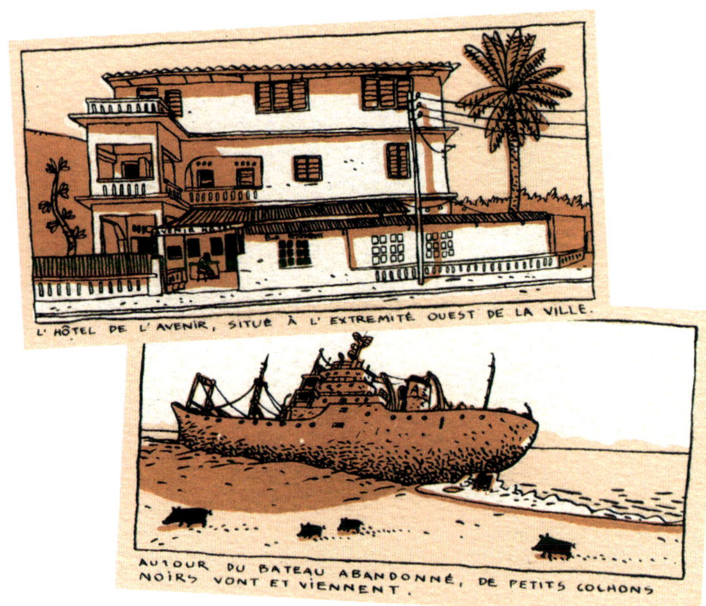

• **80 % d'humidité,** *Alain Beaulet, 1985. This 21-picture artist's book on the life of a small African hotel is by Loustal, a great lover of travel... and diaries!*

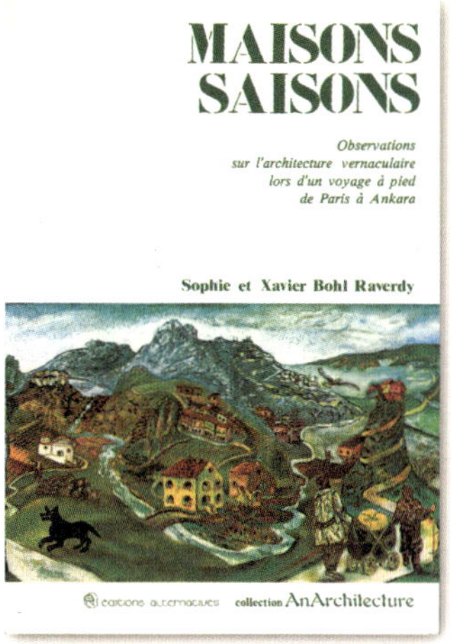

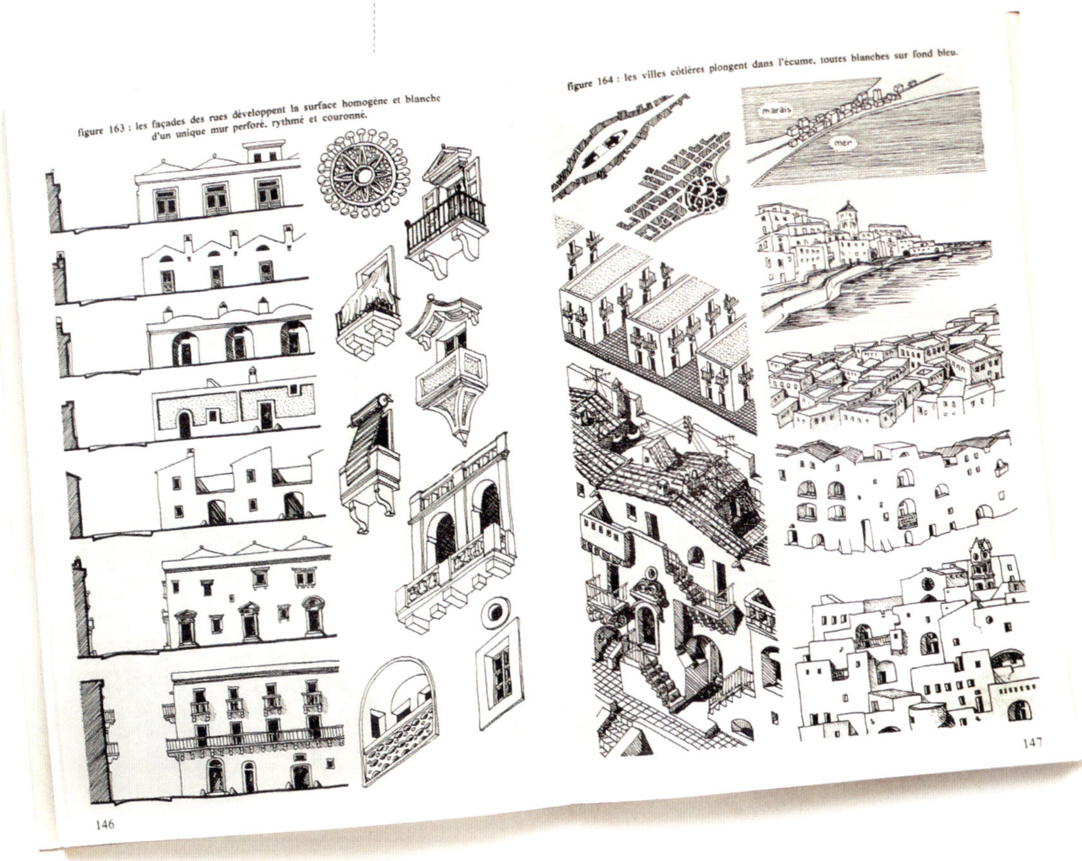

• Maisons saisons, *Alternatives, 1981.*
Sophie and Xavier Bohl Raverdy walk the road to Jerusalem. The journey narrated by Sophie is illustrated with drawings by Xavier of houses he came across.

Innovating publications, 1990 to 1995

In 1989, Jano published *Carnets d'Afrique* through Humanoïdes associés. *Carnet de voyages*, a comic album by Loustal that was created out of his travel sketches, appeared the following year through Futuropolis. Loustal, who is also a journalist for *Géo* and *Grands reportages*, created eleven works[20] for the first collection dedicated to travel sketches, which was launched in 1991 by Seuil. The same year, the "Carnets du monde" collection by Albin Michel Jeunesse, a project that was put forward by Laurent Corvaisier, paid tribute to the travel diary within the world of youth publishing in order to educate children on citizenship and safeguarding the environment. At the same time, between 1990 and 1992 Épigones's "Carnets de route" collection offered ten exploration stories to a younger audience.

Rascal and Louis Joos, illustrators for young-adult works and authors of comic strips, created the first illustrated children's logbook, *Escales: carnets de croquis*, for Pastel. In the work, sketches taken on the spot are annotated by texts that surround the image.

Janine Brégeon, a painter and writer based in Pondicherry since 1962, published one of the first travel diaries illustrated in black and white, *Un Voyage de France en Inde, 1952–1955: Jean et Janine chez les hommes*. Among contemporary press cartoonists, Cabu worked with the theme of culture clashes with *Sauve qui peut à l'Est* in 1991 and with *Cabu au Japon* in 1993, published in Seuil's "L'histoire immédiate" collection. In 1994, Monique Martin, an artist at the Palais de justice in Brussels for more than twenty years, published *Au palais*, a travel diary on the life at the court of assizes, through Casterman. A year later, Antoine Garapon and Noëlle Herrenschmidt, an illustrator for young people's works and court artist, published *Carnets de palais* with Albin Michel.

20. *Cuba, Maroc, Santo Dominguo, Guadeloupe, Seychelles, Europe, Japon, Équateur, Sénégal, Andalousie, Îles Marquises.* These titles have been grouped into a trilogy: *Carnet de voyages: 1981–1989*, *Carnet de voyage: 1991–1996* in 1997 and *Carnet de voyages: 1997–1999* in 2000.

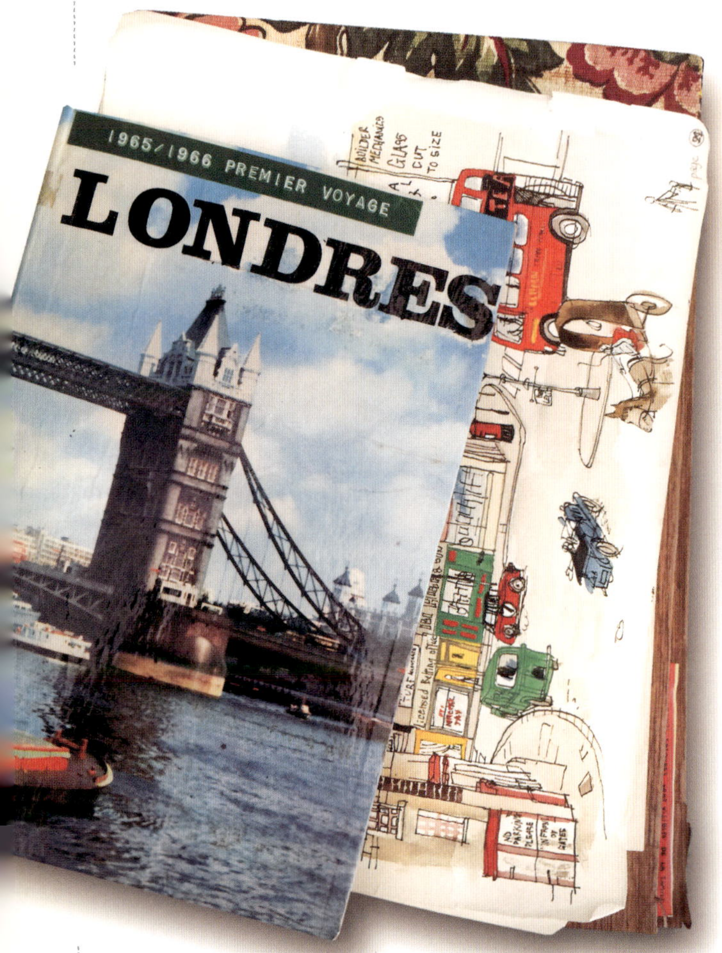

• *An illustrator and globetrotter, Alain Bouldouyre has been to more than half of the planet's 210 countries!*

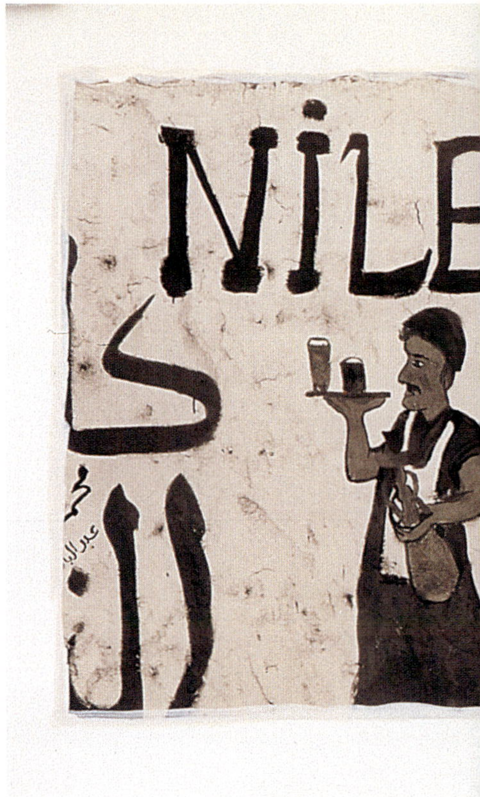

TRAVEL GUIDES AND ILLUSTRATION

Jean-Louis Pagès, creator of the Solilang guides, is the author of *Sur les chemins de la Méditerranée: aquarelles*, one of the first hybrid travel diary and guides, published in 1992 by Calmann-Lévy and Plume. Arthaud's collection "Vacances secrètes," which began in 1999 with the regions of France, branched out to Europe from 2001, while still retaining its objective of "seeing the countryside off the beaten track and cities through unusual itineraries, discovering the country at its own pace, enjoying the charm of unusual hotels or characterful cottages, tasting the specialities in auberges, restaurants and tables d'hôte that usually only the locals know about." The works now mention the name of illustrators, who include Alain Bouldouyre. He worked on three titles, which cover Scotland, Moscow and Berlin. A travel diary maker[21] since 1962, and an author of guides for Arthaud, he was also behind *Paris des poètes*, published in 2002 by Plume. Since 2000, he has been building many bridges between travel diaries and tourist guides.

---

21. Through his work he received a Zellidja award.

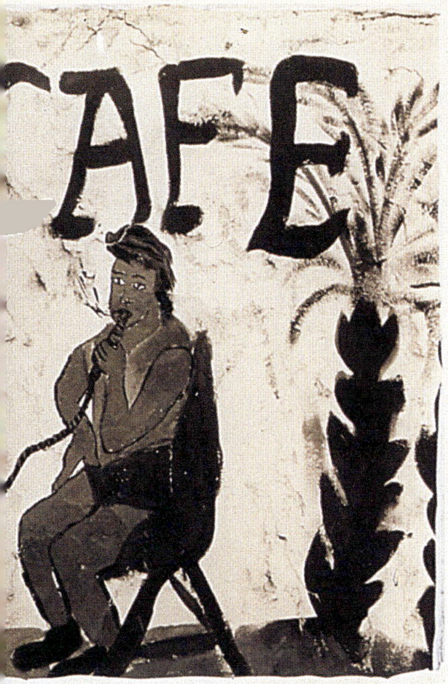

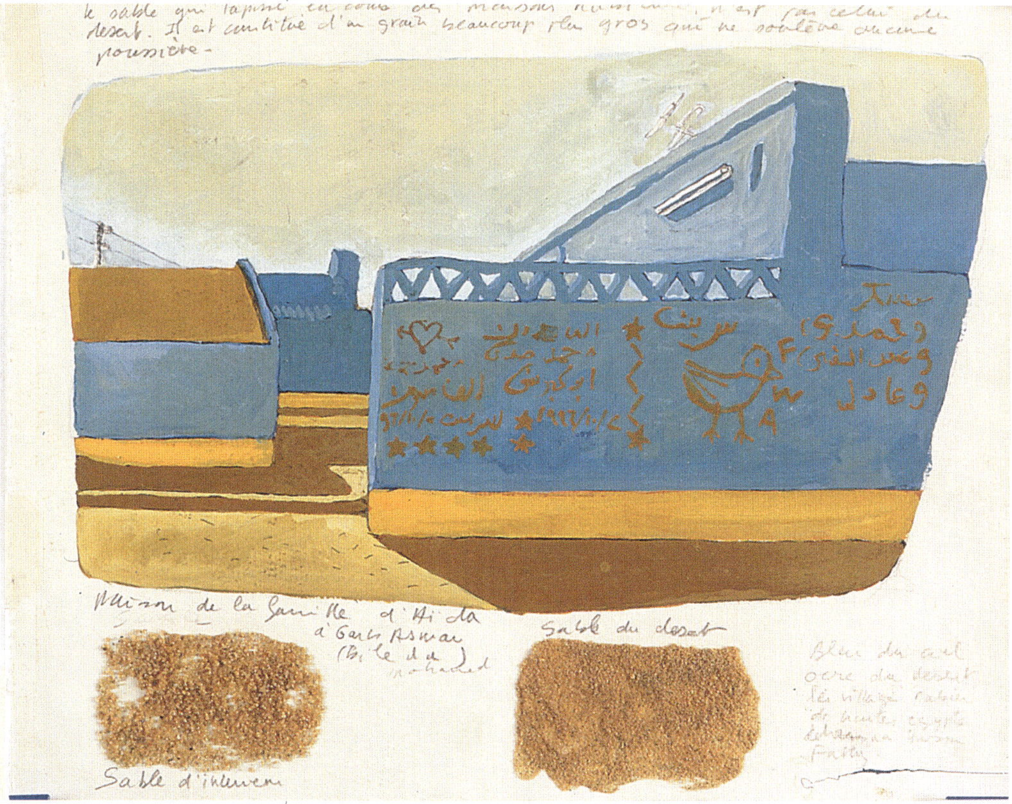

• Carnets de voyage, *Gallimard, 1998.*
In 1993, after almost 20 years at sea, Titouan Lamazou offered up diaries filled with drawings, notes, sketches, photographs and gouaches from his many trips.

Media attention for the genre from 1996

In 1996, Cornélius published Philippe Dupuy and Charles Berberian's *New York: carnets, avril–octobre 1995.* From 1997, *Les Correspondances de Pierre Christin* paved the way for drawn reportage, the outcome of a graphic exploration begun in 1984 with the album *L'Étoile oubliée de Laurie Bloom: Los Angeles, 1984*, which was coauthored with Enki Bilal. With *Impasse et Rouge: Cambodge 1970–1975* by Sera and *Palestine, une nation occupée* by Joe Sacco, comic reportage ushered in the arrival of travel reportage books. In 1998, Baudouin brought a collective of four artists[22] together around a destination—Egypt—in *L'Association en Égypte*, a project followed up in 2000 by *L'Association au Mexique* with another team, and then *L'Association en Inde* in 2006.

22. Golo in Cairo, Baudoin in Alexandria, David B. in the Siwa Oasis and Menu in Luxor.

Titouan Lamazou, a regular contributor to the genre[23] (the West Indies in 1974, the Moroccan Atlas region in 1989), published *Carnets de voyage* through Gallimard in 1988. Various publishers put out collections in the 1990s and 2000s, but two of them were truly pioneering: 1990's "Voiles" and "Carnets du littoral," launched by Françoise Chabbert and Dominique Legrain in 1996.

23. Titouan Lamazou's diaries were published in Air France's magazine between 1996 and 1998.

4. Contemporary trends

TOWARDS THE ARTIST'S TRAVEL BOOK

Like the artist's book and mail art, the travel diary remains more a form of artistic expression than a publishing genre: a work on travelling or a well-travelled work, it bears the marks of itinerancy and nomadism, and it testifies to a completed journey. Makers of travel diaries such as Stefano Faravelli, Hervé Grimal, Nicolas Jolivot, Sarah Letouzey and Gwenaëlle Trolez, as well as artists such as Frédérique Le Lous Delpech, Yvan Pommaux and Eni Looka, have invented other graphic creations, forms and dimensions that go beyond the book format. Where Nicolas Jolivot gave us both accordion albums on China and creative culinary diaries (*Nakoul: on mange à Marrakech* and *Chifan: mangeons en Chine*), Eni Looka and Dominique Penloup were inspired by mail art, and Pierre Josse has reworked the postcard.

Frédérique Le Lous Delpech on the historical logbook
"This travel diary was made by using the logbook of my great-grandfather, who was a sailor. He travelled in the Far East between 1907 and 1910. One hundred and four years separate our journey; I go through his trip with him following the rhythm of those three years. This artist's book, created out of the texts from his logbook, his postcards to his partner in Brittany, the objects he brought back from different countries, documents kept in the family's possession and old maps, was also a way to redo this journey and discover this great-grandfather whom I barely knew. It comes in the form of three large leporellos of 30 pages (each is about 4.50 m when unfolded; the page dimensions are 48 x 21 cm). It contains etchings, collage, animation and hand cutting. I started it in October 2011 and I'm trying to complete it to this day."

Eni Looka on mail art and travelogues
"I love travelling and recounting what I discovered through drawing, just like many members of my family (for several generations, many of us have travelled around while sketching and painting with watercolours). A mail-art enthusiast for more than thirty years, this is essentially the form that I use to make my travelogues. From the places I visit, I apply stamps that I make myself to the mail that I send to my friends. These are original illustrations (in pencil, pen or watercolour) that I carefully cut around with scissors, making serrations similar to the ones you see on real stamps. And it works as well in France as it does abroad... I often also do the envelope design, or else glue photos, pebbles, driftwood, plants, pieces of fabrics or other objects found on the spot to it. I have carried out my activities as a globe-trotting forger with success (almost always, my stamps arrive at their destination) in 40 countries (including the United States, Canada, Mexico, Australia, Russia, China, Mongolia, Czechoslovakia, Denmark and Iceland). And I have sometimes had fun creating nations that do not exist (Scotland, Corsica); the postal services frank the stamps without batting an eyelid!"

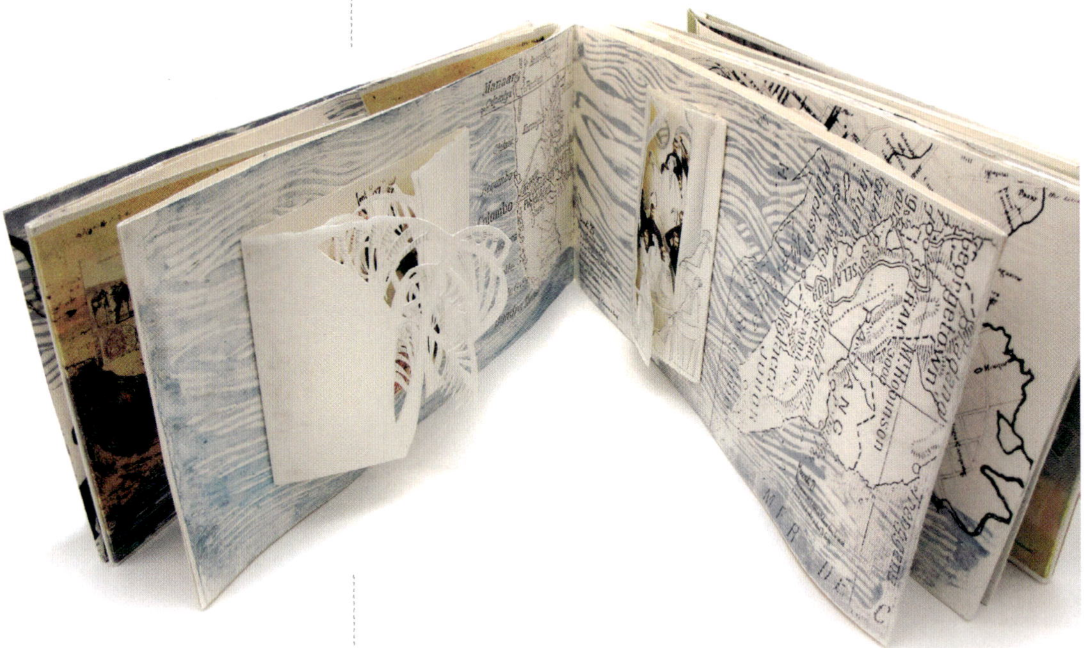

• *Frédérique Le Lous Delpech creates livres-objets that are made from paper she produces herself and that are illustrated with embossed prints.*

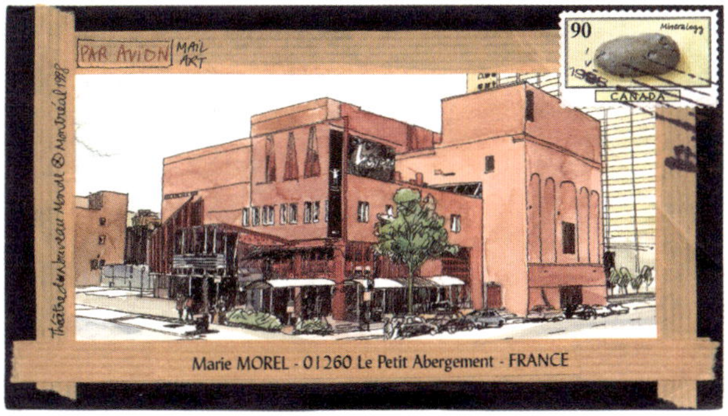

• A mail art enthusiast, Eni Looka takes advantage of trips abroad to keep travel diaries. She sends their pages by mail to her family and friends. Above, an envelope addressed from Canada.

TOWARDS DRAWN REPORTAGE

The three strengths of "thinking visually"[24]—social critique, illustrated reporting and narration—appear to be transposable to the travel diary. This filiation can be seen in the satirical drawings of *Charivari* and the illustrated reportage of the 1950s and 1960s, with the pictorial essays of Paul Hogarth, Robert Weaver and Robert Andrew Parker, which paved the way for visual journalism. From 1952, Weaver created visual essays, transforming the illustrator into a journalist who travels the world, pencil in hand. His influence at the avant-garde of American illustration could be seen in all magazines from the late 1960s. He covered the Kennedy campaign for *Esquire*. The exhibition-essay "Seeing is Not Believing" on him at the Norman Rockwell Museum, which incorporated a series of images on urban life in New York ("New York Unbound"), perfectly summarizes the artistic stance contained within the exhibition's name.

It is also the spirit of the magazine *XXI*, which brought the innovation of thirty-page illustrated reportage pieces on a topical subject, often in comic-strip or graphic-story form. Created in November 2008, this magazine came about through an encounter between a freelance editor, Laurent Beccaria (publication manager) and a great reporter, Patrick de Saint-Exupéry (chief editor). Over the course of two hundred pages, this quarterly publication made up of nine sections brings together a full range of reporting talents—novelists, journalists, photojournalists and comic artists—to understand the world, "to take time and a step back by having the space to report with total freedom" in order to "reflect reality as closely and as fairly as possible." For the first time, the graphic narrative is being treated as a successful—50,000 copies are distributed each issue—and full-fledged genre. "100% new, 0% advertising" is the publication's motto and the anniversary manifesto of its first five years in print. *La Revue dessinée* is also a quarterly magazine (digital and paper) of more than two hundred pages of illustrated news, reportage, documentaries and columns in comic form. The text-image balance changes depending on the purpose and the narrative necessity. The idea was launched by the illustrator Franck Bourgeron in the autumn of 2011 in order to retell goings-on in the world through drawing. It was announced at the Angoulême international comic-strip festival in January 2012. Since 2011, Clermont-Ferrand's Rendez-vous du carnet de voyage has offered an exhibition space called "reportage diaries," which is becoming more and more digital, following the model of the magazine *XXI*. In 2011, the Swiss press cartoonist Patrick Chappatte produced an animated reportage on southern Lebanon entitled *La Mort est dans le champ*, which was broadcast on TV Suisse and Canal+ and at a score of documentary festivals. It won an award at Sydney's Flickerfest 2012.

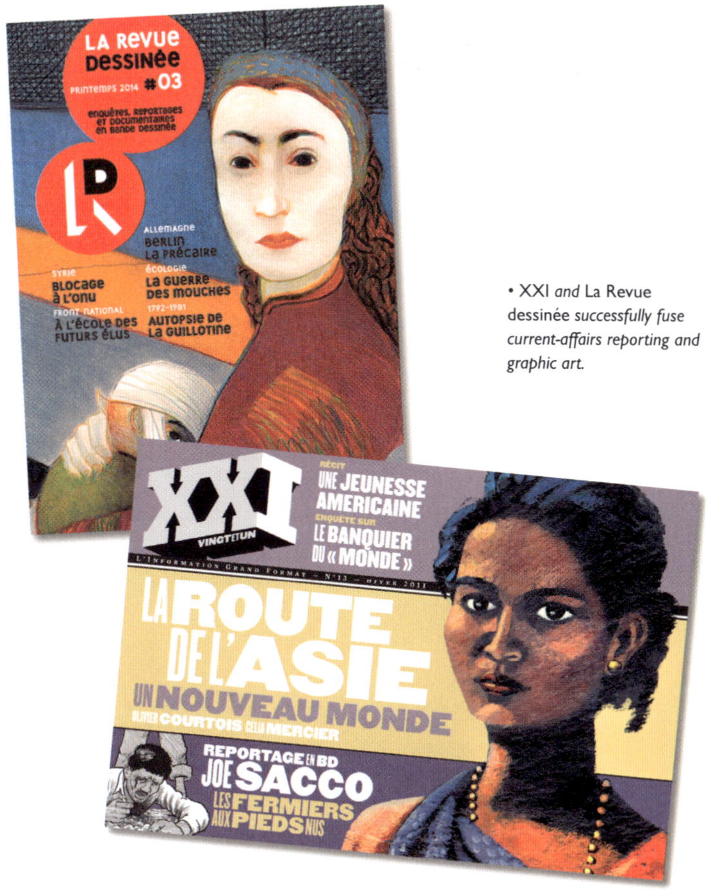

• XXI and La Revue dessinée successfully fuse current-affairs reporting and graphic art.

24. Mark Wigan, *Pensée visuelle*, Pyramyd.

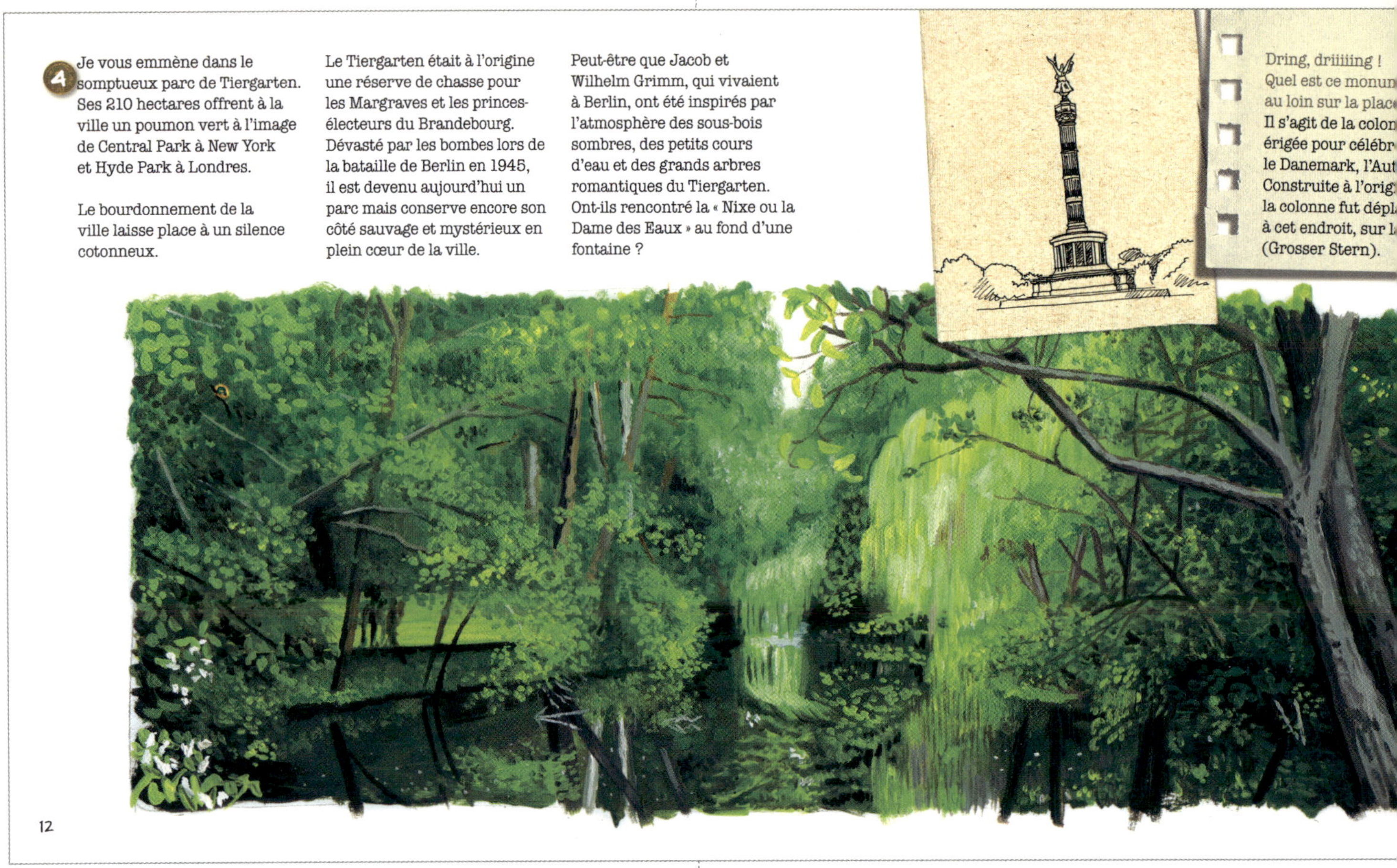

4 Je vous emmène dans le somptueux parc de Tiergarten. Ses 210 hectares offrent à la ville un poumon vert à l'image de Central Park à New York et Hyde Park à Londres.

Le bourdonnement de la ville laisse place à un silence cotonneux.

Le Tiergarten était à l'origine une réserve de chasse pour les Margraves et les princes-électeurs du Brandebourg. Dévasté par les bombes lors de la bataille de Berlin en 1945, il est devenu aujourd'hui un parc mais conserve encore son côté sauvage et mystérieux en plein cœur de la ville.

Peut-être que Jacob et Wilhelm Grimm, qui vivaient à Berlin, ont été inspirés par l'atmosphère des sous-bois sombres, des petits cours d'eau et des grands arbres romantiques du Tiergarten. Ont-ils rencontré la « Nixe ou la Dame des Eaux » au fond d'une fontaine ?

Dring, driiiiing !
Quel est ce monun
au loin sur la plac
Il s'agit de la colon
érigée pour célébr
le Danemark, l'Aut
Construite à l'orig
la colonne fut dépl
à cet endroit, sur l
(Grosser Stern).

12

TOWARDS THE ILLUSTRATED TRAVEL GUIDE

In 2009, several guides took inspiration for creativity and innovation from travel diaries. For example, *Ma Bretagne autour de Perros-Guirec* by Dominique Corbasson, both a travel diary and tourist guide, was published in 2009 by Ouest-France. The work offers a range of itineraries on foot, by bike and by boat, as well as seventy illustrations in acrylic and an assortment of tips on restaurants, beaches, markets and mooring spots. The Conservatoire du littoral's *Carnets de mission*, *Armoriques: balades de Corto Maltese en Bretagne* (Casterman/Cong sa, 2003), *City guides illustrés* (Ouest-France) and *Itinéraires* (Casterman) mix genres to communicate clearly with their tourist audience. Yann Breton does the same thing in his work *Itinéraires de voyageurs: Japon* (2012). Some illustrators of travel diaries, for example Florine Asch, have also illustrated tourist guides for Arthaud's collection "Vacances secrètes." From 2007, Alain Bouldouyre began contributing to the English-language "Authentik Books" collection, the product of a collaboration between a French publisher and an American one (Mont-Tonnerre and Globe Pequot Press). The three titles on London and three others on Paris articulate the art of living on the Old Continent: *Artistik London*, *Chic London*, *Gourmet London*, *Gourmet Paris*, *Artistik Paris* and *Chic Paris*.

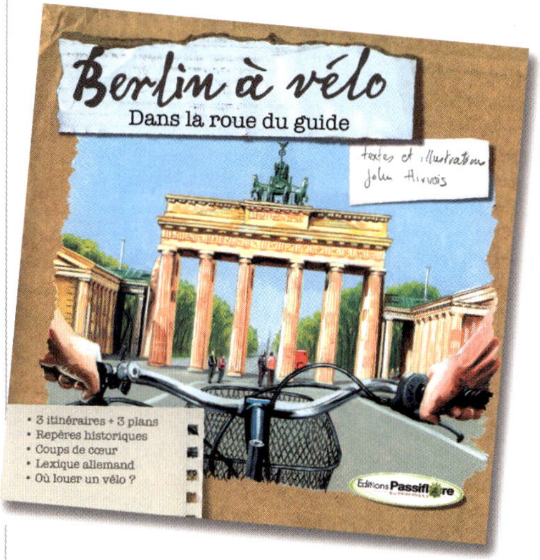

• John Hirvois, Berlin à vélo *and* Rome à vélo, *éditions Passiflore, 2013.*
Tourist guides and travel diaries have always been bedfellows. This harmony permeates the books of the "Dans la roue du guide" collection, which invites readers to discover cities using bikes.

Éditions Passiflore on the collection "Dans la roue du guide."

"This collection includes four diaries (plus two—Bordeaux and Paris—that have been translated into English) that sketch out cycling tours in Berlin, Bordeaux, Paris and Rome. The seed of the project was sown in John Hirvois's mind during a weekend in Rome. Éditions Passiflore decided to extend the concept to other destinations. With a bike you can freely roam around a city and fully enjoy its heritage. The tour routes guide the reader through a discovery of the city's monuments, parks and gardens, and especially its highlights: a typical neighbourhood, a piece of architecture, a beautiful view, a special shop and characterful people. You don't visit Berlin, Bordeaux, Paris or Rome in the same way. The development of bike paths and bike culture is not at the same level in them. The routes are meticulously plotted to allow cyclists (or pedestrians) to go on user-friendly paths. Historical commentaries and a frieze at the end of the book enrich the journey. These books provide a fresh look at the cities they cover through the pencil strokes of an author who gives it all an inviting feel. John invites the reader to follow him on an exciting path. These are books that you look at and keep looking back at. The artistic content is made from a mixture of oil paintings, pencil work and black markers: different techniques that allow the subject being drawn to be singled out and highlighted, working from memory and the sensory footprint left by the scenery passed by during the bike ride."

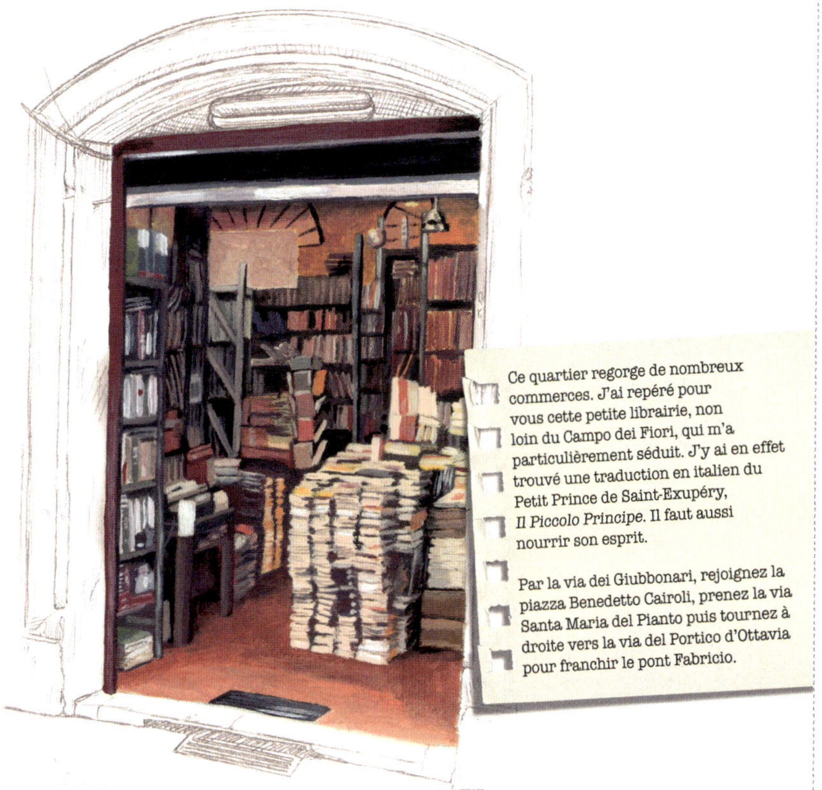

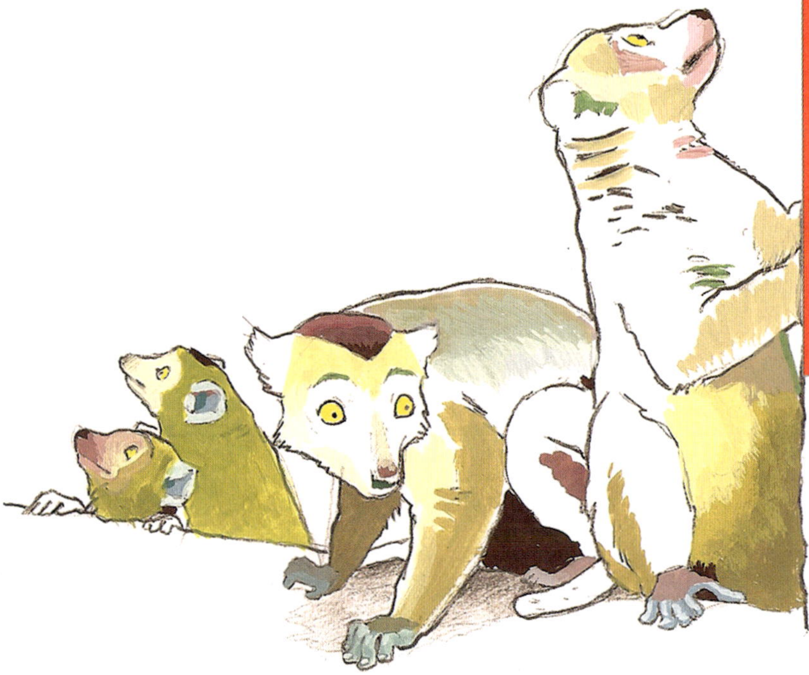

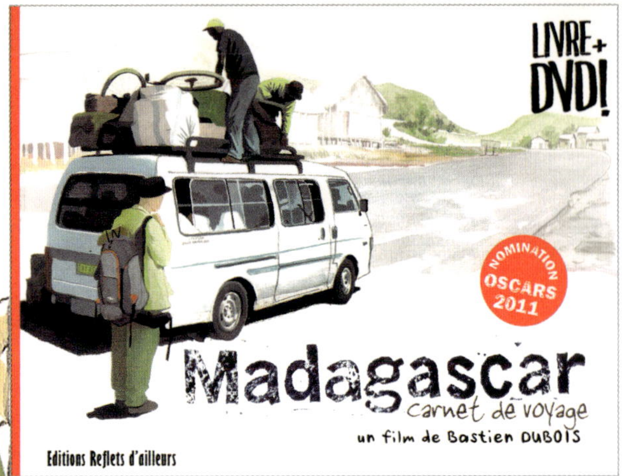

• Madagascar, carnet de voyage, *Reflets d'ailleurs, 2011. To create an animated travel diary, Bastien Dubois spent a year in Madagascar—an incredible experience that won a nomination for an Oscar in 2011.*

TOWARDS MEDIA CIRCULATION AND COMBINING ARTS

The travel diary has opened up to the performing arts, spreading and flowing from discipline to discipline. *Typographies Parallèles* is an offering from Michel Bouvet with scenography by Sandro Agostini and mise en espace by Stéphane Déplan and Laurence Delmas. During his travels around the world, Michel Bouvet photographs the streets of the towns he visits or passes through. It is a kind of "typo-trip." The travel diaries of the Galapiat circus in Argentina and Chile recount its three-month journey across Latin America from east to west—Buenos Aires to Valparaiso—in 2011.

The travel diary can allow one to discover different art forms such as textiles, as is the case with Catherine Legrand's diaries, illustrated by Satomi Ichikawa et Anaïs Guéry: *Textiles et vêtements du monde: carnet de voyage d'une styliste* and *Carnet d'inspirations textiles* (2007 and 2008). In *Indigo: périple bleu d'une créatrice textile* (2012), this designer tells the story of her two years spent travelling the world to learn about the production of indigo, the know-how of dyers, clothing and the fabrics treated with the dye. Travel diaries also extend to other visual arts such as cinema, as is the case with the "Carnet de tournage" collection of short films started in 2011 by Michel Francillon and Pascale Fontaine (Reflets d'ailleurs) in association with the Festival international du court-métrage. The first title, *Madagascar: carnet de voyage, un film de Bastien Dubois* (a book and DVD), which was nominated for the 2011 Oscars, brings to light the creation of an animated documentary. According to Michel Francillon, "this collection allows you to understand the genesis of a short film, from the first idea conceived by the author to the film's final cut. On the paths to creating and producing a film, production diaries are like travel diaries, with their notes, drawings, photos and technical information. The book plunges us into the making of the film and the construction of an individual work, and the DVD reveals a strange and fascinating work."

Street art has not escaped the attentions of the genre. In *Street Artbooks: carnet de voyages* (2012), Tristan Manco invites us to meet street artists from London to Mexico City and Bogota, who tell of their journeys into the world of street art and present, in parallel with their urban creations, the secret pages of their sketchbooks.

TOWARDS DIGITAL AND TRANSMEDIA

As an album and art book, the travel diary seeks out originality to fully bring the journey experience to life. In keeping with this desire to innovate, multimedia has helped to diversify the characteristics and dissemination of works. The "travel diary" genre is therefore constantly evolving—due to its very nature. Often viewed as a rough draft, palimpsest or work in progress, the travel diary is well suited to the artistic experimentation, research and creativity involved in the process of intermediality. Transmedia narration, a new creative challenge for the diary, focuses on the experience that the user can gain from multiple convergent media to enrich its overall vision of a fictional universe or a story. The parts of this puzzle, which are each different from one another, remain complementary because they are attached to a same base narrative reference. The audience is flung into being a "spect'actor" through stories that branch out from one medium to the other in multiple forms—film, animated shorts, video games, comics, and so on. According to the Centre national du cinéma et de l'image animée's Valérie Bourgoin, "transmedia is a global creation concept that offers a form of writing that is specific to each of the media forms that the creation calls on; these media complement each other in terms of narrative." So a transmedia travel diary could be seen as a succession of media and narratives that combines comics, blogs, publications with a global focus, photo albums and film.

Karen Guillorel on her approach

"My creative approach has two key dimensions at the moment. Firstly, there are the main themes of travel, and the appeal of travelling in particular. These are unveiled using written media, video, cartoons, comics, music, and so on. Secondly, these themes are approached through a so-called realistic universe, but also imaginary ones. Narration is fundamental to all this. The challenge of my work is to push traditionally set limits at the narrative level. Everything is still to be invented when it comes to three-dimensional space and narration, elements I've studied in the research laboratory at the ENSAD in Paris. There is the possibility of creating a gigantic narrative puzzle whose components are told through several media that correspond to one another and are stories in themselves but also contribute to a broader narrative construction, of telling big stories and epics, and of allowing self-expression through very different media. With transmedia, we are going back to the era of the storyteller."

• 6000 km du couchant au levant, *2009. Karen Guillorel embarked on a journey to Jerusalem on foot and by bike, "being relaxed about culture shock from country to country."*

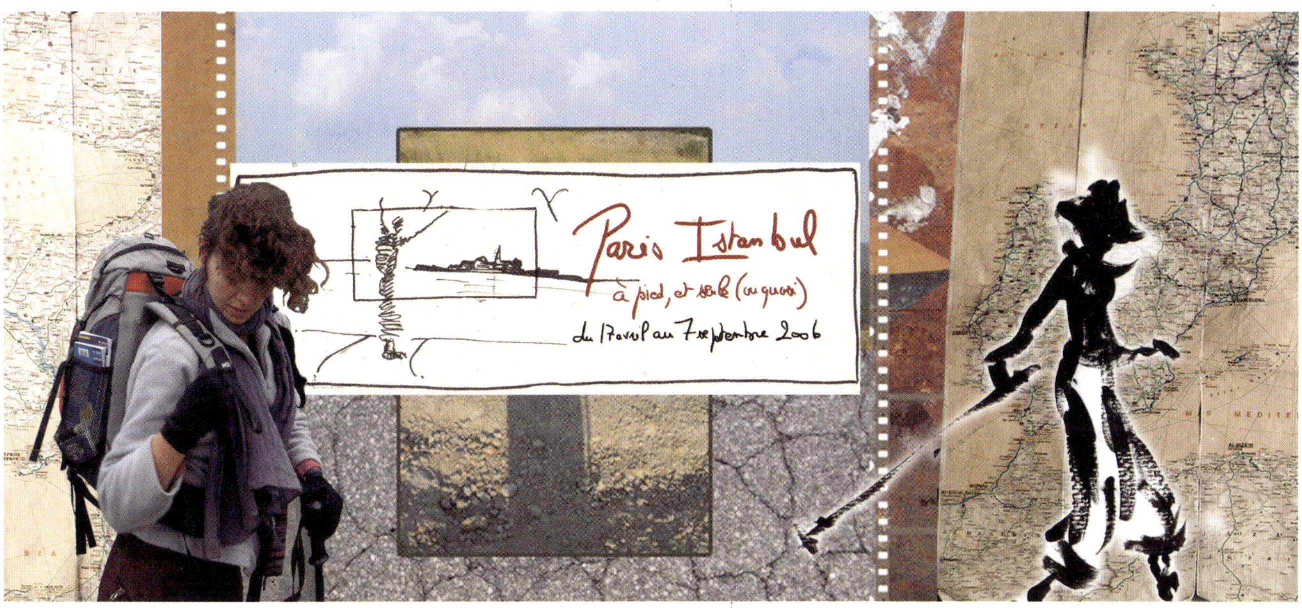

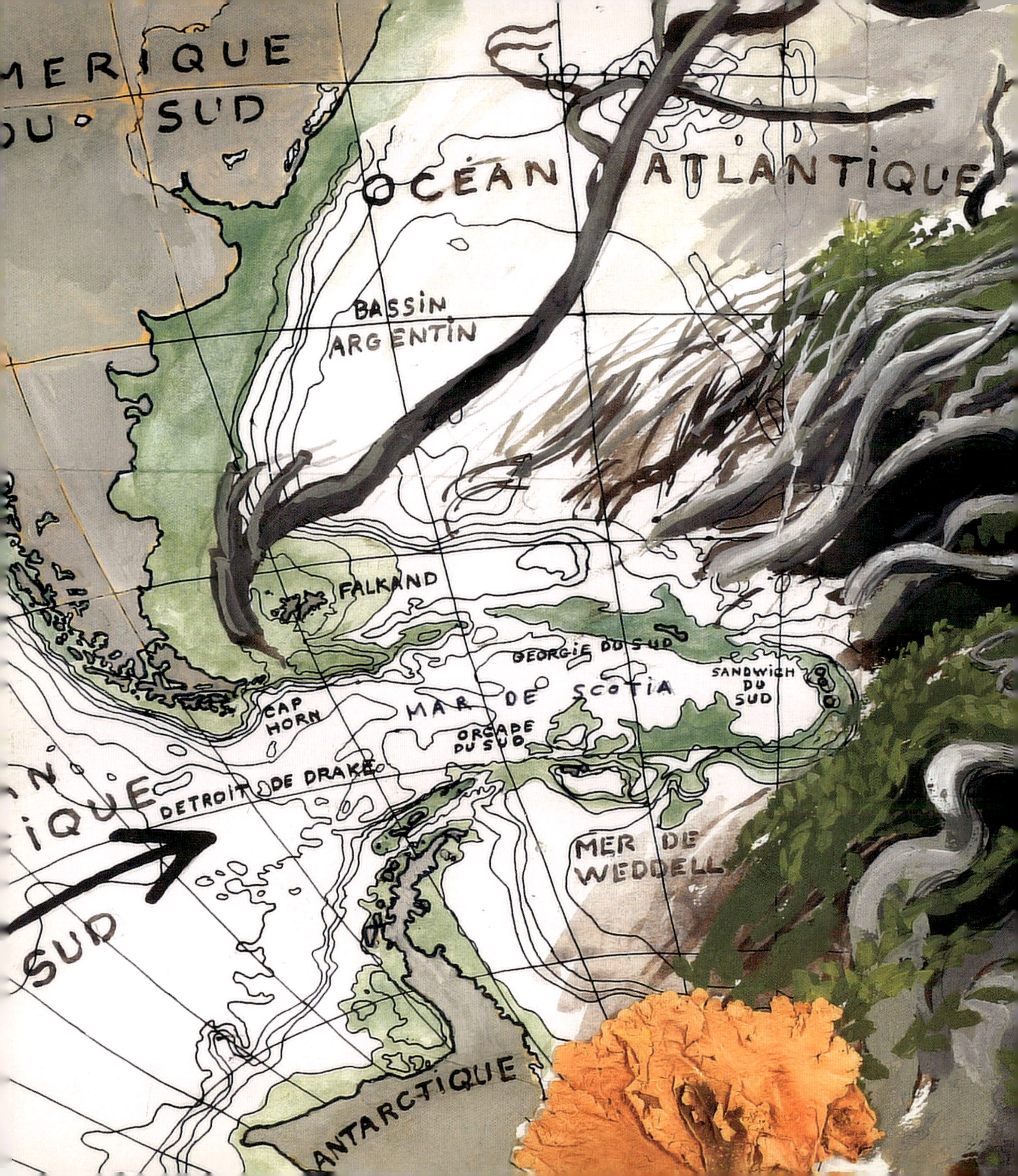
MERIQUE
DU SUD
OCÉAN ATLANTIQUE
BASSIN ARGENTIN
FALKAND
GEORGIE DU SUD
SANDWICH DU SUD
MAR DE SCOTIA
CAP HORN
ORCADE DU SUD
DETROIT DE DRAKE
IQUE
SUD
MER DE WEDDELL
ANTARCTIQUE

Artistic Techniques

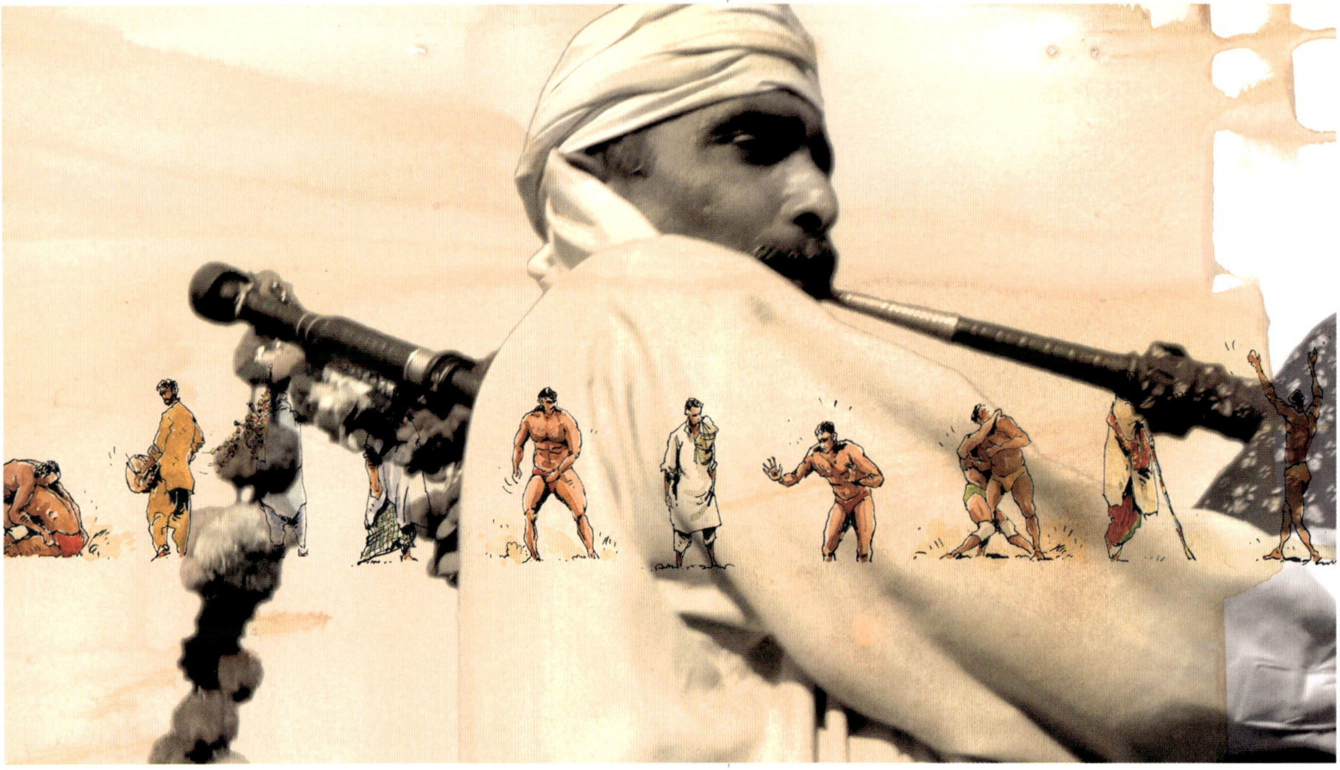

• *This representation of Pakistani musicians and wrestlers in Dubai was taken from the documentary* Journal de la mer d'Arabie *(Claire and Reno Marca, Béliane distribution) and fuses several techniques (ink, watercolour and photography).*

TRAVELLING AND LOOKING: THE ARTIST AS EYEWITNESS AND TRAVELLER

The travel diary is a compilation of fragments, sketches, a storyline and a personal testimony or take. On the visual level, the fragments represent the timelessness and duration of the past and prove the materiality of the journey through the places visited. The sketches, in contrast, capture the moment and movement, but also the realism of the scenes observed. As for the written part, the storyline establishes the chronology, the linearity of the journey and the evolution of the imaginative side. The whole thing offers a subjective and personal testimony of or look at the journey experienced—a journey of encounters with others, of cultural differences and of a search for their identities. An autobiographical tale of wanderings (in geographical terms) that is illustrated and places the image at its heart or even gives it a superior position to writing, the travel diary is a pictorial narrative of discovery—a meeting of the artist's gaze and the reality observed, between impression and perception, between the felt and the transcribed. Although it is difficult to define this polymorphic autobiographical genre, it is at least possible to accept that it undeniably sets its sights on the discovery of the Other. Involving reporting and witnessing over the whole of the mental map's itinerary, the travel diary promotes the link between the image and the text. Keeping one requires mastery of stylistic forms (such as the art of the portrait) via graphical techniques that are adapted to travelling and the capacity for sensory awakening, all in the service of a creation grounded in the sensible and completed during the journey or started with a view to being finished later on in the studio, possibly using another medium. Creativity and innovation, traits that characterize the travel diary, are expressed through the mixing of graphic arts, free expression, a patchwork aesthetic and the art of collage favoured by a number of extremely prolific artists: Arnaud d'Aunay, Cathy Beauvallet Françoise Caillette-Deneubourg, Philippe Delord, Stefano Faravelli, Giancarlo Iliprandi, Titouan Lamazou, Stéphanie Ledoux, Claire and Reno Marca, Bertrand de Miollis, Bruno Pilorget, Alan Johnston, Emmanuel Michel, Simon, Gwenaëlle Trolez and Julie Sarperi, to name just a few. The diary as an object, its form and the combination of various media also foster clever experimentation.

1. Characteristics

REPORTING AND WITNESSING

Contemporary graphic reportage is defined as the conveying of a lived experience with an assumed subjectivity "that paradoxically allows a more immediate and more in-depth understanding of the subject."[1] It stands aside for the travel diary when the border between reportage and autobiography becomes blurred: the lived reality from the individual viewpoint of the artist is no longer about journalism, but rather a sometimes very subjective form of witnessing, in which emotion can replace the quest for truth. The poet and journalist Blaise Cendrars sees reportage's art as being above all literary, with ties to poetry and the novel: "A reporter is not a mere image hunter; he or she needs to know how to capture mindsets."[2] The artist communicates the feeling and the ambience or atmosphere of the journey. Moreover, illustration does not show the event in the same way as photography does. It allows visuals that are not linked to be compiled in a single composition, such as the two panoramic images of the siege of Sevastopol during the Crimean War inserted in the war reportage or "photo-reportage" created in 1860 by Jean-Charles Langlois. The first image in this example is a photograph of no-man's land with no subject; the second is a narrative painting—which would have been impossible as a photograph—depicting all the "film" of the action at a single glance. This form of witnessing in sketch form oscillates between two ways of looking—those of the journalist and the ethnologist—and reflects the artist's feelings. The documentary challenge is therefore not just to reproduce the world, but to question it and find its revealing angles via a significant arrangement or composition, at the same time as providing a social critique.

1. Art Spiegelman on *Maus: A Survivor's Tale* (*Neuvième art*, no. 10, January 2004, CNBDI).
2. *Hollywood, la Mecque du cinéma*, B. Grasset, 1936.

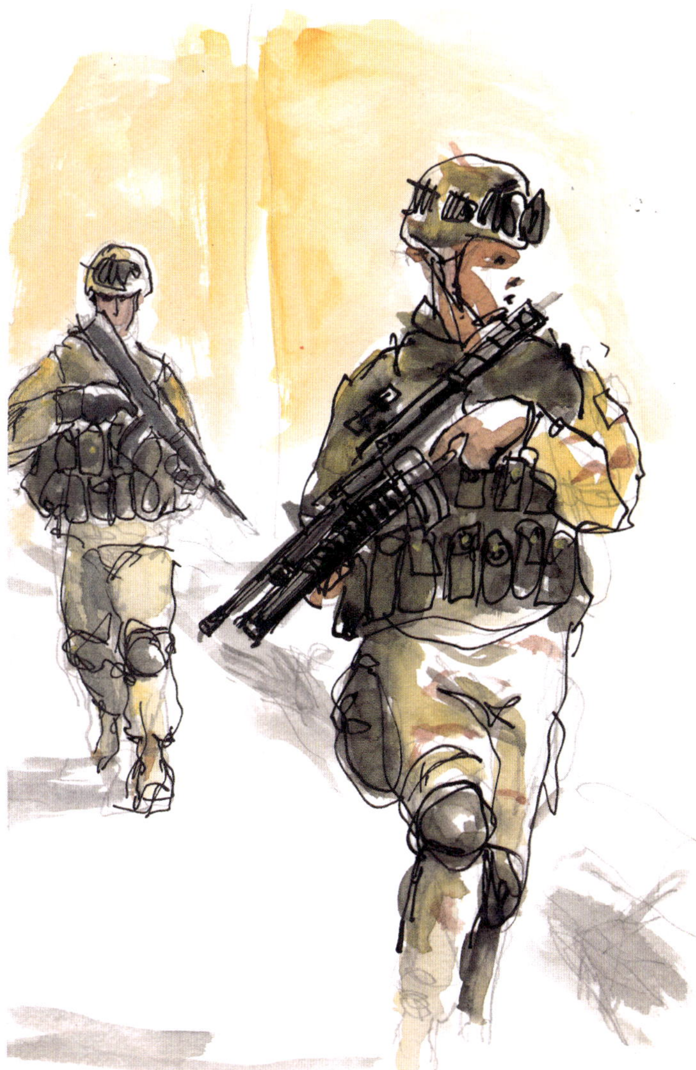

• Irak année zéro, *Gallimard, 2004.*
Shortly after the Western military intervention, Bertrand de Miollis, accompanied by the journalist Arnaud de La Grange and the photographer Thomas Goisque, set off "in search of the people of the 'New Iraq' and of their hopes, their fears and their angers."

THE TEXT-IMAGE LINK OR THE ICONOTEXTUAL

In the travel diary, the narrative is delivered through text and images—a typical method of graphic literature. Illustration makes a text clearer, illuminates it and makes it shine, therefore bringing it to the attention of a wider audience. Linked to the text, illustration blurs the lines between fiction and documentary and requires or offers an interpretation, advancing or fragmenting the information. The image can remain "at the service" of the text, thereby preventing itself from producing any distortion, metamorphosis or extrapolation of the story, or freeing and opening itself up with a narrative of its own. Pictorial expression is therefore an invitation to discover the sensible world, freeing up emotional, sensory and imaginative resources, something which is most frequently the case in contemporary album illustration.
In general, several different statuses are attributed to the image. According to Denise Escarpit[3], illustration, in its interplay with text, may variously be suggestive, serve as metaphor, strengthen the text, subvert its meaning, strengthen mythical or literary references or translate the subjectivity of the artist by way of example.
The role of the image relative to the text is therefore essential in the travel diary. The illustrated translation of a journey from start to finish serves as narrative, and geographic displacement is the connection between fragmentary visions and diverse views, hybrid images pasted throughout the album.

3. *Les Exigences de l'image dans le livre de la première enfance*, Magnard, 1973.

NARRATION THROUGH IMAGES IN DIARIES

The travel diary is defined as an album about the journey embarked upon. As such, it must graphically transcribe the entire path travelled in the composition of the image and the layout of the book. Over the pages, wanderings are expressed and movement materializes through "montage," a cinematic term for a technique used to connect two shots as a film rolls. Ellipsis, which is typical in the language of the comic, enables the mind to make the narrative link from one page to the next. Furthermore, at the very heart of the page, the telling of the journey is developed through a random reading from the text to the image or vice versa, or from the dialogue between the two, giving an account of the physical and intellectual journey of the traveller, his or her discovery of the environment and his or her meeting with the Other.
Some travel diary creators such as Stéphane Lemardelé have chosen an accordion form, borrowed from the artist's book *Every Building on the Sunset Strip* (1966) by Edward Ruscha. Lemardelé's *Sur les chemins de Compostelle* (2008), a foldout frieze of almost three metres in length, offers a watercolour presentation of the Camino de Santiago and is accompanied by a pilgrim's notebook and a travel diary. The "Carnets de Voyage" collection by the Belgian publisher Tandem, a pioneer in this field, opened the way for this form of illustrated foldout with the 1998 work *L'Été à Hiddensee* by Gudrum von Malztan.

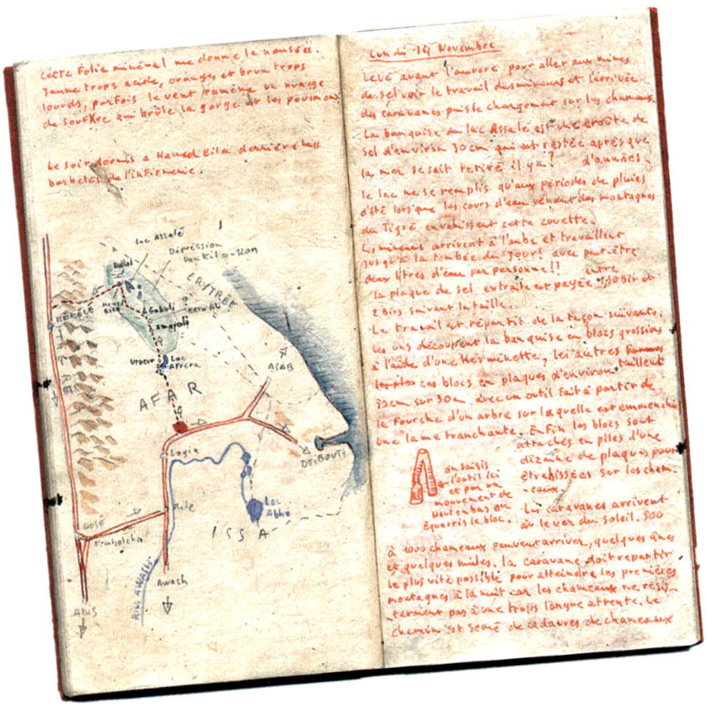

• *This map of the Bab el-Mandeb region sketched in Philippe Delord's travel diary paints the scenery of his 2009 journey to this strait between the Red Sea and Indian Ocean.*

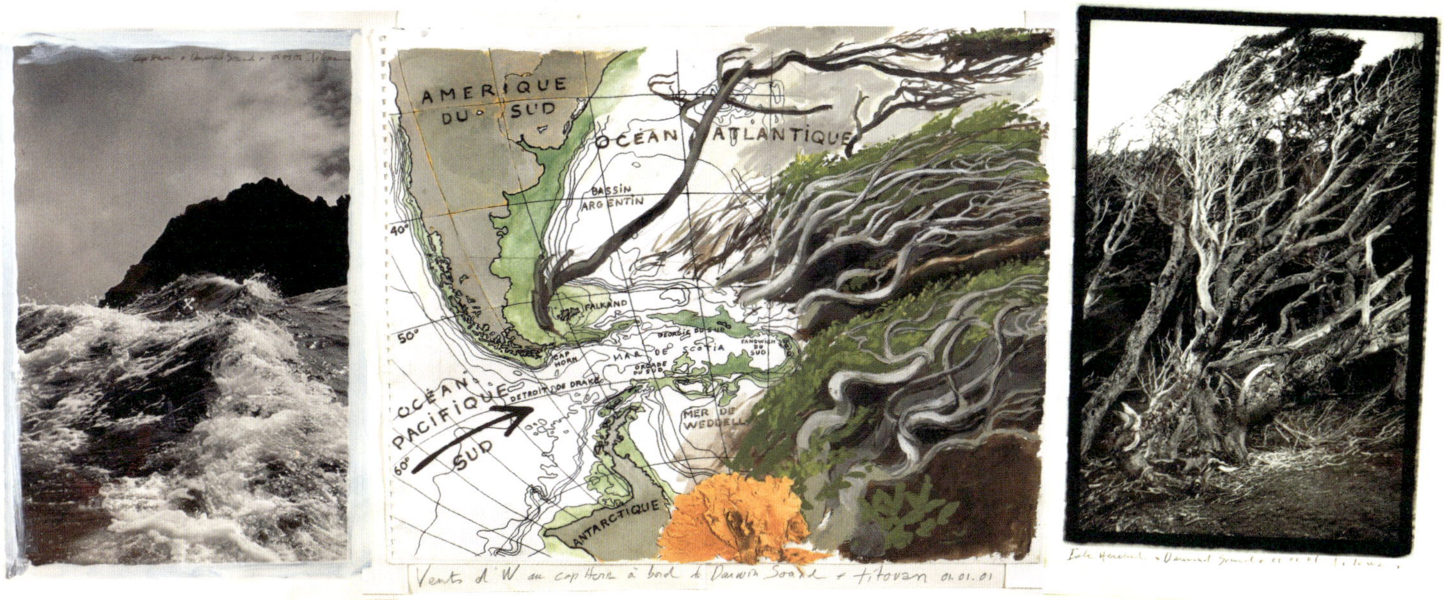

• A painter and photographer, Titouan Lamazou combines the two techniques within the travel diary. His vision of Cape Horn excellently conveys the dangers that threaten sailors who cross this "cape of storms."

THE ITINERARY AND THE MENTAL MAP

Halfway between a map of perceptions and a subjective one, the travel diary offers a journey of a lived and felt itinerary in images and text. The "perceptions" map is a complex, multidimensional synthesis that evokes the habitat, the neighbourhood and the cityscape; it is a symbiosis between the methods of geography, anthropology, sociology and art. The "subjective" map represents the vision of a person or a group of the given territory or town at a specific time. It is not based on real data (such as distance or the layout or social function of places) but on the impressions of the inhabitants and their memories, stories related to places that may or may not be intimate, spontaneous ideas and beliefs. This map indicates dreamed-up spaces as well as those of everyday life. For example, in his travel diary *Tokyo Sanpo: promenades à Tokyo* (2009), Florent Chavouet describes the soul of the Japanese capital and its inhabitants over the course of a walk in the city and of unexpected encounters across different districts, doing so through a succession of subjective maps containing urban itineraries. The map that serves as a contents page to the work introduces the journey and echoes Nicolas Bouvier's admission in *L'Usage du monde*[4] that: "It's the silent contemplation of the atlas, lying on the rug on your stomach when you're ten or thirteen years old, that really makes you want to pitch up there." Whether it is an explanatory and scientific image or an imaginary and emotional one does not matter; the essential thing is that the map describes the path in the form of signs and codes. Travel diaries offer little inventiveness in terms of cartographic representation. It is likely that the creator of the work does not dare to divert the map, a symbol of travel and indispensable tool when in the field, from its scientific function to make a visual object, limiting himself or herself to briefly indicating his or her itinerary at the start of the book, as if, ultimately, the geography had little importance relative to the artist's images.

However, some contemporary artists (for example, On Kawara, André Bay and Richard Long) have used maps as their creative format. Alechinsky calls up chimeras and monsters from the visual cues of maritime contours, borders or elevations, thus mystifying the elsewhere and fantasizing the unknown in the manner of a decorated medieval map. The poets and graphic artists Donatien Garnier and Guillaume Bullat invented a "cartography of the island fantasy" entitled *Recueil d'écueils*,[5] which was published in the form of a portolan chart that is unfolded in order to navigate between the reefs of poems by following the currents of rhymes to draw alongside the islands of fables and myths.

4. La Découverte, 2014.

5. Les bords perdus, 2008.

2. Techniques

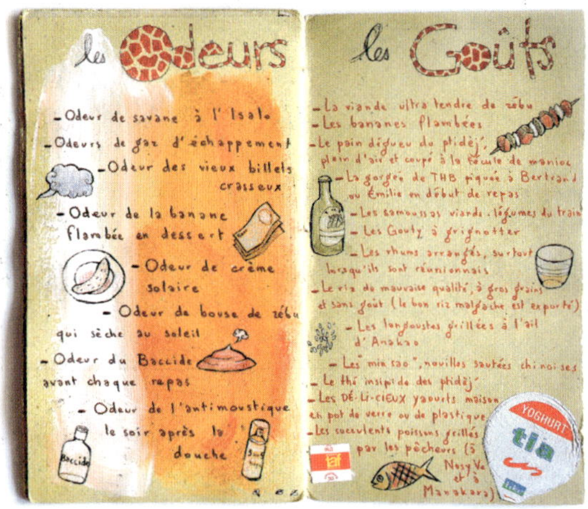

• *In her pages on Madagascar, Stéphanie Ledoux establishes "volatile and fleeting sensations," which give importance to "often neglected 'secondary' meanings."*

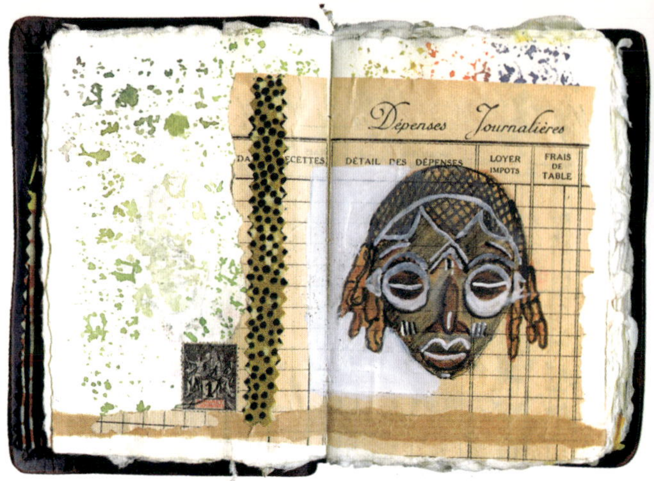

• *In* Cotonou et Ouidah, sur les traces du vaudou, *Antonia Neyrins mixes watercolour and gouache with cut elements (including old paper, loincloth fabric and stamps).*

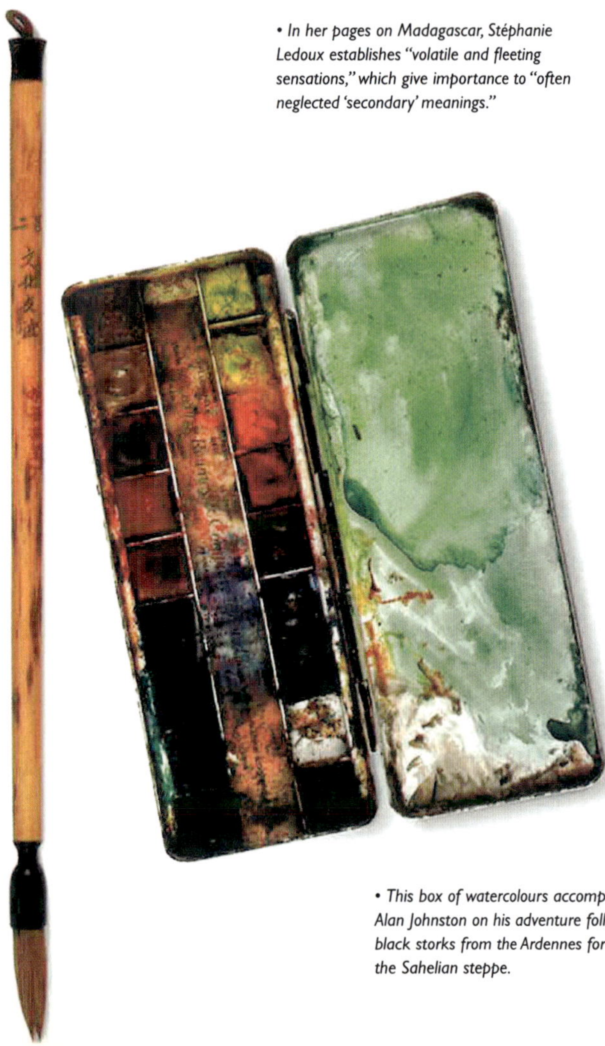

• *This box of watercolours accompanied Alan Johnston on his adventure following black storks from the Ardennes forest to the Sahelian steppe.*

ADAPTING GRAPHIC ARTS TO TRAVEL

From the eighteenth to the twentieth centuries, watercolour, the perfect travel companion for topographical illustrators and artists, ruled over the diary. Nowadays, photography allows the tourist to keep a memory of the places visited. The arts of watercolour and photography, which seize the moment experienced, are the trademark of the travel diary. The clarity of the colours and the complementarity of the stroke make watercolour a technique intended for travellers and illustrators, and therefore for travel diary artists. Following the publication of Titouan Lamazou's travel diaries in 1998, Gallimard launched a collection of books dedicated to adventuring watercolourists, among them Philippe Delord, Arnaud d'Aunay, Stefano Faravelli and Fabrice Moireau. The collection of travel diaries by Pacifique is named "Aquarelles." In 2002, Sophie Ladame reinvented the seascape, excelling at capturing spray live and creating a dialogue between photography and watercolour in *Carnets d'éole vers les Caraïbes*.[6] The artists Olivier Ploton (*La Tentation de Bénarès*) and Loïc Barreau (*Carnets de voyage: Inde-Népal*) use a mixed composition of photography and painting, inspired by the "photo-painting" of Tony Soulié. In *Rêve de déserts* back in 2000, Raymond Depardon and Titouan Lamazou superimposed their photographic and pictorial takes on the desert. Creating a dialogue across graphic arts within a visual composition is one of the creative challenges of the contemporary art of the travel diary.

6. Public's choice award at the Biennale du carnet de voyage.

AWAKENING THE SENSES

The travel diary needs to speak to all the senses—sight, smell, taste, hearing, touch—and recreate the atmosphere of the place visited. The great naturalistic voyages, on the incense route in the East, on the spice route in the Indian Ocean and to the crop-growing regions of the Americas, offer educational inspiration for producing travel diaries that are like sensory, olfactory and gustatory herbaria: traces of spices, pistils, seeds, colours from fibres and the juices of fruits and vegetables. Antonia Neyrins offers up tactile and sensation-based travel diaries that provoke a sensory and imaginative awakening in the way that cabinets of curiosities once did. Many collected documents or materials—for example, bank notes, tickets, fabric, packaging, bits of plants or spices—lend themselves to collages (following Peter Beard's model) and enrich the travel experience from a tactile and olfactory point of view—and even from an aural one, in the case of the addition of a CD of music or street or market ambiences. Nature is the source and material of inspiration in *Amani, impressions du pays Dogon*[7] by Sarah Letouzey. Its pages are teeming with organic matter, various fragments and plant pigments. Dogon architecture is evoked by the presence of stones or dried earth, while seeds glued on arrangements of images refer to merchants' stalls.

The Italian Stefano Faravelli kept diaries during his wanderings in Mali and India,[8] in which writing contributes to the creation of the image. In his latest diary, *Egitto: cercando l'Aleph, carnet di viaggio*,[9] he attempts to evoke the historical international commerce of the colonial port of Alexandria. To this end, he compiled testimonies of the past in the form of snippets of bric-a-brac archival materials inserted into the visual creation: old stamps, obsolete labels, colonial product packaging, commercial exchange notes, and so on. This desire for authenticity gives the reader the impression of going back in time and discovering the book of an explorer from the beginning of the century. The delicate watercolour, the extraordinary strokes and the rich and deep graphic composition invite the reader on a timeless journey, during which the imagination soars.

7. Boussole, 2006.

8. *Mali secret* (Gallimard, 2005) and *India per vedere l'elefante – carnet di viaggio* (EDT, 2007).
9. EDT, 2008.

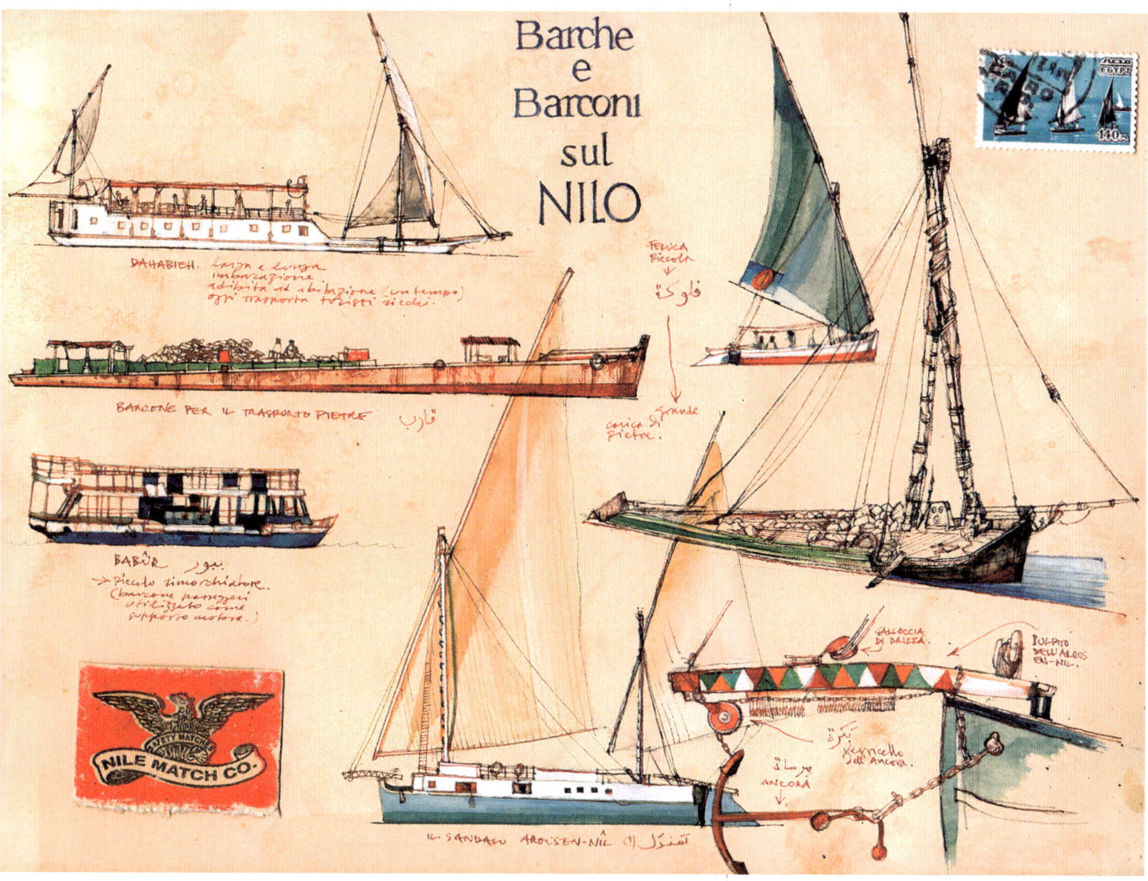

• Egitto: cercando l'Aleph, *EDT, 2008. Discovering Egypt like an early twentieth-century traveller: this is the project of Stefano Faravelli, who masterfully details Nile crafts.*

PORTRAIT ART

Inherited from Renaissance humanism, portrait art captures the physical and psychological likeness of the model. Three travel diary creators excel at it, regardless of the support medium (canvas or paper): Françoise Caillette-Deneubourg in Nepal, Sonia Privat in India and Stéphanie Ledoux in Burma. Ledoux uses the country's newspapers to bring out the person's ethnic origin and the strength of his or her features and expression.[10] In a similar vein, two painters have turned to portraits to raise awareness of indigenous peoples or ethnic minorities: Emmanuel Michel in his diaries *Guatemala, terre Maya* and *Guyane, les îles du Salut*,[11] and Patrick Singh in *Handle with care*. Since 2005, the travel diary has borrowed this pictorial genre from journalism, a middle ground between photo album and interview. For example, *Passeurs d'espoir* by Laurent and Marie-Hélène de Cherisey, published by Presses de la Renaissance, is a family album of fourteen portraits produced in the four corners of the world.

10. Some of her large-format pieces are collected in *Portaits de voyage* (Elytis, 2012).
11. Gallimard, 2004 and 2002.

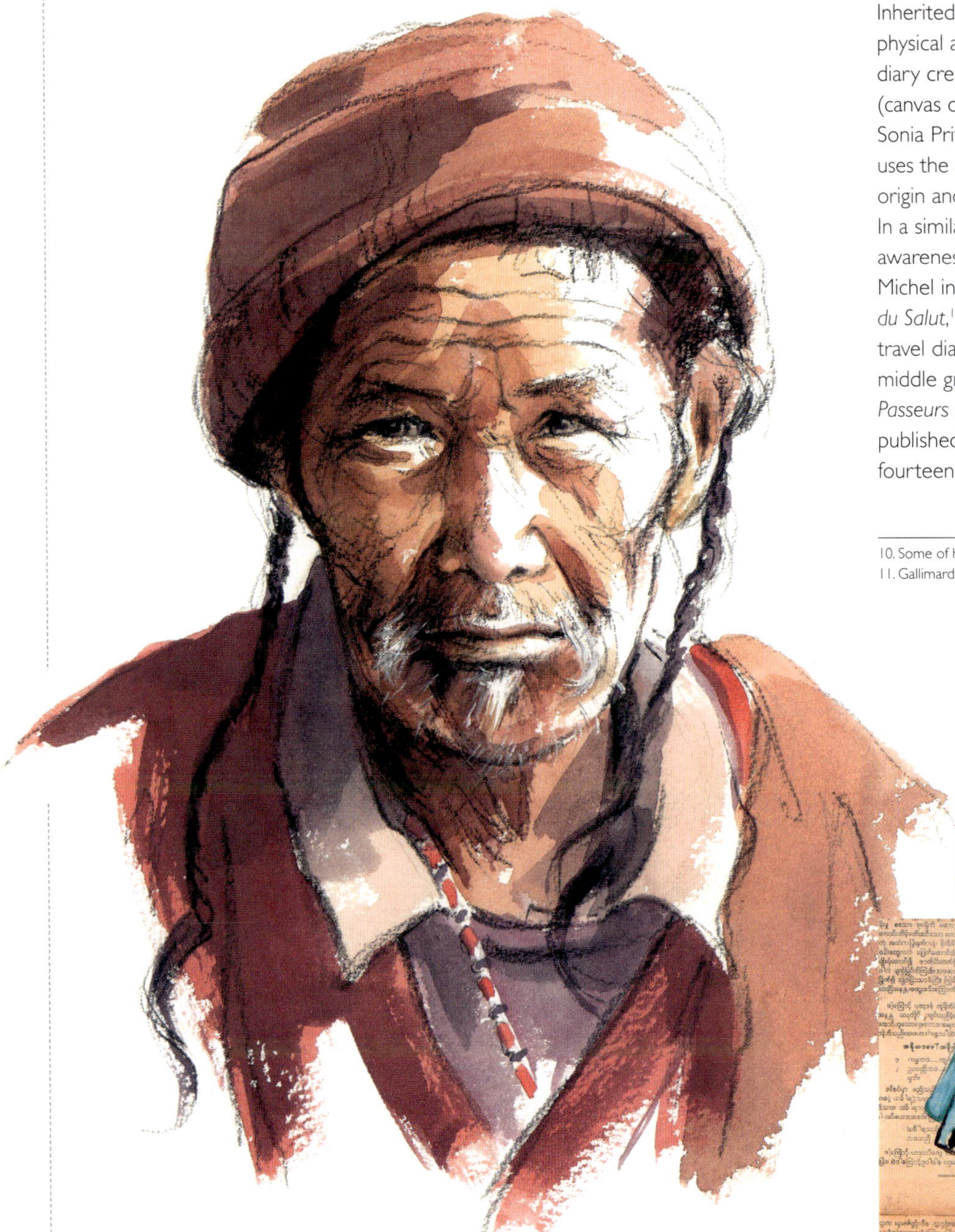

• Vies du Népal, *Magellan & Cie, 2011.*
In this work, Françoise Caillette-Deneubourg uses watercolours to capture the daily lives of the Nepalese in their "harsh and powerful environment."

• Portraits de voyage, *Elytis, 2012.*
Before completing a portrait of Nam Pan in her workshop, Stéphanie Ledoux produced several sketches of her model on the pages of her Burmese diaries.

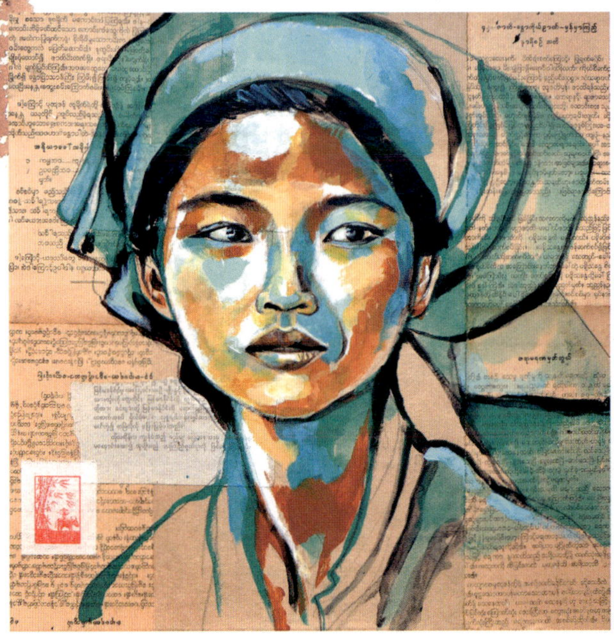

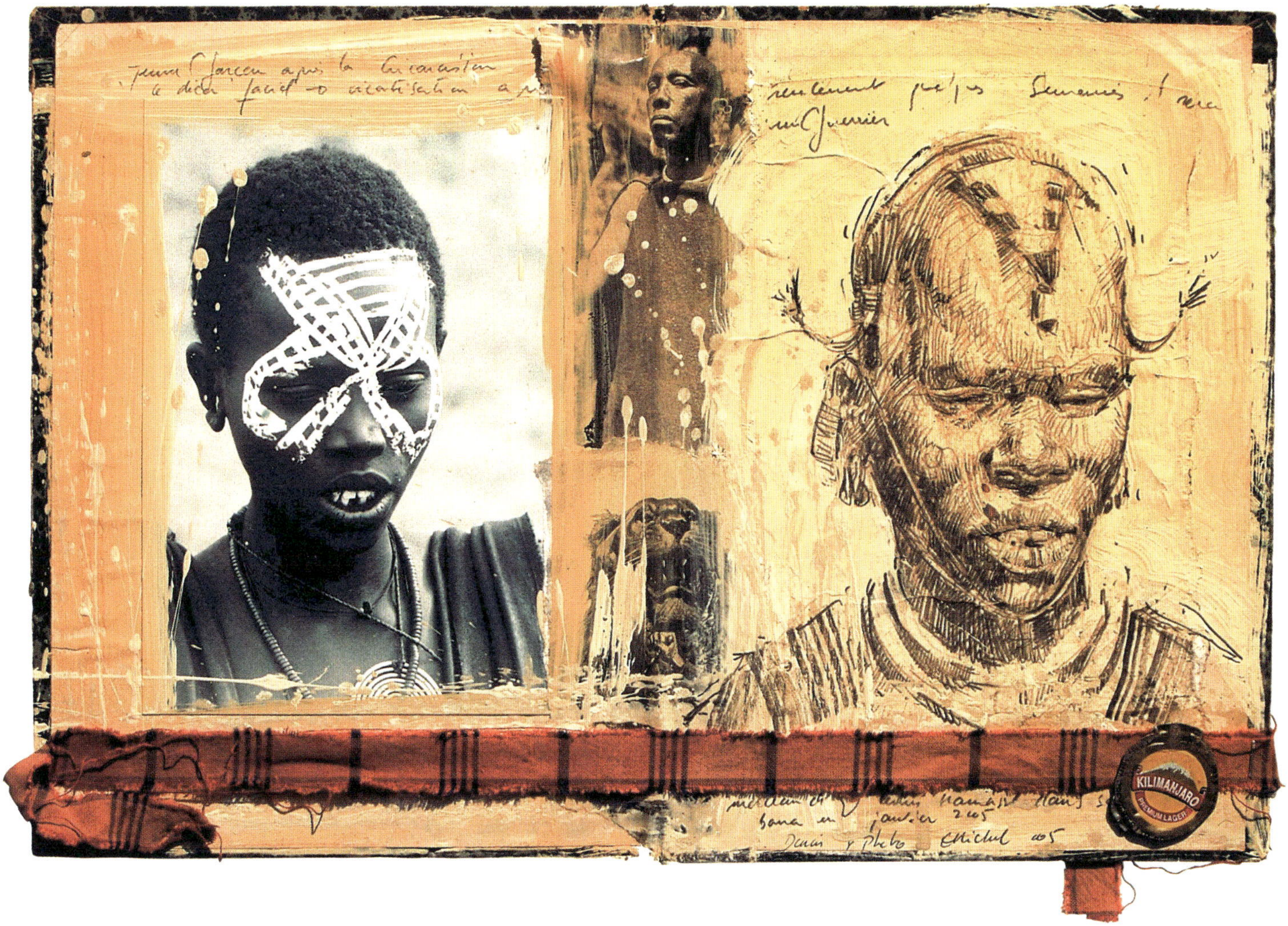

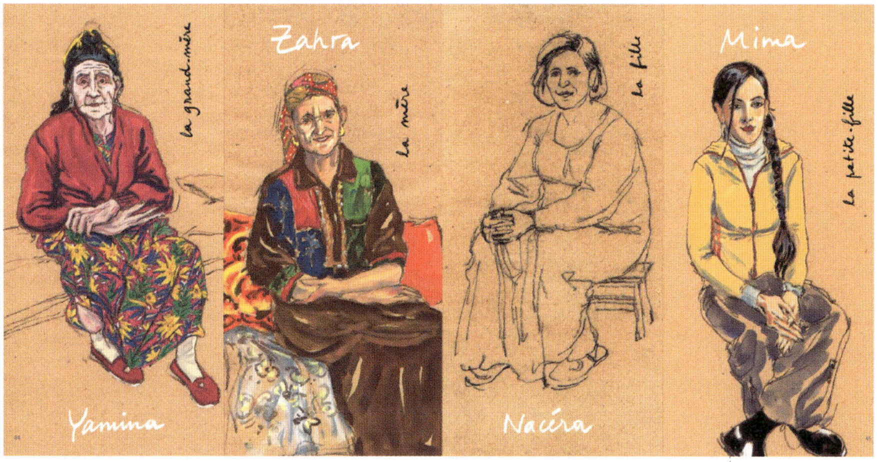

• Peintures-dessins-sculptures 1998-2005, *Éditions EM, 2005. Produced from several techniques (painting, drawing, photography and collage), Emmanuel Michel's Les Trois Âges represents three Masai from Tanzania at different periods of their lives.*

• Alger, simples confidences, *Jalan Publications, 2005. 4 generations of women from the same family, sketched in pastels by Elsie Herberstein.*

3. Travel time and creation time

GRAPHIC REPORTAGE AND SKETCHING

To capture the moment, sketching is essential. Bearing the artist's identity, it shows off a work in progress, accompanied by notes that shed a particular and even private light on the artistic process. Marianne Roth describes her practices as a travel diary maker in these terms: "The decision to leave a trace, a personal mark, is equivalent to a willingness to trap life while allowing its heart to continue beating. The notation itself poses the problem of the dialectic of the mobile and the immobile, the ephemeral and the sustainable. It grabs the truth of creation from up close."[12]

Many travel diary makers take their first steps through producing rough layouts for PR or advertising agencies. In "Le carnet de voyage: croquis, notes, reportages,"[13] Guy Mathias breaks down sketching into five areas: the sketchbook (learning drawing based on imagination and observation), the ideas or work notebook (sketches to form documentation and research), the private notebook (personal notes and humorous notes will that are not shown to others), the project notebook (accompanying a project and prior to the completion of a work, comic, film, building and so forth and for compiling research, documentation, various notes, rough layouts, and so on) and the daily sketchbook (for an artist or illustrator's daily practice so they can "get their hand in").

12. *De l'ailleurs à l'œuvre*, Peter Lang, 2007, p. 115-116.

IN THE FIELD AND IN THE STUDIO

The art of sketching, which allows us to capture reality on the spot, stands in contrast to the art of creating in the studio, which produces a reworked and enriched book that is a collection of selective impressions and memories, in which memory does its work or the imagination takes precedence over reality. Metamorphizing, assimilating, transforming and distorting reality

13. SCEREN-CRDP d'Alsace, L'iconograf, 2004.

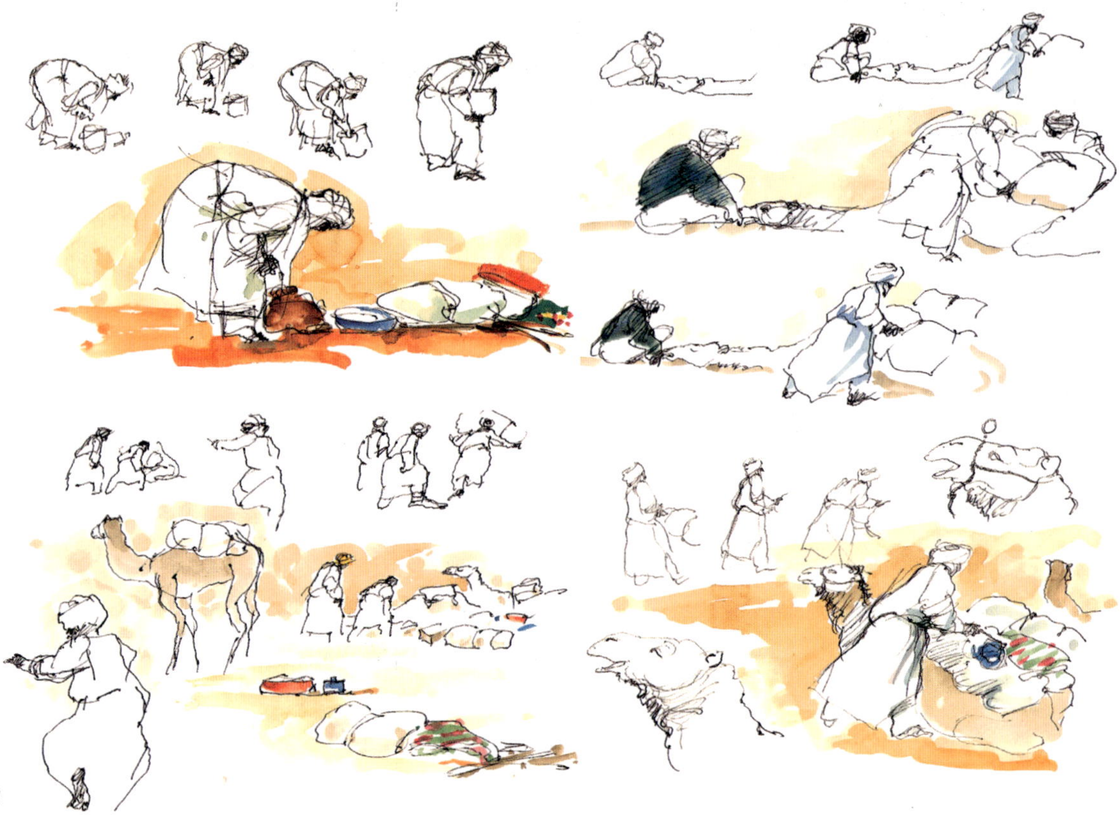

• Viaggio in Sahara, *Nuages, 2009.*
Giancarlo Iliprandi has completed fourteen travel diaries on the Sahara and its inhabitants!

is to relive the journey—an opportunity for a fresh look. These two time frames for creation—one in the field and the other in the studio—can both complement and also exclude one another. Some travel diary makers (for example, Cathy Beauvallet, Elsie Herberstein, Giancarlo Iliprandi, Reno Marca, Bertrand de Miollis and Damien Roudeau), prize in situ sketching and avoid later alterations to preserve the spontaneity of the account, something that is dear to their ethics of seeing the journey as part of the artistic process. For these artists, the book's art takes place while travelling and ends there. Other artists (Stefano Faravelli, Gildas Flahault, Geneviève Hué, Sophie Ladame, Simon and Gwenaëlle Trolez) prefer to return to their creation in the studio to set the fruits from elsewhere against a form of critical distance, the filter of memory and the work of time, and aim for a renewed creativity. This work is accompanied by reading, research and thinking that deepen the artist's take relative to that of the traveller, with the artist offering a different expression of his or her travel impressions. The two time frames—that of capturing reality and the external on the trip, and that of impregnation and interiority in the studio—are essential for producing an artwork. This dual approach, in the immediacy or in the long term, results in a generic separation. The first is in the tradition of graphic reportage and photography, where perception and reporting need to be as close as possible to the authenticity of the experience. The second feeds on the legacy of painters and artists who rework impressions and feelings to reflect reality artistically.

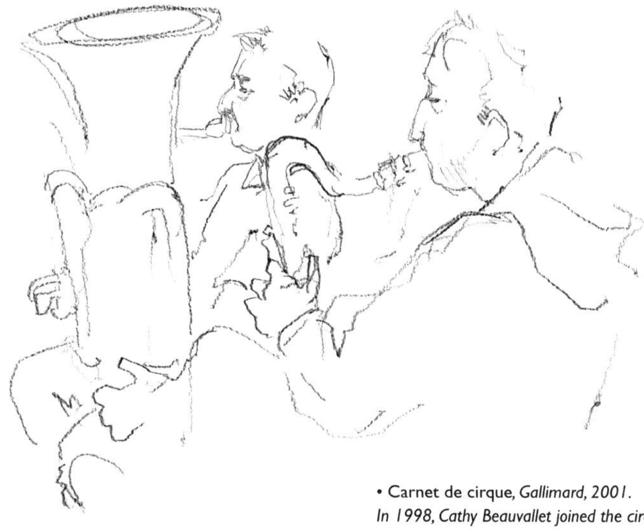

• Carnet de cirque, *Gallimard, 2001.*
In 1998, Cathy Beauvallet joined the circus artists of Que Cir que and captured the atmosphere of a troupe with a "simply human story" in her diaries.

THE CONCEPTUAL APPROACH

The travel reportage book is a diary for remembering and observing as well as a project and research diary. The process of collecting, inventorying, observing and surveying produces a personal database that facilitates projection, innovation and creativity. This approach works in six phases:

1- observation and perception in the field (discovery of the environment);
2- interpretation (a heuristic approach in which subjectivity is exercised);
3- retranscription (fragments, notes in text and image form and spatialization);
4- verification (back and forth between theory and field);
5- development of the secondary document (analysis, verification and information);
6- sharing the book (external feedback, comparison and commentary).

The diary allows the sensory discovery of reality as well as questioning and imagining. Its aim is the transcription and construction of symbols, bringing into play creativity and cultural competency. A personal tool for research and inspiration, this diary suited to mobility is a structured memory of the lived experience that allows projections into the future. It refines the creator's way of looking, awakens emotions and puts thoughts in motion to construct a humanistic culture. It sensitizes the critical spirit according to its own cultural codes: the journey, through the change of bearings and the meeting with the elsewhere and other cultural references that it brings, has an impact on the force of questioning.

FROM THE PALIMPSEST TO THE FUTURE WORK

The travel diary is also the palimpsest-like expression of a future work. Taking notes and making sketches in it reveals the creative act: testimonies, vestiges, marks, fragments, unfinished and rough elements, collages, variations and models. It offers a rich legacy, with many painters having kept "sketch and inspiration diaries" during their travels: Dürer in the Netherlands, Bruegel or Da Vinci in Italy, Turner in Venice, Delacroix in Morocco, the Orientalists (for example, Roberts) in the Middle East, photographers such as Maxime du Camp in Egypt, and so on. As Damien Roudeau suggests, "With the diary, whether it is the private diary or a chaotic notepad, you enter the studio or the kitchen, places where graphic ideas are born." This medium therefore raises an issue of poiesis, a philosophy of creative behaviours that is the process of a reflective consciousness of the conception of a work and that examines the notions of intention, of doing, of finality and of completion. This philosophy may form the foundation of a typology of the travel diary based on a differentiation of creative acts—the journey and the experience lived on the ground trigger the creative act of the diary and distinguish it from other albums.

4. Artistic innovation and creativity

THE MIXING OF GRAPHIC ARTS AND FREE EXPRESSION

The travel diary offers up all the graphic and visual arts with a freedom of genres, styles and techniques to deliver a message through text and images. The alliance of different graphic or pictorial processes (for example, calligraphy, typography and drawing, material and photography techniques) characterizes the work of the travel diary maker. The same technique can be mastered in different ways, depending on the style and talent of the artist. For example, watercolour lends itself to the portraits of Noëlle Herrenschmidt, Geneviève Hué, Sophie Ladame and Titouan Lamazou, and to movement and transparency for Cathy Beauvallet; it produces light and impressionism for Jean-Loup Eve; it serves Stefano Faravelli's thoroughness and accuracy and Giancarlo Iliprandi's liveliness of gestures and strokes; and it highlights the originality of Sophie Ladame's angles and Reno Marca's depth and realism. But other media are also prized: Elsie Herberstein uses pastel and Emmanuel Michel and Geneviève Hué use paints; collages are added by Anne Steinlein and Simon, newspaper cartoons by Bertrand de Miollis, cartoon-style sketches by Troub's or Yann Le Béchec, reworked photographs by Olivier Ploton, and so on. Artists' different takes therefore produce highly creative books. Inspired by the artist's book, Marion Lesage (*Sais-tu où va le soleil: traces d'Afrique* and *L'Inde à fleur d'âmes*[14]) enriches her painter's perspective with impressions from a native poet, whereas Véronique Groseil and Marie-Véronique Boissard observe their daily lives in the pages of *Marché à rêveries: brocantes en Picardie* (Martelle, 2008) and *Amiens: jardins* (Librairie du Labyrinthe, 2005), playing with overlays and effects of weathered and distorted materials. Reno Marca loves using traditional techniques (pencil, watercolour and inks) and contemporary tools (graphic tablet, video and image editing software) in equal measure to seek out other graphic forms. Reno's approach is a way to offer new visual expressions (crosses between photography and drawing) to push the boundaries of the genre.

14. Éditions de La Martinière, 2008 and 2004.

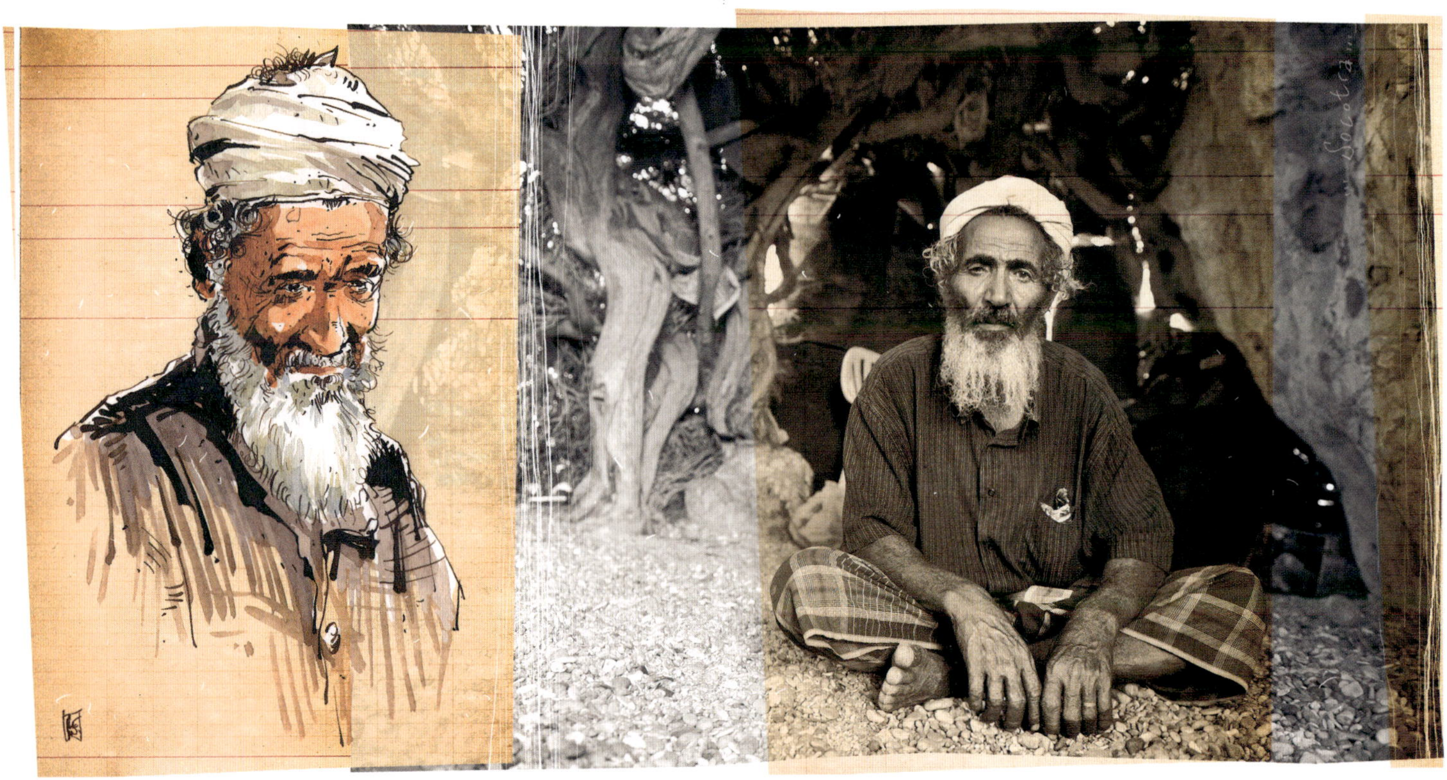

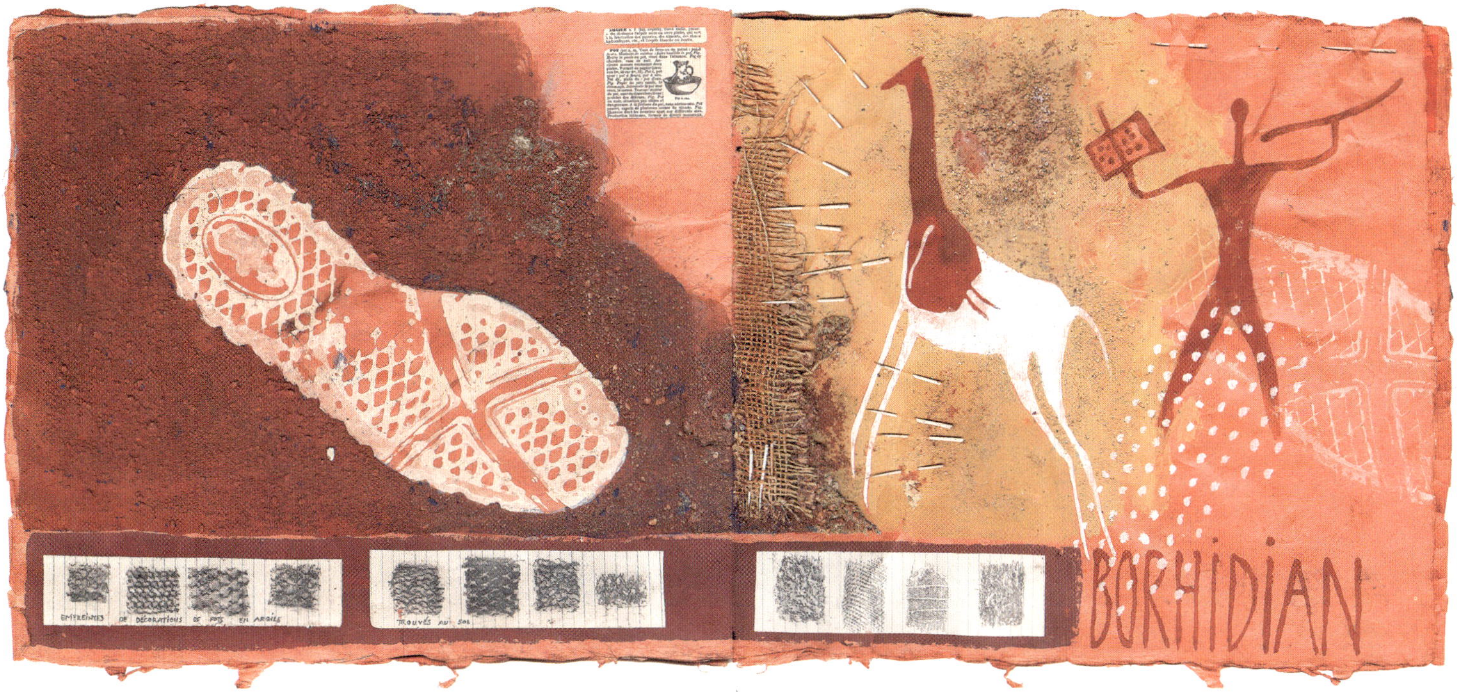

• Sahara, marche avec moi, *Alternatives, 2009. The sand, feathers, tubes of paint and more, all pasted on the pages of Simon's book, recount the artist's steps alongside Lakhdar, his Tuareg guide.*

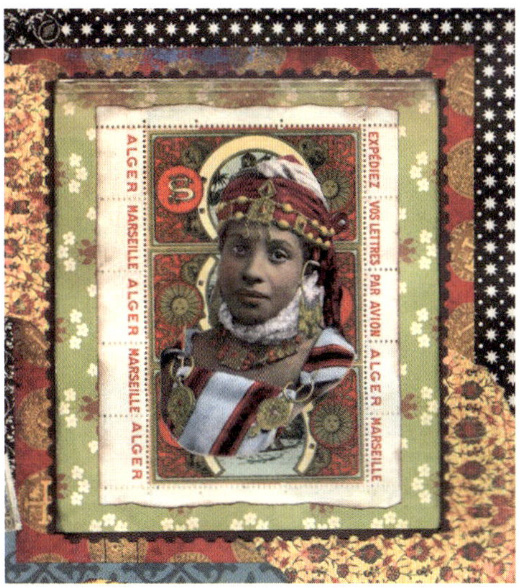

• Algérie, mon amie, *Magellan & Cie, 2008. Having tried collage through keeping a travel diary, Gwenaëlle Trolez developed this technique through her "vintage" illustration of books and stationery.*

• Journal de la mer d'Arabie, *Éditions de La Martinière, 2012. Reno Marca combined pencil, watercolour, photography and computer graphics to make a portrait of this old man from Shoab (Socotra Island, Yemen).*

THE PATCHWORK AESTHETIC AND COLLAGE

As a visual creation, the travel diary can be composed of drawings, photographs, motifs, graphics, assorted materials, collages of authentic documents or testaments (fragments and signs). In *Sahara, marche avec moi* (Alternatives, 2009), Simon uses a diverse range of techniques to provide each page with a different picture, which may be a watercolour, a painting, a collage, and so on. The approach gives rise to an original work that rewrites reality through a thoughtful handling of composition, selection, distancing and positioning. The assemblage of the fragments collected or created defines the style of the artist, who can play with both the depth of the image and its spatial composition and becomes a cartographer, interpreting the world according to a subjective Western perspective that is imbued with exoticism and sometimes produces "geocaricatures"[15] that are exaggeratedly picturesque but rich in signs and meaning.

15. Laurent Gervereau, *Inventer l'actualité: la construction imaginaire du monde par les médias internationaux*, La Découverte, 2004.

Contemporary trends prize the art of collage and images dear to pop art. The naturalist and visual artist Gwenaëlle Trolez collects and makes arrangements out of old papers and photographs as well as authentic postcards. She uses all of these things to produce an original, old-fashioned-looking, vintage visual composition, presenting a very Western, even exotic vision of the Algeria or Japan of the previous century (*Algérie, mon amie* or *L'Explorateur, le Photographe et le Missionnaire, Japon*, Magellan & Cie).

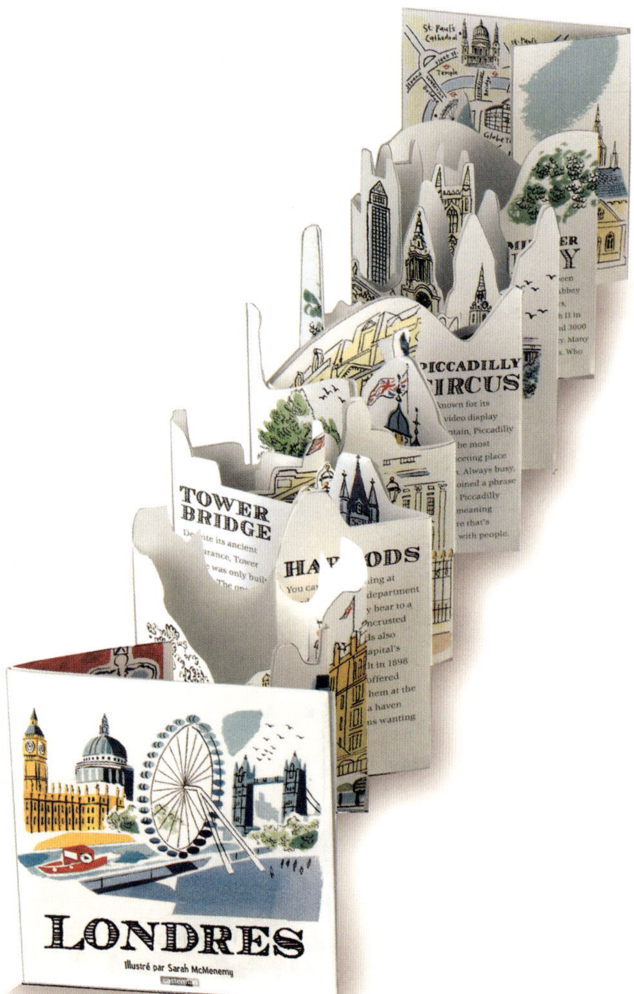

• The "Petit pop-up panoramique" collection by Casterman Jeunesse is an invitation to discover the monuments of the great cities of the world (Paris, London, New York, Berlin, Rome and so on) in a foldout format, illustrated by Sarah McMenemy and Kristyna Litten.

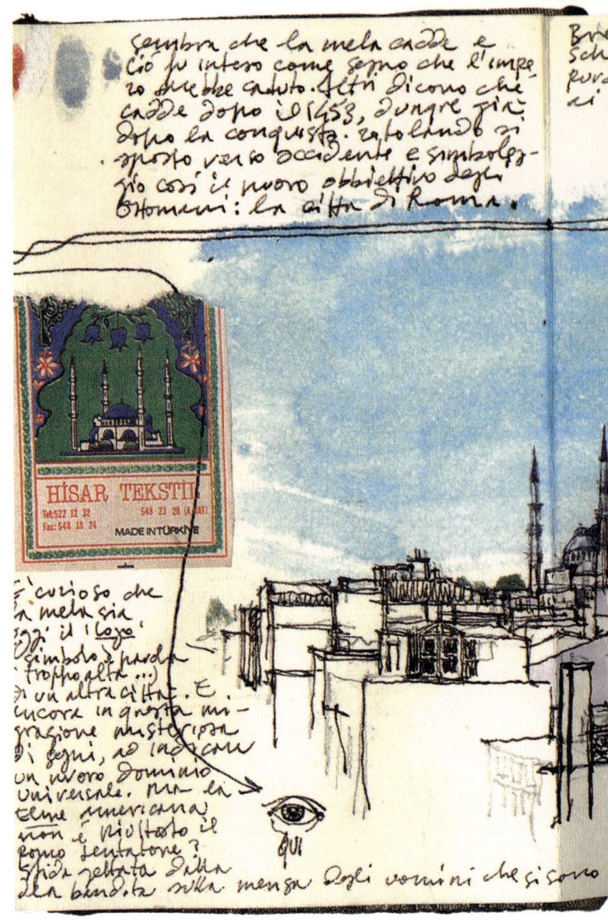

THE LIVRE-OBJET AND DIARY FORMS

Heir to the artist's book, the travel diary blends into the current trend for the original and cherished "livre-objet." It is created using specific production processes and is sometimes accompanied by an object (CD, DVD, and so on) related to the work's theme. Causing surprise and wonder, the travel diary lends itself to arrangements, collages and other relief decorations that are found in pop-up books, and to the elaborate cuts-outs and models found in contemporary book sculptures and artists' books. While travel diaries may be relatively understated in their respect for the format of the original medium chosen by the artist, they can lend themselves to a more evocative exploration of forms, taking, for example, the form of a suitcase or a trunk, or an object that symbolizes wandering and nomadism (such as a compass or a passport) or local cultures (such as a hookah or a teapot). It is clear that the trend for books in box sets has barely been used by this type of editorial production; it is as though the travel diary itself is enough on the formal level, and that any other addition could be detrimental to its evocative power.

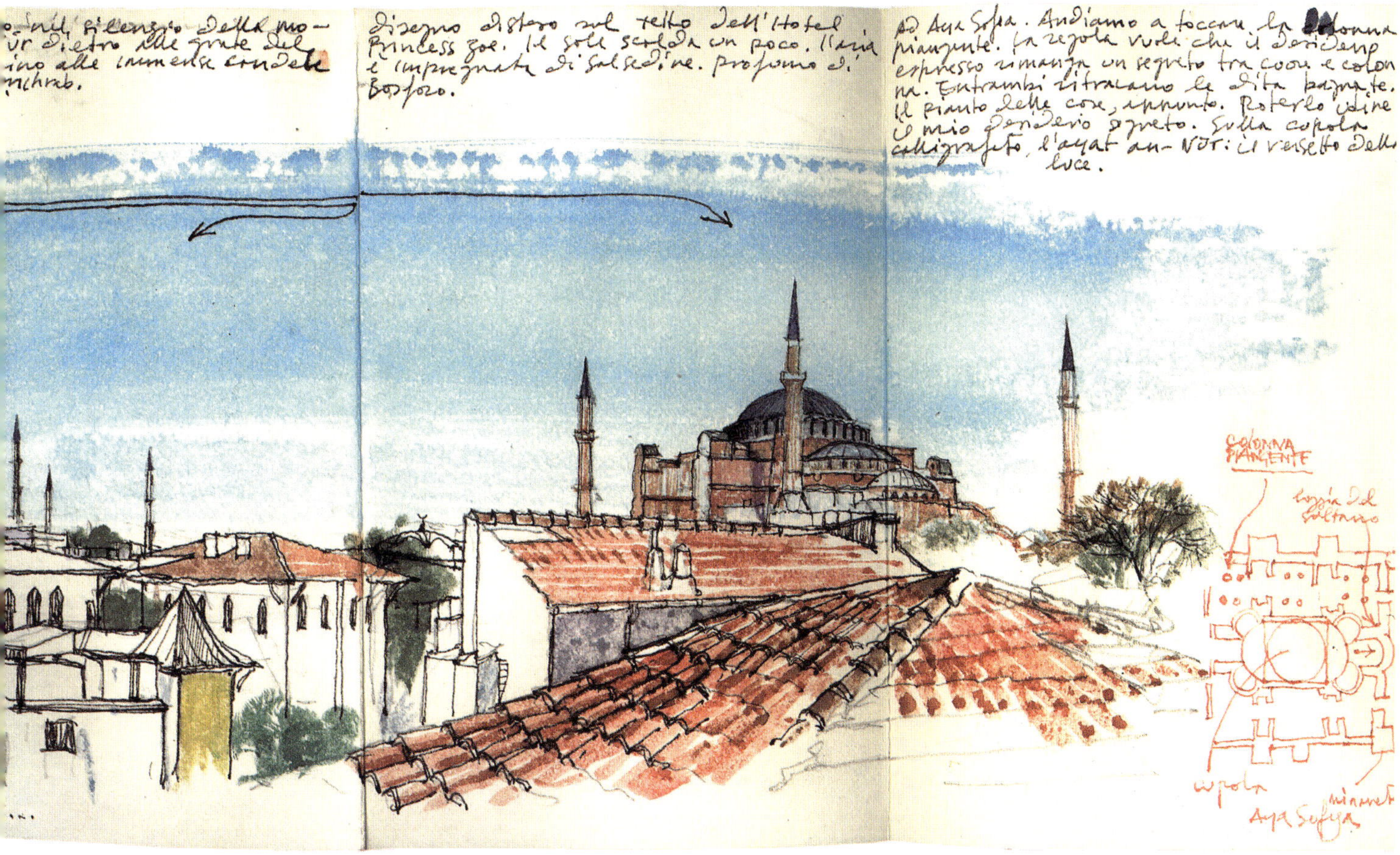

• *Stefano Faravelli customizes his travel diaries, creating panoramic views using an accordion structure.*

COMBINING MEDIA

To prolong the sense of immersion experienced in the countries visited, travel diaries have embraced multimedia storytelling, combining the book with formats such as CD or DVD. In *Carnet de route Paris-Tokyo* (2004), Laurent Granier and Philippe Lansac share the soundscape of the Silk Road. In 2005, Christine Ammour offered up a collection of songs in a self-published book entitled *Timoun: la famille Lebga*. Philippe Puget and Marc Ingrand produced a CD of excerpts of concerts and musical practices captured live in the book *Au rythme du Raga de Calcutta à Bombay* (Bachari, 2008). In 2009, the "Buddha Bar" collection saw the light of day with the release of a CD-DVD, *Travel Impressions*, that was a sort of musical travel diary. Produced by Frédéric Spillmann and Daniel Masson, the idea of the work is to recreate the experience of "walking across Asia" through sound and visual impressions. Drawing on media flows, Alain Tercinet and François Lè Xuân created *Notes de voyage: les musiques de Corto Maltese*, "an attempt at a sonic illustration of the adventures of a gentleman of fortune," using the narrative from Hugo Pratt's albums in a musical accompaniment for the hero. Another significant combination, "diary plus comic reportage" compiles narrative techniques and graphic literature. Following this model, *Sous le ciel d'Atacama* (Casterman, 2011) offers parallel narratives from Pierre Cristin and Olivier Balez.

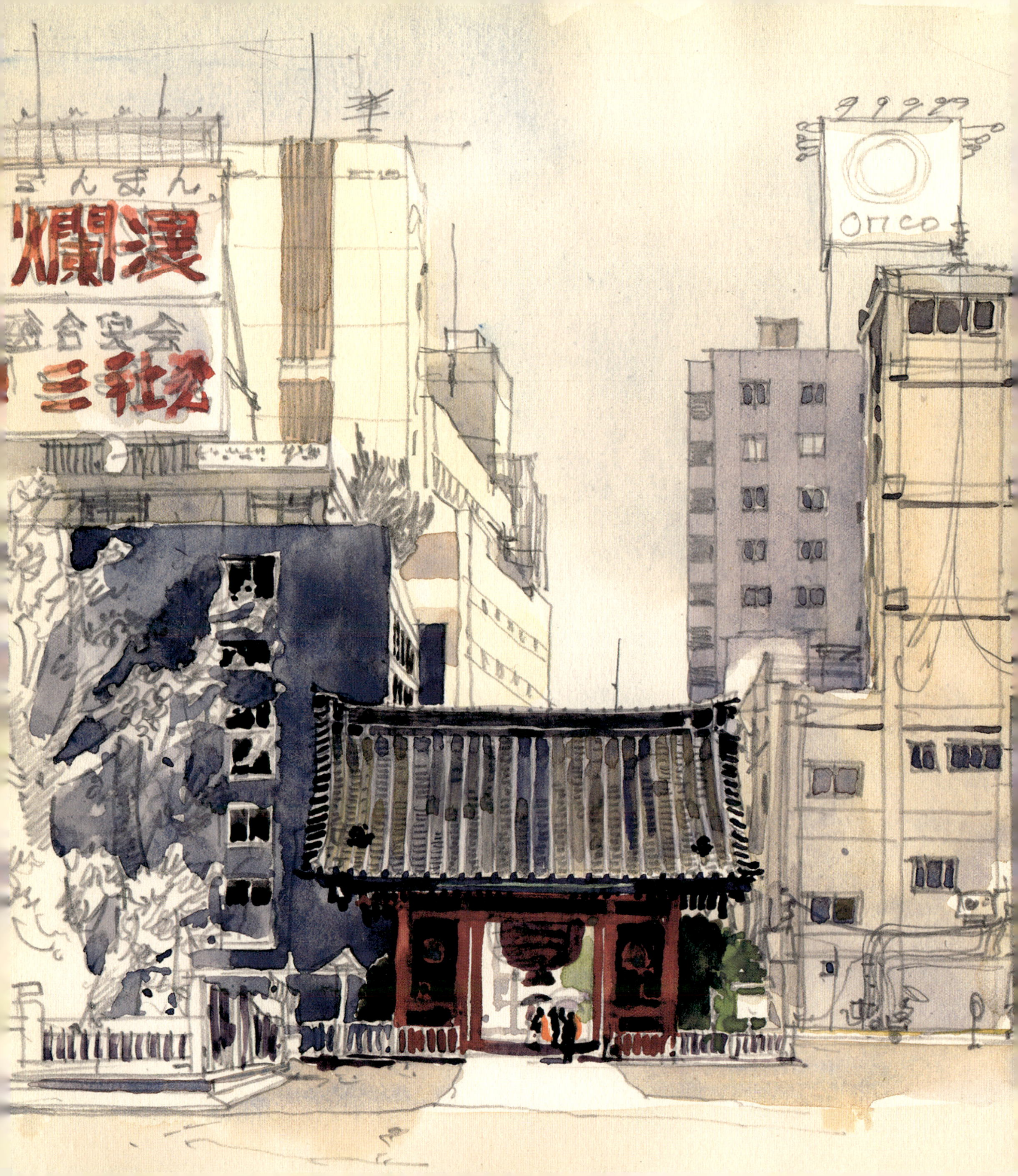

Types of travel diary

A GENRE OF ARTS, WRITING AND TRAVEL

Sustained since the 1990s by an amazing appetite for the genre, the publishing scene for travel diaries in France is unique, probably due to the fact that the country's culture is shaped by both an artistic tradition centred on the visual arts and an interest in the outside world and geography. A technological renaissance fostered by a multiplicity of media formats, which has opened up the genre to all kinds of journeys and travel diaries, has also become part of this heritage. This production has experienced several metamorphoses since the 1950s, including greater exposure since the 1998 publication of Titouan Lamazou's *Carnets de voyage*. Although the travel diary sometimes draws on its scientific past, it has become a medium for personal expression and popularization, whatever the type of journey being made or its objective. The impressions made are freed from the obligation of authenticity and objectivity, allowing a dream-like exoticism or a Gauguin-style ethnological reflection.

All in all, the travel diary is the autobiographical account of a trip in which images take centre stage or are even predominant compared to writing. They are the pictorial narrative of a discovery that shows the place of the traveller. Its story is characterized by the quest undertaken (its theme, the discovery made and its purpose), the expression (the technique, images, writing and the text-image relationship) and the intention (target and take). In seizing on the travel diary, adventurous artists, digital diary keepers, cartoonists, journalists, filmmakers and producers of television (*Échappées belles*, *Carnets de voyage d'Envoyé spécial*) and radio (*Au détour du monde* on France Inter) have continuously developed the format. With its diverse range of techniques, its variety of points of view and its multiplicity of themes, the travel diary nowadays has a broad typology that is dominated by reportage, a handling of patrimony and multimedia creations.

• **Paysannes**, ***La Boîte à bulles*, 2013.**
Les Carnettistes tribulants challenge clichés on agriculture and female farmers through their beautiful portraits of women in what proves to be an exotic work.

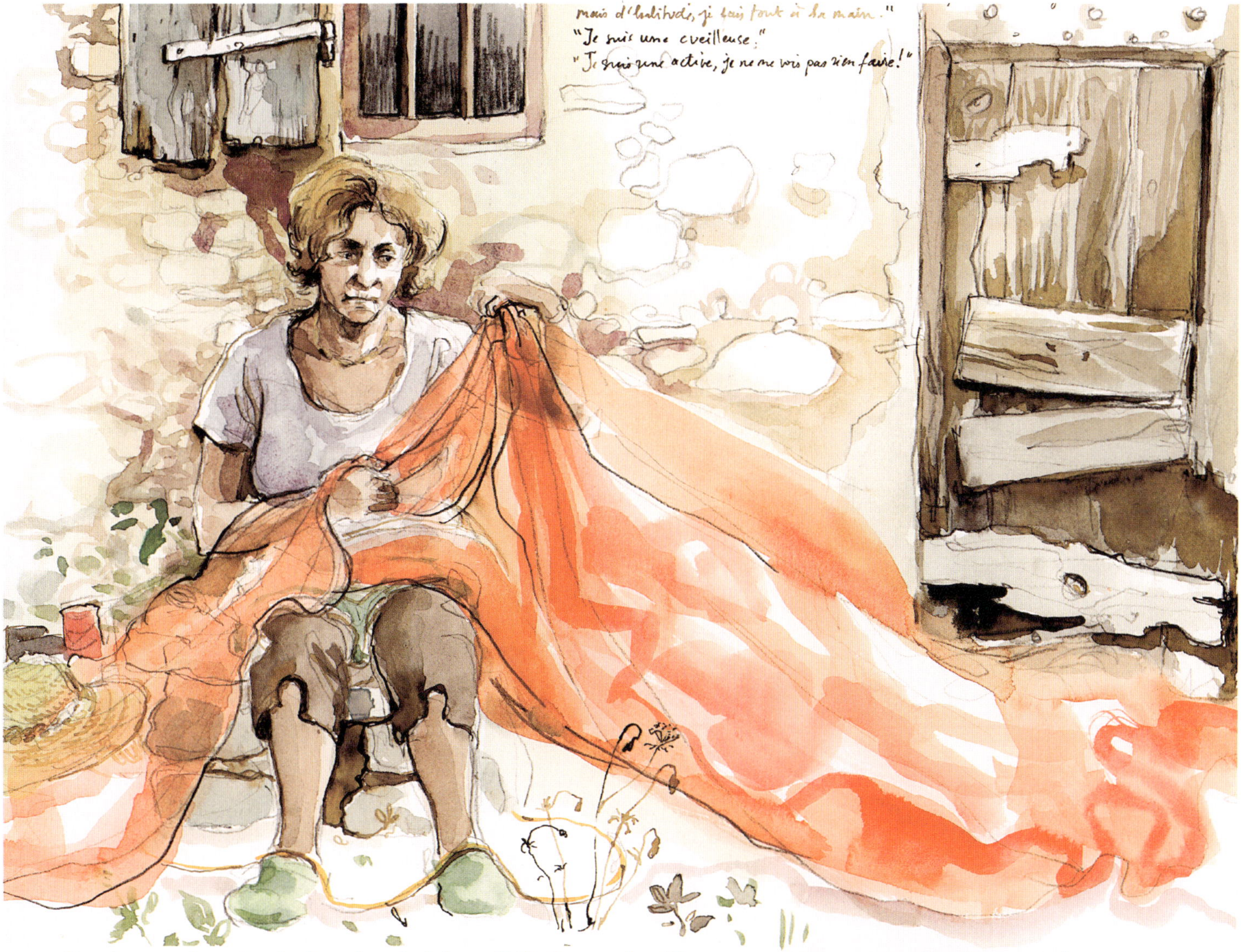

MONIQUE répare les filets en vue de la récolte en novembre

début, c

De retour vers la maison, les bras chargés de la cueillette du repas de midi, nous apercevons par la porte restée entrouverte le sanctuaire où scintillent les fusées inoxydables, comme sorties des aventures de Tintin : les cuves rutilantes et précieuses dans lesquelles se conserve la médaille d'or liquide. Nous y sommes. L'endroit est simple mais efficace. Totalement propre et aseptisé. Rien d'inutile ne traîne. Tout semble d'un futurisme à la limite du démodé. Façon tableau de bord de voiture de course. Fascinant !

Deux jours sur place s'avèrent bien trop courts pour parcourir l'étendue des passions et des pratiques de Monique et Lionel. Les discussions qui s'engagent nous invitent au rapprochement. Chaleur et générosité sont rassemblées autour de la table, tandis que nous dégustons les merveilles préparées par Monique. La salle à manger domine la vallée et l'horizon semble vaste et appétissant.

« Avec ce métier il faut savoir tout faire ! Couture, cuisine, truc-truc.... »

« Là, je vais me servir de la machine, mais d'habitude, je fais tout à la main. »

1. Reportage diaries

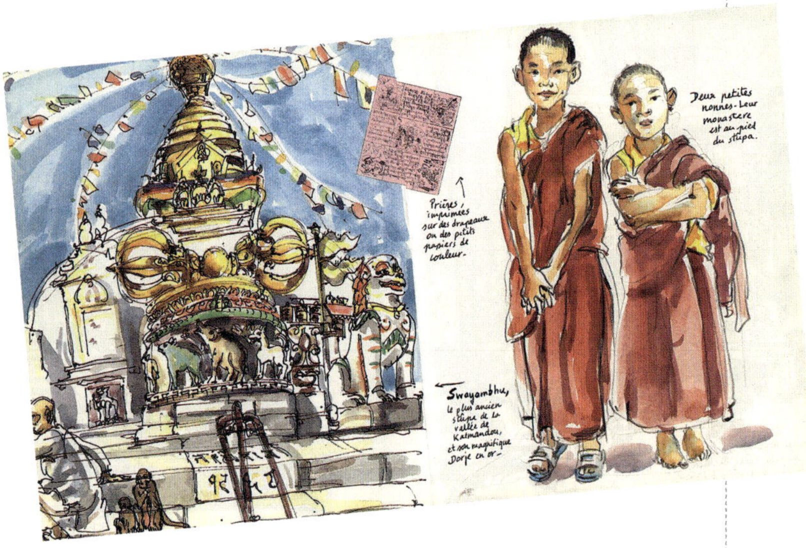

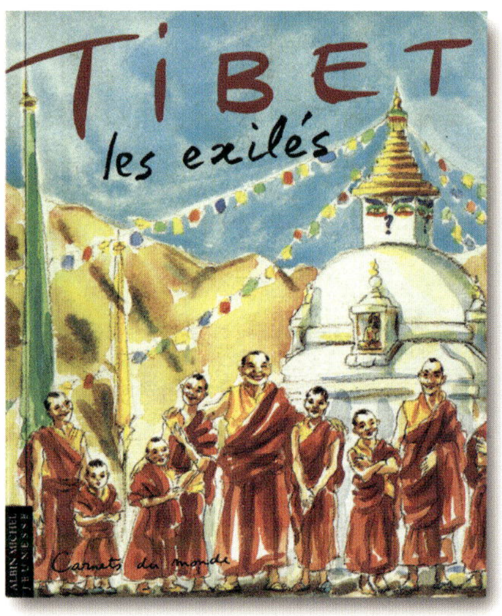

• *Created by Frédéric Houssin and Anne Bouin, "Carnets du monde" is home, among other works, to Sandra Davidson and Elsie Herberstein's* Tibet, les exilés.

REPORTAGE DIARIES AND "CARNETS DU MONDE"

The now-defunct collection "Carnets du Monde" was launched by Albin Michel Jeunesse in 1991 at the initiative of Laurent Corvaisier, an illustrator from the Arts décoratifs whose classmates included Laurent Lolmède and Elsie Herberstein. Four perspectives were offered: society, business, environment and science and technology. These were the first works to be "drawn on the spot" (a term used in the cover title) by an illustrator. They were copublished with the Cité des sciences et de l'industrie. The first three titles were intended to defend human rights from a sociological perspective: *Turquie – sur les chemins kurdes* by Marie-Odile Pagniez and Laurent Girault, *Algérie – filles et garçons* by Imache Tassadit and Anne Tonnac and *Afrique du Sud – le jour et la nuit* by Ariane Bonzon and Elsie Herberstein. The back cover of *L'Offensive du Sahara* by Tarik Oulehri and Laurent Corvaisier reads, under a captioned watercolour of the sand houses of Tarfaya: "Sahara: our reporters in the dunes of the Western Sahara. A daily journey among men who fight against the sand." This reference to drawn reportage, to travelling in the field and daily journalism are all undeniable evidence of the travel diary genre. The work contains three complementary double-pages. One is entitled "points of reference," which provides a history in the form of illustrated vignettes and which serves as an introduction. The two others, entitled "extents" and "situations," explain the scientific movement of the dunes and provide a concluding watercolour map. The preface presents the two authors, an academic and an illustrator, as two reporters, offering photographs, professional histories and motivations. In 1992, *Off-shore en mer du Nord,* illustrated by Yann Le Béchec, was billed in its subtitle as a "travel diary."

In the space of three years, the collection extended to twenty-four titles, which were intended to educate young readers about citizenship and the environment. The titles included *Bangladesh, cyclones à Chittagong* by Christophe Blain, *Dans le sillage des boat people* by Noëlle Herrenschmidt, *Formule I, Afrique du Sud, le jour et la nuit* and *Tibet, les exilés* by Elsie Herberstein and Sandra Davidson, and *Sahara, l'offensive du sable* by Laurent Corvaisier.

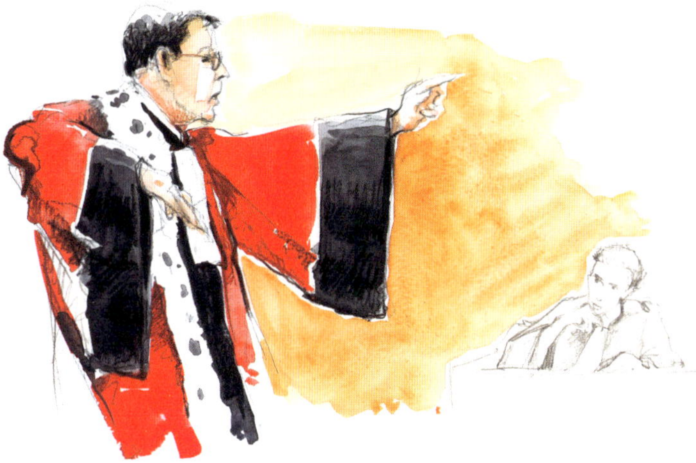

ILLUSTRATED COURT DIARIES

Noëlle Herrenschmidt, an illustrator for children's works since 1971 and a court sketch artist, published *Carnets de palais* in 1995 with Albin Michel. She became interested in portraits through drawn reportage, which she discovered in 1980 in Calcutta when sketching the life of Mother Teresa. She also produced reportage in Hong Kong and then Vietnam, following in the footsteps of the boat people. For her, reporting is instantaneous, and therefore ethnographic: "I recount moments of life. Sometimes they are brief—just the opposite of a beautiful and polished drawing. In *Carnet du Palais* (1995), *Carnets de prisons* (1997), *Carnets de la gendarmerie* (1998), *Carnets du Vatican* (1999), *Carnets du Jubilé: pèlerins de Rome à Jérusalem* (2000)[1] and *À la vie, à la mort: l'hôpital* (2003, Gallimard), this artist, as a witness and messenger, aims to "let people who have never had a chance to speak out do so, and to show places that are frightening." But she is known above all for immortalizing trials[2] in the press: the trial of Klaus Barbie for *La Croix* in 1987, as well as the trial of Paul Touvier in 1995, the trial of Maurice Papon, the contaminated blood trial and the Dumas trial, all of which were published in the newspaper *Le Monde*.

In her eight instalments of *Carnets du Palais: regards sur le Palais de justice de Paris*, Herrenschmidt shows "the inside and out of the judicial setting... moments, situations and atmospheres that give the palace its complexity and make it a place for memory and emotion—a unique place." Her different diaries, which retrace her journey through the Palais de justice, capture the atmosphere of the judicial world: the civil court, the accused's path through the system, the criminal court, the court of assizes, the life of the palace, the Ordre des avocats, the court of appeal and the court of cassation. After three years spent sketching in the courts of assizes of Blois and Orléans, Cathy Beauvallet breathed new life into this form of reportage in 2004's *Cour d'Assises, et si demain vous étiez juré?* (Jalan Publications), which introduces the reader to these often inaccessible places of solemnity. The book provides an educational introduction to members of the jury and justice professionals, who talk about their role and their civic engagement, and it details in chronological order the steps—letter, summons, hearing, deliberation, verdict and post-trial—of the judicial enterprise. A book filled with reportage and encounters, this training tool for the future juror equips him or her to scrutinize the evidence.

1. All these works were published by Albin Michel.
2. With the assistance of the author Michel Zaoui and the photographer Antoine Garapon, Noëlle Herrenschmidt revisits this period in the book *Mémoires de justice: les procès Barbie, Touvier, Papon* (Seuil, 2009).

Cathy Beauvallet on *Cour d'Assises, et si demain vous étiez juré?*
"It's not a journey, but a place where destinies, human stories to be resolved and individuals to be defended, supported or accused meet. This work is the fruit of commissions for press illustrations. The interviews conducted by Olivier Cirendini make it a touching vehicle for the humanity expressed by each individual, marked by their different doubts or questionings. The book subsequently became used for teaching purposes."

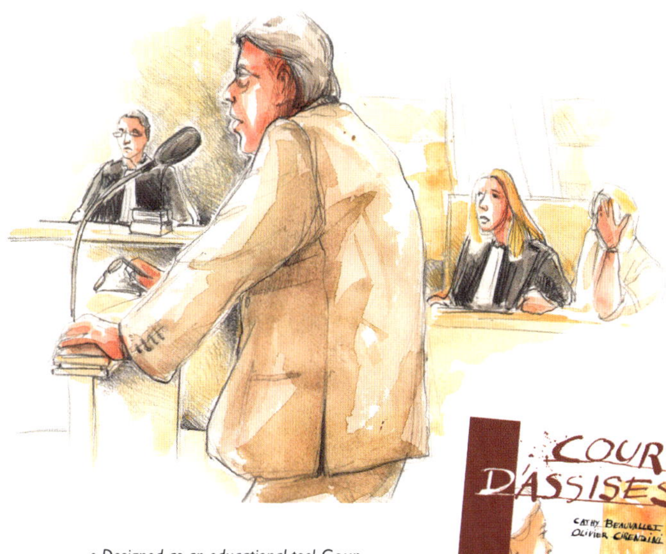

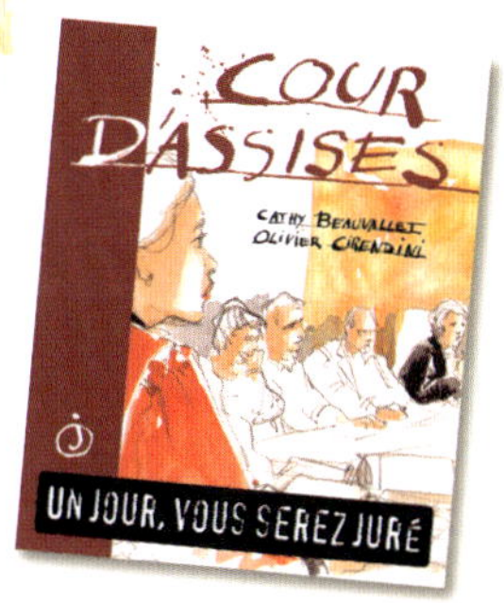

• *Designed as an educational tool,* Cour d'assises *offers a journey through the "unknown land" that is the court of justice.*

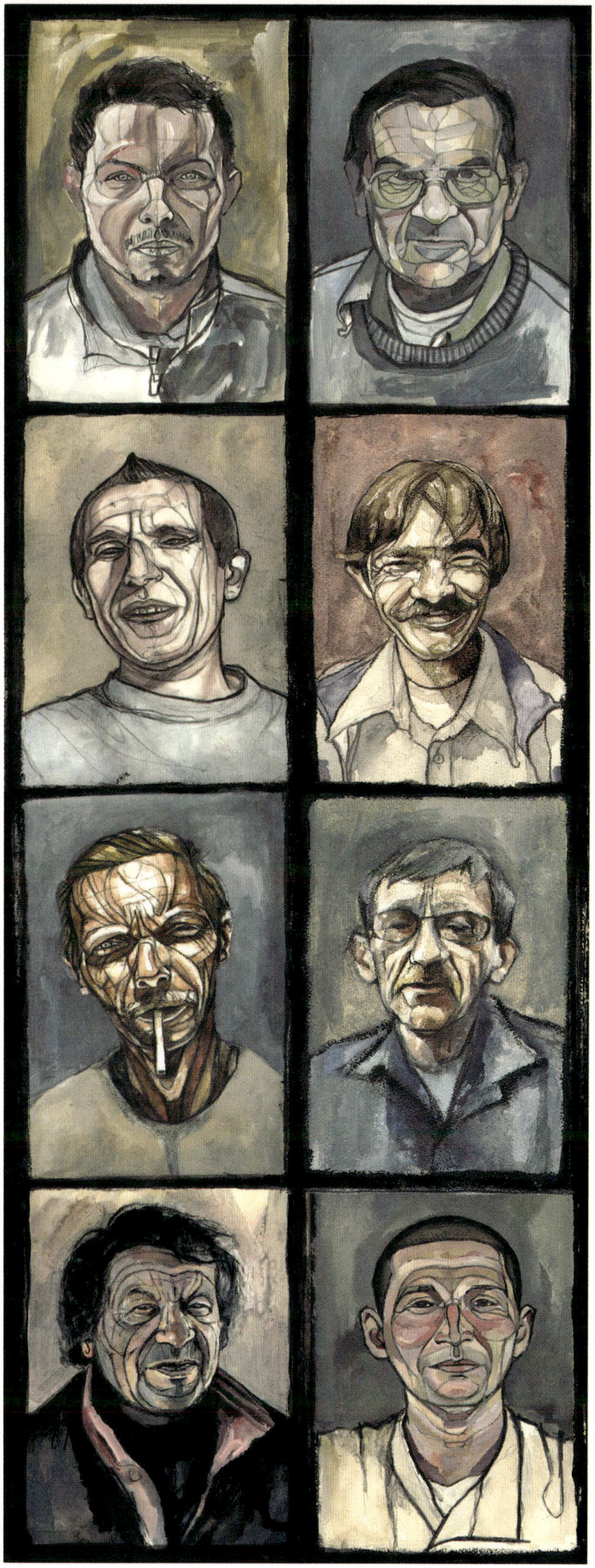

• De Bric et de broc, *Parole et silence, 2006. The illustrator Damien Roudeau adopted the approach of an ethnologist to blend in among the members of an Emmaüs community of ragpickers.*

DIARIES ON SOCIETY

In 2001, the Lille-based publisher Sansonnet offered up two books of sociological reportage: *Les Mains bleues: 501 blues* by François Saint-Remy, on the closure of the Levi's factory in northern France, and *En regard de Sangatte: refuges* by Denis Lecat. Comic artists have presented works of graphic reportage: *La Bouille* by Troub's (Rackham, 2002) describes the last home distillers, and *Moloch* by Michael Matthys (Frémok, 2003) looks at the steel plants of the city of Charleroi. Damien Roudeau, a member of the collective Les yeux du monde, fits in with this tradition with his books on the history of a strike in Cholet in January 2007 and on the musicians of the Paris metro. His projects tend to be pieces of graphic reportage, whether the subject is a housing estate from the national programme for urban renovation in the process of demolition or renovation or humanitarian subjects such as Doctors of the World or Chinese women who work in prostitution. His last published diary, *Têtes de pioche: la Provence au rythme des chantiers de jeunes,*[3] describes a youth project in the Alps. Fabrice Bloch gets the subject matter for his various pieces of graphic reportage from Romania. For example, he focuses on the bloody march of the miners of the Jiu valley to Bucharest in *Les Gueules noires de Roumanie*. In another vein, *Suivez les enchères* opens the doors of the Hôtel Drouot auction house and gives auctioneers and buyers from Saint-Ouen or abroad the chance to speak. Following the lead of Noëlle Herrenschmidt, Elsie Herberstein published a book on homeless people, *Viens chez moi j'habite dehors*, with Jalan in 2004. In this book championing "the transmission of human stories at a time when social tragedy is becoming trivialized," she collects the comments of the impoverished users of Paris's shelters. She uses the method of "participant observation" advocated by Bronislaw Malinowski and the Chicago school of sociology in the 1920s. Under this method, the researcher plunges into social life by sharing the way of life of the communities, and in order to better understand them, he or she takes daily notes in the form of images or texts, implementing a relationship of immediacy. The ethnologist blends into a group whose language and customs he or she learns and practices in order to transcribe them as they really are and gather objective material, stripping himself or herself of all a priori ideas and becoming a member of the society under

3. Les Alpes de lumière, 2009.

• *Through her "little drawings" recorded in the diaries she kept at a centre for vulnerable people, Elsie Herberstein helped visitors to Compagnons de la Nuit to rediscover their identity.*

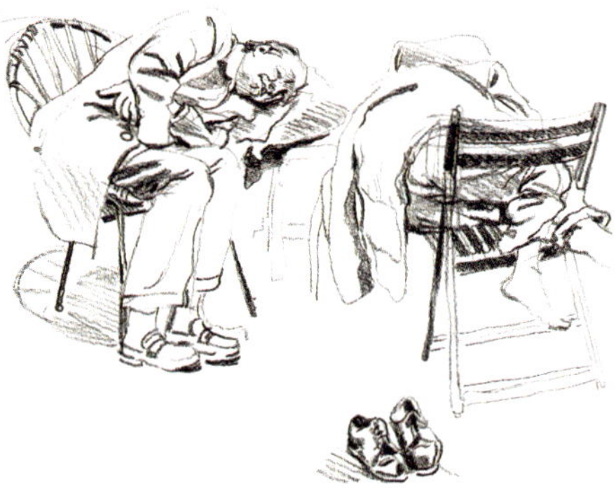

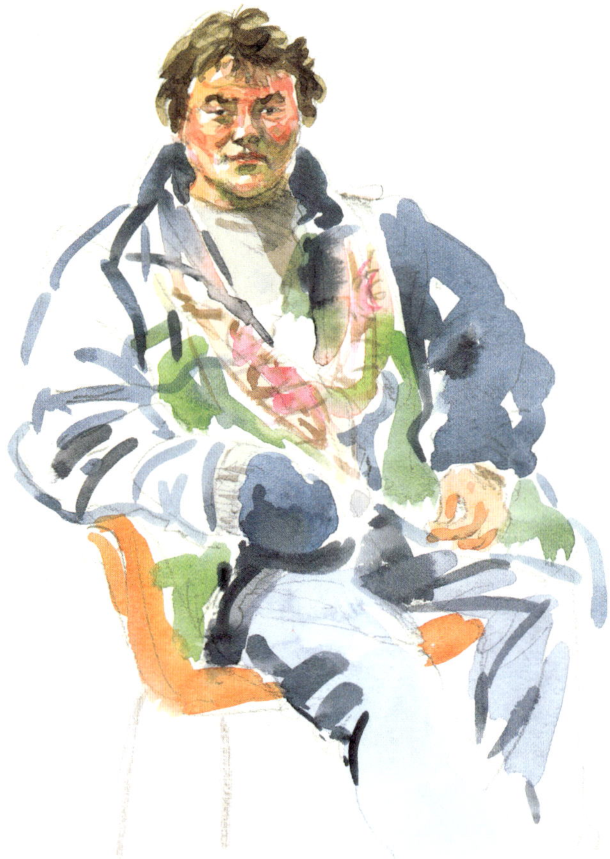

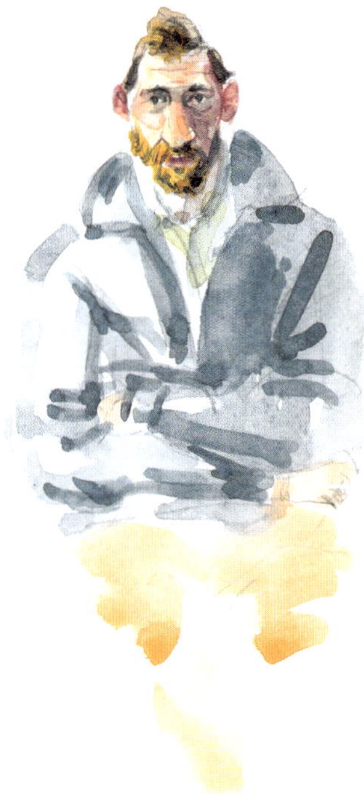

study. Damien Roudeau uses such methods to share the life of the Emmaüs community of ragpickers in his book *De bric et de broc: un an avec les compagnons du partage* (Parole et silence, 2006). Edmond Baudouin and Troub's turned reporter-sociologists for L'Association, becoming specialists in reporting from the world's "hot spots": Ciudad Juarez in Mexico (*Viva la Vida, los sueños de Ciudad Juárez,* 2012) and Colombia (*Le Goût de la terre,* 2013). In addressing immediate environments,[4] the travel diary follows the evolution of anthropology and ethnology, which today have turned towards social, cultural and economic otherness in France. The artist, in the role of a mediator who makes a hidden reality visible, highlights the perspective of the excluded and brings it to our collective attention. His or her work thereby acquires the status of an ethnographic, documentary and reflective consideration of the Other, who is examined within his or her own culture and his or her difference or marginality.

4. "The tourist between the cracks" referred to by Jean-Didier Urbain, *L'Idiot du voyage, histoires de touristes*, Plon, 1991.

Elsie Herberstein on *Viens chez moi j'habite dehors*

"I started going to the Compagnons de la Nuit outreach project in 1994, without any particular idea in mind. The approach taken by Pedro Meca (the priest who founded the association) really appealed to me. It's a place that is open to all, regardless of the time or how many. Both homeless people and those with accommodation go to this place where instead of blankets and beds there is an intimate setting designed to let people get to know one another, talk, play cards and participate in writing workshops or lectures. In short, it's a place that offers nourishment other than food or drink, providing a friendly cocoon where people can put their feet up and be welcomed not because of their shortcomings but because of their qualities, which are concealed behind the anonymous and exclusionary label of 'homeless.' I immediately felt at ease in this curious and genuine place.

I got into the habit of going there one or two nights a week. Initially, the people there did not know that I was an illustrator. They knew me at first as 'Elsie, non-homeless and a friend of La Moquette.' The first visitors gave the places the name 'La Moquette' ('The Carpet') because there was a carpet in the basement, and when you're on the street, this detail has a real luxury to it. Then, one day, I gradually pulled out my diary and a few pencils and I timidly started to sketch there and then. My drawings sparked a half-admiring, half-amused curiosity. I don't know who was the first person to ask me to do a portrait, but then everyone wanted to have a turn and get one done. These improvised sittings in a corner of the room created the conditions for an atmosphere of trust and dialogue. As the collection of portraits grew, we hung them on the wall, and I made colour photocopies that I gave to my models. One of them told me as I was putting fixative on the freshly dried watercolour: 'It's amazing. It's really me, it looks like me, and I look good as well.' That remark really struck me because I suddenly realized that these small drawings captured their identity but also allowed them to take back a beautiful and empowering image of themselves."

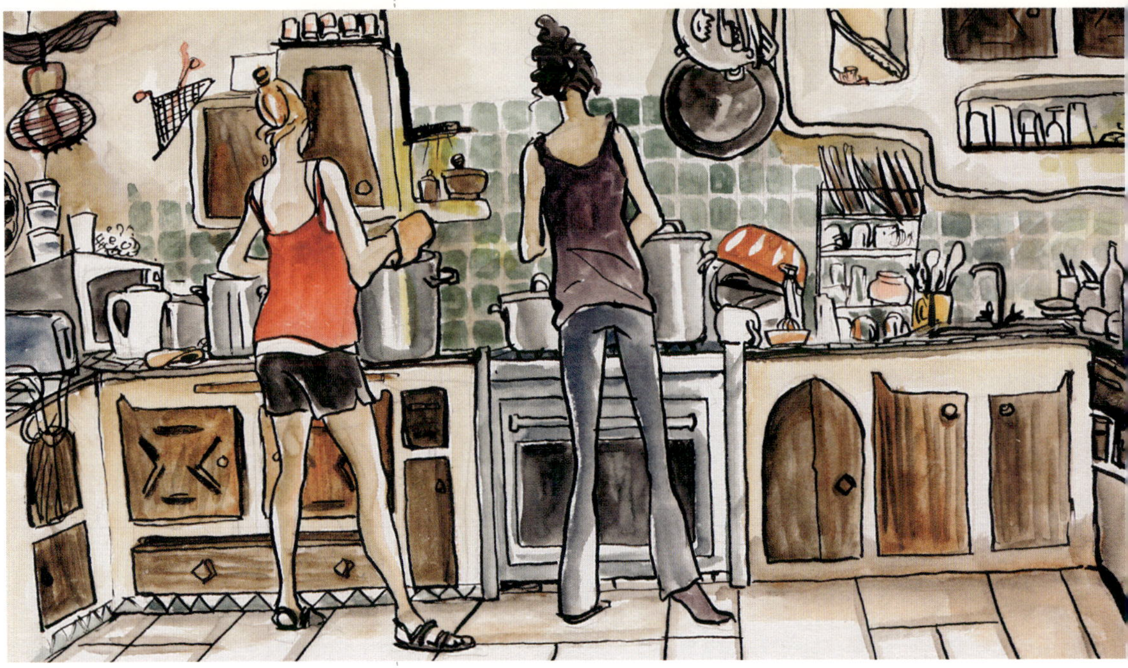

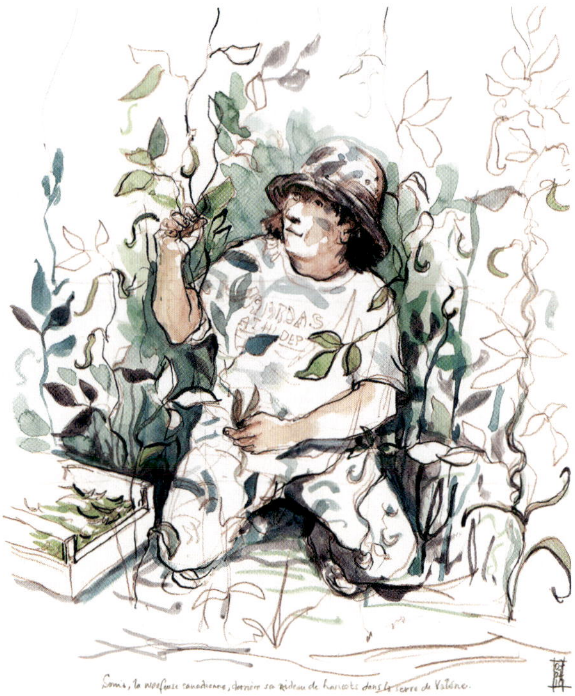

• Paysannes, *La Boîte à bulles, 2013.*
Between culinary tasks (preparation of pesto) and farming (the bean harvest), women farmers took the time to confide in Les Carnettistes tribulants.

DIARIES FOR ENCOUNTERS AND PORTRAITS

Since 2005, the travelogue has borrowed the portrait genre—between photography and interview—from journalism. The association Les Carnettistes tribulants ushered in this type of book through two collective works: *Vivre vieux: carnets de rencontres* (Alternatives, 2009) and *Paysannes: carnet de rencontres avec des femmes engagées* (La Boîte à bulles, 2013). The first of these is a taboo-breaking examination of the issue of old age that went against the dominant discourse on the subject. Sharing the daily lives of retired people, the authors collect in words and images their art of ageing—their activities, places and passions. The second book[5] describes the life of women pastoral and agricultural farmers and wine growers to show the changes in their professional and rural environment. Encounters, exchanges, the subjects' stories and the things they share punctuate this work in which the journey takes place through going beyond the clichés, though the richness of the exchanges and through the sensitive and open take of each artist in his or her quest for the Other—an approach initiated by Noëlle Herrenschmidt in her diaries published with Albin Michel. In 2005, Elsie Herberstein, Cathy Beauvallet and Damien Chavanat (in collaboration with Jérôme Pruneau) revealed the town of Sète to us through the sports event associated with it, namely water jousting. This festive occasion is used to collect the people of Sète's stories, which are transcribed through portraits and words in *Sète, surprenant voyage* (Jalan Publications). The same year Jalan also published *Alger,*

5. Les Carnettistes tribulants were commissioned to do this work by CIVAM (Centre d'initiative pour valoriser l'agriculture et le milieu rural).

simples confidences by Elsie Herberstein and Zahia Hafs, a book of portraits highlighting the ethnographic and historical aspects of Algiers's neighbourhoods (Casbah, Bab el-Oued, Bologhine, Belcourt, El-Biar and the fishing port) through a polymorphic perspective. For the author Zahia Hafs it was a journey to discover her roots and a trip off the beaten path to draw attention to the preservation of tourist areas.

Elsie Herberstein on *Alger, simples confidences*

"We stayed in Algiers three times and during three different seasons in 2004 and 2005. We didn't want to make a nostalgic or backward-looking book on the city's architecture, heritage or picturesque parts. Instead, our intention was to provide a portrait of Algiers today, reborn after ten painful years of terrorism. The inhabitants of Algiers whom we encountered randomly in our explorations of the city's streets each showed us their area, opened the doors of their homes and welcomed us into their families. In my previous books I had preferred white paper and watercolour. But in Algiers, I realized that watercolour was too soft and transparent to reproduce the character and contrasts of a city that, while definitely white and blue, also displays the full range of earthy and yellowy Sienna and ochre tones, sometimes with a splash of vermilion. So I chose a recycled beige-brown paper that already had an irregular texture that was similar to a whitewashed wall. And instead of watercolour, I used gouache, which is smoother and thicker and which becomes dull and powdery like pastel as it dries. I used larger diaries and paper formats for this technique. It takes longer to implement because you have to take out your tubes and have a palette, but I had more time than I would have had on a trip that involved lots of travelling, and we also took three consecutive trips for the same purpose. My passion for architecture is as strong as it is for portraits. The Algiers diary combines portrait sessions, scenes of everyday life drawn on the spot and views of the Casbah and the prettiest architectural jewels that the various districts of Algiers have to offer."

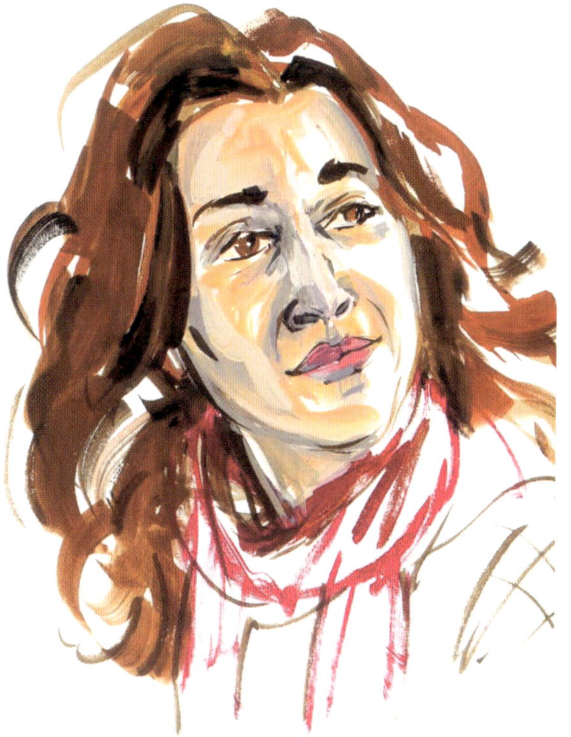

• Alger, simples confidences, *Jalan Publications, 2005. To put an end to postcard portrayals, Elsie Herberstein and Zahia Hafs went to rediscover the districts of Algiers, guided by their inhabitants.*

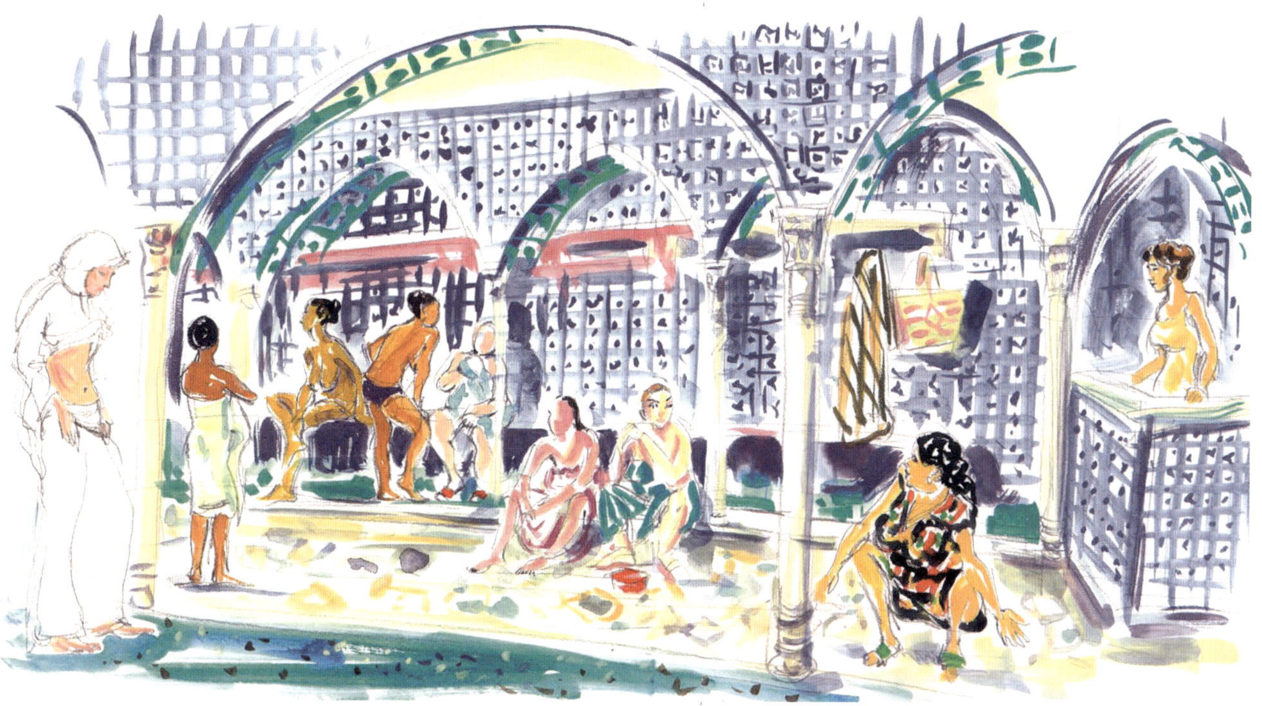

HUMANITARIAN DIARIES

Following the example of *Carnet de mission, prostitution et épidémie de sida à Phnom Penh* by Nicolas Lainez (2006), humanitarian missions can also be a theme for travel diary makers. Tian Keu, a Cambodian refugee in France, revealed his homeland to three illustrator friends (Lisa Mandel, Sylvain Rondet and Lucie Albon) through an educational theatre project for hearing-impaired children. He wanted to give an account of the project through a travel diary, and the experience resulted in *Sept mois au Cambodge* (Glénat, 2003). Geneviève Marot, also from Cambodia, runs painting workshops with an NGO in the streets of Phnom Penh. She uses a sketchbook to collect watercolour and collage portraits of street children (*Cambodge: dans les rues de Phnom Penh*, Gallimard, 2003). She contributed to *Carnets de la Salagane*,[6] which was published under the aegis of the humanitarian organization Aide et Action. It tells the story of a round-the-world sailboat voyage undertaken by a team of five

6. Portes du monde, 2003.

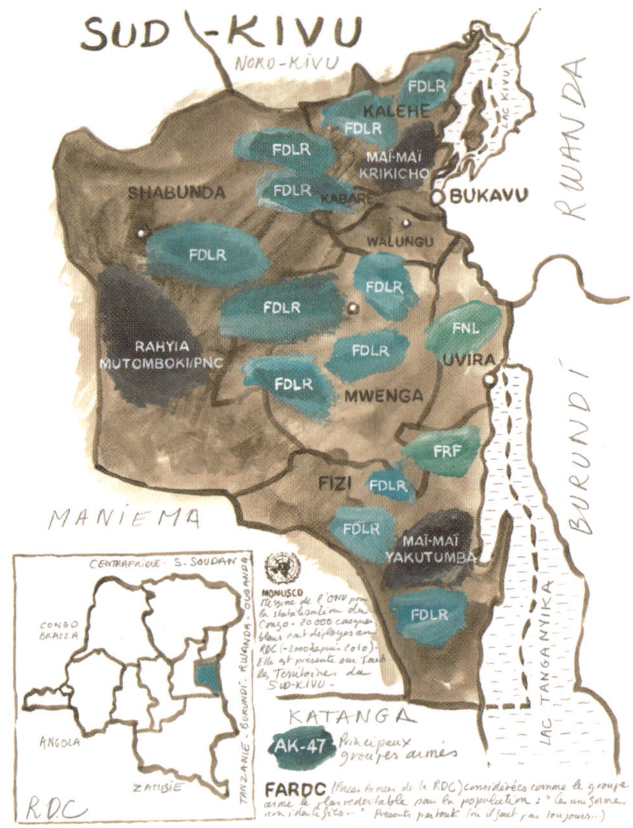

"Ici nous avons peur, là-bas nous n'avons rien": Bukavu ou la valse des réfugiés. Premier séjour à l'aube de 2005.

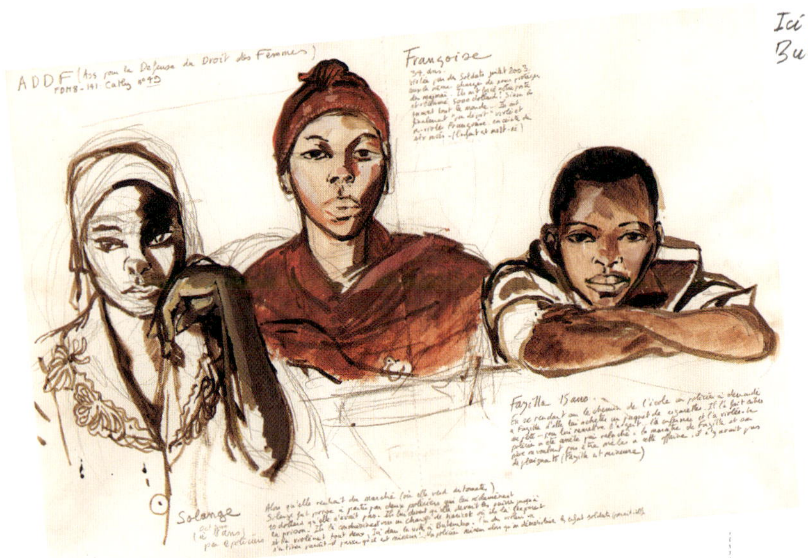

• Ténèbres au paradis, *Gallimard, 2011. After* Zoé Zoé femmes du monde, *Titouan Lamazou gave a voice to Congolese women in a politically torn country.*

young people of different nationalities to discover the beauties of the world—and its injustices. In *Ténèbres au paradis* (Gallimard, 2011), Titouan Lamazou paints portraits of Congolese women who are variously victims, activists, refugees and workers, which are accompanied by texts from Congolese, French and Belgian writers. Six years after *Zoé Zoé femmes du monde* (Gallimard, 2007), Lamazou wanted to give women a voice once more. The voices he recorded are supported by commentaries from specialists on this complex geopolitical region.

In 2009, as part of a Franco-Palestinian artistic exchange between France's overseas cultural centres and the Clermont-Ferrand Rendez-vous du carnet de voyage, the illustrator Bruno Pilorget, the author Véronique Massenot and the photographer Marc Abel travelled to Palestine to reveal a little-known land. The exhibition of their work, from Hebron to Nablus and Ramallah, offered the authors the opportunity to meet people and converse with them: "The Palestinians feel as though they are hardly recognized, and they really want to be listened to. So it was very easy to

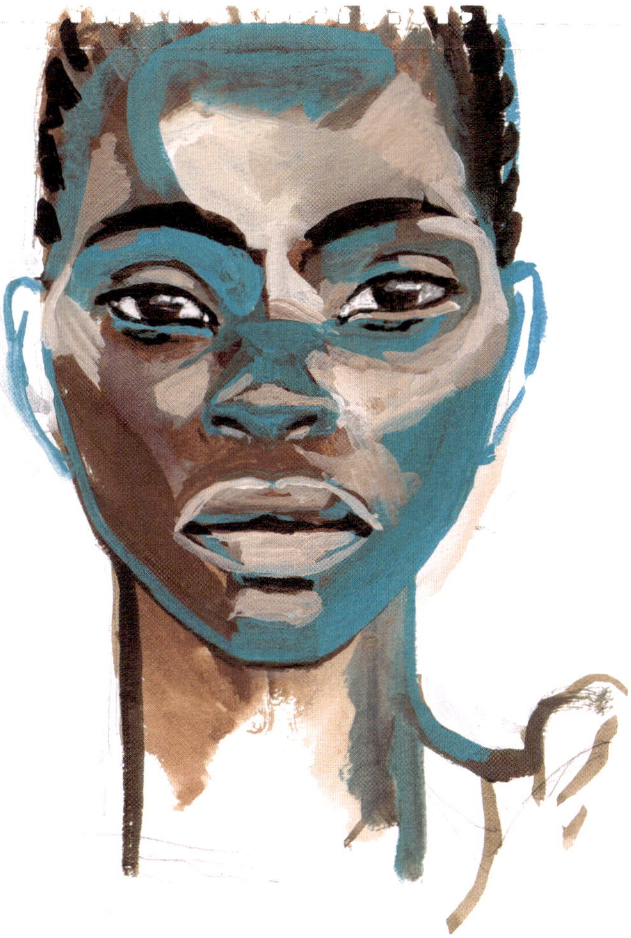

approach them. Interviews, in situ portraits, photo reportage—we had plenty to do!"[7] The participants were also able to reveal a Palestinian identity through an artist's take: "We are not journalists, we are artists, but we worked in a journalistic form."[8] This endeavour gave rise to the work *Salaam Palestine! Carnet de voyage en terre d'humanité*, which was published by La Boîte à bulles in 2013 and won the Grand Prix Michelin, the Médecins Sans Frontières favourite award and Prix Club de la presse during the Clermont-Ferrand's fourteenth Rendez-vous du carnet de voyage. The presentation of the book was accompanied by an exhibition and a film to encourage interactions with the public.

Bruno Pilorget on *Salaam Palestine! Carnet de voyage en terre d'humanité*
"My Palestine diary made me evolve towards travel reportage diaries. They always recount a trip, but of course, not so much from a wanderer's perspective. Invited in 2008 to do touring workshops in towns with young people, I was stupefied to see the realities of the situation, and so I started a book. I had to give an account in my own way through producing a book. I returned in 2009, accompanied by a writer and a photographer. Each of us had our own field and sensibility, but these were brought together for the same subjects. We set out with the idea of doing a portrait of a little-known Palestine, as it is lived and recounted by the Palestinians themselves, with ourselves sticking to our position of artists, far removed from weighty geopolitical diatribes. When we returned, we had a lot of work to do over a period of four years to bring together the texts, drawings and photos in a clear and consistent layout and in the spirit of our trip as a threesome. The content and the form of the book were equally important."

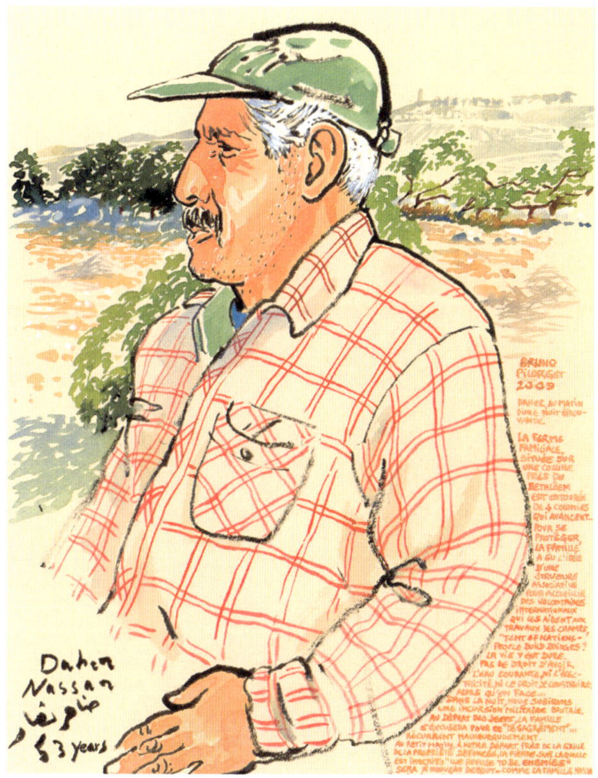

• Salaam Palestine, *La Boîte à bulles, 2013. The portrait of a "little-known" Palestine "lived and told by the Palestinians" sets the media representations of this country shaken by war straight.*

7. Bruno Pilorget.
8. Bruno Pilorget.

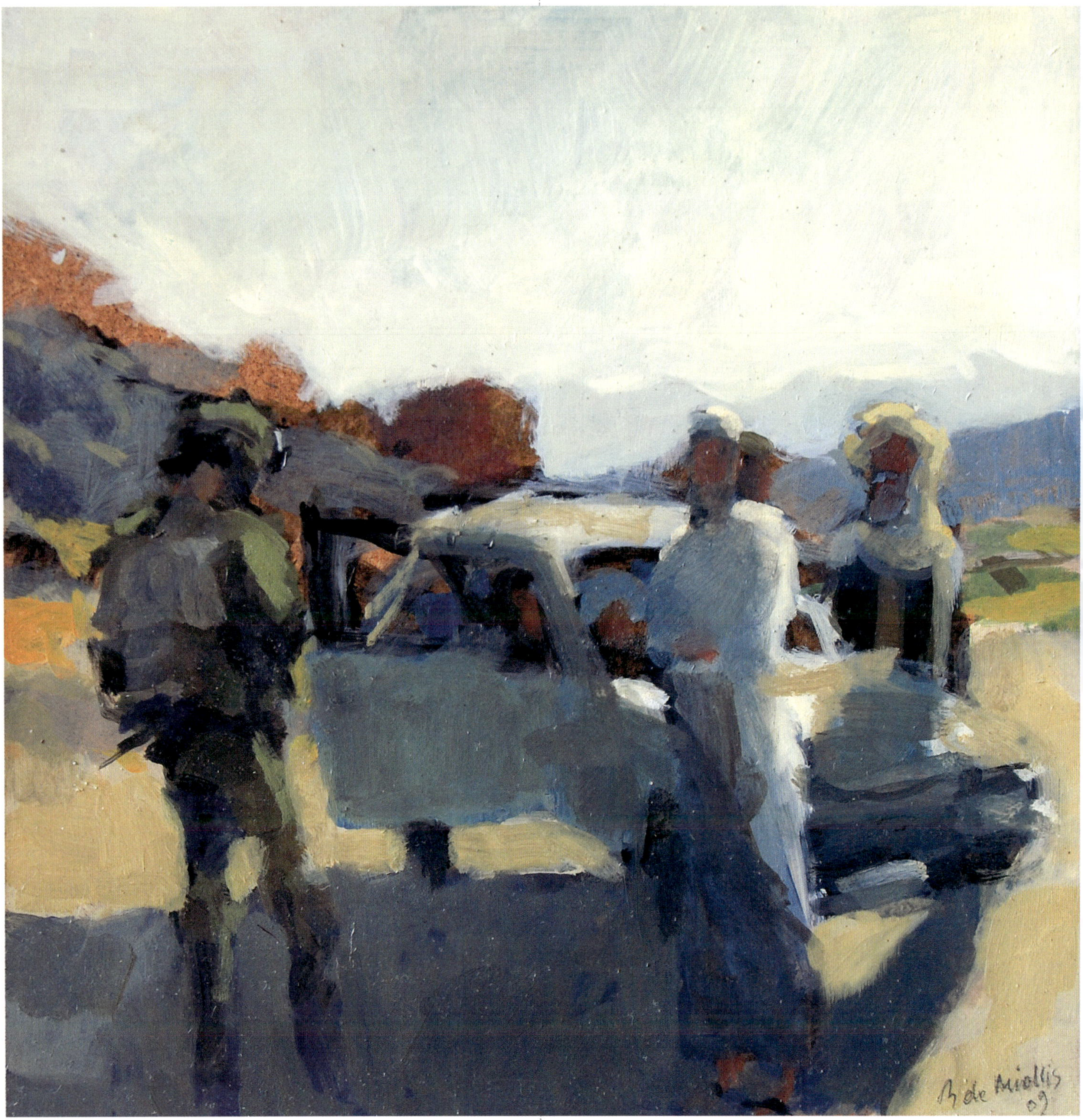
B de Miollis
09

WAR DIARIES

Comic-strip artists were the first to engage in a graphic reportage of war. Back in 1995, Séra became the first comic author to report on a conflict, that of the Khmer Rouge in Cambodia, in *Impasse et rouge: Cambodge 1970-1975* (Rackham, 1995) and *L'Eau et la terre: Cambodge 1975-1979* (Delcourt, 2005). Following on from this, Joe Sacco, an American journalist and illustrator, broadened this trend by recounting the reality of daily life for Palestinians in the occupied territories in two volumes: *Palestine: A Nation Occupied* and *Palestine: In the Gaza Strip.*[9] Jean-Paul Mari[10] and Yann Le Béchec offer an interpretation of the Israel-Palestine conflict that came to them following their interactions with people living out their daily lives in a war zone. Their stories are told in *Israël Palestine: carnets* (Jalan Publications, 2004). The first illustrator to focus on the Serbo-Croat conflict in the former Yugoslavia is the journalist Aleksandar Zograf. In *E-mails de Pancevo* and *Bons baisers de Serbie*,[11] he tells of his experiences in Belgrade during NATO's bombing campaign. Joe Sacco also produced books on the conflict: *Stories From Bosnia #1: Soba* introduces us to an engaged artist; *Safe Area Goražde: The War in Eastern Bosnia 1992–1995* describes the suffering of the last Bosnian enclave in the Serb zone; and *War's End: Profiles from Bosnia 1995–96* combines two stories from his work in the former Yugoslavia, one of which focuses on the one-of-a-kind Soba, a painter and rock star, while the second is about Radovan Karadzic. Meanwhile, in his *Notes from a Defeatist*,[12] Sacco shares his thoughts on being a war reporter during the twentieth century's armed conflicts. *Afghanes* by Titouan Lamazou (Gallimard, 2009) records the testimonies of war widows of various ethnic origins (including Tajik, Uzbek, Sikh and Pashtun women) and their fates during twenty-five years of Afghan conflict. The work is complemented by an analysis of the country's complexities by Bernard Dupaigne of the Muséum national d'histoire naturelle, a specialist on Afghanistan.

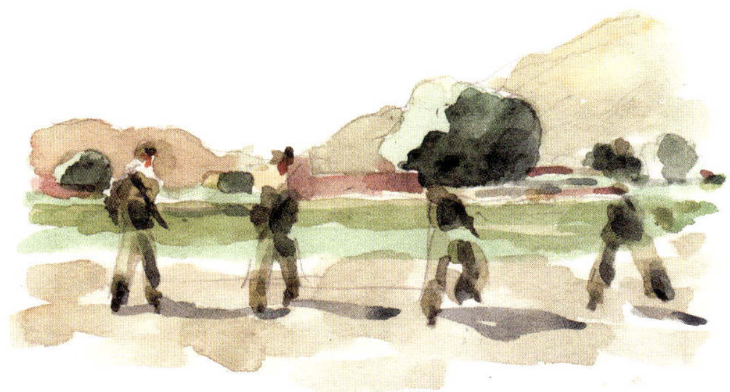

The reporter Arnaud de La Grange put his name to *Irak, année zéro* (Gallimard, 2004), an illustrated album of photographs by Thomas Goisque and drawings by Bertrand de Miollis. The contents, geographically divided into three parts (the Centre, North and South), evokes a documentary. The different takes, chosen by the photographer and illustrator, are organized like a storyboard—wide-angle photography meets watercolour medium shots, press drawings or pencil sketches of details—and contribute to a tracking-shot effect between images and texts. The photography affirms the lived experience, while the drawing and watercolour emphasize the timelessness, so that the representation is not reduced to "the immediate events." There was another instalment of this threefold reportage-focused publishing project in 2009 with the publication of *Haute tension: des chasseurs alpins en Afghanistan*, to which Sylvain Tesson also contributed. This story gives a day-by-day account of the first six months of combat between the 27e bataillon de chasseurs alpins and the Taliban in the Kapisa region. Its personal accounts and portraits provide an understanding of the activities of these seven hundred and fifty French soldiers in Afghanistan as they help a people to restore peace, as well as explaining the difficulties of their struggle.

9. These two works were published by Fantagraphics Books in 1993 and 1996.
10. This reporter is the author of *Carnets de Bagdad*, published by Grasset in 2003.
11. L'Association, 1999 and 2000.
12. Fantagraphics Books, 2003.

• Haute tension, *Gallimard, 2009. After* Irak année zéro, *Bertrand de Miollis and Thomas Goisque, accompanied by Sylvain Tesson, recounted the 27e bataillon de chasseurs alpins's fight against the Taliban in Afghanistan.*

Bertrand de Miollis on *Haute tension: des chasseurs alpins en Afghanistan*

"In a military context and in a theatre of operations, making a 'war diary' is to adopt the eyewitness's take on history in the making. It is about recounting events with a personal and sensitive eye and doing so as well as possible. Drawing takes time, which is sometimes problematic, and for this reason it requires a summarizing of information. Ultimately, this subjective reality is in fact imbued with the conditions encountered at the time of producing the drawing: urgency, fear, the cold, the warmth, discomfort, and so on. The drawing is therefore a suggested way of looking at reality. Depending on the person doing the drawing, it can be sweet or violent, disincarnate or human. I personally love using my drawings to reveal just the essentials and leave a lot to the imagination. On the ground, my approach is to be constantly alert, to spend a lot of time observing and to draw broad scenes when I can be at ease, and quick little scenes when that's all I can do. Working from memory allows me to draw what's before my eyes and what is already gone. I try to reconstruct multiple and varied pieces of information so that my reportage is as rich as it can be."

DIARIES OF CULTURAL AND GEOPOLITICAL DIVERSITY

These diaries often provide a different take on sensitive geographical areas that have fallen under the spotlight of the news. Bernard Ollivier, a retired journalist, set off on his own to meet the peoples living along the old Silk Road, which is now an international geopolitical hotspot. His years of adventure, from the Mediterranean to Xi'an in China, are described in his trilogy *Longue marche* and were followed up by a new journey, during which the author took as a companion the painter François Dermaut (*Carnets d'une longue marche: nouveau voyage d'Istanbul à Xian*, Phébus, 2005). In 2011, Emmanuel Guibert and Frédéric Lemercier used images and texts to tell the story of the different journeys taken by the reporter and photographer Alain Keler among the Roma in Europe, particularly in France and Italy, to better understand the difficulties encountered by this stateless community. *Zoé Zoé femmes du monde* by Titouan Lamazou is an examination of the status of women around the world. Since 2001, the author has been drawing and photographing women whom he has met during his travels and who have led exceptional lives. Lamazou records their stories and portraits and introduces a wide range of cultural diversity in terms of religion, way of life or societal change.

Journal de la mer d'Arabie[13] reveals Claire and Reno Marca's journey to Socotra island. Having set off without any preparation, this pair of adventurous artists allowed chance to shape their escapades. This is how they discovered the dhows, the wooden boats that transport goods between the shores of the Arabian Sea, heirs of ancient trade between Africa, Arabia and India. Passing through Yemen and the Sultanate of Oman, the authors headed towards India in search of the sites where they are built. Empowered by their twelve years of experience in "illustrated reportage," Claire and Reno Marca give images a central position, with text fitting in peripherally in the form of comments. The recounting of their journey, the fruit of a significant amount of postproduction work, is organized within skilfully composed page spreads that create a dialogue between drawing and photography and between black and white and colour.

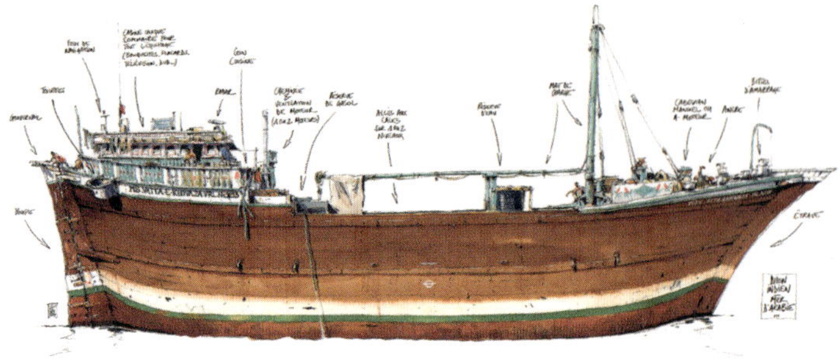

13. Published by Éditions de La Martinière in 2012, this book was awarded the Prix Pierre Loti and the Prix de l'ATJ in 2013.

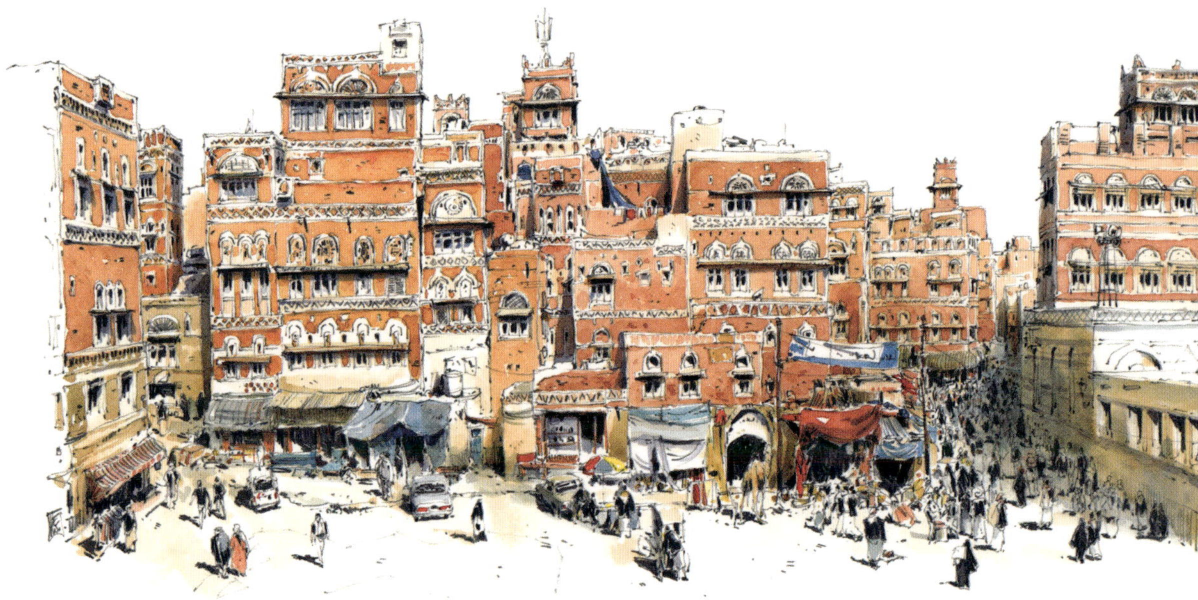

• ***Journal de la mer d'Arabie**, Éditions de La Martinière, 2012. Going in search of Indian dhows (above) carrying trade between Dubai and Somalia was what took Claire and Reno Marca through Yemen, the Sultanate of Oman and India.*

• ***Journal de la mer d'Arabie**, Éditions de La Martinière, 2012. Right, the district of Bab el-Yemen in Sanaa (Yemen), captured in watercolour by Reno Marca.*

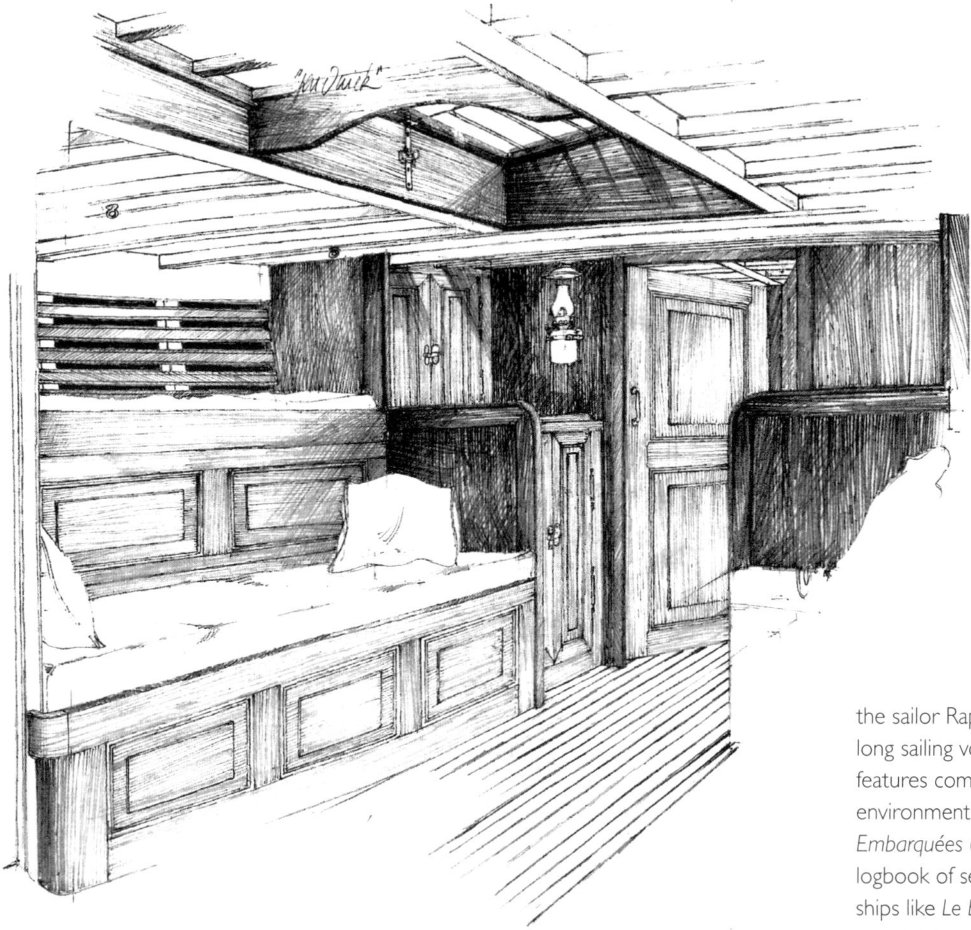

• Pen Duick, *Gallimard, 2000.*
Éric Tabarly's boat, Pen Duick, *as seen by Marc P.G. Berthier (left, the wardroom; below, layout plan and cross section).*

SEAFARERS' LOGBOOKS

Following in the wake of the seafaring geographers of the eighteenth century, Erik Hesselberg, a young Norwegian architect, used sketches to capture the story of the expedition of the *Kon-Tiki* to the Polynesian Islands. This gave rise in 1952 to *Kon-Tiki and I*, published by Rand McNally. The "*Voiles*" collection of albums republished Sahib's and Mike Peyton's comedy albums at the end of the 1970s (*Plaisir d'humour ne dure qu'une marée*), and then called on renowned watercolour artists, who were often official naval painters like Marin-Marie, Marc P.G. Berthier and Titouan Lamazou. The illustrator Christophe Blain, who completed his national service in the navy, showed the daily lives of drafted men aboard a warship in *Carnet d'un matelot* (Albin Michel Jeunesse, 1994). The travel diary therefore seems linked to seafarers' experiences. And that includes women as well as men! Sophie Ladame, a skipper and illustrator, excels in the art of watercolour, as evidenced by her Caribbean seascapes in *Carnets d'Éole vers les Caraïbes*, which were produced on her sailboat. She continued her artistic work by illustrating the book *Dialogue avec la mer: retour en terres de Bretagne* (Le Toucan, 2007) by the sailor Raphaella Le Gouvello, which recounts a month-long sailing voyage with twenty-six stops in Breton waters and features commentary by a specialist of flora, fauna, coasts and the environment. Having collaborated with Isabelle Rosenzweig on *Embarquées* (Magellan & Cie, 2009), Sophie published her own logbook of seafaring adventures[14] on board traditional sailing ships like *Le Belem*, *Le Renard* and *La Grande Hermine*. The work is a veritable watercolour ode to the maritime world.
The technical version of the maritime logbook has been in existence since the sixteenth century. The logbook kept by Bernard Moitessier in 1968 on board the sailboat *Joshua,* which collects over a thousand maritime secrets, is a perfect example of such works.

14. *Grisée de mer*, Moea éditions, Saint-Malo, 2011.

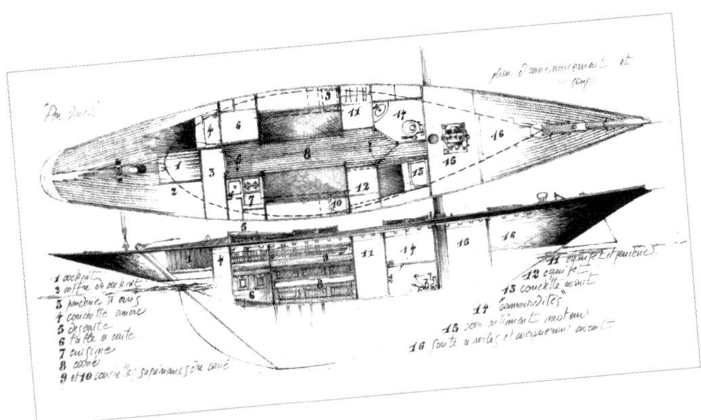

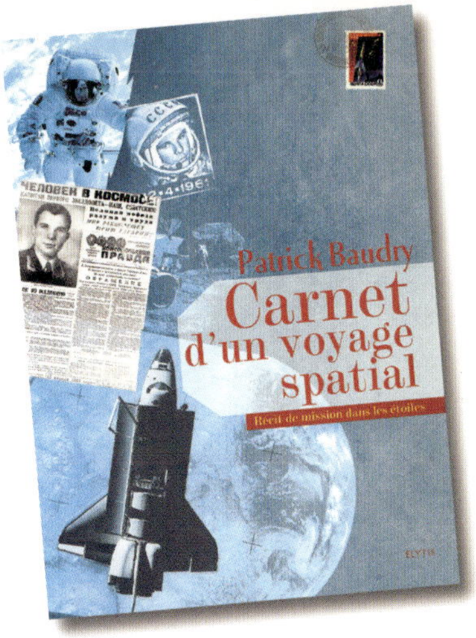

• Carnet d'un voyage spatial, *Elytis, 2007.*
The memoirs of Patrick Baudry, or the realization of the universal dream of seeing the Earth from space.

SCIENTIFIC EXPEDITION DIARIES

Following in the footsteps of Paul-Émile Victor, the anthropologist and geographer Jean Malaurie made it to the geomagnetic North Pole in 1951. He brought back two diaries from his expedition: a travel journal that gave details of his itineraries, and a rich ethnological collection of many sketches (for example, tattoos, objects, costumes and igloo plans), which was a way for him and the Inuits to share things with one another, with each drawing in the book. In 1997, at the request of the magazine *Grands reportages* and the Institut français des pôles, Christophe Blain set off for Adélie Land. He would return with what would become *Carnet polaire* (Casterman, 1997). *Carnets de Sibérie: Mammuthus expéditions*[15] by Benjamin Flao and Bernard Buigues (Glénat, 2002) is an account of the scientific mission charged with collecting the DNA of the Jarkov Mammoth. The expedition "Arktika" (2000–2004) was led by Gilles Elkaim, who travelled 11,000 kilometres without motorized means, from the North of Norway to the Bering Strait. The expedition was the subject of an online travel diary. Nicolas Vanier's "Odyssée sibérienne" between Irkutsk and Moscow reveals the taiga and tundra over a distance of more than 8,000 kilometres. Mixing personal papers and scientific iconography provided by NASA, *Carnet d'un voyage spatial* offers the astronaut Patrick Baudry's recollections from flight STS-51G of the Space Shuttle *Discovery*. Current expeditions, some of which have taken place at the initiative of the Société des explorateurs français and the Société de géographie, have also been reported through online logbooks or narratives. In 2005, Jean-Louis Étienne's expedition, which was tasked with describing the flora and fauna of the atoll of Clipperton Island in the Eastern Pacific, was the subject of a young-adult book, *Les Aventures d'Elliot et Basile à Clipperton*.[16] In general, logbooks illustrated with photographs are a common tool for scientific research. For example, between 2006 and 2008, Stéphane Lévin, a member of the Société des explorateurs français, planned three scientific expeditions to be undertaken with secondary-school students from Toulouse. These led to the creation of the logbooks *Voyageurs des sables*, *Voyageurs des glaces* and *Voyageurs des fleuves*, which were published by Loubatières. More recently, in *Mission Tara océans*, Sophie Nicaud, a biology researcher, traces her five-week experience on the team of oceanographers, biologists and physicists on board the *Tara* for a 2009 global study on plankton, marine viruses, bacteria and jellyfish.

15. Grand Prix 2003 of the Biennale du carnet de voyage.

16. Texts and illustrations by Elsa Pény-Étienne, Seuil Jeunesse, 2005.

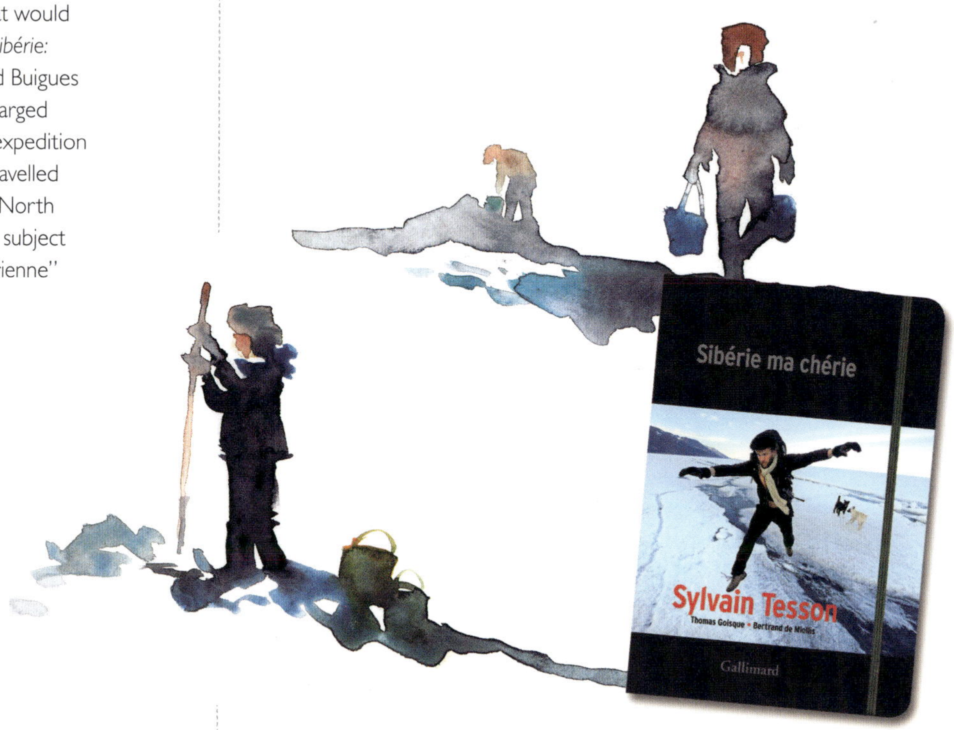

• Sibérie ma chérie, *Gallimard, 2012.*
The trio behind Haute tension *reunited in Siberia, bringing back with them a geographical diary that was intended as a "declaration of love to a country that brought [them] joy and taught [them] so much."*

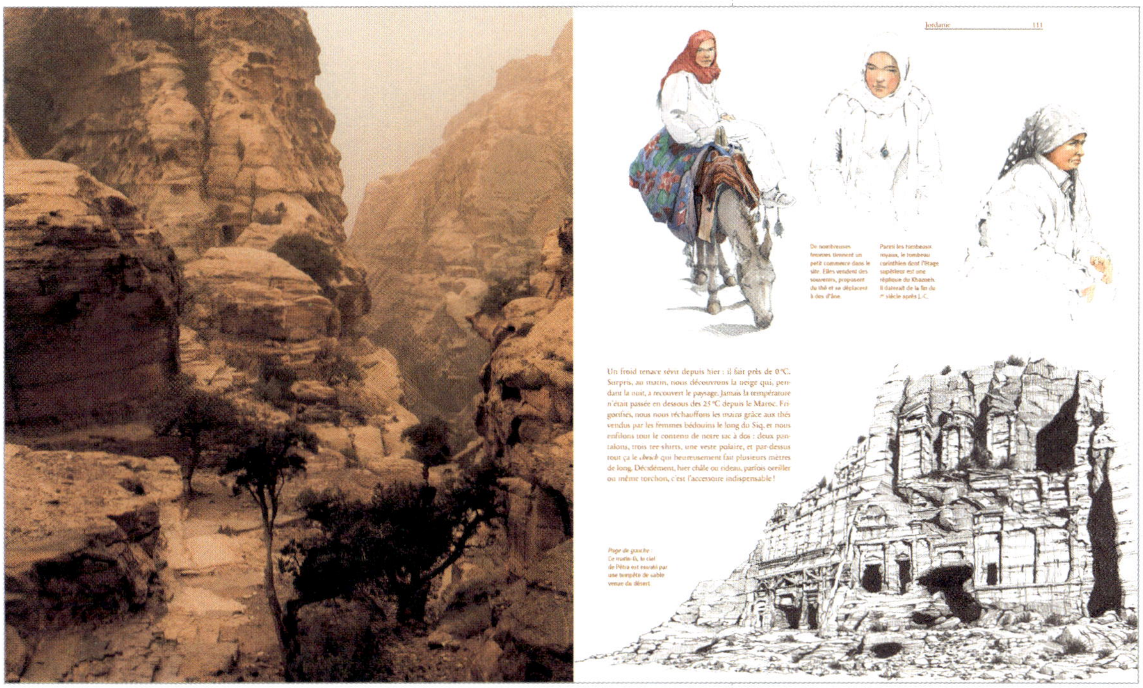

• *Trois ans de voyage, Éditions de La Martinière, 2012. Or 18 months of work to capture Claire and Reno Marca's journey through 25 countries on 4 continents.*

GEOGRAPHERS' DIARIES

Inspired by reports of scientific expeditions, the geographer and writer Sylvain Tesson, who took trips to Russia over a period of twenty years, produced a travel diary entitled *Sibérie ma chérie* (Gallimard, 2012) in collaboration with Thomas Goisque and Bertrand de Miollis. This trio, who travelled thousands of kilometres from Yakutia to the Bay of Bengal and spent six months on the shores of Lake Baikal, compiled news, stories and reports as they followed the path taken by a Gulag escapee. This geographic angle on the travel reportage book corresponds to the inductive approach of geography and ethnology, which go from the field and local experience to establish a more general law. Every book that contributes to this research records a point of view, and such works taken as a whole allow observations to be compared and then lines of thought towards a more general explanation to be elaborated.

Claire and Reno Marca's diaries on Algeria, Madagascar and Saudi Arabia are distinguished by the breadth of the documentation that they draw on. Their first long-distance trip is recounted in *Trois ans de voyage*[17] (Éditions de La Martinière, 2012), a travel reportage diary with a documentary dimension that gives an account of a journey through twenty-five countries and four continents. Each country is described from a geographer's point of view, placed in an international geopolitical context and analysed on the basis of its political, social and economic situation. This journal, which offers a personal and intimate view, is compared to media perspectives and juxtaposes the feelings of the authors out in the streets and those of local residents with government policy in each state. A geography book of the contemporary world, *Trois ans de voyage* fits into the great tradition of early twentieth-century encyclopaedias that compiled the reports of the Société de géographie's expeditions around the world. "Packed with more than 700 illustrations and a wealth of maps, this story of a unique adventure is an unusual travel diary and a lavish and exciting first-hand atlas of a reenchanted world" that required seven years of reflection on travelling—two years of preparation, three continuous years on the road and eighteen months of working with a small editorial team.

17. Prix Amerigo Vespucci at the Festival international de géographie (2006) and Prix du jury at FIDLAS (2007).

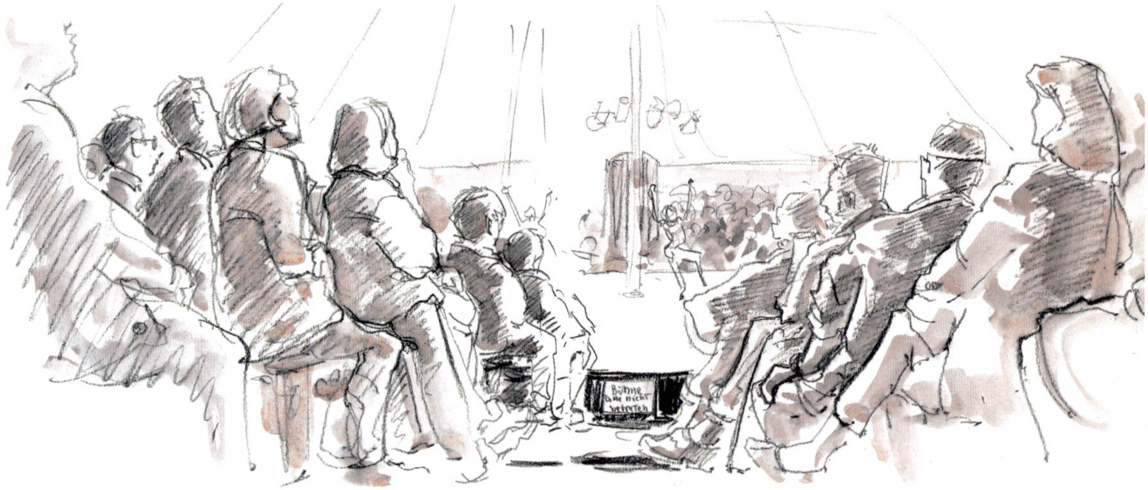

PERFORMANCE DIARIES

The theatre lovers Cabu, Alain Léonard and Gérard Vantaggioli produced a diary of comedy and critique at Avignon's Festival Off (*Festival off Avignon*, Avant-scène théâtre, 1989), which they had attended for many years. These trailblazers opened the way to other diaries on the performing arts, for example the circus, the subject of choice for Cathy Beauvallet (*Carnet de cirque* with Manu Reisch, Gallimard, 2001) and Michel Costiou (*Le Cirque: reportages graphiques*, IDLivre, 2006). These authors, who are well known for the quality of the sketches they have made of dance,[18] opera and orchestra performances, offer up "performance diaries." Cabu produced the first pieces of music reporting for *Hara-Kiri* on the Parisian cabarets from which the young singers of the era emerged (for example, Brel, Boby Lapointe and Gainsbourg) before developing a passion for jazz (*Cabu in jazz: carnets de jazz*, éditions Du Layeur, 2004 and *Cabu swing: souvenirs & carnets d'un fou de jazz*, Les Échappées, 2013). In 2007, Vincent Besançon produced the first festival diary, *Le Festival de la Chaise-Dieu: le carnet de voyage musical* (Rouergue, 2007), using his pencil drawing to cover the forty-seven concerts of the fortieth edition of Chaise-Dieu's festival. Bullfighting also has its place in the performing arts and performance diaries, in the form of *Toreros* by Enrique Lasserre (Rouergue, 2003), *Carnet de voyage en corridas* by Jacques Brianti, Cathy Beauvallet and Nathalie Cloutier (Atlantica, 2008) and *Carnets taurins* by Jean-Pierre Formica (Actes Sud, 2012).

Nem, le Nouvel Ensemble moderne: un parcours d'ensemble contemporain 1989–2009 (Lorraine Vallaincourt Montréal, 2009) brought about the meeting of three different but complementary artists: Lorraine Vaillancourt, conductor and artistic director of the Nouvel Ensemble Moderne; Cathy Beauvallet, an illustrator who specializes in reportage illustration; and Nathalie Cloutier, a painter and photographer. All three collaborated on a work of art to celebrate the Nouvel Ensemble Moderne's twentieth anniversary.[19] While Cathy Beauvallet's performance took the form of producing pencil sketches of the musicians during concerts, rehearsals and moments of working or interacting with the public, Nathalie Cloutier took inspiration from the music to create pictorial and photographic works that reveal the musicians' movements and gestures. These two forms of visual expression come together over the pages of the work: on-the-spot drawings show a figurative reality with a specific duration in time, while the paintings open up a more indecisive temporal reality. Suggesting a lived emotion, the paintings offer an abstract narrative construction, whereas the drawings reveal a more descriptive emotion. The texts that bring us the musicians' views are by Lorraine Vaillancourt and Nathalie Cloutier. Cathy Beauvallet has also undertaken this form of performance at various festivals—Avignon's Festival de jazz and Lignières-en-Berry's L'Air du Temps—thereby opening this genre up to all the arts and making it push the boundaries of reportage, sketchbooks and art books.

18. Dance was what inspired Michel Costiou's album *La danse: reportages graphiques* (IDLivre, 2006), while Cathy Beauvallet has also focused on Argentine tango.

19. Montreal's Nouvel Ensemble Moderne, a chamber orchestra founded in 1989, brings together fifteen musicians in residence from the Université de Montréal's music faculty.

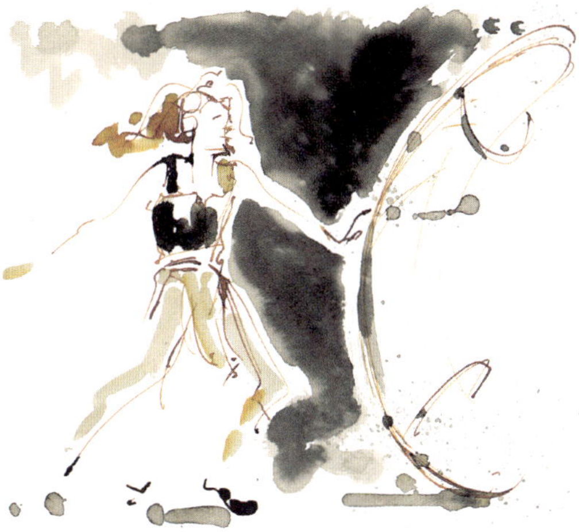

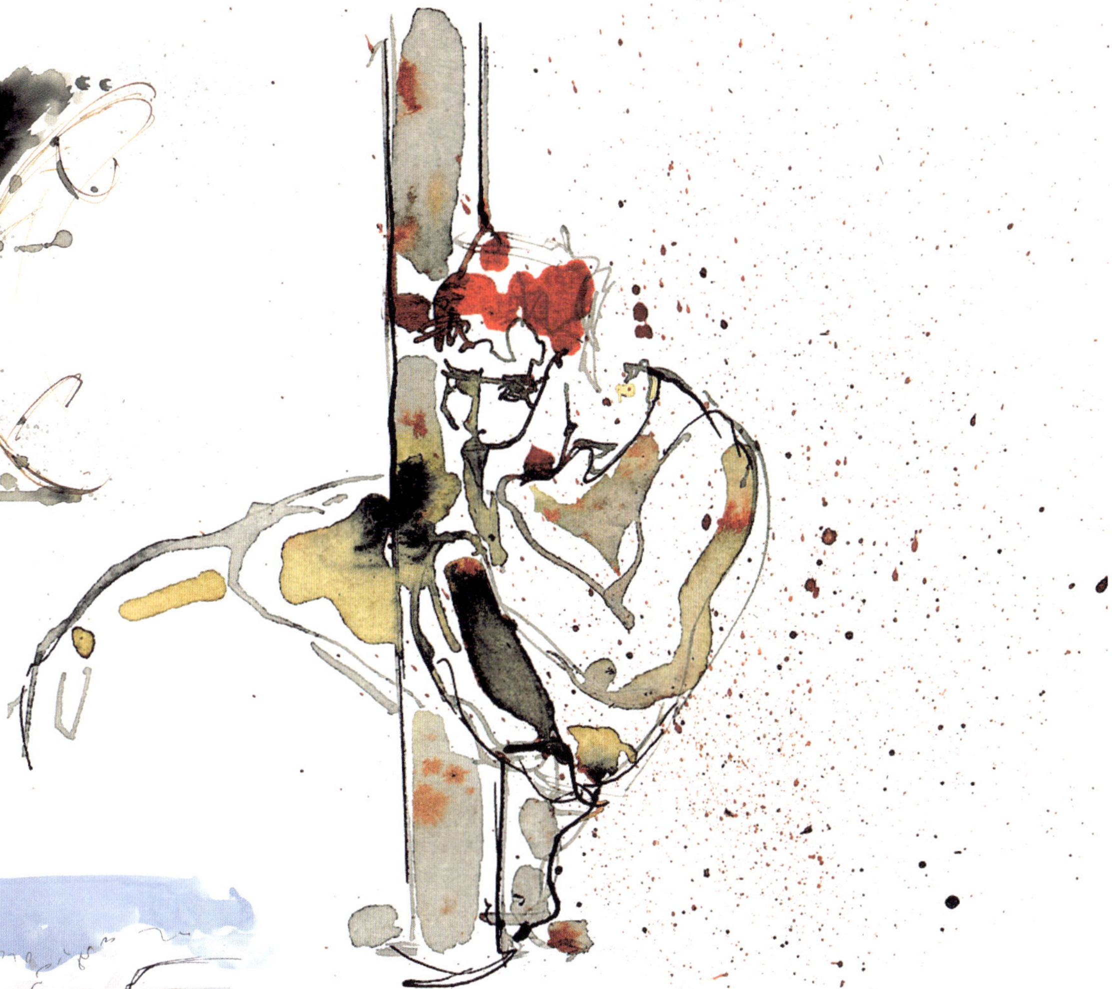

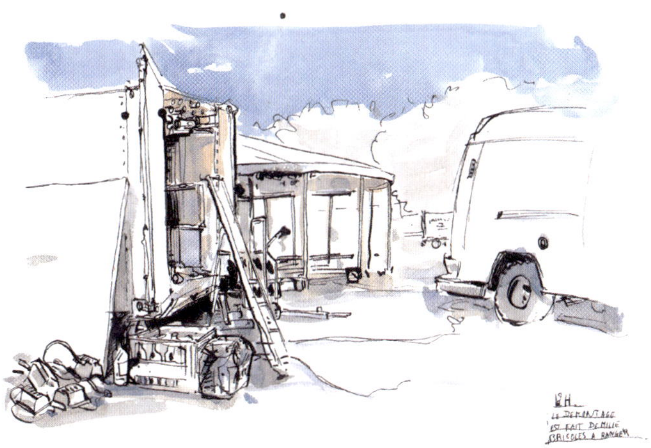

• Carnet de cirque, *Gallimard, 2001. Whatever field she explores (for example, the circus or the music festival), Cathy Beauvallet has enjoyed developing a certain performance art by capturing the artistic events that she attends in real time.*

Cathy Beauvallet on her approach

"The living is the focal point of my work; the strokes and the marks are a breath of its expression and its ephemerality. As an expression of life, performances allow us to not be tied down and let a shared moment of poetry, harmony, humour and humanity penetrate the space of representation. A music or dance performance becomes a journey, and drawings and paintings are expressions of the poetic moment. At festivals, drawings are immediately displayed, and the narrative gradually unfolds through them collectively. This is the case at various festivals, such as Lignières-en-Berry's L'Air du Temps for contemporary music, Avignon's jazz festival, or Chartres's dance festival."

and on *Carnet de cirque*

"This was a personal tribute to a contemporary circus. Three magnificent artists in the midst of their tour, performing their show with dexterity and poetry, presented me with me an opportunity to follow them over the course of three years while I drew them; I didn't originally intend to produce a book. It was about translating movement into drawing. For a long time, I had admired the extreme gestures that you can see in Hokusai's sumo wrestlers, and Toulouse-Lautrec's take on La Goulue. So I had the idea of seeking out a circus. The only thing I wanted to convey in my drawings is the humanity that these three express with such simplicity. And I wanted to access this simplicity with pencil strokes."

2. Carnets de patrimoine

REGIONAL HERITAGE DIARIES

Sites, views and coasts can be promoted through the pictorial arts and the aesthetics of the "picturesque" landscape. Great patrimonial treasures can also be shown through travel diaries, which can serve as a "postcard" and collection of views of a particular region and convey its identity. Lizzie Napoli embarked on such an adventure in 1987 with the publication of *Carnets de voyage en Provence* and *Une aventure au Mont-Saint-Michel*. These were followed by three diaries for Édisud (*Escale à Saint-Malo*, *Provence*, *Escale en Corse*) and a number of works published by Équinoxe, including *Cueillettes en Provence* (1995), *Mon voyage à Sète, Cordes et l'abbaye de Sénanque* (1996) and *Ma Provence* (1997). In her works, ink drawings are partially coloured to attract attention to a particular element of decoration or architecture that has been selected by the artist. Her original style can be found in several collections with evocative names: "Cités du Midi," "Carrés de Provence," "Mosaïques," "Carnets d'ailleurs," "Mes carnets" and "Carrés de France." Her works were the first to have the description of "travel diary" in their subtitle. Michel Duvoisin subsequently offered through the same publisher an invitation to revisit the heritage of the French regions, specializing in this type of book. Rediscovering the paths travelled by the impressionists and outdoor painting are cherished themes for travel diary makers and tourists in search of images to seize and keep in their memories. Accompanied by Solange Louvet, Arnaud d'Aunay set off for places in Normandy that have inspired painters (*Escales d'artistes*, Gallimard, 2003) in order to capture the light that was so valued by Delacroix, Monet, Whistler, Sickert and Braque. Provence has managed to highlight its sites, stretching from the Montagne Sainte-Victoire to the Mediterranean coast, that have been painted by (among others) Cézanne, Van Gogh and Matisse. Following in the footsteps of famous people or writers is also a way to promote local heritage. In 1995, Arnaud d'Aunay[20] explored the Morvan region, on the trail of his forefather Vauban,

20. Vauban, génie maritime, Napoléon, Empereur des Îles, Empereur d'exil and Vézelay: colline d'éternité were all published by Gallimard (2007, 2006 and 2002).

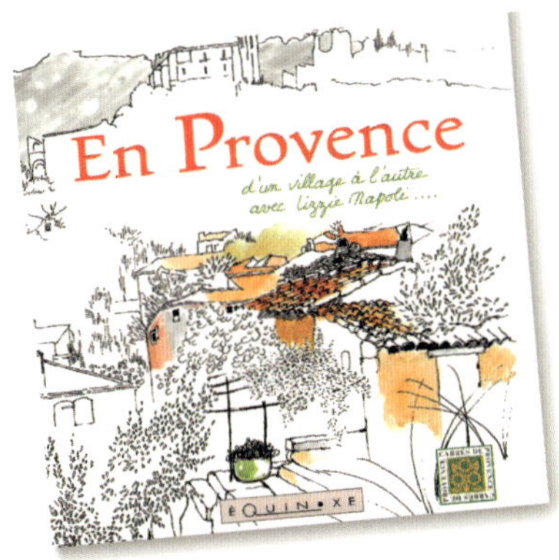

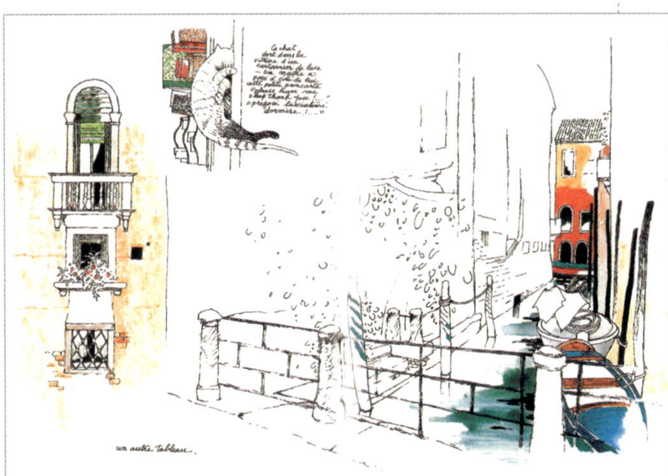

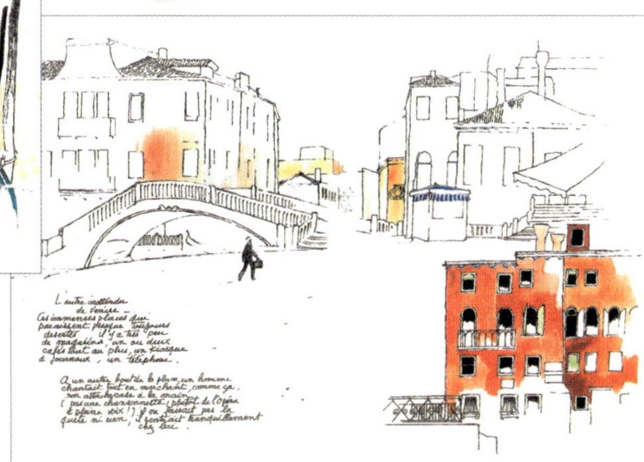

• *Venise, Équinoxe, 1998. Lizzie Napoli was the first artist to offer her sketches to publishers. She quickly established herself as a key travel diary artist, as her numerous publications with Équinoxe and Édisud demonstrate.*

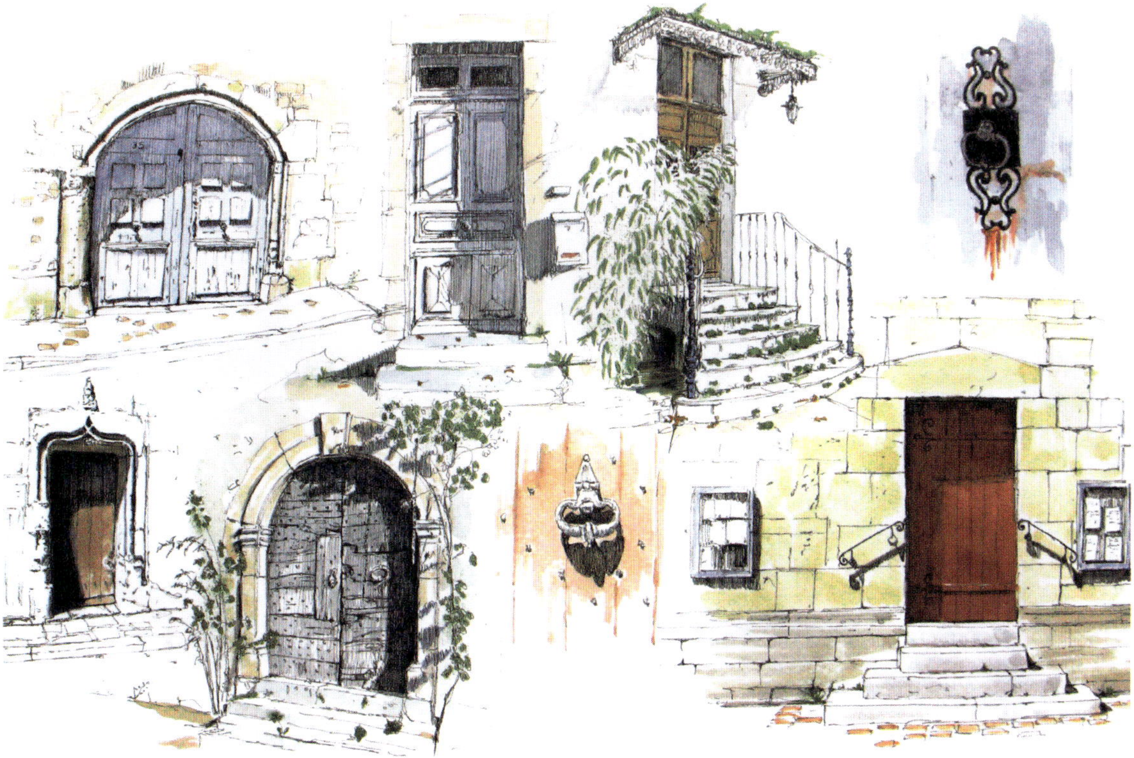

• Vézelay: colline d'éternité, *Gallimard, 2001. Arnaud d'Aunay roamed the city looking for surviving traces of a rich history.*

in *Vauban, seigneur de Bazoches*, while in *Vauban, génie maritime* (Gallimard, 2007) he surveys fortifications spread over 3,000 kilometres of coastline between Dunkirk and Antibes. This artist then followed Napoleon from island to island in *Napoléon, Empereur des îles, Empereur d'exil* and discovered Vézelay and its basilica, a masterpiece of Burgundian art, in *Vézelay, colline d'éternité*. The publisher Gallimard has encouraged heritage books and the discovery of the natural environment with the help of naturalist artists.[21] Illustrators' and painters' takes on the coast have been highlighted in Ouest-France's "L'itinéraire du peintre" and "Regard d'artiste" collections. Within these works, Yvon Carlo paints watercolours of the ports of Brittany, Charente and Gironde; Dominique Darras does the same for Flanders, the Opal Coast and the Bay of Somme; Marie-Madeleine Flambard is drawn to Provence and its villages; Isabelle Issaverdens sketches the most beautiful sites along the Channel and Perche as well as the banks and shores of the Loire and Normandy; and Gilles Ronin illustrates Paris and the castles of Périgord.

21. These themes are found in particular in the collections "Carnets du littoral" and "Carrés de jardin," which were created by Françoise Chabbert and Dominique Legrain.

After Paris, Brittany, Provence and the Loire Valley are the three most popular tourist areas in France, and there are therefore many books that are focused on them. Fluctuating between painter's diary and travel guide, all have in common the use of watercolour. Although French artists have produced most of the works on these areas, travel diary makers from other countries have also proven to be popular among publishers. The publisher Ouest-France has created an original collection, "Le lecteur de l'imaginaire," which provides an opportunity to see foreign artists' takes on France's regions.

Arnaud d'Aunay on his approach

"The travel diary is a singular object that offers up the world's plurality. The free, unique, spontaneous and thoughtful transcription of ties to other people, objects and surprising things requires attention and humility. This understanding of the Other through the removal of the self allows the artificial and the mundane to be avoided. We leave behind our blurred vision as all these other horizons enlighten us. This subtle passage between reality and its translation is an art in its own right. From an idea, which might be historical or improvised, though never imposed, I try to feel the rhythms, colours and waves that emerge from my journeys. The world is polyphonic, and I have many different methods. My job is to invent the most beautiful score to make it loved. It takes a lot of time—weeks and months—to succeed in producing a good travel diary."

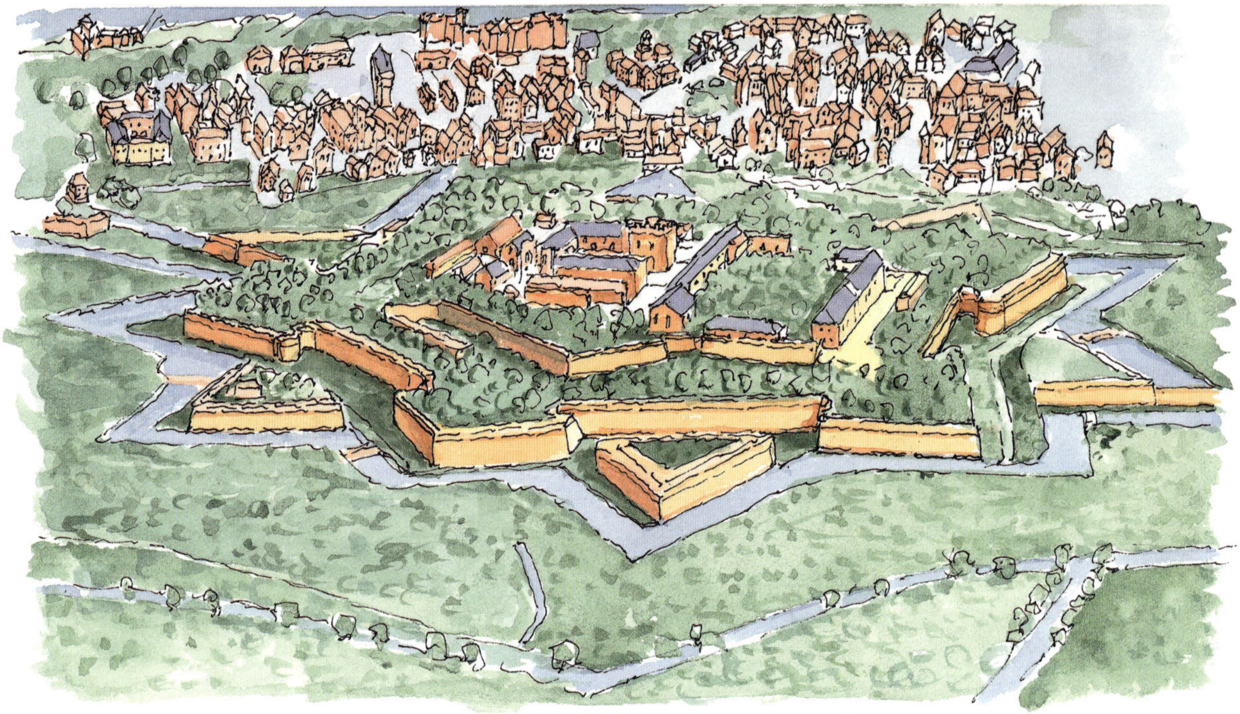

• *Vauban, génie maritime,* Gallimard, *2007. For this architecture diary, Arnaud d'Aunay travelled across 3,000 km of coastline in the footsteps of his ancestor Vauban, "a man of war who became a man of the sea."*

ARCHITECTURE DIARIES

In 1981, Éditions Alternatives published *Maisons saisons: observation sur l'architecture vernaculaire lors d'un voyage à pied de Paris à Ankara* by Sophie and Xavier Bohl Raverdy. This painter and architect duo set off for Jerusalem in 1979, and they recorded their journey through landscapes and architectures to Ankara. Keeping a diary allowed them to "share their emotions and their visions in this book of architecture in which painting, poetry, houses and seasons naturally blend together." Works by many other architects then appeared. Paul Rudolph, Albert Laprade, Aldo Rossi and Christian Dardennes had books published as part of a pioneering collection by the Société des éditions régionales that charts the evolution of Paris's *Grands Projets* (*Le Grand Louvre: dessins de chantier – 1991-1993*). Alain Bouldouyre's three years of drawings from 1990 document construction in the city of Lyon as it aspired to become an international metropolis (*Lyon: carnet de chantier*, Horvath, 1993). In 2007, Gildas Chassebœuf made use of the diary form to record the rehabilitation of former industrial land, bringing together memories of the former paper industry, protected natural space and a hub for cultural and artistic creation (*Carnet de chantier dans la vallée des papeteries*, Coop Breiz, 2007).

In parallel to in vivo architectural reportage, a patrimonial dimension has also developed through books that contain authentic or archival documents, ethnographic or historical research and surveys collected by diary-making architects. The travel diary is therefore a mechanism for using an artistic and sensible perspective to raise awareness about safeguarding world heritage. Charles Chauderlot shares his fascination for Beijing in his two books (*La Cité interdite: le dedans dévoilé* and *Pékin, les derniers jours 1996-2006*[22]), through which he uses drawings to immortalize the last *hutongs* prior to their destruction. His journey through old Beijing is an essentially iconographic one, captioned here and there with excerpts from the work of novelist Lao She.

Both in France and elsewhere, many Unesco heritage sites are the subject of books (*Angkor, carnets du Cambodge* by the architect Vincent Besançon, *Vauban, génie maritime* by Arnaud d'Aunay).

22. These two books were published by Éditions du Rouergue in 2006.

Fabrice Moireau,[23] an architectural history enthusiast, uses watercolours to capture the atmospheres and illuminations of important heritage sites. The major French cities are also covered by travel diaries, which serve as key tools for communicating with toursits. In *Lyon, ville ouverte* (Beaux-Arts, 2003), Micheline Colin arranges her paintings within a panorama based around the four elements: "Water, finally rediscovered, a source of exchanges and convergence. Earth, a mixture of heritage and greenery, recognized... as a model of continuity in the urban installation. Fire, which allows the people of Lyon to combine passions and an appetite for invention. And finally air, which has abandoned soot-filled skies for colour, light and transparency."[24]

Fabrice Moireau on his Japan diary

"I have an affectionate relationship with Japan. Little by little, a Japanese friend opened my eyes up to its culture as I took various trips to the country in the 2000s. He showed me the treasures of his city, Yokohama. And he took me to see the monster city that is Tokyo. Using watercolour as my only method of representation, I painted the wonderful traditional wooden architecture of Yokohama, Tokyo, Kyoto and Kamakura. The absence of symmetry is synonymous with balance in movement. I lost myself in gardens of reconstructed nature and countrysides in miniature, in which each thing is in its exact place. I became aware of this millennia-old aesthetic, this restraint of means that strangely has so many parallels with the "design" of Western modernity. While drawing, I let myself go with the joy of travelling, with the endless surprises that human beings—who are so diverse, so different in Japan, and so endearing—reveal. These pictures have never been published. They reflect some of the most beautiful trips I have taken."

23. *Paris*, *Vallée de la Loire*, *Venise*, *New York* and *Rome*: all these titles by Fabrice Moireau were published in Pacifique's "Aquarelles" collection.

24. Régis Neyret.

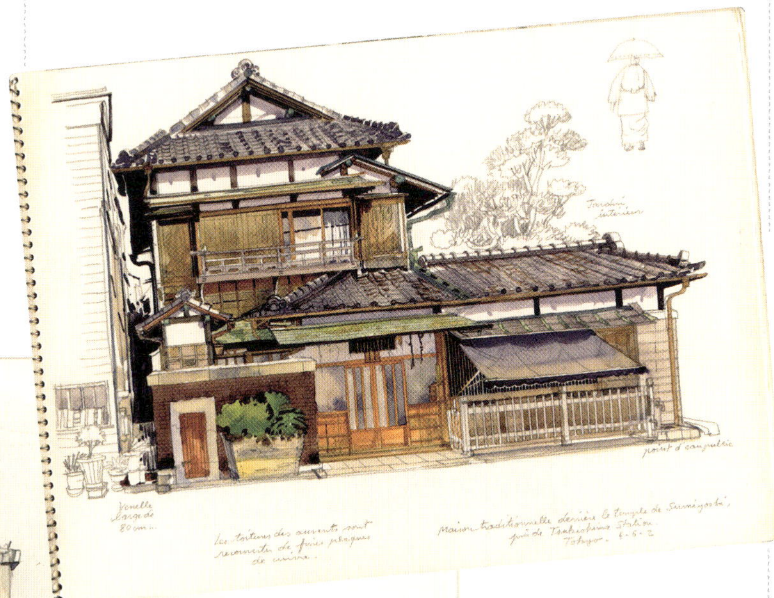

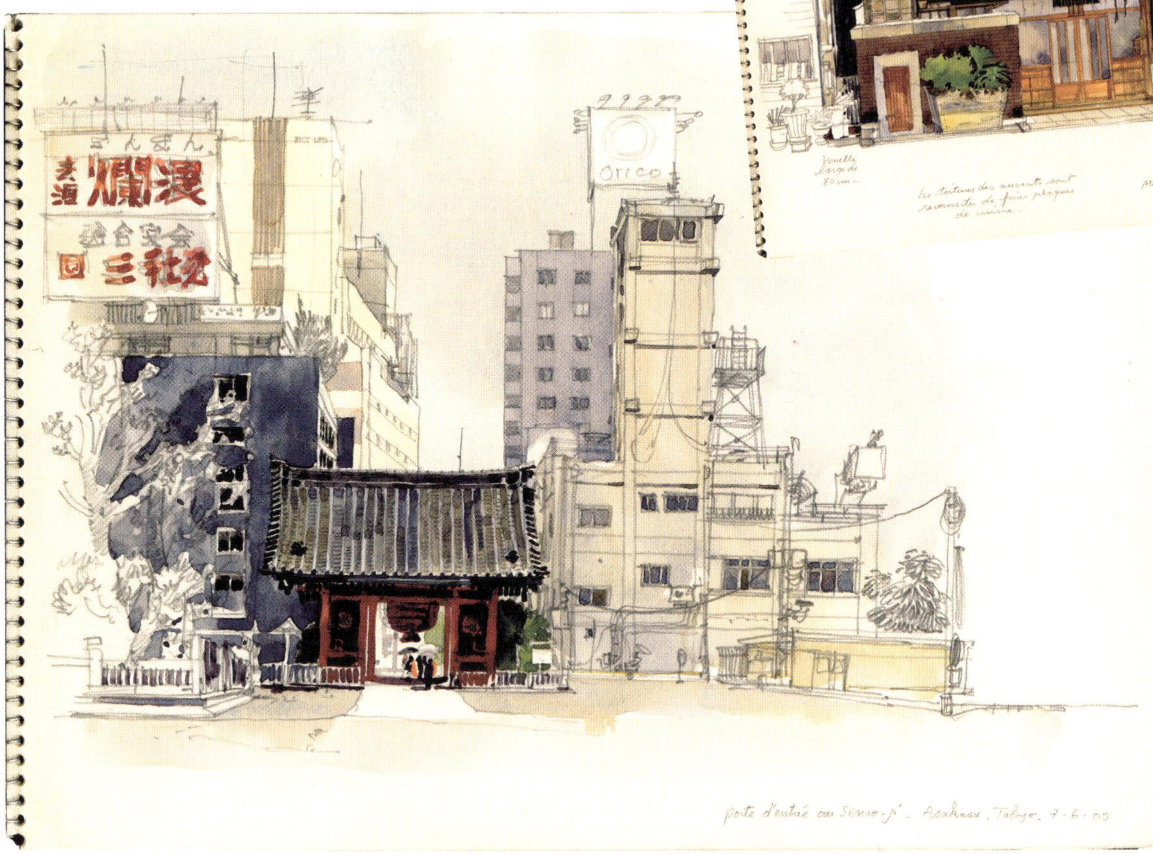

• *Following Félix Régamey and Mathurin Méheut, Fabrice Moireau was inspired by Japan and its traditional architecture during "one of the most beautiful trips [that the artist has] made."*

MEMORY DIARIES

In *Les Carnets de Renefer*, Raymond Fontanet (1879–1957), a painter and illustrator, bears witness to the life of the *poilus* (French infantrymen) during World War One in the form of thirty illustrated letters that he sent to his eight-year-old daughter. Somogy published a facsimile of them under the title *Belle petite monde: histoire de poilus racontée aux enfants* (2006). Dark and apocalyptic drawings by the young Otto Dix had also left an impression on people's minds owing to their highly expressionist intensity. Having signed up in 1914, he translated the chaos and cruelty that prevailed on the battlefield—the trenches, barbed wire, craters, corpses and mutilated landscapes—into drawings. The *Carnets de guerre, 1914–1918* (Hersher, 1996) by Ernest Chaussis, Gaston Lavy, Paul Mencier and André Mare complement this vision of hell in chronicle form. Finally, Mathurin Méheut's diaries (*Mathurin Méheut: 1914–1918, des ennemis si proches*)—probably the best known—describe life on the Western front, from Dunkirk to Toul, and are illuminated by letters that the artist sent to his wife.

World War Two also inspired a number of illustrated private diaries, notebooks and chronicles. A student at the HEC and performer in the US Army during the winter of 1944–1945 in Lorraine and Alsace, Jacques Law de Lauriston recounts the epic of the Leclerc Division, the 2nd Armoured Division, from its landing in Normandy in August 1944 until the capture of Hitler's Eagle's Nest in Berchtesgaden on 5 May 1945. *La Misère aux yeux de fou: notes et dessins de déportation*[25] and *Sauvé par le dessin: Buchenwald*,[26] diaries kept by deportees, reflect the daily martyrdom of the victims of Nazi barbarism; their drawings in extremes of inhumanity show us the horror of the camps and are irrefutable evidence of the genocide. Raphaël Esrail, president of the Union des déportés d'Auschwitz, explains the approach taken in the book *Des miettes et des étoiles* (2012): "Thomas Duranteau invites us into the heart of a representation of the Shoah, woven around a meeting between graphic art, memory and history, a representation that works through the senses and demands that we imagine. In this unlikely diary, we follow him through the memory sites—Auschwitz, Birkenau, Majdanek and Treblinka—whose complexity he renders through a striking artistic approach."[27]

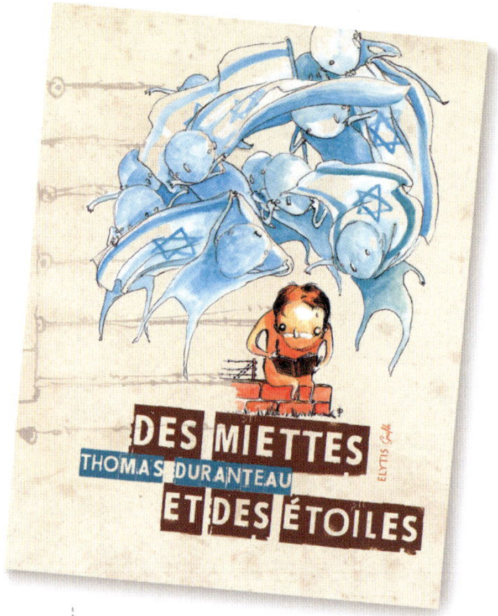

• *Des miettes et des étoiles, Elytis, 2012. Thomas Duranteau collects notes and engravings, drawings and quotations, cartoons and poems to retell the journey of the victims of Nazism, 70 years after the Holocaust.*

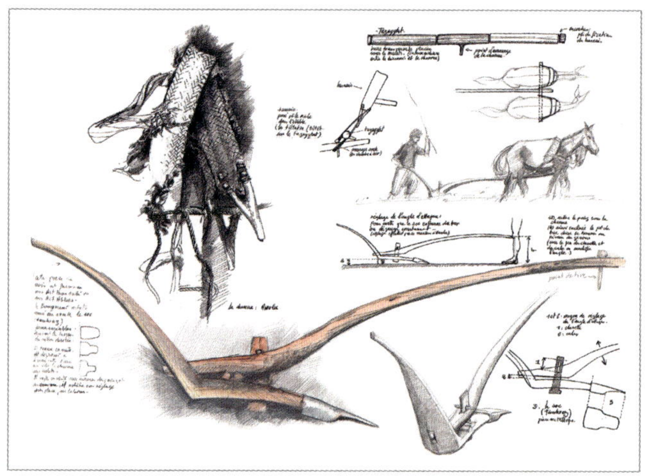

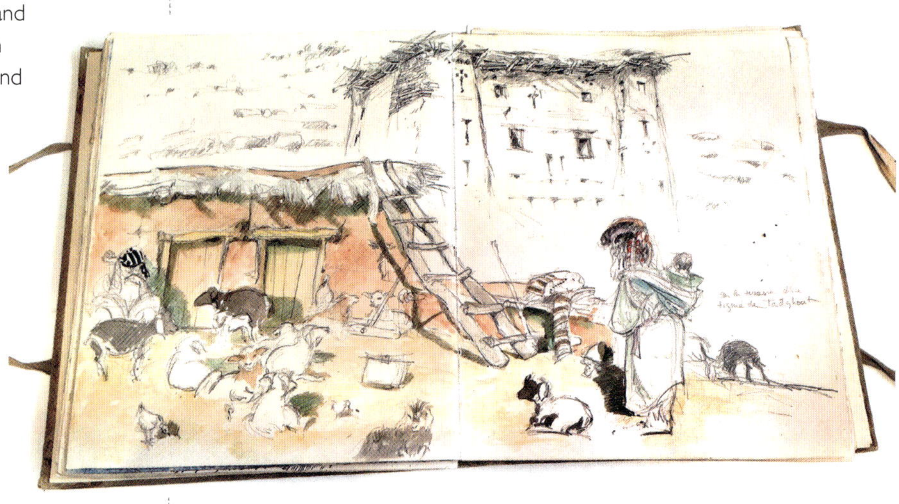

25. René Baumer, BGA Permezel, Lyon, 2004.
26. Walter Spitzer, Favre, 2004.
27. From the preface of the work.

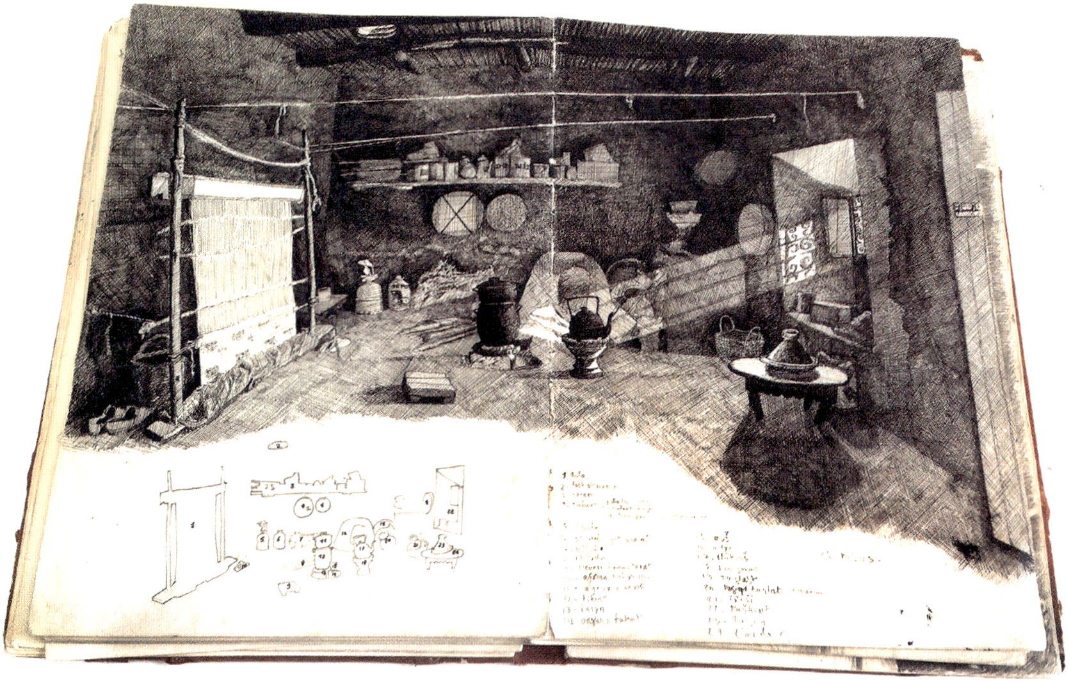

• Onze lunes au Maroc, *Gallimard, 2012. While studying traditional Islamic ornamentation, Titouan Lamazou and Karin Huet discovered the way of life of the Berber villages of the Moroccan High Atlas. Theirs was a journey to the limits of ethnology, rich in texts, drawings and photographs.*

ETHNOGRAPHIC DIARIES

The first "ethnographers" tried to work out what was the most appropriate support medium for their research: travel diaries, notebooks, sketchbooks, harvest books, and so on. Writings on exploration should be considered in the context of the history of ethnography and ethnology-anthropology. And the travel diary places at the centre of its approach the ethnographer's eye, observations and inquiries, heralding the beginnings of visual anthropology and sociology prior to the use of photography. This filiation explains the long-standing interest in travel diaries in current fields of ethnology at home, which has taken the form of the use of graphical and sociological reportage with a more documentary than artistic purpose. The first travel diaries, which were packed with sketches and surveys, were published with the goal of popularizing ethnology—well before the public had developed a taste for this type of publication. *Sous les toits de la Terre (1988)* and *Un hiver berbère* (1990)[28] by Karin Huet and Titouan Lamazou were published ten years before the success of *Carnets de voyage*. *Les Carnets de voyages de Stéphane Peyron* appeared in 1998 as part of the show *Dans la nature*, which was broadcast on Canal+ from 1993.

A documentary angle combined with an ethnographic take is called on in a number of publications, including *Les Carnets d'Amazonie* by Claudie Baran (Flammarion, 2004), *Les Carnets de Papouasie* by Nicolas Garnier (Hazan, 2000), *Tibet, le pèlerinage impossible* by Michel Peissel (Éditions de La Martinière, 2005) and *Marrakech: culture populaire de la médina* by Hassan Jouad and Elzbieta Jouad (Éditions du Rouergue, 2007). And we shouldn't forget *Nos âmes sauvages*, a hybrid of a travel diary and a comic strip, in which Johanna Schipper describes her shamanic initiation in Ecuadorian Upper Amazon (Futuropolis, 2008), with shades of Gauguin 's experience of Polynesia in *Noa Noa*. If the work of Elsie Herberstein and Zahia Hafs (*Alger, simples confidences*) adopts a similar approach, Catherine Legrand's ethnographic mission (*Textiles et vêtements du monde: carnet de voyage d'une styliste*) confirms the relationship between the methods of ethnology and those of the travel diary (portraits, interviews, samples, and so forth). Whatever the culture being considered and the place chosen, the goal is to preserve the memory of a changing world and to bear witness to threats to traditions. Accordingly, in *Une saison de chasse en Alaska* (Paulsen, 2014), the journalist Zoé Lamazou and the illustrator Victor Gurrey describe a whaling season in the far North of Alaska. Immersed among the Inupiat of Point Hope, they draw attention to the consequences of global warming and oil production.

28. These works were brought together under the title *Onze lunes au Maroc* (Gallimard, 2012).

These autobiographical accounts evoke a dialogue between two cultures. This is the case, for example, with *Née quelque part* (Delcourt, 2007), in which Johanna Schipper, who was raised between two cultures in Taiwan,[29] shares her ambivalent take on the island. Many travel diary makers whose families came to be based in France return to their countries of origin and offer accounts of this return to origins, which is sometimes experienced as an initiatory journey. Examples of such works include Leïla Sebbar's *Mes Algéries en France: carnet de voyages*, Tian Keu's *Sept mois au Cambodge*, Bénédicte Nemo's *De Saint-Louis à Ziguinchor* and Geneviève Hüé's *Mes carnets d'Indochine*. Foreign artists wishing to discover French culture have been just as busy. See, for example, *Un Japonais à Paris*, an account by Akio Suzuki that is illustrated by Cabu (Belfond, 1988), and *Un Américain en balade* (Casterman, 2005) by Craig Thompson. Chinese, Mongolian, Russian and Haitian painters have grasped this format to describe Brittany and Normandy in their own styles within the "Le lecteur de l'imaginaire"[30] collection published by Ouest-France. Flirting with reportage, press cartoons offer a humorous look at political and economic events and society. Cabu deployed his full range of talents in a series of books published with Seuil from the 1990s: *Cabu en Amérique*, *Sauve qui peut à l'Est*, *Cabu au Japon*, *Cabu en Chine* and *Cabu en Inde*. These were then followed by *Cabu, dessinateur reporter* (Vent d'ouest, 2007) and *Voyages au bout du crayon* (Flammarion, 2011).

Like travelogues, travel diaries reflect a perception of the elsewhere that is transcribed through the filter of the traveller's culture. This vision is influenced by the type of journey being undertaken, the context of creation, or the culture of the artist himself or herself. Between anthropological approach, artistic slant and journalistic analysis, the diversity of points of views on the same given experience contributes to intercultural understanding, which can be seen in action in *Gratte-ciel & soupe de nouilles* by Les Carnettistes tribulants (2011), which weaves together the different takes of ten French artists on China.

29. That of Taoist China, studied by her sinologist father, and that of her Dutch mother.

30. Collection created by Henri Bancaud.

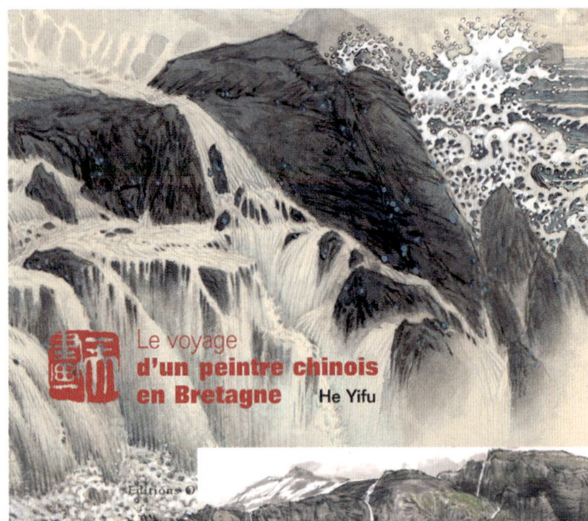

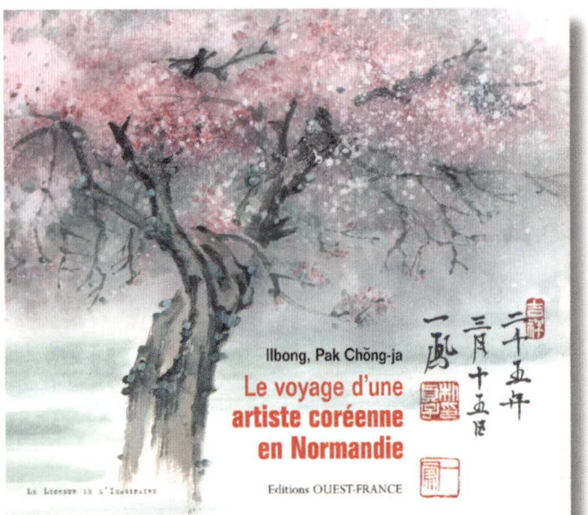

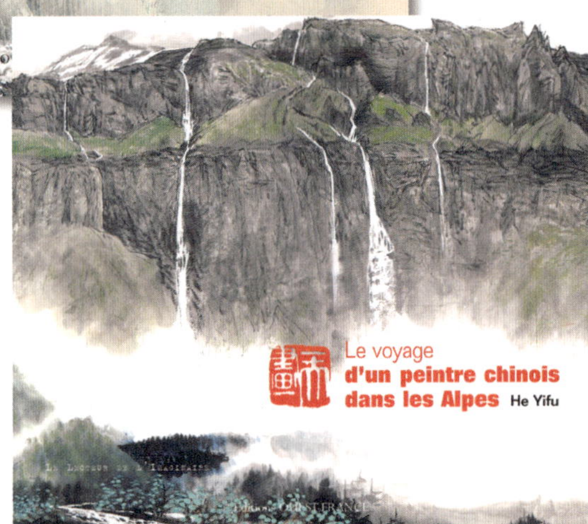

• Ouest-France's collection "Le lecteur de l'imaginaire" brings together travel diaries on the regions of France as they are seen by foreign artists, who use the traditional techniques of their country of origin.

CULTURAL EXPEDITION DIARIES

In the tradition of history's cultural expeditions, travel diaries provide a day-to-day retelling of great contemporary escapades. *Portes d'Afrique* is an eight-month maritime adventure to twelve African ports, narrated by writers, photographers, filmmakers and travel diary makers working under the aegis of the newspaper *Le Figaro*. *Sillages d'Afrique* (Gallimard, 2003) is an invitation to discover Africa through an exploration of its ports—memory sites of slavery—and a multitude of meetings and interactions. *Paris-Kaboul: expédition scientifique et culturelle sur les routes de la soie* (Hoëbeke, 2004) brings together the accounts of seventeen participants (including scientists, authors, journalists, photographers and artists) involved in a surveying and exploration mission to three archaeological and natural sites in Afghanistan that are threatened by conflict situations. In *La Boudeuse en Amazonie: carnets d'expédition* (Glénat, 2005), the explorer Patrice Franceschi describes his four-year sailing voyage around the world to meet people whose lives revolve around water, in the company of sailors, scientists, writers, filmmakers, illustrators and divers. Finally, *Opération Lapérouse – journal de bord à Vanikoro* (Éditions de Conti, 2008) is an account of the expedition led by the Association Salomon to crack the mystery of the disappearance of the frigates of Lapérouse. The naval painter John Pendray, who was part of this adventure, illustrated the daily research with a touch of British humour in *Sur les traces de La Pérouse: carnets d'expédition à Vanikoro* (Glénat, 2006).

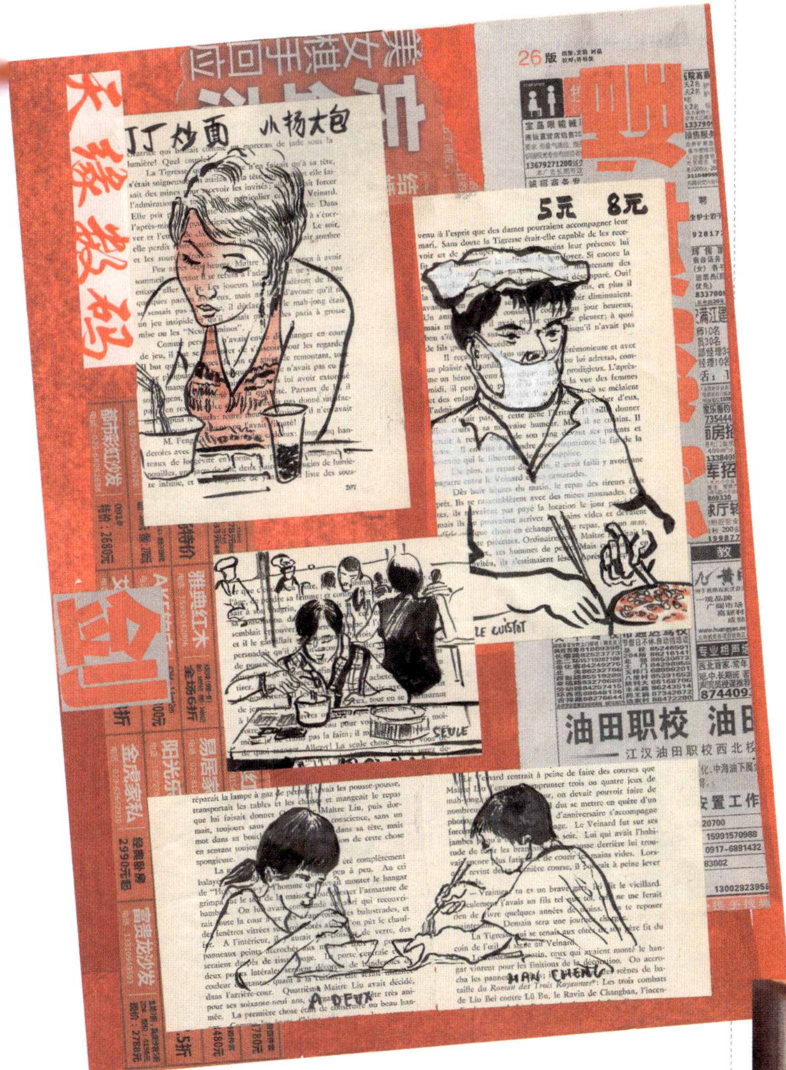

• Gratte-ciel & soupe de nouilles, *Les Carnettistes tribulants, 2010. The tribulations of 10 artists in China: a stay "of total freedom and immersion" to evoke the country with sensitivity and without the usual clichés.*

Simon on *Gratte-ciel & soupe de nouilles*

"There were elements of us producing journalism, because as we drew we were in contact with people with a critical and engaged perspective on reality. The artist shows the process behind what he or she is observing; passers-by or natives then once again see the places that they had stopped seeing. In fact, he or she tips a bucket of fresh water on a routine reality, thus making visible what had stopped being seen. Like music, drawing is a tool for immediate communication."

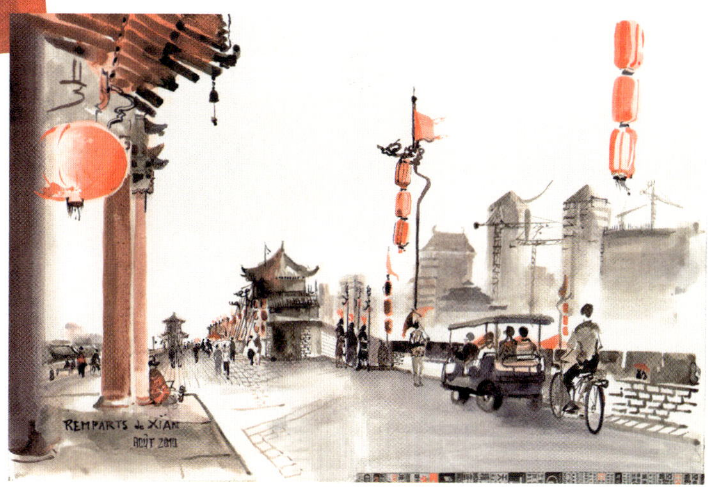

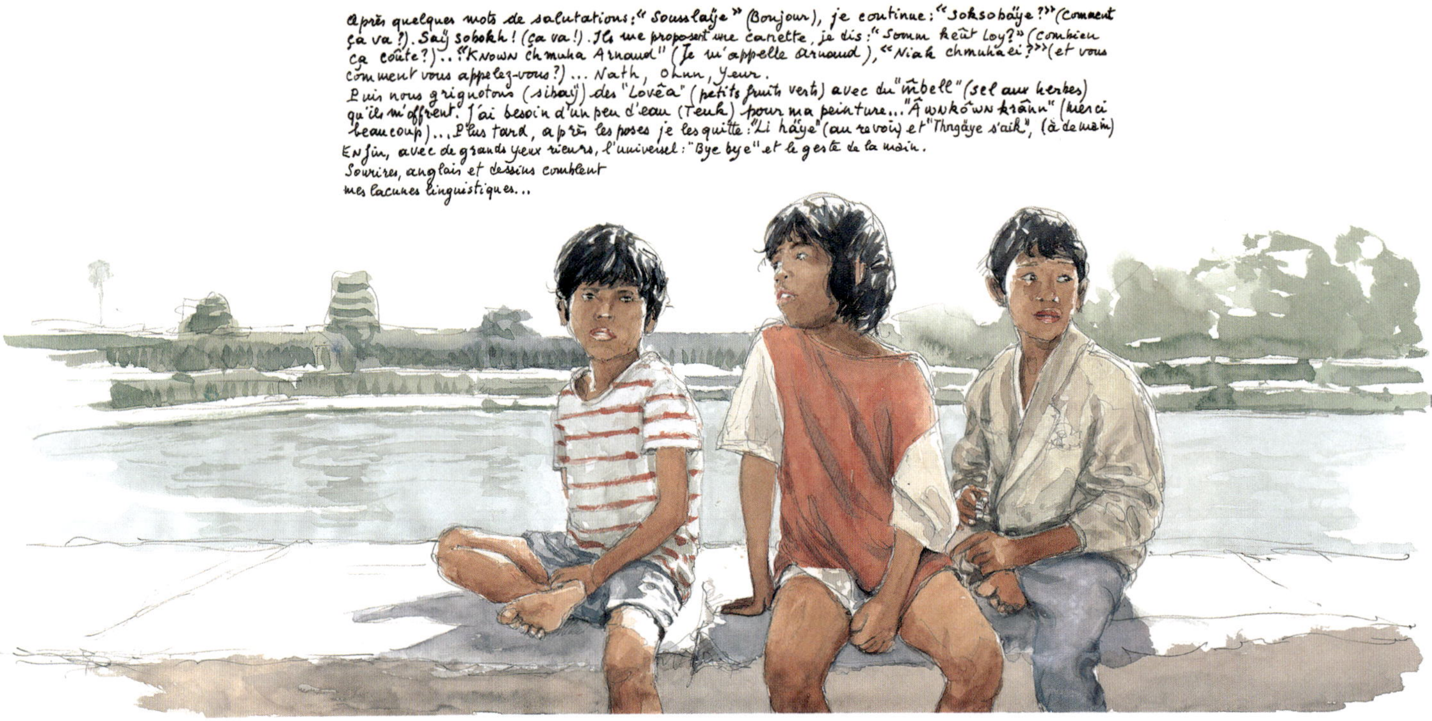

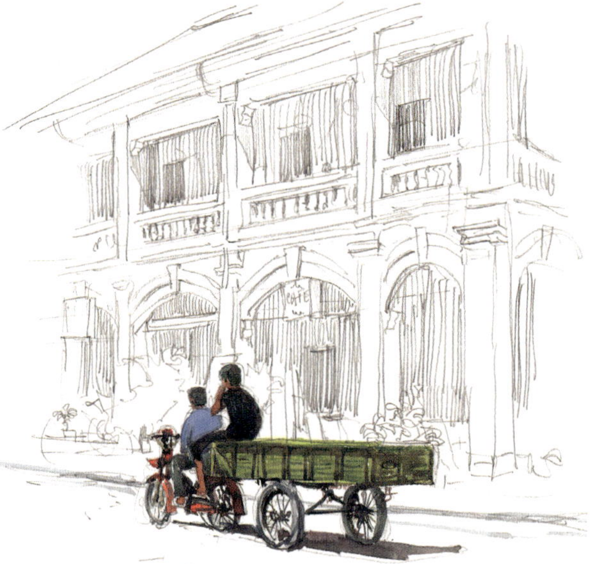

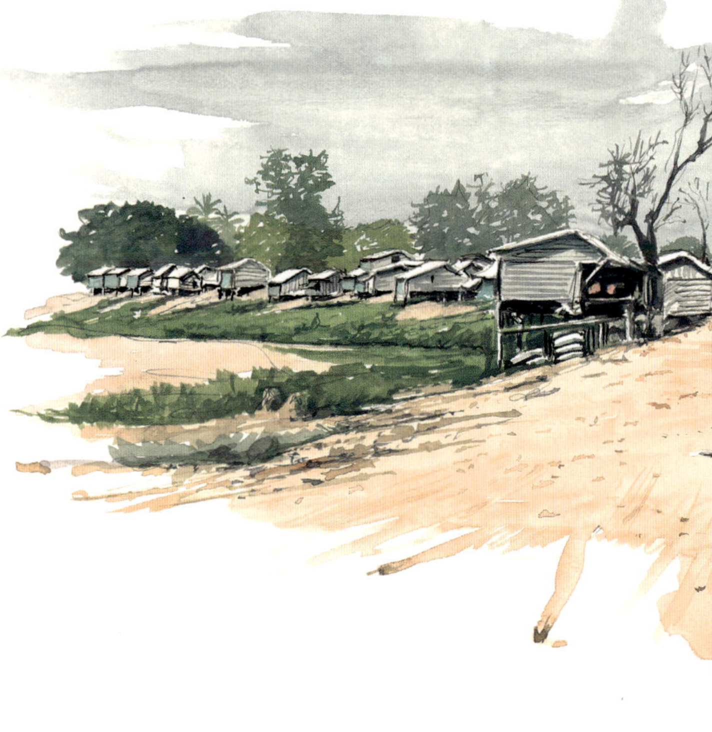

• Au fil du Mékong, *Gallimard, 2004. Arnaud d'Aunay set off to discover Vietnam along the Mekong River, "navigating between ancient history and the contemporary world." Views of Siem Reap and boys in Angkor Wat.*

ITINERARY DIARIES

The major trade routes, such as those for spices and incense, are the main theme for a beautiful range of creations: *Carnet d'une route de la soie ou l'invitation aux voyages* by Arthur R. David (Artisans-Voyageurs, 2005), is a narrative of a journey by mountain bike from Carthage to Dunhuang, and *Voyage d'un cyclopède sur la route de la soie* by Pierre Robin (Reflets d'ailleurs, 2012), is a diary of a backpacker's encounters in sometimes hostile lands. Legendary routes have also inspired television shows (for example, *Échappées belles*). And the peregrinations of hippies in India have left a great impression on travel diary makers and other backpackers on idealistic quests. In *Trip indien* (Elytis, 2012), for example, Pascal Grellety-Bosviel evokes this youthful journey in the 1970s, which contributed to the beginnings of Médecins Sans Frontières. If Asia is the preferred destination of travel diary makers, India has been mythologized by great travellers,[31] and it alone has inspired more than twenty travel diaries.

31. Alexandra David-Néel (1868–1969), Ella Maillart (1903–1997) and Nicolas Bouvier (1929–1999).

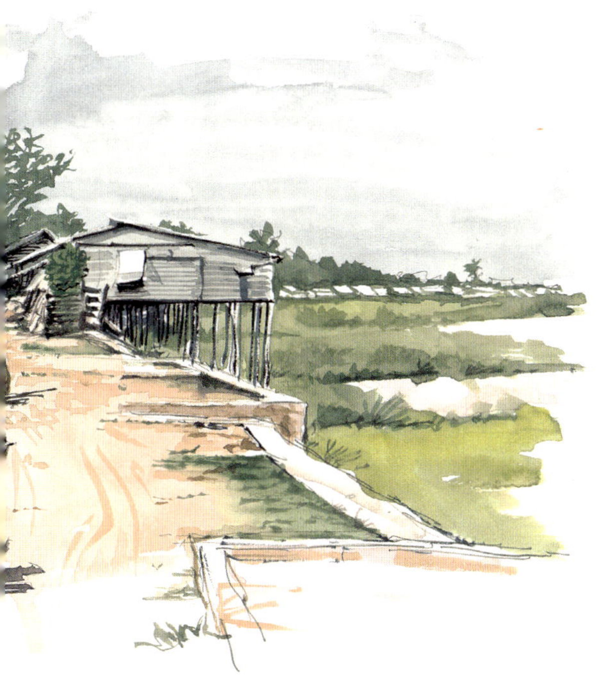

An essential element of these journeys in unknown lands is the method of transport, which conditions a particular form of discovery and to a greater or lesser extent dictates the routes followed by travellers. While they are more restrictive than merely moving about on foot or by bicycle, the train, sailing, the hot-air balloon or the sled also offer pleasant surprises. Each means of transport gives rise to a different type of diary. Going down a river is the most common route: Miquel Barceló and Arnaud d'Aunay did just this, the former on the Niger, the latter on the Mekong (*Au fil du Mékong de Saïgon à Angkor*, Gallimard, 2004). Since 2002, the Camino de Santiago has been the subject of over fifteen books. One of the first of these was by Anne Le Maître (*Du Puy à Conques par le chemin des pèlerins*, Rouergue, 2002). It mixes text, ink sketches and watercolours, which are interspersed with geographical and historical information on the places passed through. *Un artiste chinois, pèlerin de l'art, sur les chemins de Compostelle* (Ouest-France, 2005) by Ji Dahai uses the techniques of traditional Chinese painting, while *Compostelle, il n'est que de partir* by Jacques and Pierre Patureau (Atlantica, 2005) uses watercolour to depict the walking route at its origins. Finally, *L'Épopée de Compostelle* by François Tallandier (L'Instant durable) provides a very thoroughly documented patrimonial and historical vision.

Cultural itineraries (routes of castles, vineyards or writers) in Europe are described in some diaries. The watercolour painters Martine Salvatge, Christine Laverne and Georges Bronner show us the seaside resorts of the Pays d'Auge in the company of Marcel Proust.[32] Walking in the footsteps of an artist, a writer or a scholar is an amazing way to discover a region or a country, and it is the option chosen in Garde-Temps's offerings (for example, *Voyage en Égypte sur les pas de Flaubert* and *Voyage au Tibet sur les pas d'Alexandra David-Néel*) and those by Presses de la Renaissance (for example, *Sur les pas de Georges Sand*, *Sur les pas de Colette* and *Sur les pas de Léonard de Vinci*). Outside the realms of the travel diary and within the confines of the artist's book, Vertige Graphic published the correspondence of Arthur Rimbaud in Africa (*Lettres d'Afrique*) and a selection of poems by Rudyard Kipling in works illustrated in watercolour by Hugo Pratt.

32. *En passant par Houlgate: sur la Côte fleurie avec Marcel Proust* (Cahiers du temps, 2000) and *Proust et la Côte fleurie* (Cahiers du temps, 2003).

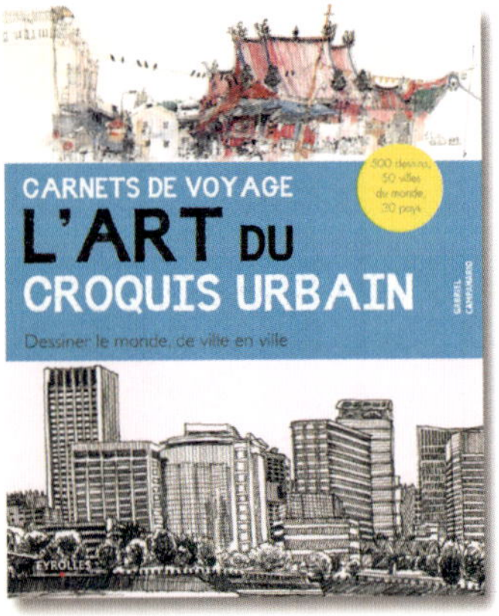

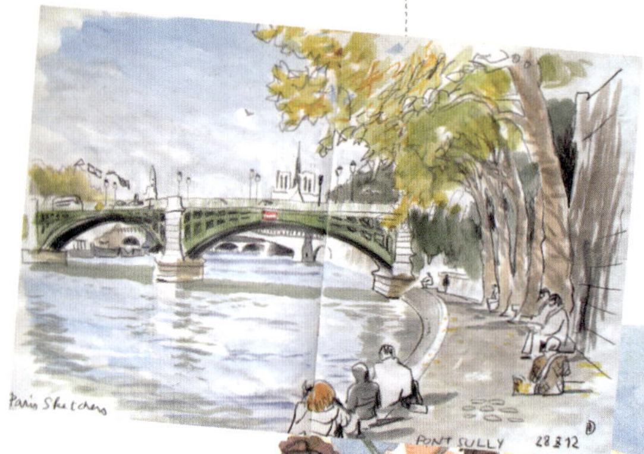

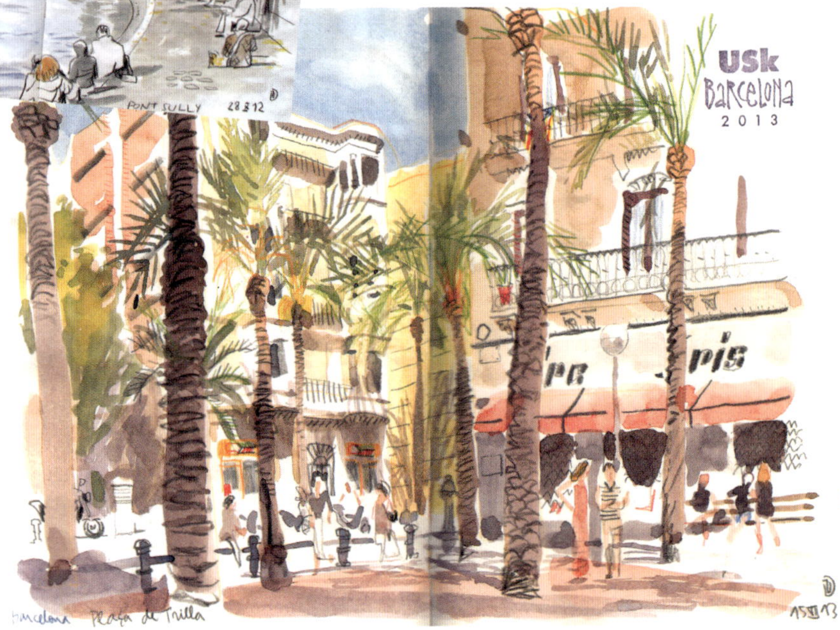

• Carnets de voyage – l'art du croquis urbain, *Eyrolles, 2013. Paris and Barcelona as seen by the Urban Sketchers, an association founded by Gabriel Campanario, an illustrator at the* Seattle Times, *whose objective is to promote the art of drawing from in situ observation.*

URBAN DIARIES

At the request of local governments, around thirty travel diaries on French towns have seen the light of day. Their aim is to promote heritage, renovate the image of their outlying areas and develop periurban tourism. The heart of Paris has been the subject of numerous publications, some of which have been translated into English for foreign visitors: *Revoir Paris* by Cabu (Arléa, 1996), and *Bon baiser de Paris* by Nathalie Lété and Frédéric Rey (Rouergue, 2004), which combines graphic arts, photographs and souvenirs presented in the form of collages. The suburbs opened up to graphic arts and diaries from 2001. Joëlle Jolivet offers an offbeat look at her home of Ivry in *Vues d'Ivry* (Cornélius, 2001). The collective work *Banlieue nomade: carnets de voyage autour de Paris* (Alternatives, 2006) by Les Carnettistes tribulants is the fruit of three years of wanderings in the suburbs and far from the stereotypes conveyed by the media, in order to take a new look at a space with undefined limits. With the same intention of making a city known beyond prejudices of it, *Saint-Denis, portrait sensible* (Magellan & Cie, 2008) was born out of a collaboration between thirty amateur and professional diary makers. Damien Roudeau shares this approach in *Villiers rebelle: carnet de rencontres à la Cerisaie* (La Boîte à bulles, 2014) by giving a voice to the inhabitants of the suburbs stigmatized by the riots of 2007: "Clichés about the 'working-class areas' give way to the real description of the inhabitants: *Villiers Rebelle* is above all a book about exchanges and encounters. Transcribed dialogues and vivid watercolours recreate the atmosphere from Damien Roudeau's visit, whose defining features were not violence and crime."[33]

Across the world, the association Urban Sketchers has promoted the artistic, narrative and educational value of in situ drawing and created links between "sketchers" worldwide. Its members, through sharing their sketches on blogs or community sites, show "the world of drawing through drawing," transcribing graphically and collectively the daily life of the explored city on the model of American cartoonists Robert Crumb and Will Eisner. In France, Dupuy and Berberian, authors of *New York carnets* (Cornélius, 1996), continued their urban explorations with *Barcelone carnets* (Cornélius, 1999).

33. Vincent Henry.

ARCHAEOLOGY DIARIES

The tradition of surveying archaeological sites, characteristic of the tour of Italy and the nineteenth century's poetics of ruins, has not had much of a new lease of life within contemporary publishing. Indeed, not many travel diaries on this science were published after *Un archéologue en Arabie* by Vincent Charpentier and Sophie Méry, with "on-the-spot drawings" by Marc Lacaze, which was published in 1991 in the "Carnets du monde" collection for Albin Michel Jeunesse. However, a breach was opened up at the end of the 1990s thanks to the artist Philippe Delord, who produced a book on Louis-François Cassas, an eighteenth-century French illustrator who completed the survey of Alexandria's archaeological sites in 1785. In *Alexandrie – sur les pas de Louis-François Cassas* (Gallimard, 2001), Delord captures the picturesque monuments of the past and tries to find fragments of them in the port area and close to the site of the future library. He continued this work on the island of Cyprus (*Regards croisés sur Chypre – sur les pas de Louis-François Cassas*, Gallimard, 2004), where he explored the places drawn by his predecessor in order to show the vestiges of 8,000 years of civilization.

Reflets d'Ailleurs launched a collection on archaeological sites, "Carnets de fouilles," following the publication in 2012 of the album *Dans le sable de Saqqara*, a chronicle of an archaeological excavation site that was illustrated by Catherine Adam. *Mille ans d'histoire aux portes de Clermont-Ferrand* presents the archaeologist Kristell Chuniaud's fieldwork during a nine-month excavation in the Clermont area's Trémonteix to unearth Gallo-Roman and medieval remains. Scientific documents, explanatory drawings and photographs mingle with Catherine Adam's surveying to help us to understand this fascinating profession. Outside the publishing world, the educational services of some archaeological museums make diaries available to young visitors to help them to discover the museum's collections.

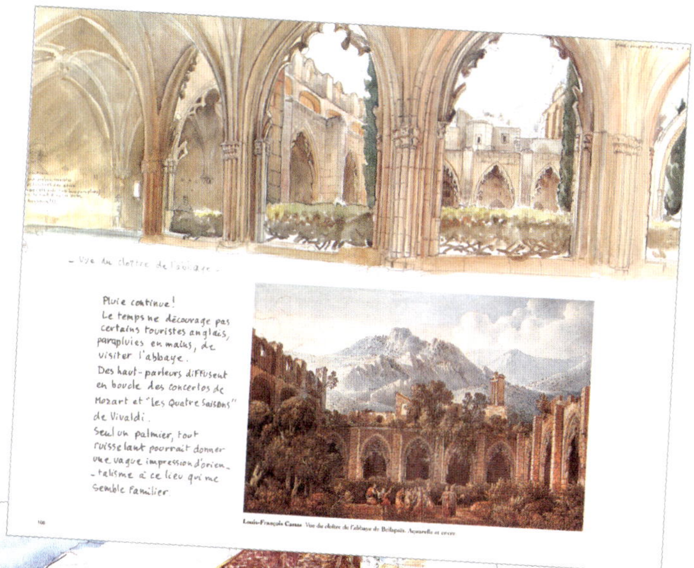

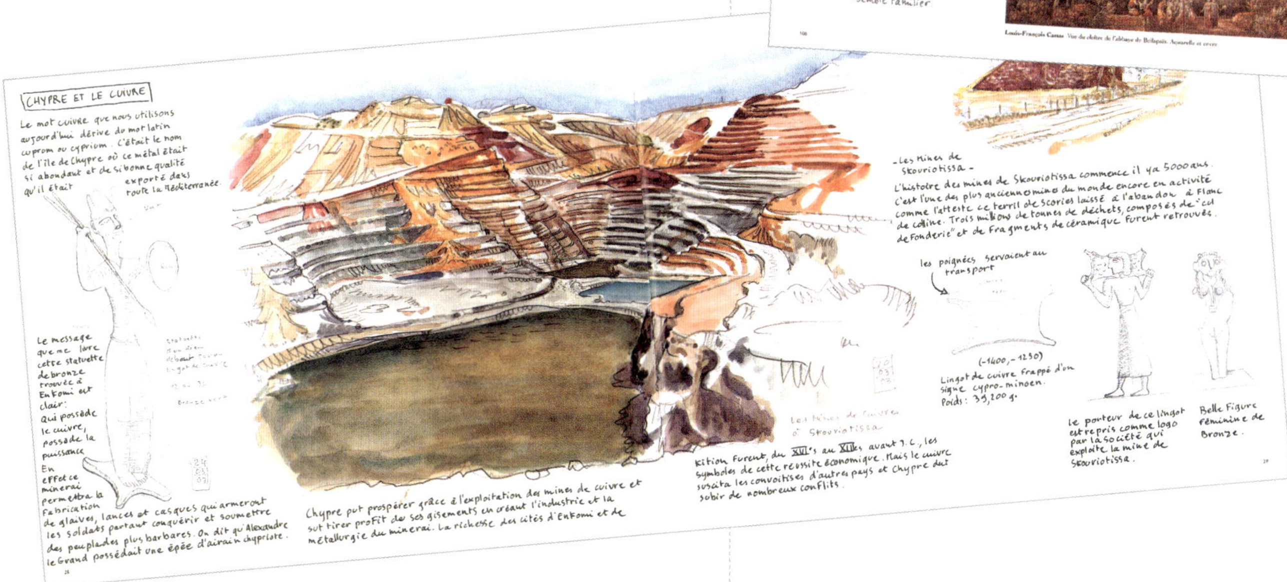

• *Regards croisés sur Chypre*, Gallimard, 2004. *Having walked in the footsteps of Louis-François Cassas in Alexandria, Philippe Delord moved on to Cyprus, breathing new life into the practice of archaeology drawing.*

GEOLOGY DIARIES

The favourite medium of the great English watercolourists, eighteenth-century topographers and geologists or geomorphologists (Alcide Dessalines d'Orbigny, Paul-Émile Victor, Charcot and Théodore Monod), geology diaries examine physical geography through maps, surveys and scientific diagrams. A teacher and researcher in the earth sciences and an amateur watercolour painter, Georges Bronner creates diaries that serve as geology guides, for example *Guide géonautique, de la rade d'Hyères à l'Esterel* (2004) and *Du delta du Rhône à la rade de Toulon: guide géonautique* (2006). His book *De la Durance aux monts de Vaucluse: géoballade, du paysage à la géologie* (2010)[34] offers a geological walk in the Lubéron Regional Park to explain its geological architecture, discover traces of life in rocks and fossils and reveal the human footprint on the landscape. Its watercolour pictures capture the colour differences between soil and rock and volumes and reliefs through multiple viewpoints (from aerial views to field sites). The complementarity of the descriptive and explanatory images, of the card cuttings and of the structural diagrams serves a pedagogical approach based on the representation of landscapes (outcrops, natural profiles, panoramas), and naturalistic illustration (rocks, fossils, thin sections) and scientific illustrations (tables, sections, diagrams). The line between guide and travel diary is sometimes a thin one. Christine Laverne, an earth sciences researcher, made the seven international ocean drilling campaigns in which she participated between 1979 and 2005 into the subject of her reportage diaries. In her watercolour-illustrated diaries (*Forages sous le Pacifique*[35]) she describes life at sea, teamwork and the professions of this particular working environment. The geology diary is therefore reminiscent of the scientific expedition diary.

Georges Bronner on his approach

"Field diaries were essential for missions in which everything was recorded, day after day, and in which each observation point was numbered and positioned on a map or aerial photo. (GPS did not yet exist and it was difficult to obtain satellite images.) It was only on my last mission to northern Mauritania in 2002 that I had the benefit of new technologies. The field diary is a journal, a confidant, a reminder and a draft for a report or thesis. It must be weatherproof—only pencil can survive a dip in seawater (something I know from experience)."

34. All these books were published by Jeanne-Laffitte.
35. Atlantica, 2008.

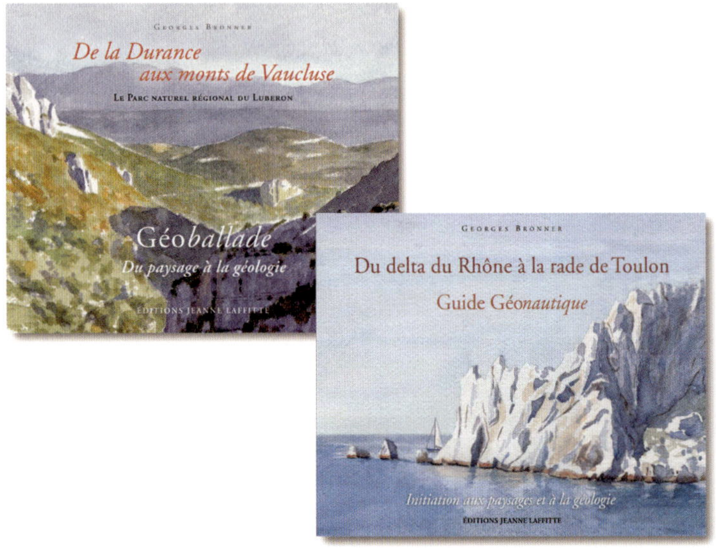

• The works of Georges Bronner, teacher and researcher in earth sciences and amateur watercolourist, study the geology of the Provençal coast between L'Estérel and La Camargue.

NATURALIST DIARIES

In the tradition of the great ornithologists of the nineteenth century (Jean-Jacques Aubudon, John Gould), three naturalists have made the world of birds their speciality: Alan Johnston, Denis Chavigny and Denis Clavreul. A naturalist field artist, Alan Johnston was involved in several scientific expeditions to New Guinea (botany) and Africa (ornithology) prior to illustrating diaries from 1996 (*La Baie du Mont-Saint-Michel*, Gallimard Jeunesse). Inspired by Peter Beard and wildlife naturalist Kim Donaldson, his goal is to raise awareness of the environment in Africa; he has undertaken scientific expeditions to the continent with Denis Clavreul. These adventures led to the publication of travel diaries for Gallimard: *Magie d'Afrique* by Denis Clavreul and *Au pays des cigognes noires* by Alan Johnston. Having illustrated *Carnets d'un naturaliste au fil de la Loire* (Nathan, 2001), Denis Chavigny concentrated on ornithology with the publication of three volumes with Delachaux et Niestlé: *Un jour, un oiseau: mille croquis de terrain* (2001), *L'Album des oiseaux d'Europe* (2001) and *Le Carnet de l'ornithologue* (2003). Among these naturalist illustrators, Denis Clavreul is a specialist in the environment who has published thirty travel diaries since 1995 and done illustrations for fifteen documentaries. He produced two titles for the "Carnets du littoral" collection (on Corsica and the Luberon) and three works on gardens published in Gallimard's "Carrés de jardin" collection (*Les Jardins de Villandry*, *Les Jardins ouvriers* and *Les Jardins de l'île de Batz*).
Vincent Desplanche, an illustrator of young-adult works, is also fond of in situ observational drawing based around hiking or natural heritage sites (*Les Calanques de Marseille à Cassis*, *Au fil du Lot*, *Le Parc de la Tête-d'or*, Gallimard).

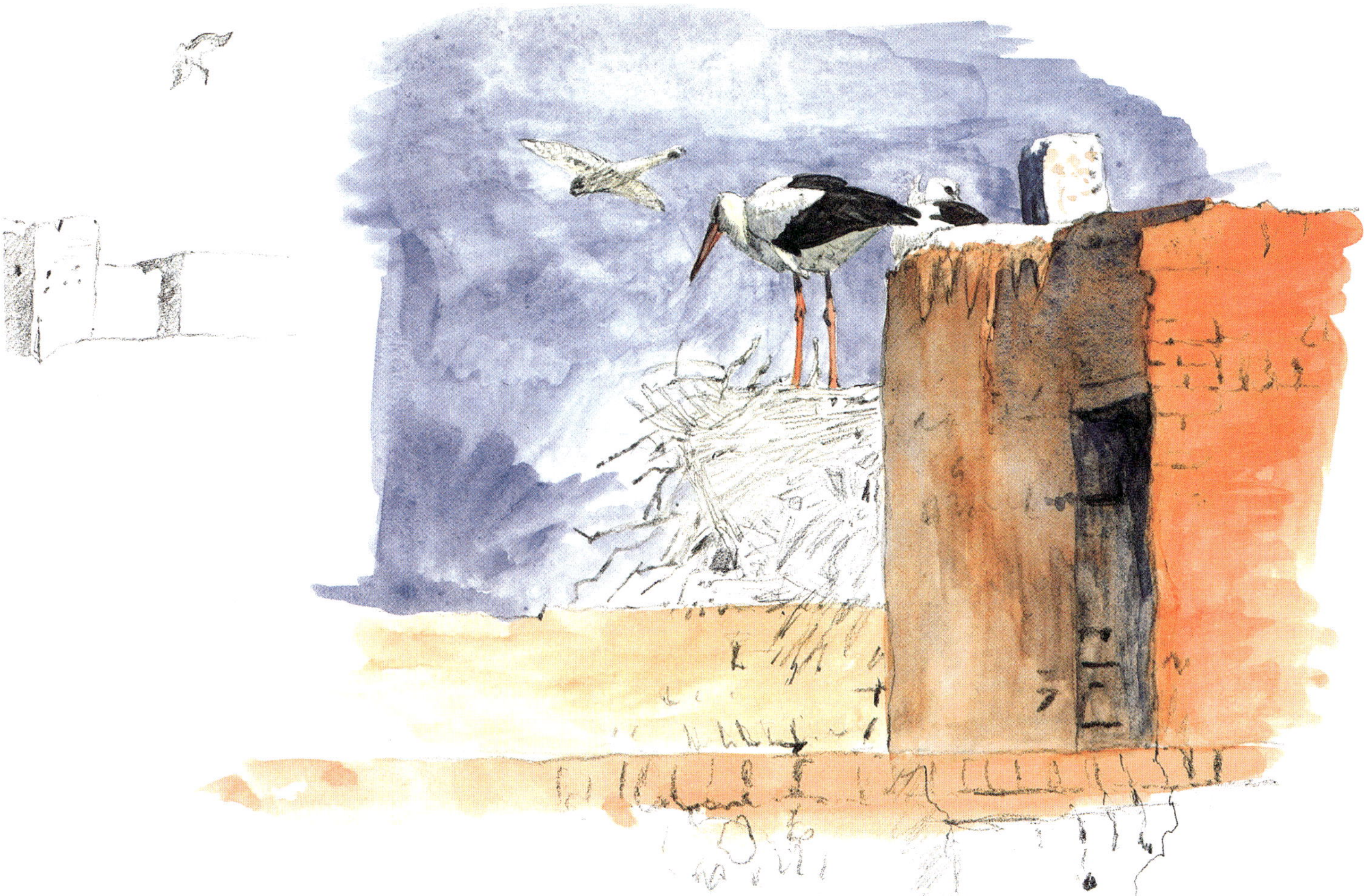

• Au pays des cigognes noires, *Gallimard, 2000. While following the migration of the black storks, Alan Johnston also directs readers' attention to the flora and fauna of the country crossed by these colonies of birds.*

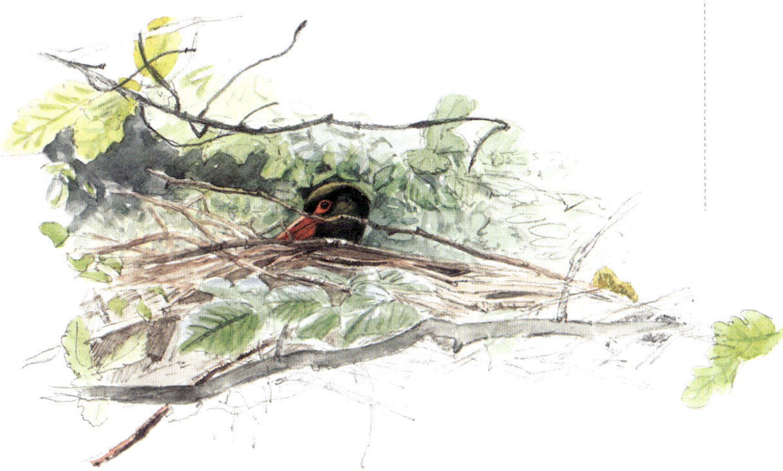

Alan Johnston on *Au pays des cigognes noires*

"This (almost) parallel journey by men and birds is a true travel diary that follows the migration of black storks from the Luxembourg Ardennes to the Sahel, passing through Senegal, Mauritania, Burkina Faso, Niger and Togo. This book is a compilation of seventeen diaries filled with sketches and seven pocket diaries of field notes taken during three years. It tells the story of birds fitted with Argos transmitters. While looking for the GPS locations, we found a large group of eighty wintering storks, among them Anne and François—a bird couple that I had drawn at home! Following scientists who were in turn following storks was not always easy because each of us sometimes had very different goals! In this book I wanted to turn my attentions to the often very rich flora and fauna that surround the storks. The chronological order of the story invites the reader to go from one place to another, and I tried to rebuild the sensory environments that I experienced. Here the documentary art is charged with a healthy dose of subjectivity!"

DIARIES ON FOODS AND FLAVOURS

Diaries can cover areas of heritage that are either tangible or intangible—including the culinary arts, one of the first cultural markers for the traveller. In 1989, Lizzie Napoli illustrated *Cuisine traditionnelle de Savoie*, a book of culinary heritage written by Paul Vincent (J.-P. Gisserot, 1989). In *Roma 44* (Rouergue, 2002), Pierre Janneau invites readers to follow him in his search for the ingredients of a recipe for pasta, a pretext for a gourmet stroll through Rome's neighbourhoods. In 2004, Patrice Fender provided an evocation of Brittany and Provence based around the recipes of Valérie Seguin.[36] Among books that combine world cuisines and travelogues, the watercolours and pencil sketches in May Angeli's *Souks et saveurs en Tunisie* (Sorbier, 2007) guide us through the markets of Tunisia and present the country's recipes and sayings. In *Une cuisine grande comme le monde: 60 recettes pour voyager tout autour de la Terre* (Rue du monde, 2007), Alain Serres and Zaü record recipes from five continents that are enlivened with representations of food and the characteristic landscapes of the various countries. Finally, *Carnet de la cambuse: les recettes de Corto Maltese* by Michel Pierre and Hugo Pratt (Casterman, 2007) presents recipes inspired by the travels of Corto Maltese. *La fabuleuse cuisine de la route des épices: 60 recettes et histoires parfumées aux plantes, aux fleurs et aux épices du monde* (Rue du monde, 2009) gives authors Alain Serres and Vanessa Hié the opportunity to teach young readers the history of the spice trade. Meanwhile, Nicolas Jolivot, a culinary illustrator, produced *Chifan: mangeons en Chine* and *Nakoul: on mange à Marrakech*, published in 2012 by L'Apart. In investigating markets across the world and their products and recipes, culinary diaries draw on reportage diaries. *Rungis: voyage au coeur d'un marché d'exception* (Éditions de Marque, 2011) offers an overview of occupations and sectors of activity of a single market through text, photographs and illustrations. Drawing on his experience as a reporter and travel diary maker, Bruno Pilorget tackles food through a travel diary project on the culinary practices of immigrant communities in France.

36. *Bretagne, carnet de cuisine* and *Provence, carnet de cuisine* (Gallimard, 2004).

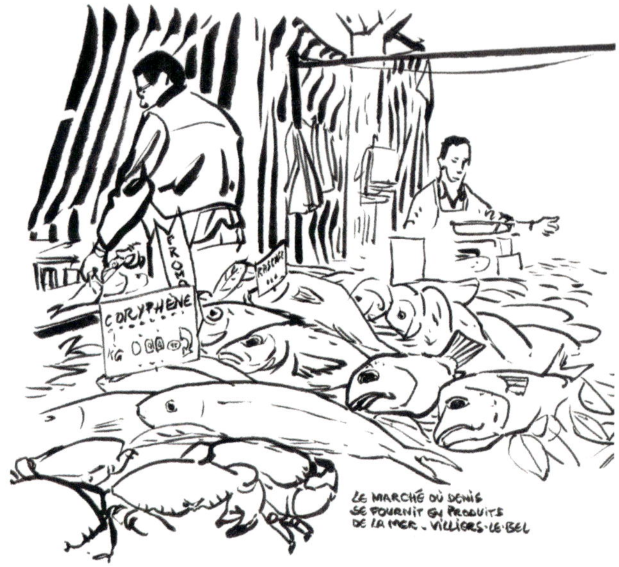

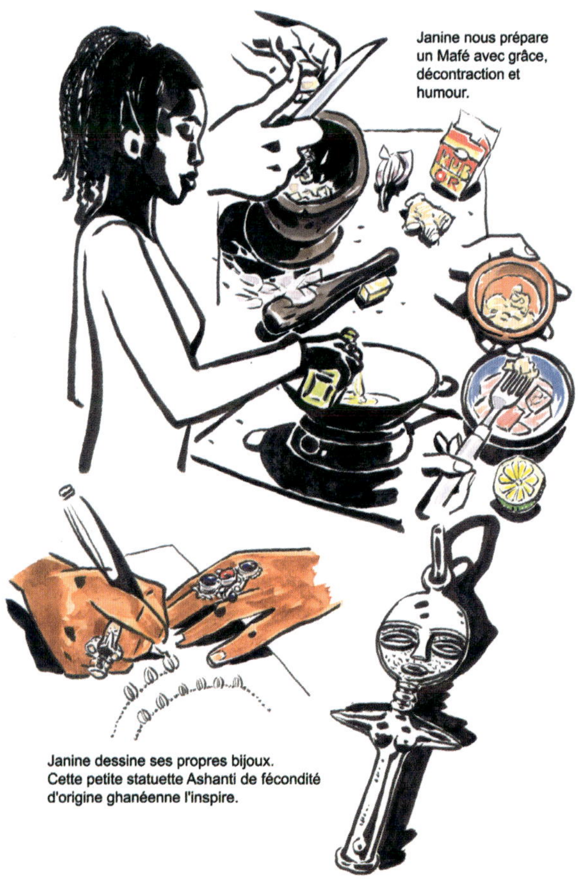

• *In this still unpublished "lovely project" by Bruno Pilorget, the preparation of a meal is a pretext for confiding and conversing in a friendly atmosphere.*

Bruno Pilorget on his culinary diary project

"At the request of a publisher, over several weeks in 2010, I went to meet twenty or so families from different cultures, accompanied by two young writers: Insa for Paris and its suburbs, and Samira for Lille and its surrounding area. The idea for me was to produce in situ drawings of the people who hosted us—of their profiles, their history, their environment and, if possible, their dreams. These were followed up by more sophisticated drawings in the studio. But the high point was drawing the preparation of a meal from their country of origin. After the cooking, we ate together, if possible with family or friends, in order to get to know them even better. We had the pleasure of 'travelling' through Senegal, Mali, Vietnam, Brazil, Cameroon, Indonesia, China, Palestine, Algeria, Kabylia, Morocco, Spain, Sicily, Guadeloupe, Martinique, Argentina and more. Thanks to Samira, for example, I had the privilege of experiencing a wonderful moment with the amiable Fatima, who lives by some dark waste tips. As though it were a dance, and only protected with cloths, the young woman grasped the boiling couscoussier with her body and swiftly plunged her hands into it to locate its contents. Fatima is blind. Her husband arrived from work. He's also blind. During the evening, their little girl, who can see, began to draw on a wall with her felt tips, throwing me defiant little glances. A very embarrassing situation quickly evaporated when I asked if I was allowed to draw on the walls like the little one! However, this lovely publishing project unfortunately didn't come to fruition."

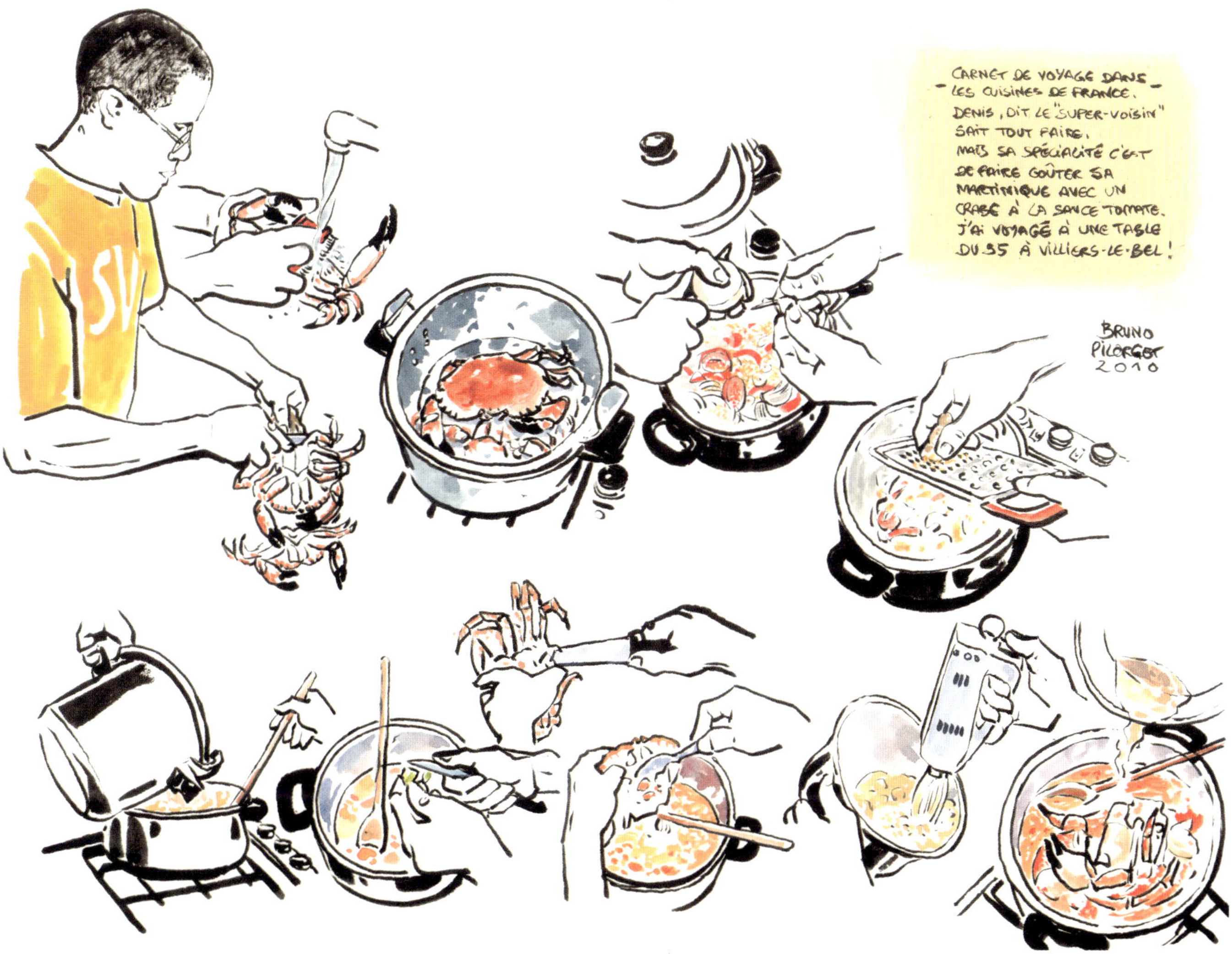

3. Intermedia diaries

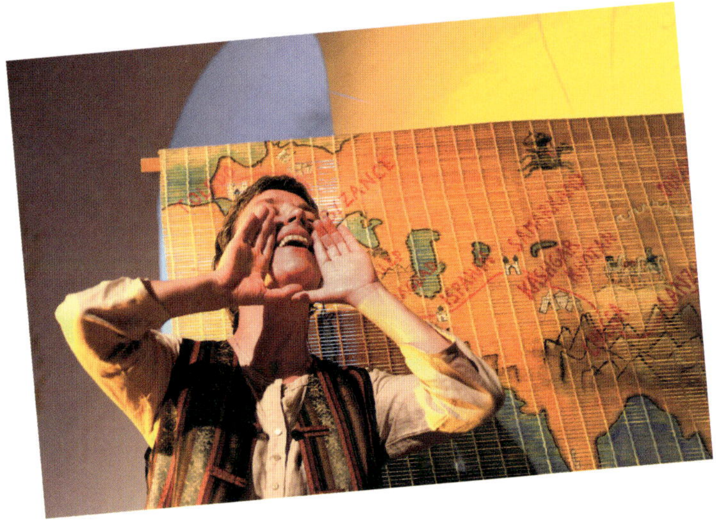

EXHIBITION AND INSTALLATION TRAVEL DIARIES

In 2007, Titouan Lamazou created an audiovisual travel diary for the Musée de l'homme, consisting of portraits in watercolour and interviews with exceptional women. The project was an adaptation of his *Zoé Zoé femmes du monde*. The exhibition, a real installation, presented, through a considered scenography, ethnographic objects that immersed visitors in the atmosphere of the featured countries. *Zoé Zoé femmes du monde* also inspired the play *Traversées* by Jessica Ashford and Jehanne Gascoin, which pays tribute to Lamazou's work by drawing on several artistic disciplines. The exhibition "Sept milliards d'autres" presents video portraits from the four corners of the planet by the photographer Yann Arthus-Bertrand. The space is organized in a village of yurts, which the visitor is invited to wander through, abolishing "the reality of the borders established by men, a symbol of the difficulty of living together." The free choice of route is in itself a form of travel diary, in which the filmed meetings pass by one by one.

TRAVEL DIARIES ON STAGE

Carnet(s) de Chine [je rêvais d'aller à Kashgar] (2010) is not, according to its authors,[37] either a "cinema-concert", or a lecture on "discovering the world." It is, in fact, "a multidisciplinary artistic offering; a living, contemporary and accessible travel diary, mixing cinema, readings by writers and travellers, music and dance; a dialogue that invites us to relive the journey together." This show, created out of a real journey, is an opportunity to discover minority (Uyghur and Tibetan) cultures and music on screen and through the creators' on-stage music, dance and dramatized reading performances. Mixing different artistic disciplines, the travel diary can take the form of installation and performance, opening up to a virtually unlimited space for creation. Other travel diaries draw on staging or theatrical adaptation, as is the case with the previously mentioned *Traversées*. Following in the footsteps of Blaise Cendrars, Philippe Rousseau offers a work that takes the form of a poetic monologue of the wintertime Russia of the Trans-Siberian railway, from Moscow to Lake Baikal. Having first been performed on stage, this initiatory journey was then published under the title *Passeport pour une Russie: mes pas captent le vent* (Elytis, 2010). Philippe Bichon adopted the opposite approach. Using his travel diary on Iran,[38] he created a performance of music and images on the oud.

37. Emmanuelle Troy, Virginie Perret, Erik Baron, Thomas Bienabe.
38. *Iran*, Elytis, 2012.

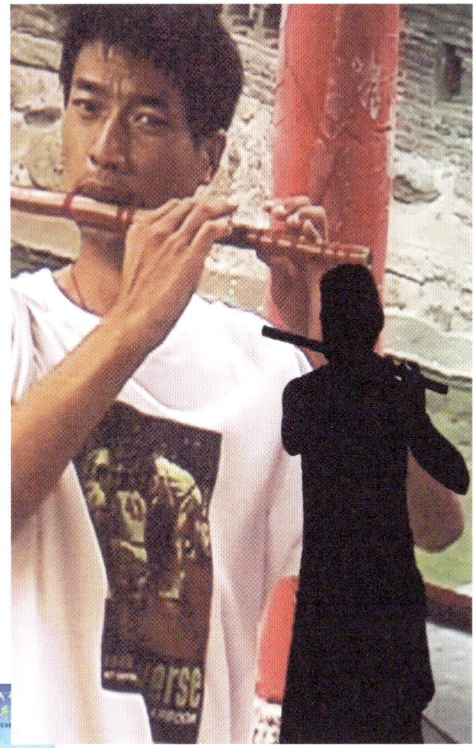

Emmanuelle Troy on *Carnet(s) de Chine*

"Carnet(s) de Chine, a transdisciplinary work, creates an unusual dialogue between cinema, the readings of writers and travellers, music and dance. It is based on a long trip to China, Turkestan and Tibet. What things remain from ephemeral encounters between a traveller and 'those who live there'? How can the porosity between here and elsewhere, between the past and present and between the real and imaginary be turned into a sensible experience? Playing on the multiplicity and complementarity of views, it invites us to relive—far from the clichés of the genre—the journey together and to let it live on. On the screen, there is a film recounting a journey to meet the Chinese, Uyghurs and Tibetans and to discover their music and their cultures. On the stage, there is an actress and dancer, along with two musicians. Our passport is their imagination, some paper, a few strings, and memories of the tales of Marco Polo, Alexandra David-Néel and Colin Thubron. There are feelings, questions, outbursts, surprises and wonderful encounters along the way, here and there, and all the while the music and dance come together, from one continent to another."

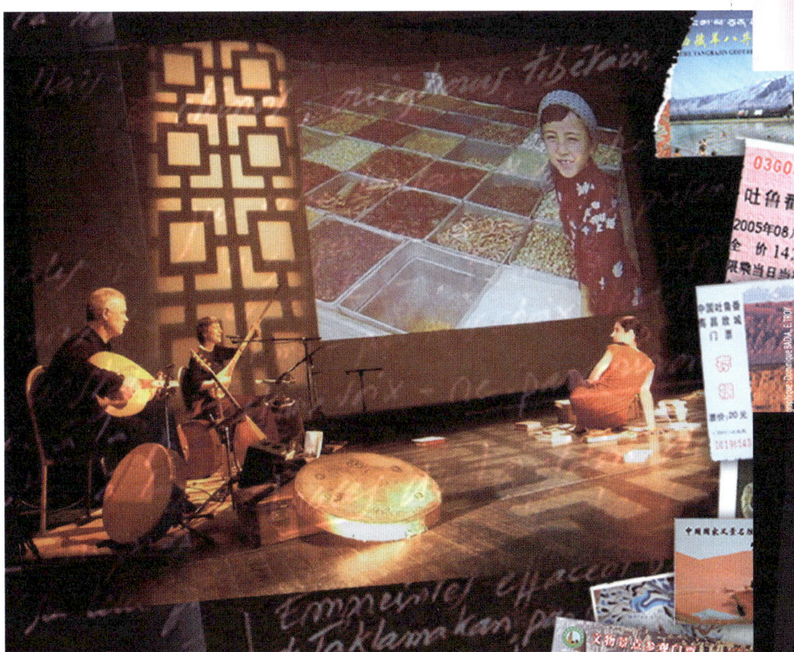

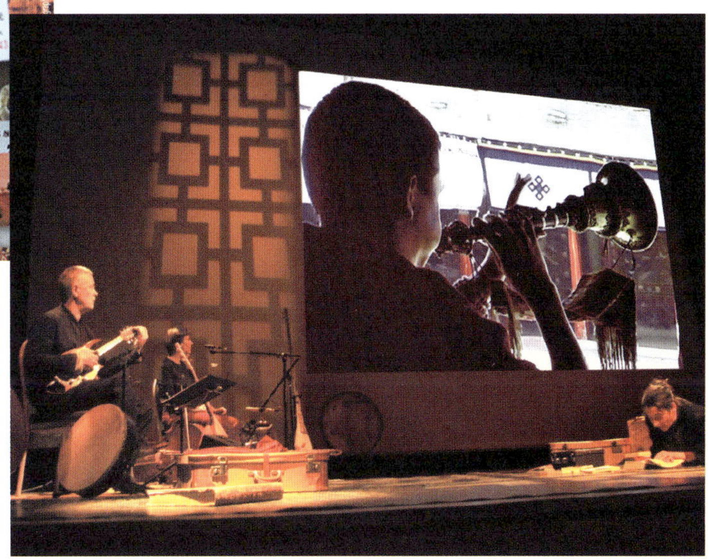

• Trans-eurasienne *(2013, opposite) and* Carnet(s) de Chine [Je rêvais d'aller à Kashgar] *(2010) turn the travel diary into a living spectacle in which performance arts (music, dance and theatre) mix with images (photography and film sequences) and writing.*

AURAL TRAVEL DIARIES

In 2004, in a diary entitled *Rajasthan* (Éditions du Garde-Temps, 2004), Éric-Roux-Fontaine journeys to the origins of Gypsy culture based on the texts and music of Thierry "Titi" Robin and Sergio G. Mebius. Over the course of three years, Philippe Lansac and Laurent Granier travelled 120,000 kilometres and across twenty-eight countries from Paris to Tokyo, a journey that is the subject of their *Paris-Tokyo: carnet de route* (Garde-Temps/France bleue, 2004), a travel diary that is enhanced by a CD of interviews, sounds, noises and music recorded along the way. The composer Bruno Letort gives an account of his travels in Russia, Belarus, Ukraine and Slovenia through a collection of sound samples. A multimedia journey created through musical works (string quartet and field recordings) and photographic documents, *Ea(s)t* (Sonagramme, 2004) traces a journey along the Volga River, to the town of Saratov. In 2008, Indian musicology inspired *Au rythme du raga: de Calcutta à Bombay* (Bachari, 2008), a book and CD by Philippe Puget and Marc Ingrand that brings together excerpts from concerts recorded in the North of India. Bruno Blum set off to Jamaica on the trail of reggae, which he captured through montages and video and music recordings. Finally, Nadine Marchal, a visual artist and fabric designer, and Stanislas Pierrel, a guitarist and composer, offer a bilingual diary covering the world (for example, the United States, Russia, Mauritania, Mali and Cuba) that consists of texts of songs and interviews with people involved in the protection of the environment and that is accompanied by a CD: *Graines de rencontres, Seeds of encounters* (Bichromia-Armonia, 2007). At the fringes of the travel diary, the photographic and multimedia album *Mégalopoles* (Éditions du Point d'exclamation, 2007) is an innovative work that stems from the collaboration of five artists[39] from various fields (photography, videography, illustration, scenography and music). This musical diary, produced by Bruno Letort, captures the aural impressions experienced during various trips to five cities (New York, London, Paris, Moscow, Bombay and Tokyo)—kinds of "aural postcards" that are illustrated by images from the album *La Fièvre d'Urbicande* by Schuitten.

39. Isao Tanaka, Charles René, Julie Heath, Valérie Anisimov.

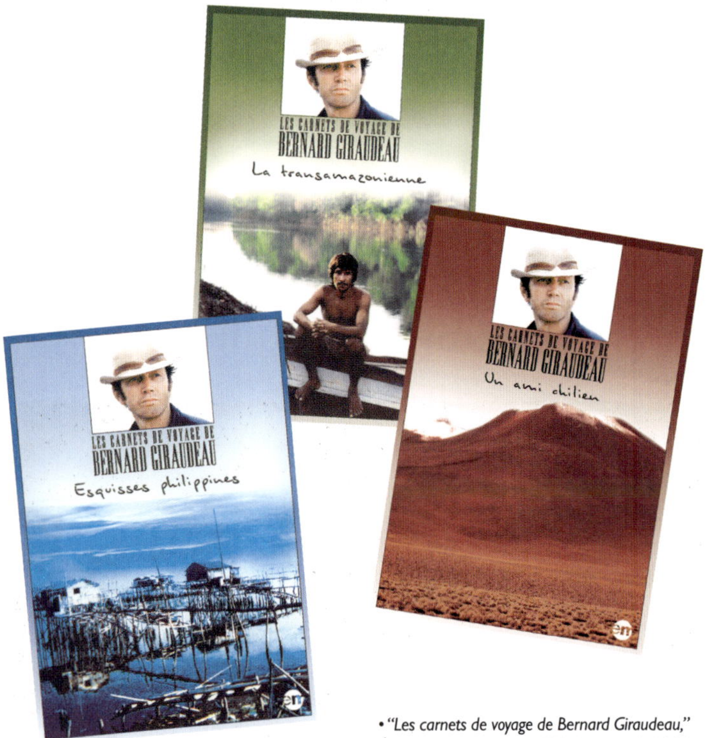

• *"Les carnets de voyage de Bernard Giraudeau," Éditions Montparnasse, 2000. In the early 2000s, the writer and actor Bernard Giraudeau turned director, taking viewers to richly human lands.*

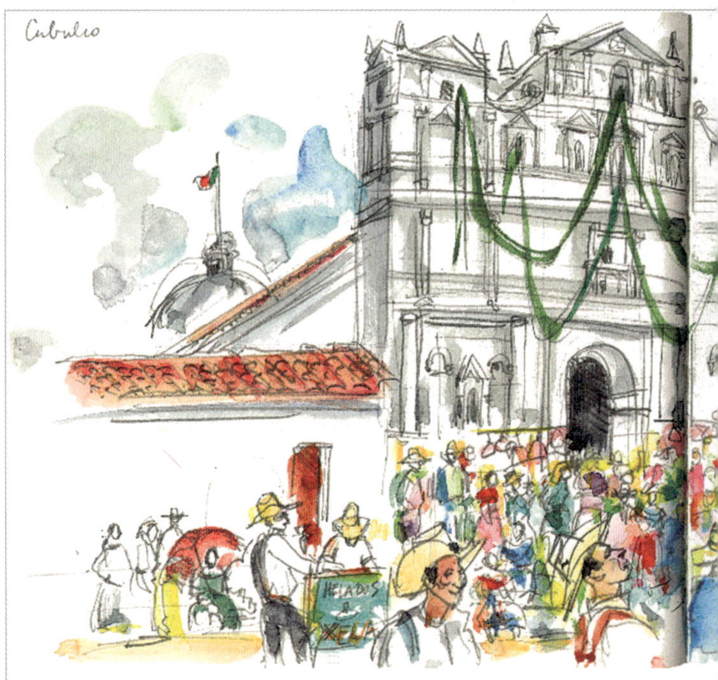

AUDIOVISUAL TRAVEL DIARIES

The intermedia travel diary borrows from audiovisual, film and digital forms. Inspired by the diary's work-in-progress aspect, television shows (*Thalassa* and *Echappées belles*, for example) have redefined themselves, billing their reportage pieces as "carnets de voyage" ("travel diaries"). This is the case, for example, with Jean-Louis Porte and his *Carnets d'Inde: le cinéma*, (2002) *Carnets de Chine* (2002), *Carnets d'Égypte* (2004), *Carnets d'Asie: Cambodge, Viêt Nam* (2007), *Carnets d'Amérique* (2008) and *Carnets du Japon* (2010). Diaries also come on DVD, a format for projects that have a tourism angle. The collections "Des trains pas comme les autres" (produced by the I.N.A. between 1993 and 1997) and "Carnets d'ailleurs" (2005) by Éditions Montparnasse combine invitations to travel and reports for a mainstream audience on the attractions of the elsewhere. One of the genre's pioneers, Bernard Giraudeau, offers a more authentic and sensitive vision that is in line with the great writers and travellers with his "Les carnets de voyage de Bernard Giraudeau" trilogy (Les Films de la saga, 2000). Priscilla Telmon and Marianne Chaud treat us to out-of-the-ordinary diaries. Telmon, a reporter, favours hiking in the show *Le Sens de la marche* (France 5) or walking in the footsteps of Alexandra David-Néel in *Voyage au Tibet interdit* (la Bonne Pioche Production). Meanwhile Chaud, a filmmaker and ethnologist, set off in 1999 to Zanskar to discover Buddhist cultures. She produced three ethnographic diaries on the back of this experience: *Himalaya, la terre des femmes*, *Himalaya, le chemin du ciel* and *La Nuit nomade* (Arte-Zed, 2008, 2009, 2012). Camera on his shoulder, Antoine de Maximy opts for the backpacker's diary, appreciating the countries he visits through trying out the hospitality of the locals in each episode of "J'irai dormir chez vous." The series "Les Routes mythiques des Échappées belles" (France 5) presents twenty first-hand journey diaries. The collection "Carnets de voyage: exploration aventure" (Gédéon Programmes-Arte GEIE, 2007) makes use of the concept of graphic and audiovisual reportage and follows the journey, discoveries and drawing sessions of an artist abroad.

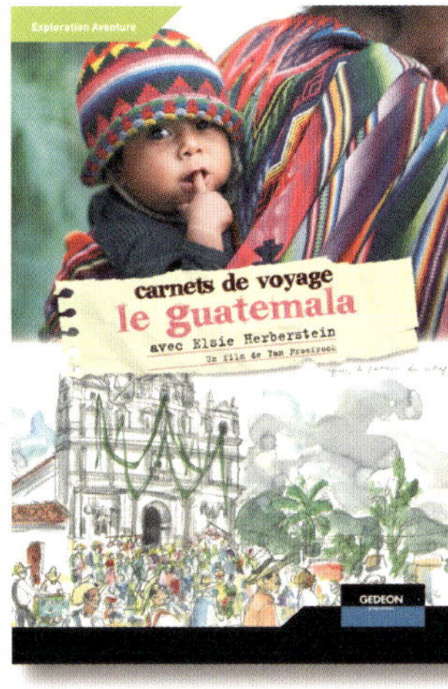

• "Carnets de voyage," Gédéon programmes. Like Damien Roudeau in Scotland or Carla Talopp in Cuba, Elsie Herberstein took her graphic reporting skills to Guatemala (images from the trip can be seen on this page) and also Namibia.

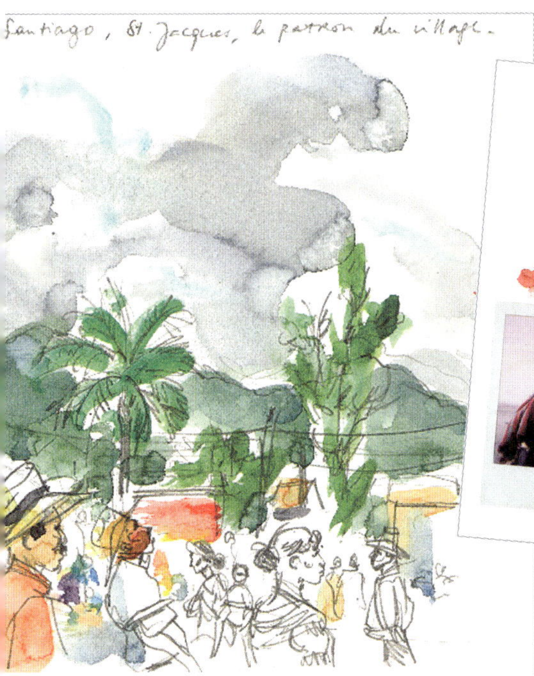

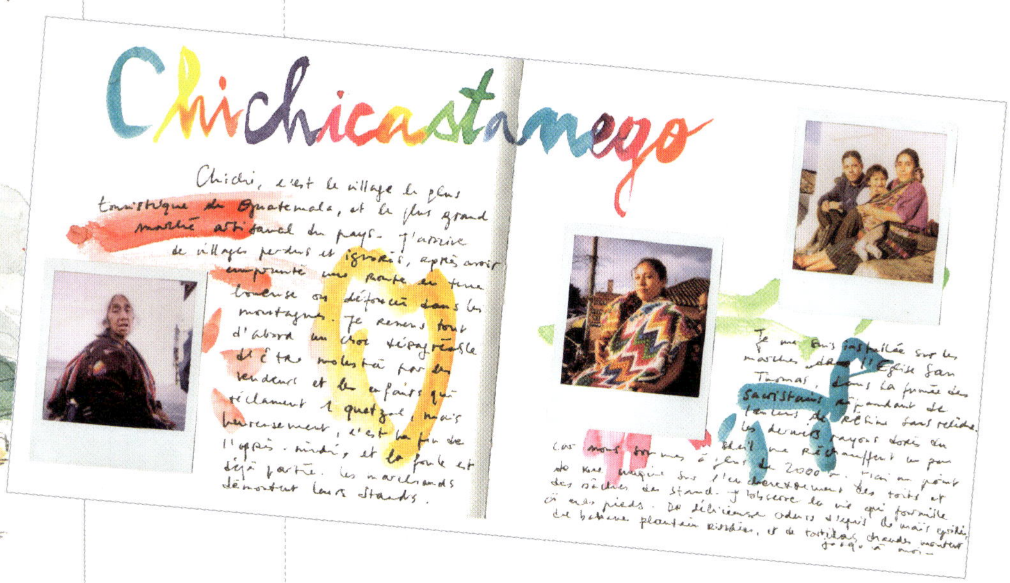

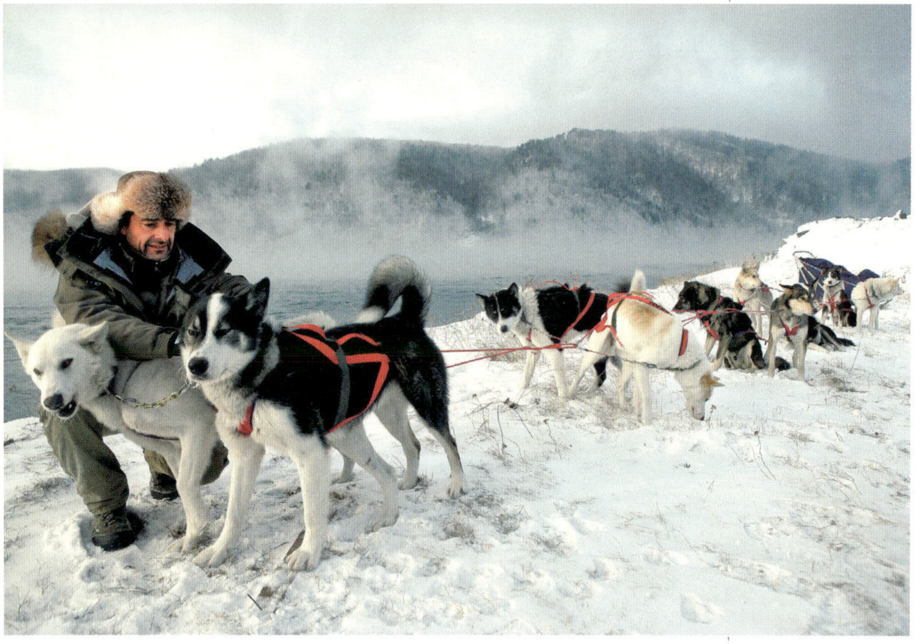

• *Nicolas Vanier's escapades—here he is checking his dog team during his "Odyssée sauvage" (2014)—lend themselves readily to multimedia.*

MULTIMEDIA DIARIES

Travel diaries on CD-Rom, which first appeared in 1999, tend to take a documentary approach (*Sur la route de la soie autour du XIIIe siècle: une voie de l'humanité vers une culture de la paix* by 3001 multimédia, ART 3000 and the Centre culturel Saint-Exupéry de Reims). Educational CD-Roms seize upon the theme of travel to go back through time and refresh memories (*Astrolabe: l'aventure océanienne* by Alain Néris[40] or *Île de Gorée et esclavage* by Pierre Pommier[41]). But the transition from CD-Rom to DVD will really unleash the possibilities of the multimedia book and allow the same content to reinvent itself on different media. Travel diaries on scientific expeditions have been transposed from one genre to another. In 2006, the "Odyssée sibérienne" successively took the form of an album (published by Le Chêne), a documentary (Nathan), a DVD that in particular features a logbook (with an animated map showing the fourteen stages of the expedition) and finally a game, "Quatre défis du développement durable: sur les traces de... l'odyssée sibérienne – Nicolas Vanier, le rêve utile."

40. Mémoire d'images, Lasermédia, 1995.
41. IUT de Bordeaux III, Renaudel Multimédia, 2003.

DIGITAL AND ANIMATED TRAVEL DIARIES

Julie Sarperi's *Carnets de Traverses* (2009) opened up travel diary makers' productions to digital art. The animation-orientated *Madagascar: carnet de voyage* by Bastien Dubois, the installation-based *Carnet(s) de Chine* by Emmanuelle Troy and the "cinema-show" have driven a current of technical innovation that allows the experience of the elsewhere to be shared with everyone. Through podcasts, the experiences of a trip can be simultaneously passed on. *6 000 km du couchant au levant* by Karen Guillorel is a diary in which videos, illustrations and photographs mingle with one another. It also uniquely depicts the author's dreams via a digital composition of mosaic images and the artist's path on a screen divided into multiple windows (a split-screen effect), allowing several actions to be followed at the same time and providing the benefit of several simultaneous points of view.

Madagascar, carnet de voyage by Bastien Dubois, which offers turning pages and drawings that come to life, offers the reader/viewer the chance to relive a journey in 3D. This digital creation has received numerous international awards and was nominated for an Oscar in 2011. David Lopez makes uses of the same principle in *Entre Mexico et Guatemala,* which alternates between animated cartoons, 3D and watercolours over the course of the narration. Gauthier Mesnil-Blanc combines narrative and fiction in *Éphémérides: Petites histoires éphémères dans le Grand Nord.*

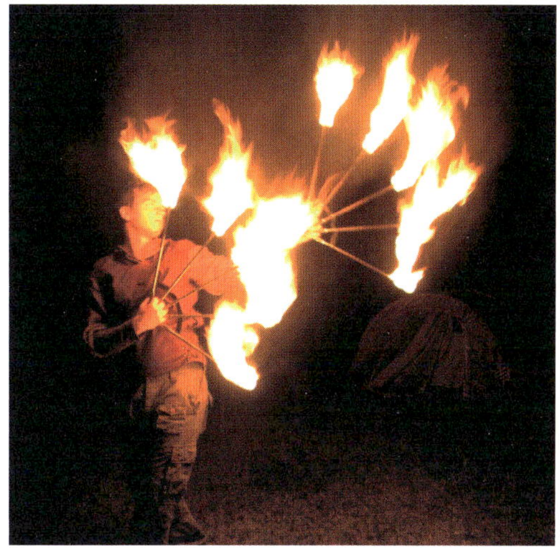

Bastien Dubois on *Madagascar – carnet de voyage*

"Camera mapping is the most frequently used technique in the film. It allows a drawing or a texture to be pasted over a 3D form by projecting them through a virtual 'projector.' Take the example of this head: I first modelled it in 3D. I calculated from the point of view of projector A an image synthesized with the mesh lines of the 3D that I printed. I then painted a gouache texture following the forms of my model. Once the painting had been scanned, I used projector A to paste the drawing on the volume. The now textured volume can be deformed and animated, and we can now move, to a limited extent, thanks to the camera B, to perceive the volume. From a single painting, we therefore have an animated sequence that can be as long as we wish, which is a great time saver. To avoid having a face that is too rigid, we can use four or five identical drawings that are on a loop instead of just one. So what we get is a small vibration that gives the illusion of a frame-by-frame piece."

WEB DIARIES

When launching the project "Trancybériennes: un cybervoyage au long cours" (which would become "E-Troubadours") in 2008, Karen Guillorel capitalized on the resources offered by the Internet to allow the public to accompany her on a journey carried out on foot, even offering those wishing to join her to do so using GPS coordinates. Through a virtual identity ("Nout Eales"), she created "a connection between the spheres that we often keep apart: the real and virtual worlds."

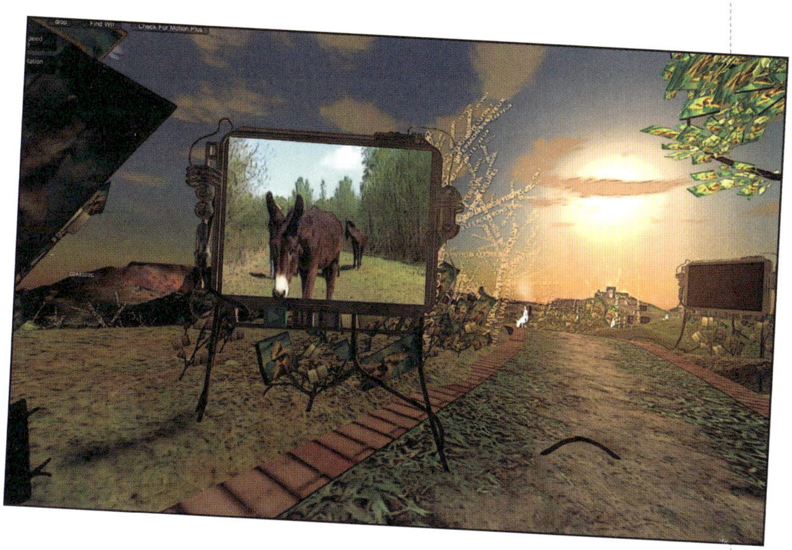

• The "E-migrations" project (above) by Karen Guillorel and Yann Minh transposes their real experience on the roads between Barcelona and Amsterdam ("E-troubadours"—opposite) into a real-time 3D digital travel diary.

Karen Guillorel on the "E-troubadours" project

"During the summer of 2008, I went on foot from Barcelona to Amsterdam with my travel companion Vincent Radix. We were accompanied by two donkeys, Chaman and Grand, who carried a library of books that were exchanged along the way, and in particular a work dedicated to travel: 'Traverses, livre voyageur.' This trip offered a link between nature and technology: the path taken every day for four months with the donkeys and with everything that daily life on the road brings with it was also punctuated by meetings in virtual worlds that we had while using random connections that we found out on the road. In these virtual worlds, anyone could ask questions through avatars. But above all, they could participate in this journey in other ways, such as offering a pictorial, aural or interactive work related to the trip in the virtual world. They could even walk with us, because we wore a geolocation tag that allowed people to locate us on the map and join us for a collective trek along this path through Europe. We called this journey 'E-troubadours,' as in 'electronic troubadours,' in reference to the troubadours of eras gone by and to our inner nature having been shaped by video games and the twenty-first century. A poet, 'E-troubadour Marco' had in fact already taken this name in the 2000s."

✏ http://www.traverses-lelivre.com

Karen Guillorel on the "E-migrations" project[42]

"E-Migrations is a real-time digital 3D travel diary that describes the E-Troubadours journey of 2008 as a continuation of the literary experience 'Traverses, livre voyageur.' How could a multimedia journey between nature and technology be recorded without designing an innovative and interactive story? 'E-migrations' in fact needed a period of reflection before being set as a digital installation that transported the viewer into an immersive 3D world generated by computers, a reflection of the imaginary world of this trip. Any new mediums of expression that I come up with complement the spirit of adventure that drives travellers, though this doesn't prevent me from continuing to draw, paint and make films. 'E-migrations' incorporates many black and white drawings into over 90 minutes of edited videos of the journey. With the help of a small joystick or keyboard, viewers wander at their own pace in the world of trees made out of books, which move gently under sun and rain alike; they head as they please to the silhouettes of the travellers and their encounters or view the videos that are dotted along the route."

✏ http://www.e-migrations.net

42. The idea and the production were by Karen Guillorel, and the graphic design of the real-time 3D world is the work of Yann Minh. The installation received support from France's Civil Society of Multimedia Authors ("Brouillons d'un rêve").

in un banchetto di contenie compro, da un commerciante songhai un flacone di collirio prodotto a Mumbai per l'esportazione in Arabia. Orienti globalizzati.

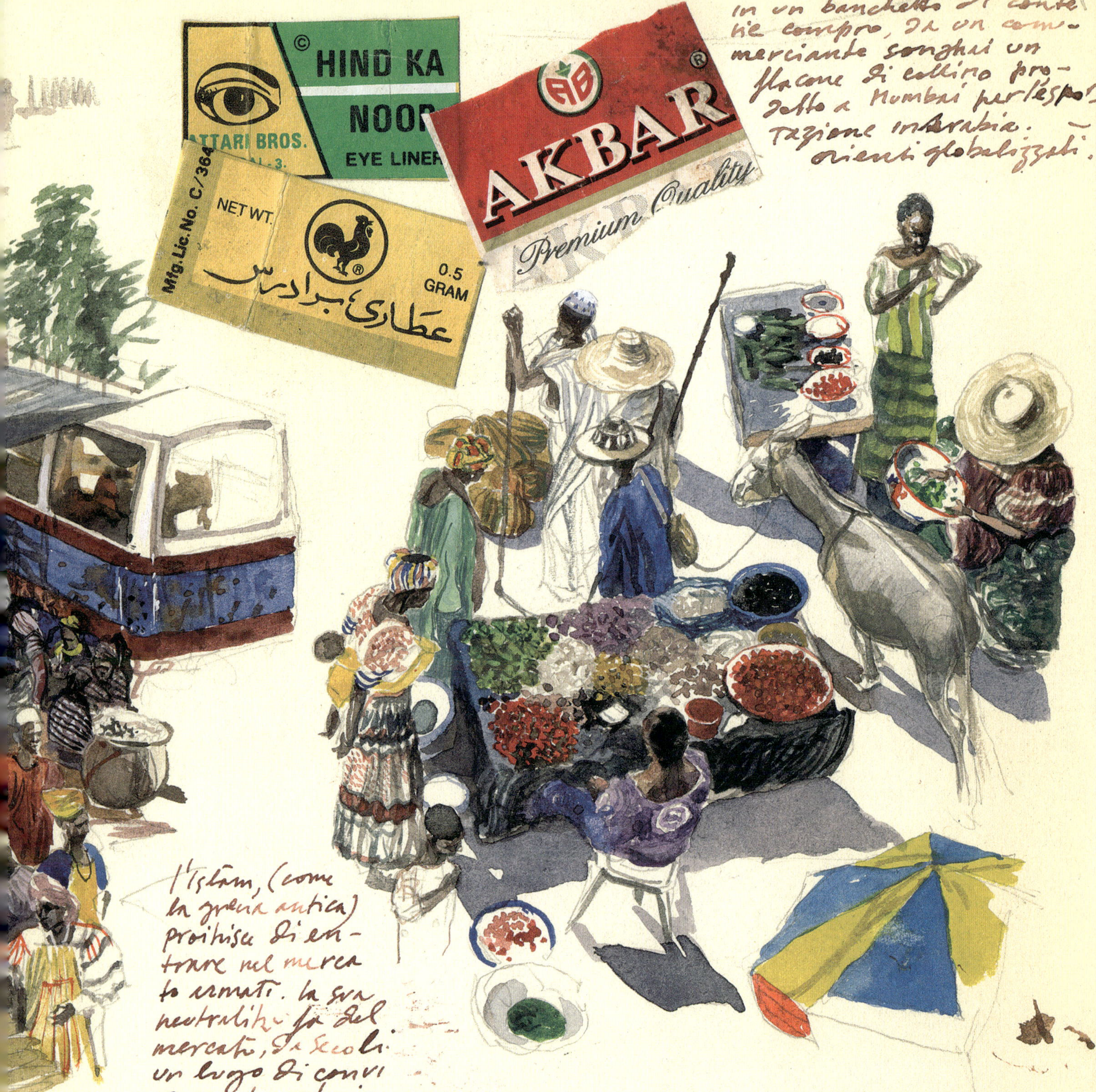

l'Islām, (come la grecia antica) proibisce di entrare nel mercato armati. La sua neutralità fa del mercato, da secoli un luogo di convivenza tra etnie diverse. Così la bancarella di un Bozo (con le sue nasse e i pesci secchi) se ne sta a fianco di una donna Dogon con il suo sacco di cipolle. I Peul con il loro bestiame commerciano con i Songhai importatori di prodotti cinesi.

Travel diary artists

Bruno Pilorget

Thanks to Delacroix's and the young Méheut's travel drawings, I dared to make my first diaries on trains, and then on Senegal. Later, in Asia, the experience finally offered me a release from the technical constraints of in situ drawing, allowing me to fully enjoy the surprises and sensations of the travel diary. I set out with an empty book and in the hope of beautiful meetings that are guided by emotion and aesthetics. I draw without a safety net—without a pencil or a rubber—creating lines or colour directly, so everything is relaxed, fluid and pure. This remains a difficult art to execute with ease or luck, or to master during difficult moments or bad weather. It's something that is sometimes done in front of many people who are proud, entertained or moved that you are interested in them and their world, family, house, boat, work or landscape—their history. I love this complicity. It always makes something happen—funny, touching or surprising stories that are told through a small text next to the drawing. And if possible, the people who are in the portraits sign my drawing. For me, getting out is essential—it reenergizes and enriches me. True drawing done in situ and the ethic behind doing it make for a great passport. This sort of drawing allows exchanges between people and creates a sense of welcoming; it offers memories of atmospheres, sounds and smells. This is its wonderful reward. My travels in Palestine made me evolve towards the more demanding reportage travel diary. I started making a diary in the West Bank in 2008, after I was invited by the Consulate of France in Jerusalem to meet young people there. I went back in 2009, accompanied by the writer Véronique Massenot and the photographer Marc Abel. We set out with the idea of doing a portrait of a little-known Palestine, as it is lived and recounted by the Palestinians themselves, with ourselves sticking to our position of artists, far removed from weighty geopolitical diatribes. The book, Salaam Palestine! Carnet de voyage en terre d'humanité, *was published by La Boîte à bulles in 2013.*

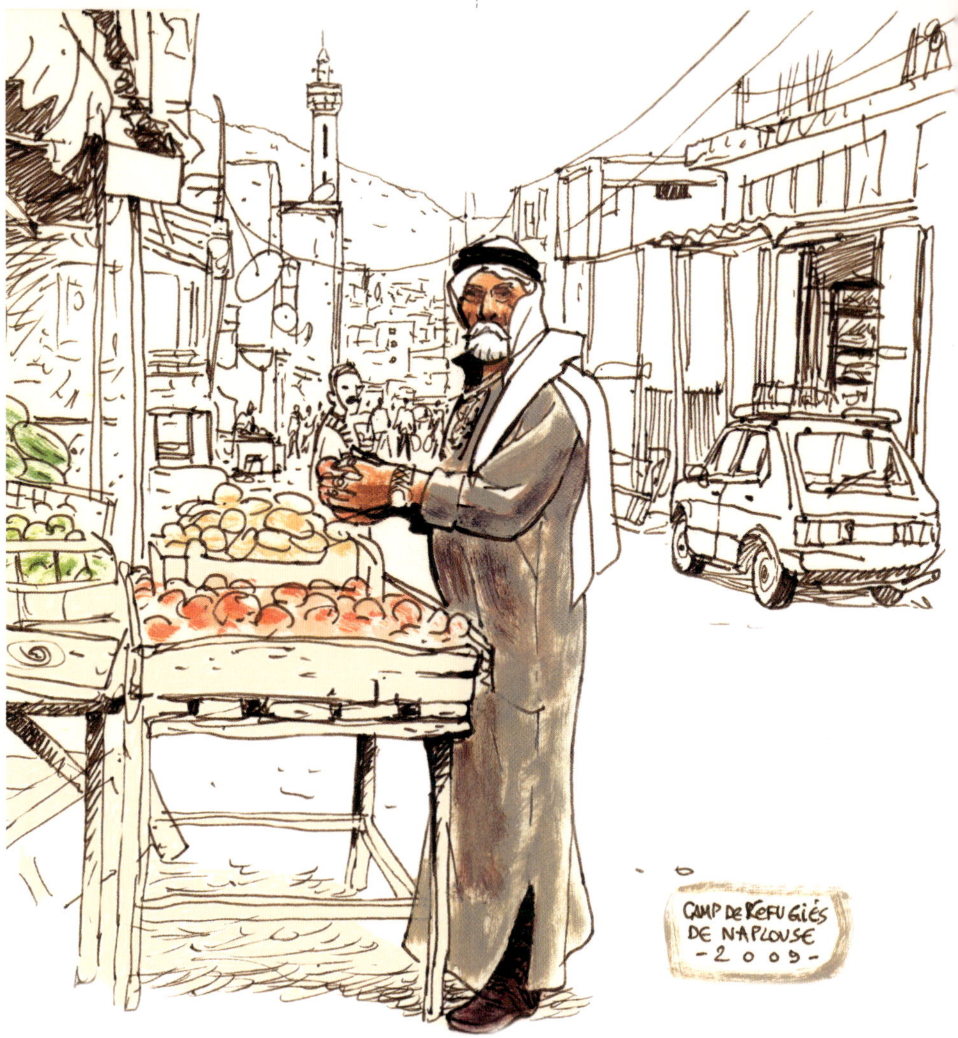

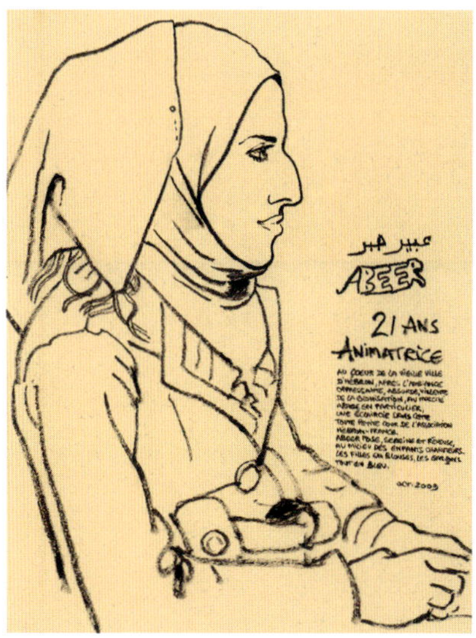

• During his travels (in this case in Palestine), Bruno Pilorget drew "without a safety net" to get to know local people.

www.bruno-pilorget.com
Carnets de voyage
Salaam Palestine! Carnet de voyage en terre d'humanité
(La Boîte à bulles, 2013)
Le Journal de Victor Dubray au Viêt Nam
(Mango Jeunesse, 2011)

Bertrand de Miollis

Bertrand de Miollis likes big experiences. Among other things, he has followed the French military in Afghanistan, criss-crossed "post-Saddam Hussein" Iraq, ridden a motorcycle over the ice of Lake Baikal and sailed on a Chinese junk. His taste for adventures that require a real personal commitment, his painter's take and his ability to slip from one world to another make his approach particularly unique, rich and fertile. *I love travelling, observing, reconstructing and being an eyewitness to my age. In a military context and in a theatre of operations, making a "war diary" is to adopt the eyewitness's take on history in the making. It is about recounting events with a personal and sensitive eye and doing so as well as possible.*

Sibérie ma chérie (Gallimard, 2012)
Aphorismes dans les herbes et autres propos de la nuit (Éditions des Équateurs, 2011)
Carnet de voyage en Arménie and *Carnet de voyage au Cambodge* (Gédéon Programmes, 2007)
Irak année zéro (Gallimard, 2004)
Paris-Kaboul, une expédition scientifique et culturelle sur les routes de la soie (Hoëbecke, 2004)
Silllages d'Afrique (Gallimard, 2004)
De Saigon à Saint-Malo: visions de la jonque Sao Mai (Transboréal, 2000)

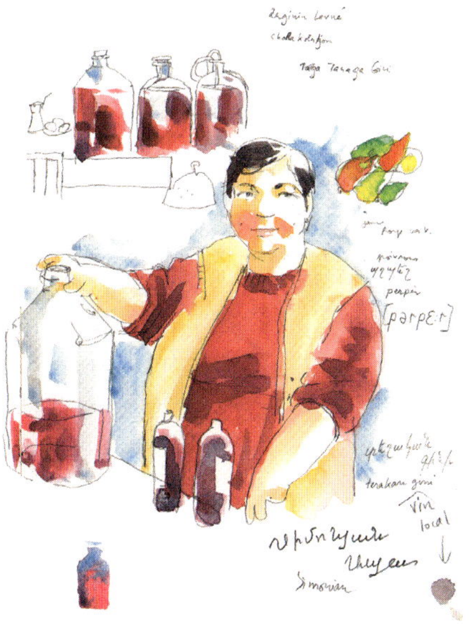

• Carnet de voyage en Arménie, *Gédéon Programmes, 2007. Bertrand de Miollis's illustrations invite us to discover Armenia, a country with a very clear identity and rich landscapes.*

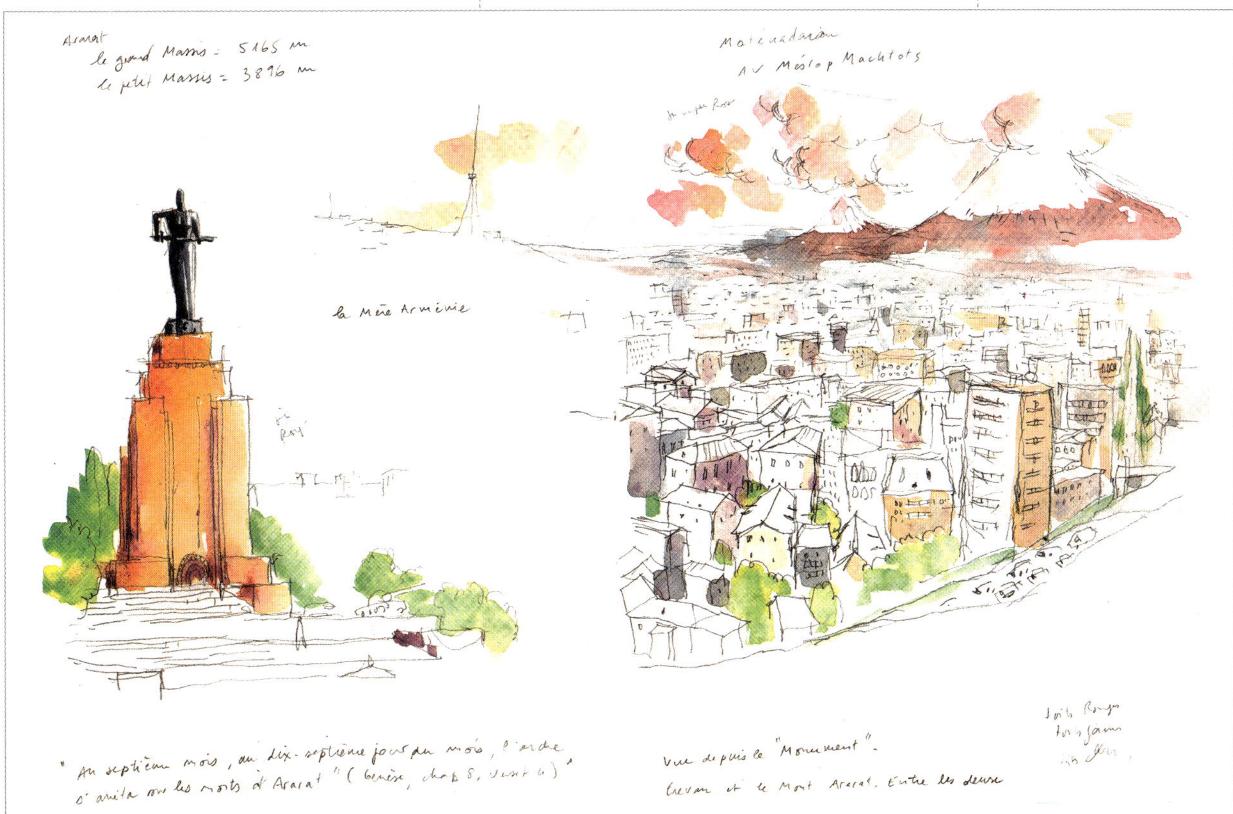

Cathy Beauvallet

After studying at the École nationale supérieure des arts décoratifs de Paris (ENSAD), Cathy Beauvallet soon became interested in travel and reportage drawing. She has produced several publications and works on the back of the encounters she has had with the performing arts world, including *Carnet de Cirque* (Gallimard, 2001). Her press drawings from the court of assizes were republished in *Cour d'Assises, et si demain vous étiez juré?* (Jalan Publications, 2004). In 2008, a trip to Quebec for an artist residency gave rise to *Carnet de Charlevoix* (Les Heures Bleues, 2008). While there she met the conductor of the NEM, who asked her to follow its European tour, which is retold in *NEM, le Nouvel Ensemble moderne: un parcours contemporain, 1989–2009* (Lorraine Vaillancourt, 2009). Cathy Beauvallet has a great sensitivity for artistic performance, and since 1999 she has covered it at various festivals (dance, contemporary music, jazz), at which she simultaneously exhibits all of her drawings, which give the closest and most precise rendering of the movements, in the performance spaces themselves.

www.cathybeauvallet.com

Other titles

***Sète, surprenant voyage* (Jalan Publications, 2005)**

***L'Ampleur du labeur: Cacao, un village hmong* (Ibis rouge, 2004)**

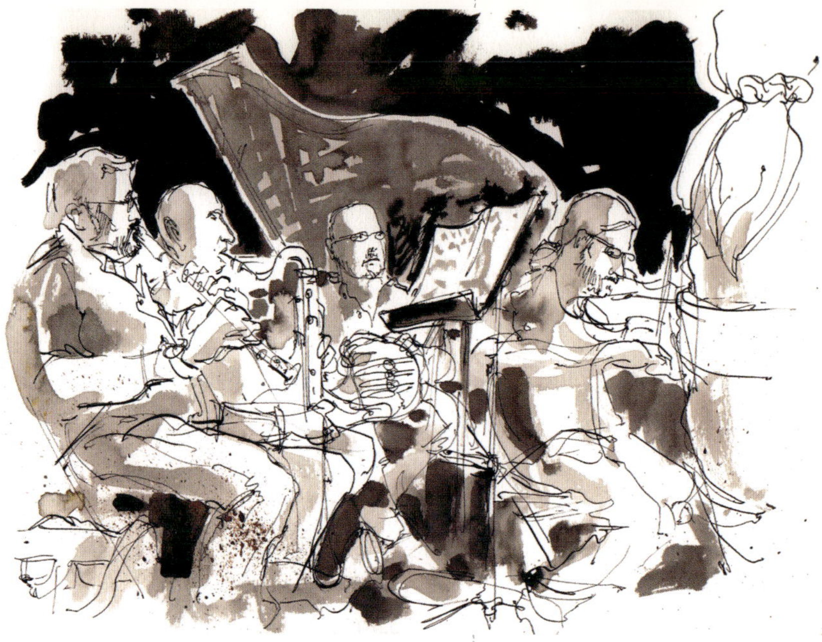

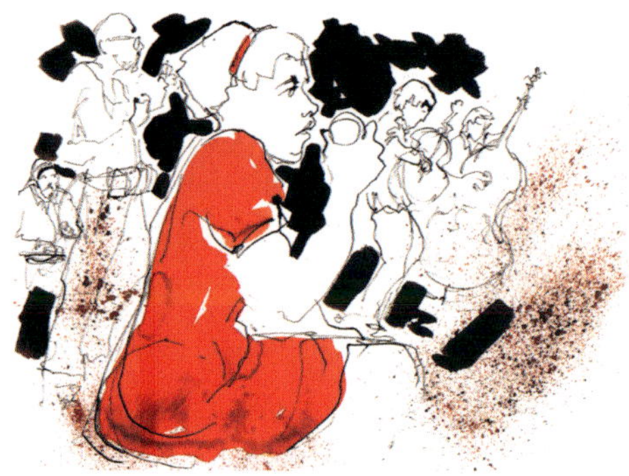

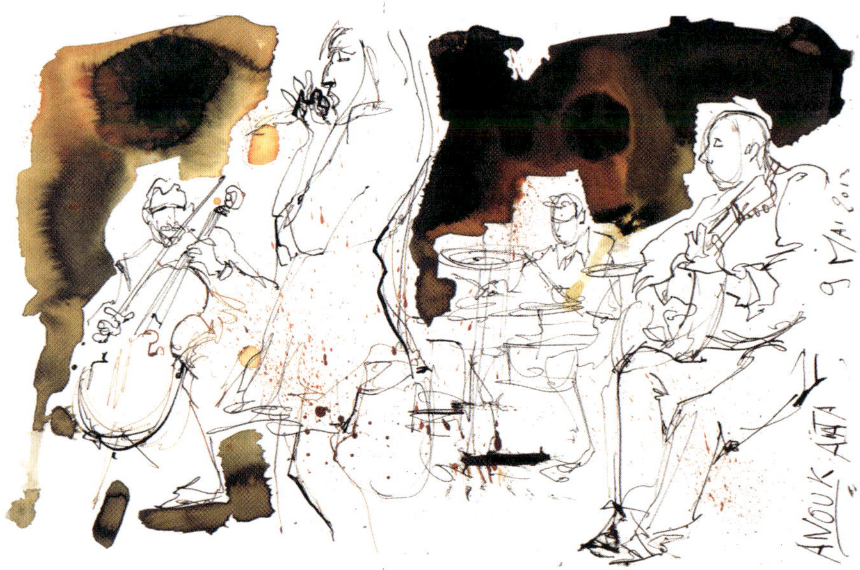

• The NEM orchestra, Moriarty (above, right) and Anouk Aïta, sketched "live" by Cathy Beauvallet.

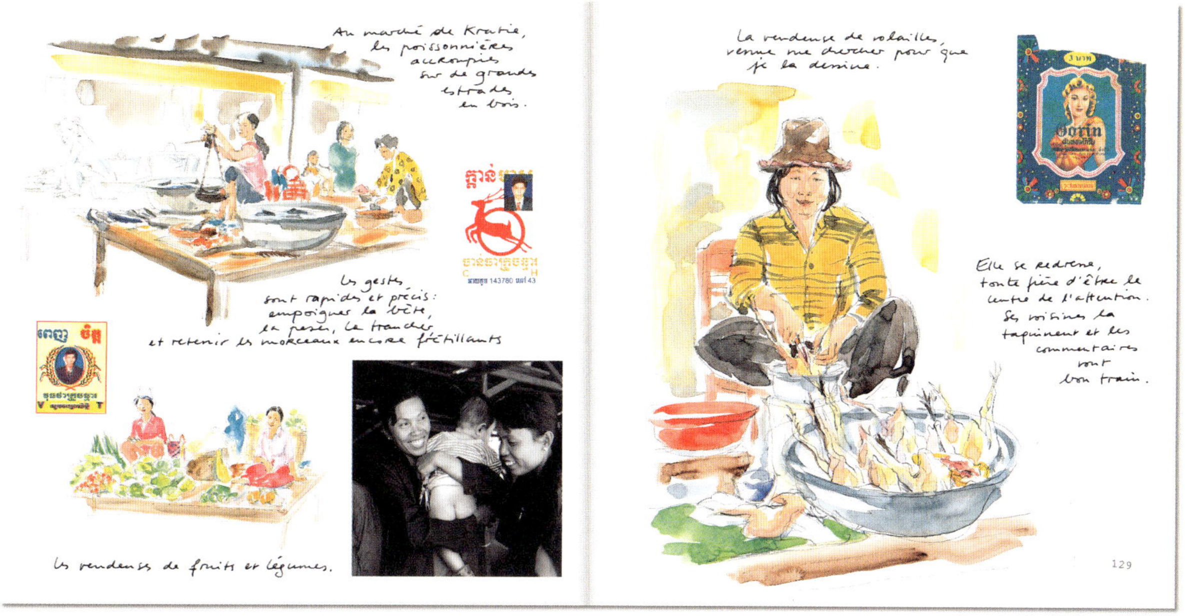

Elsie Herberstein

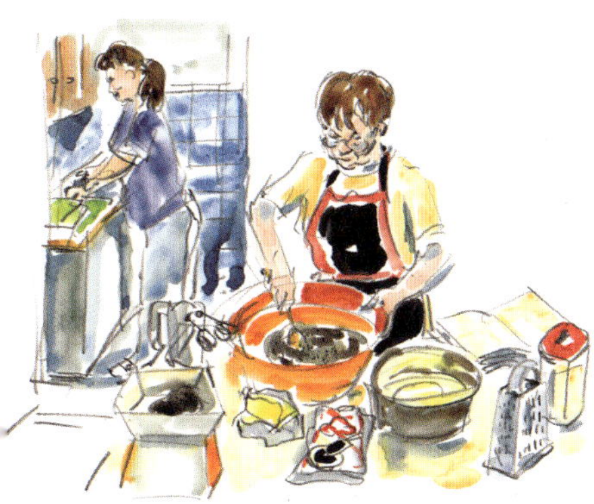

• Cambodge, carnets de voyage, *Seuil, 2003 (above) and* Les Carnets de Minna, *Seuil, 2008. A virtuoso travel diary artist, Elsie Herberstein also published this collection of recipes with a fascinating and tragic family history.*

Elsie Herberstein has been drawing since she was a child. After studying at the École nationale supérieure des arts décoratifs de Paris (ENSAD), she became an author and illustrator of travel and reportage diaries. South Africa, Tibet, Zanzibar, Cambodia, Algiers, Namibia and Guatemala are some of the far-flung destinations that have given rise to books published by Albin Michel, Gallimard, Seuil, Flammarion and Jalan Publications. She was involved in two documentary films for Arte that mix from-life sketches and stories. But her explorations have also led her to the street and to La Moquette, a venue for the homeless, where she became a volunteer and kept a logbook, *Viens chez moi, j'habite dehors: un voyage chez les sans-abri*. And she's also travelled to the French coast, where she has produced accounts on twenty port towns for Bayard Presse, which were then published in collected form by Flammarion.
She then went to the Czech Republic, Israel and the United States for *Les Carnets de Minna*, a historical documentary work published by Seuil. This followed on from a documentary film by Anne Georget that tells the story of a collection of recipes that were written in the Theresienstadt concentration camp by Minna Pächter, a Czech Jew, and that were passed from hand to hand for a quarter of a century before reaching Minna's daughter in New York. In recent years, Elsie has produced illustrated accounts in hospitals based on patients suffering from different diseases. These books were published and distributed free of charge to families and doctors. In parallel, she has published a few young-adult albums, and she teaches sketching at Strate, a design school in Sèvres.

✏ www.labonneminetoutelannee.com

Other titles

Carnets de patients (Narratives, 2008–2014)
Saint-Valery-en-Caux: les hommes et la mer (Magellan & Cie, 2010)
Ports de France (Flammarion, 2007)
Carnet de voyage en Namibie and *Carnet de voyage au Mexique* (Gédéon Programmes, 2007)
Sète, surprenant voyage (Jalan Publications, 2005)
Alger, simples confidences (Jalan Publications, 2005)
Cambodge, carnets de voyage (Seuil, 2003)
Zanzibar, carnets de voyage (Seuil, 2000)
Tibet: les exilés (Albin Michel Jeunesse, 1993)
L'Afrique du Sud (Albin Michel Jeunesse, 1991)

Damien Chavanat

After studying communications, Damien Chavanat decided to become a freelance illustrator. He is self-taught, and he began in the young-adult publishing sector but then very soon moved into press work. He has collaborated with many magazines, and in particular with the newspaper *Le Monde* and its publications. At the same time, he has been involved in graphics and art direction in the publishing world. Elsie Herberstein, Justin Creedy Smith and he make up the trio "Les Trois Moustiquaires," which published *Zanzibar* and *Cambodge, carnets de voyage* (Seuil, 2000 and 2003). With Jalan Publications, he created the "7e Œil" collection of four small diaries that cover, amongst other places, Egypt and South Africa.
He has written and illustrated young-adult works, including a "road book," *Il était une oie dans l'Ouest* (Sorbier, 2007), and he has worked on several reportage diaries related to business and industry.
In 2011, he started a blog that serves as a graphic and creative laboratory.

✏ www.labonneminetoutelannee.com
Other titles
Ports de France (Flammarion, 2007)
Sète, surprenant voyage (Jalan Publications, 2005)

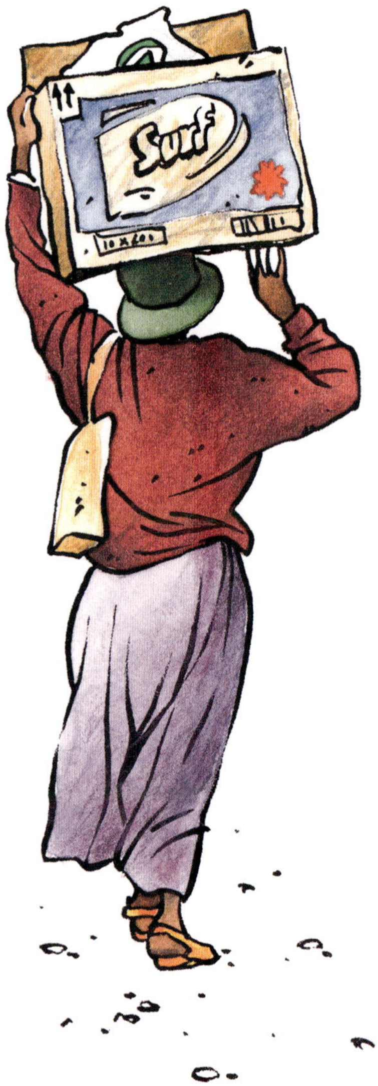

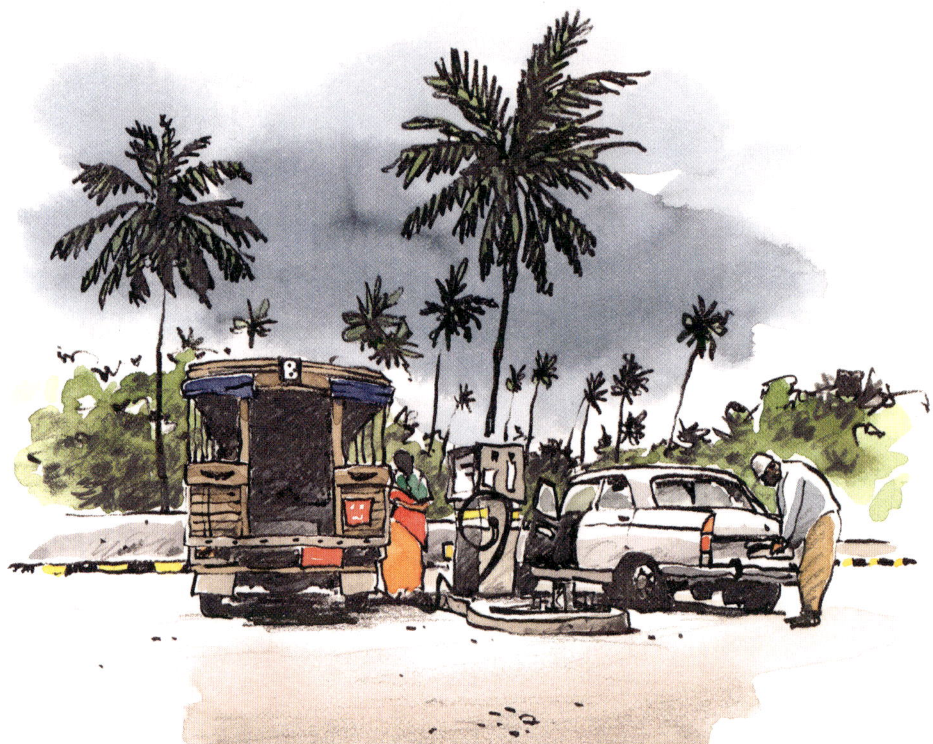

• Afrique du Sud *(above) and* Zanzibar *(opposite), Jalan Publications, 2003. After initially being a press cartoonist who stayed close to home, Damien Chavanat became a travel diary maker and travelled the world with his offbeat take on things.*

Noëlle Herrenschmidt

Born in 1940, Noëlle Herrenschmidt began drawing in 1971 for the youth imprint of Bayard Presse. She discovered reportage in 1980 through Mother Teresa in Calcutta, and then while in Hong Kong and Vietnam in 1990. Through these experiences she turned to watercolours for the first time and then never looked back. She dived into the judicial world in 1987, covering the Barbie and Touvier trials for the newspaper *La Croix*. From 1997, she worked as a court illustrator for *Le Monde*, working on the Papon, Dumas, Clearstream and infected blood trials. At the same time, for the past twenty years, she has explored closed-off spaces to discover, through drawings and first-hand accounts, how they operate and the men and women who live and work in them. Book by book, she paints a day-to-day picture of our society in its essential institutions: justice, health, religion and, nowadays, politics. Since 2010, she has been producing long-term accounts of the law's institutional pathways, for example in the Council of State, the Prime Minister's office, the National Assembly, the Senate, the Élysée Palace and the Constitutional Council.

✏ http://noelleaquarelle.wix.com/noelle

L'Assemblée nationale au bout du pinceau (Assemblée nationale, 2013)
Sceaux: au fil du temps, au fil des jours (Ville de Sceaux, 2013)
Corps et âmes: itinéraires spirituels en France (Éditions de La Martinière, 2009)
Mémoires de justice: les procès Barbie, Touvier, Papon (Seuil, 2009)
Carnets du lycée Lakanal (Ville de Sceaux, 2005)
L'Hôpital, à la vie, à la mort (Gallimard, 2003)
Carnets du Jubilé: pèlerins de Rome à Jérusalem (Albin Michel, 2000)
Carnets du Vatican (Albin Michel, 1999)
Carnets de la gendarmerie (Albin Michel, 1998)
Carnets de prisons (Albin Michel, 1997)
Carnets du Palais (Albin Michel, 1995)
Dans le sillage des boat people (Albin Michel Jeunesse, 1993)

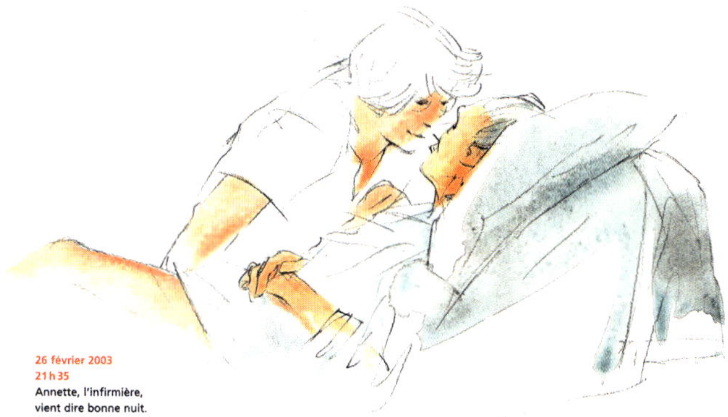

26 février 2003
21h35
Annette, l'infirmière, vient dire bonne nuit.
– Est-ce que vous voulez que je ferme la porte ?

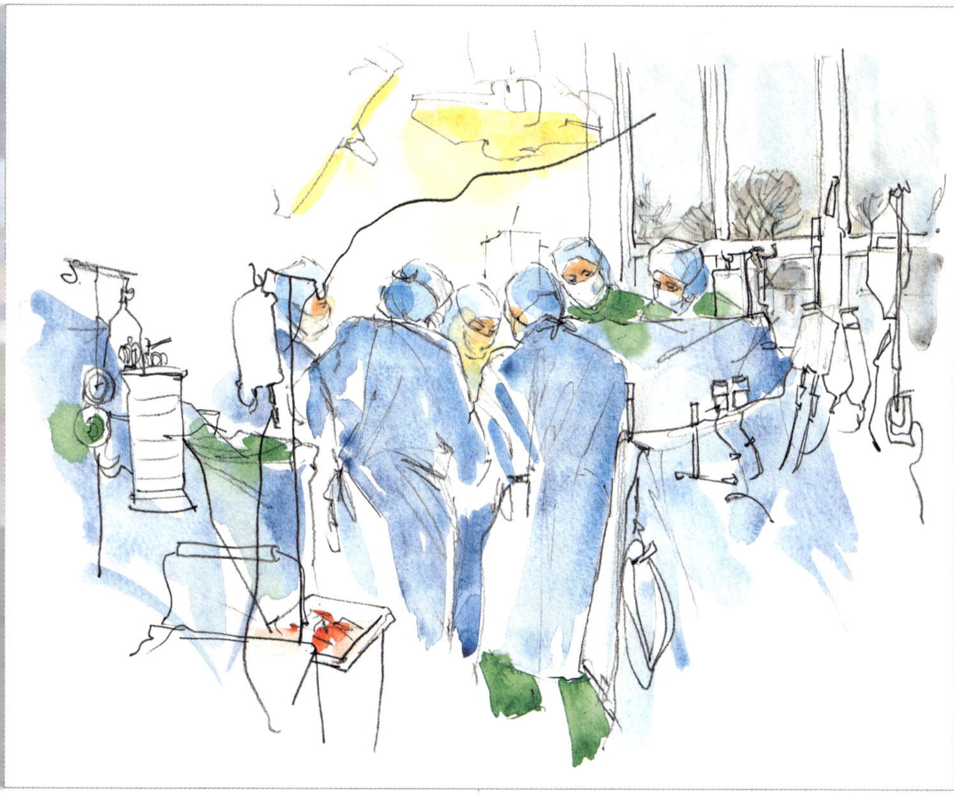

• L'Hôpital, *Gallimard, 2003. The fruit of three years of reportage work, this beautiful book shows the daily life of a hospital, a place of suffering and death where we can also learn to live and to grow, and even sometimes to laugh.*

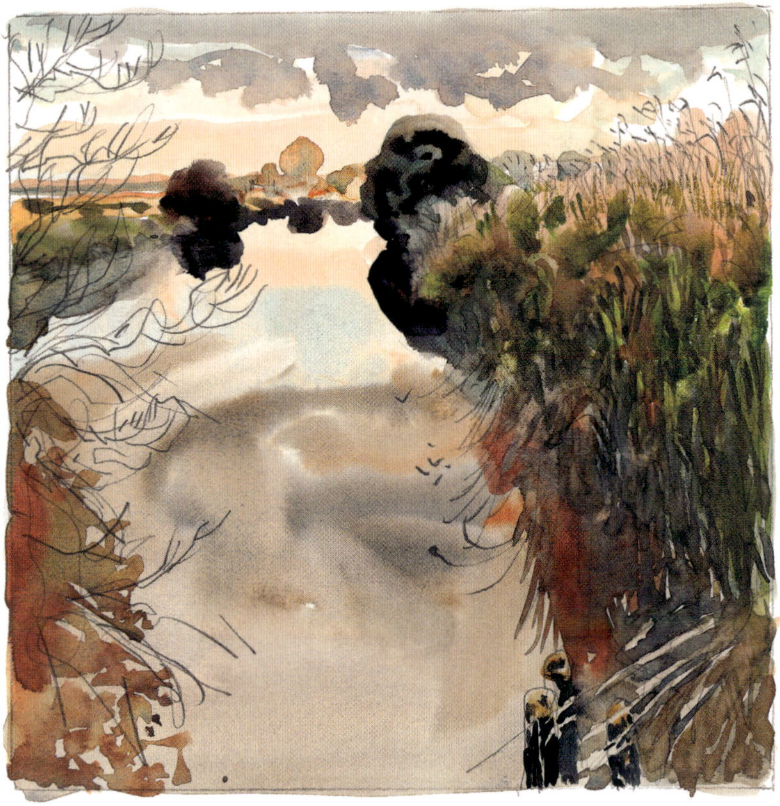

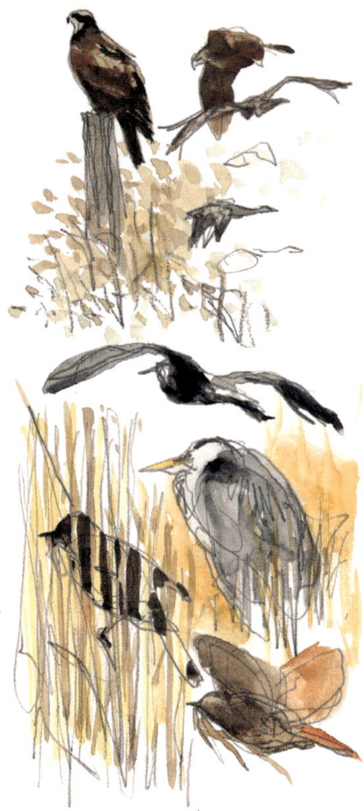

• *For* Rochefort et l'estuaire de la Charente, *the Conservatoire du littoral invited me to work for three years along the Charente estuary. The uniqueness of this area lies in the fact that the exceptional architectural heritage of* Rochefort *and its surroundings is intimately tied to the landscapes, the diversity of the natural environment and the human activities that take place in an estuary.*

Denis Clavreul

My books are a bit like portfolios composed of drawings and watercolours that have been made during various stays in a country, a national park or a near- or far-flung region. I explore and enthusiastically observe the landscapes, plants and animals, as well as the people and the places where they live. My passion and my knowledge of nature reinforce this ecological and global approach to life. Aware of the progressive degradation of the environment, above all what I like to do is express the beauty of my discoveries. My "journeys" are those of a surveyor: I travel through the seasons, sensitive to variations of light on a tree, to the behaviour of an insect, or to the lichen on a stone. Faced with the unexpected and the diversity of what inspires me to paint, I "capture" from real life without the use of photography. I love new challenges like this. Little by little, over the course of the journey, I become familiar with the places I go to and their inhabitants through the rhythm of their activities. Drawings and paintings follow one after the other, slowly creating a sensitive portrait of a territory, of what we can see in it at first glance and what is more discreet, more secret, more timeless. The conception of the work extends this long fieldwork. I have to choose from the images, find a consistency and create variations without there being a beginning or a real end. When I write I am alert to the trap of tittle-tattle. The quality of a travel diary is shaped as much by what it reconstructs as it is by what it suggests or conjures in the reader's/viewer's imagination.

✏ www.denisclavreul.com
Among other travel diaries
L'Agriate (Albiana, 2014)
Carnets de Bretagne (Équinoxe, 2013)
Le Mont Saint-Michel: quelques jours en été et *Le Mont Saint-Michel: quelques jours en hiver* (Équinoxe, 2010)
Rochefort et l'estuaire de la Charente (Équinoxe, 2008)

Alan Johnston

I've been crazy about making diaries since the age of thirteen. My diaries (I've made more than 200) reveal a real artistic practice that, among other things, provides the raw material for my published books. Sometimes the works in my diaries focus on a specific theme, making them "artists' books." My work as an artist and naturalist has allowed me to travel everywhere in the world, and thanks to my longer artist residencies, my most recent books are more like "places diaries" that take you on a journey. But the book Au pays des cigognes noires *(Gallimard, 2001) is in my opinion particularly interesting because it retells an (almost) parallel journey made by men and birds! It's a true published travel diary that follows the migration of the black storks of the Luxembourg Ardennes to the Sahel, passing through Senegal, Mauritania, Burkina Faso, Niger and Togo. This book is a compilation based on seventeen diaries filled with sketches and seven pocket diaries of field notes taken during three years.*
"Sketching Kijimadaira" is a diary in progress. Four artist's residencies in the Japanese village of Kijimadaira over the four seasons allowed me to produce 200 sketches in several diaries. India inks, oils on canvas and works on paper made up the raw material for a "places diary" that both takes the reader on a journey and, I also hope, invites him or her to stop from time to time for moments of "zen" contemplation. It features eagles and rare plants as well as studies of the rice or even the "weeds" that I observed for the first time.

Other titles
Le Marquenterre: d'une hirondelle à l'autre (Équinoxe, 2012)
Carnets d'un naturaliste en Normandie (Val d'Orne) (Nathan, 2001)
Au pays des cigognes noires (Gallimard, 2000)
La Baie du Mont-Saint-Michel (Gallimard, 1996)

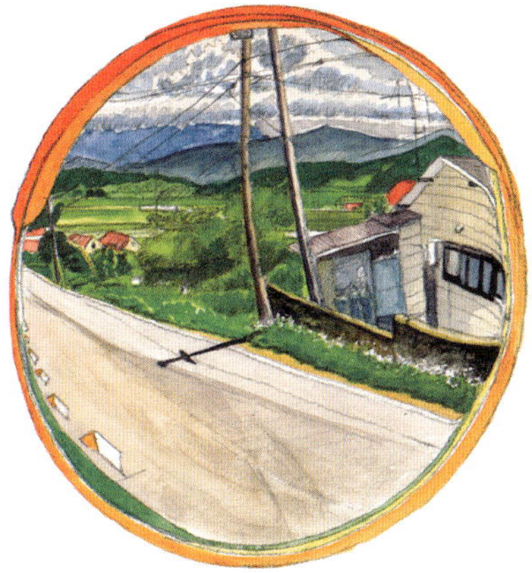

• *Here Alan Johnston presents unpublished illustrations from the diaries he kept during an artist residency in Kijimadaira, Japan.*

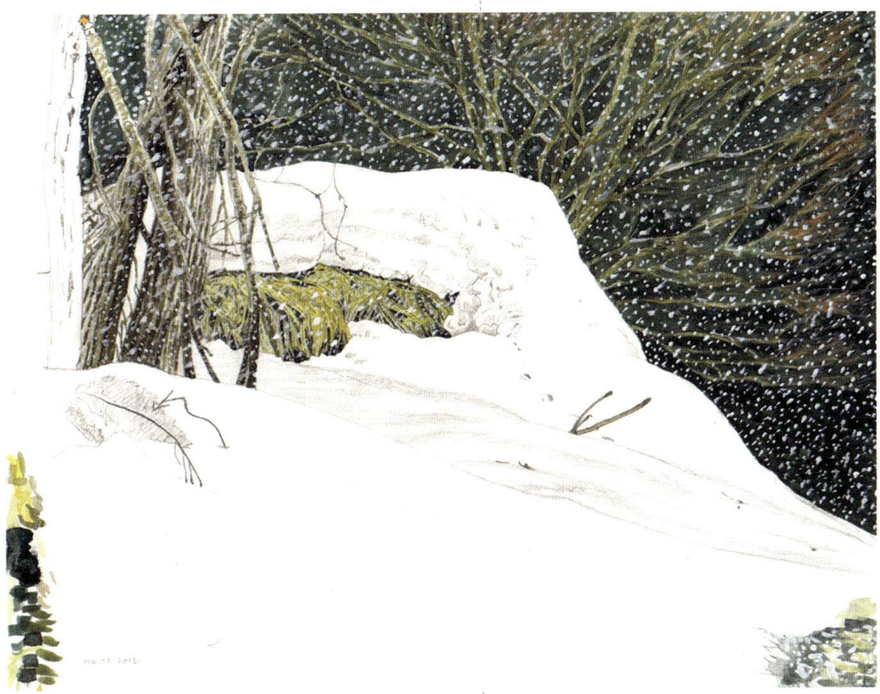

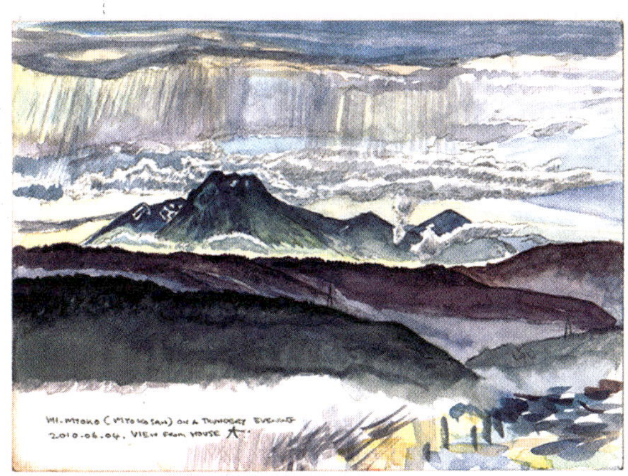

Arnaud d'Aunay

Travelling painters, with their child-like eye, collect, capture and translate all manifestations of reality. They forget the devouring jaws of daily obligations to delve into the intoxicating pleasure of discoveries. They become all conquering—and also conquer themselves. Their materials are sheets, pencils and colours. With so little, they set about decoding the man-made world and finding the invisible. A travel diary is ultimately the result of a rampage fuelled by curiosity, the quirky and the unexpected—a pathway over which collusion with reality and people and echoes from the past reverberate.
In keeping with this spirit, I imagined routes linked to a person (Vauban, génie maritime), *a magical place* (Vézelay, colline d'éternité) *or an era* (Escales d'artistes, de Dieppe à Saint-Valery-en-Caux).
Vauban, génie maritime *(Gallimard, 2007)*
The protector and inventor of France's borders left his mark on the age of Louis XIV. Like my ancestor, I "roamed the coast" to immerse myself in it and especially to find surprising treasures between Dunkirk and Antibes. Walls, fortifications and glacis—nothing was overlooked in safely protecting our "domain." They make up a colossal work that has become sacred.
Vézelay, colline d'éternité *(Gallimard, 2002)*
This key Christian site, which has had a profound impact since the earliest times, has called on curious and wandering painters and historians (for example, Bernard Pujo) who are eager to understand and to decrypt the beauty of this hill. You can truly feel, experience and perceive this place. History has brought together and preserved a unique Unesco-listed site.
Escales d'artistes, de Dieppe à Saint-Valery-en-Caux *(Gallimard, 2004)*
This is a section of Normandy's coast that I surveyed with the historian Solange Louvet. This alabaster border has flashes of magic and a subtle and changing light. Many artists have come here. Its undulating paths, hidden-away villages, secret gardens and hanging valleuses—places that reveal the perfect symbiosis of sky, sea and art—have been captured in writing and painting.

www.arnaud-daunay.com
Other titles
Napoléon, Empereur des îles, Empereur d'exil **(Gallimard, 2006)**
Au fil du Mékong, de Saigon à Angkor **(Gallimard, 2004)**
Les Indes françaises, Pondichéry, Chandernagor, Yanaon, Karikal et Mahé **(Gallimard, 2000)**

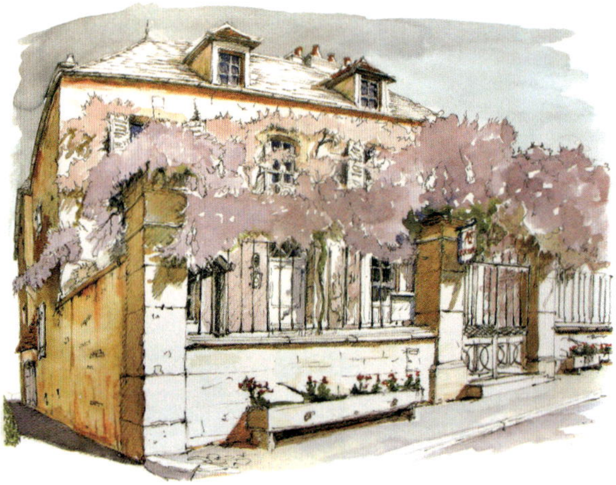

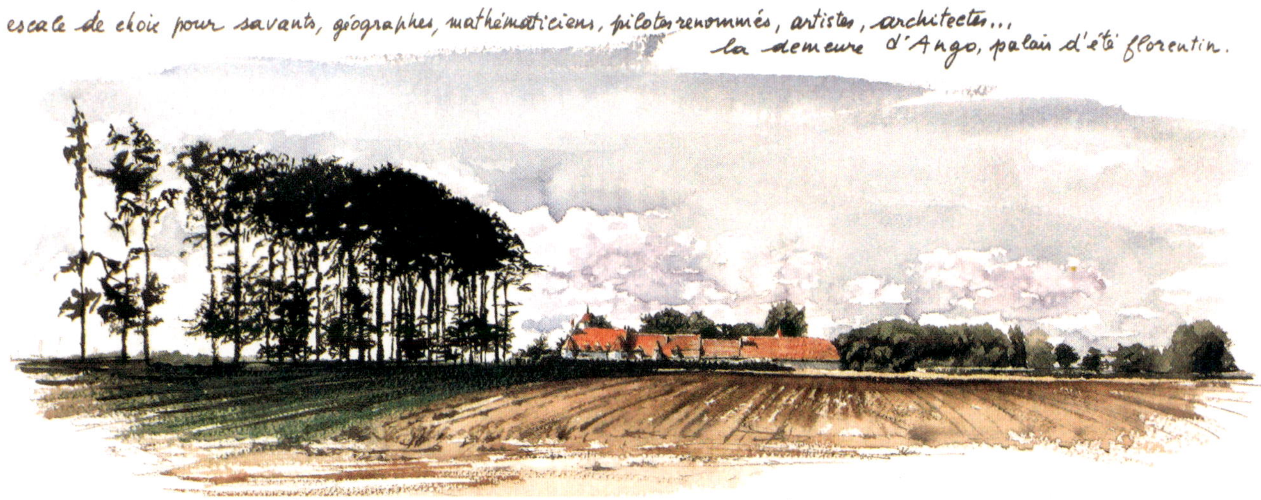

Philippe Delord

I have always loved painting and drawing outdoors. Later on, while travelling in far-off places, I continued this habit. I therefore selected solid diaries that can withstand the vicissitudes of the journey. Through my drawings, bit by bit my diaries begin to look like picture books produced day by day. When I return home, I usually put these books on the shelves of my library or studio. Long after, when the memory of the trip fades to the point where I begin to doubt it happened, the book will be there to tell me that it wasn't a dream. Sometimes, for more ambitious projects, I strive to pursue an idea and put it to the test through my trip. This is what I did in Cyprus and Alexandria, where I tried to find the views of an eighteenth-century illustrator, and I did it after reading Henry de Monfreid's books when I travelled to the countries around Bab el-Mandeb, chasing whispers of adventure. I also did it in Japan, when I went in search of the vestiges of the Tokaido road, "drifting on the river like a gourd" to follow the meandering path of the Floating World. During my first visit to Alexandria, I just saw an Egyptian metropolis that I found somewhat disappointing compared to all of Cairo's Eastern riches. Back in Touraine, I discovered the drawings that Louis-François Cassas made of it in 1785, thirteen years before France's Egyptian campaign. Cassas brought back a portfolio of fifteen drawings to France from his trip to Alexandria. These are the drawings that, two centuries later, guided me during my exploration of the city.

✏ ***Regards croisés sur Chypre dans les pas de Louis-François Cassas*** **and** ***Alexandrie: sur les pas de Louis-François Cassas*** **(Gallimard, 2004 and 2001)**

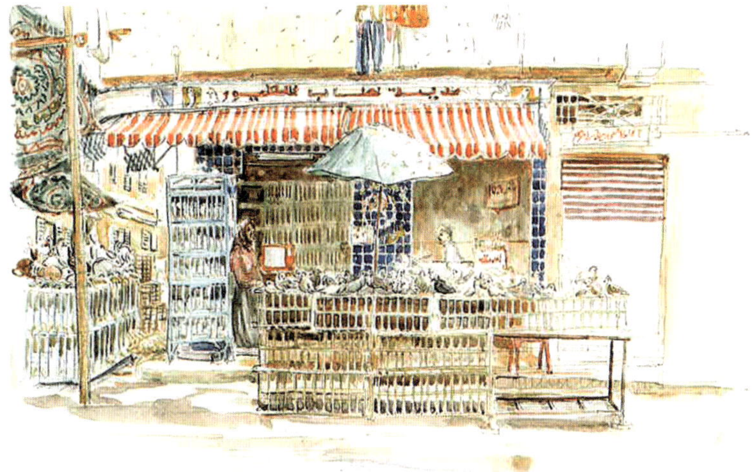

• Alexandrie: sur les pas de Louis-François Cassas *(Gallimard, 2001).*
Outside of archaeology, Philippe Delord sketches small businesses on the streets of Anfushi.

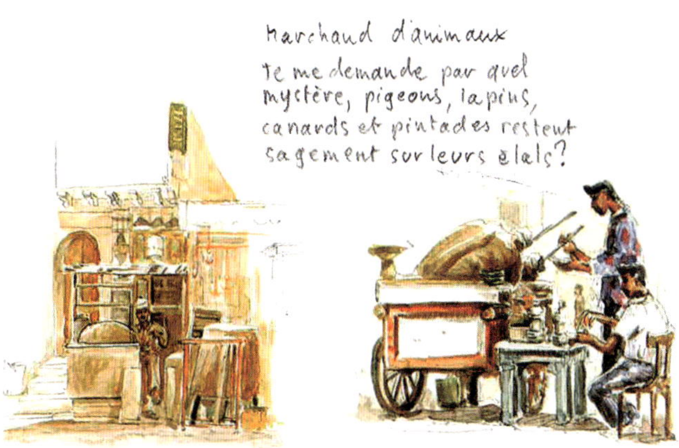

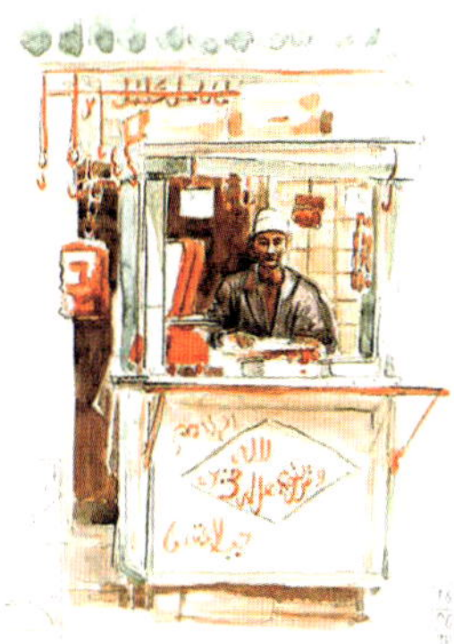

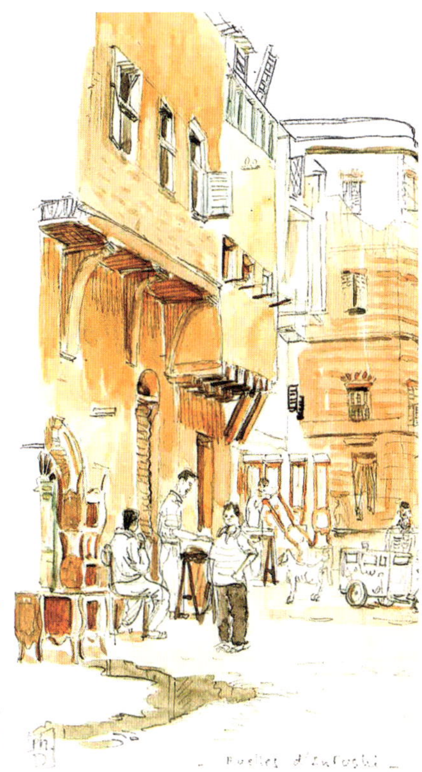

Giancarlo Iliprandi

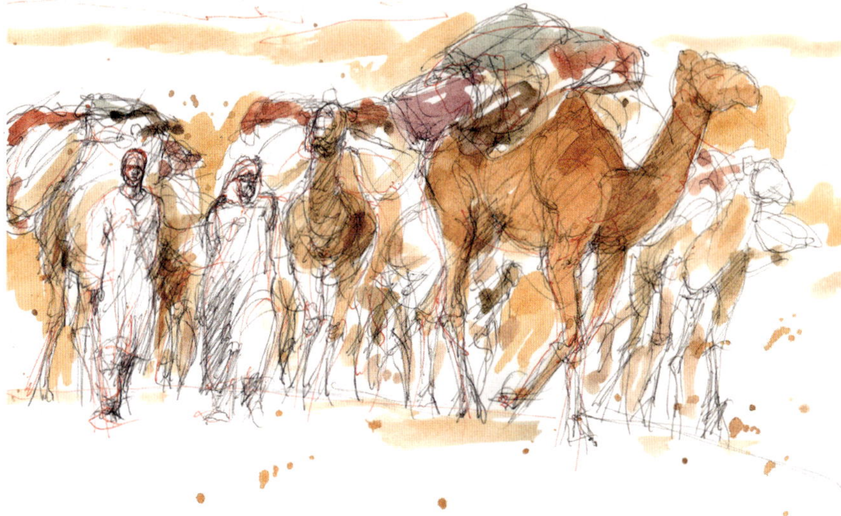

This teacher at the Politecnico di Milano likes to be defined as a "Milanese designer of the old generation" (he was the winner of the grand international prize at the thirteenth Triennale di Milano in 1964, he was president of the International Council of Graphic Design Associations from 1991 to 1993, and he won the ADI's Premio Compasso D'Oro for his career achievements in 2011). He is fascinated by the Sahara, which he first visited twenty years ago and to which he has devoted fourteen books. He has attended the Rendez-vous du carnet de voyage de Clermont-Ferrand since its earliest years, where he exhibits his watercolours of the wind, dune movements, caravans and the Tuareg people.

He captures the moment, the heat haze and bright light of the desert, where all life is precious and rare. In his diaries, which offer encounters with memories from countries that the author has travelled through, colour blends with signs, landscapes, animals and turbans. *Le Tibesti* is a tribute to Sahara's Tibesti Mountains, a now-forbidden desert corner. *Sahara* is a magical encounter with the Azalaï salt caravan at a forgotten oasis in the Ténéré, and then in the Bilma salt mines via the Grand Erg dunes. *Namibie* reveals a desert and the red dunes that run through it, beyond which one imagines a world without tourists, an air of crystal and long, incredibly straight and dangerous roads that traverse the bush. *Madagascar* takes us on a discovery of this large island in the East of Africa locked in a fight for self-preservation, and of its flora and fauna and its markets where the colours of the flowers mingle with the stylishness of its old ladies. *Portofino* evokes memories of a trip in the company of Maupassant's writing.

✏ **www.giancarloiliprandi.net**

Un inevitabile ermafrodita: a proposito del cosiddetto carnet de voyage (Luglio, 2013)
Viaggio in Namibia (Voyage en Namibie, Nuages, 2011)
Nero e bianco. Disegni e acquarelli da Bali (Spazioinmostra, 2009)
Viaggio in Sahara (Voyage au Sahara, Nuages, 2008)
Aria di portofino (Archinto, 2007)
Sahara, trie diari di viaggio (Autocircuito, 2007)
Oman, il paese dei sultani (Polaris, 2001)
Il sapore della foglia d'acero dal Ganata (Graphice Nava, 2001)
Orrizonte perduto – diario dal Tibet (Grafiche Nava, 2000)
New York, inclusive tour (Alberto Maroota Editore, 1978)

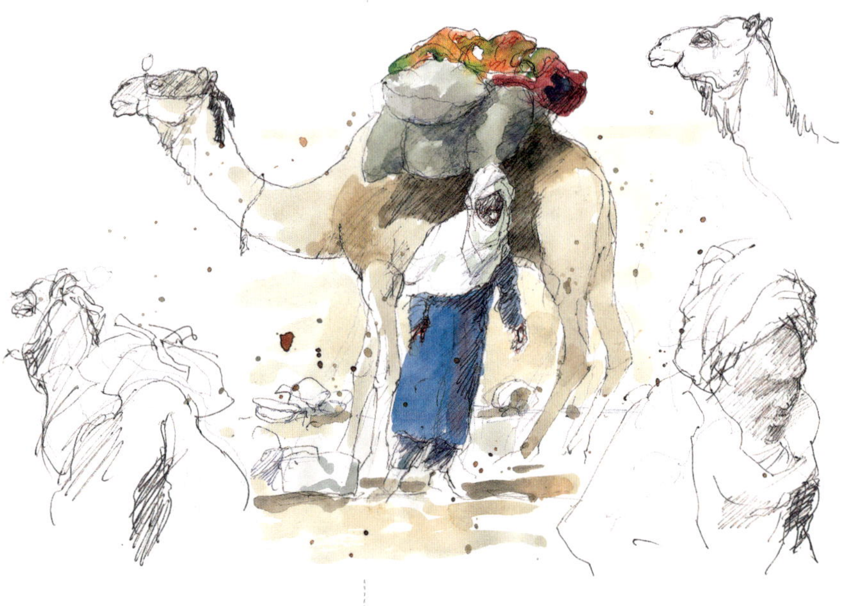

• **Voyage au Sahara,** ***Nuages, 2008.***
In this second book devoted to the Sahara, Giancarlo Iliprandi used watercolour to capture memories of his encounters with people and caravans.

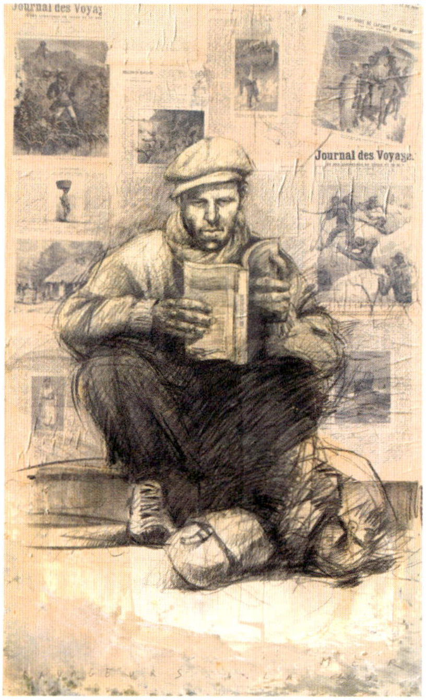

Emmanuel Michel

Emmanuel Michel was born in 1970. After training to be an art restorer, he focused exclusively on painting and sculpture, getting most of his inspiration from his travels across the continents. He has been exhibiting his works in France and abroad for over twenty years. He lives and works in Puybegon, in the Southwest of France. There are several books on his works.

www.emmanuelmichel.com
Cuba New York: peinture, sculpture (Elytis, 2013)
Tibet, Mongolie: grands récits de voyageurs sur les routes interdites (Elytis, 2011)
Mongolie, Tunisie, Tanzanie: peintures sculptures (Éditions EM, 2009)
Un cargo aux Marquises (Éditions EM, 2006)
Emmanuel Michel 1998–2005: peintures et sculptures (Éditions EM, 2005)
Guatemala, terre Maya: de l'Altiplano à la côte caraïbe (Gallimard, 2004)
Guyane: les îles du Salut (Gallimard, 2002)
Emmanuel Michel: peintures sculptures (Ramsay, 1998)

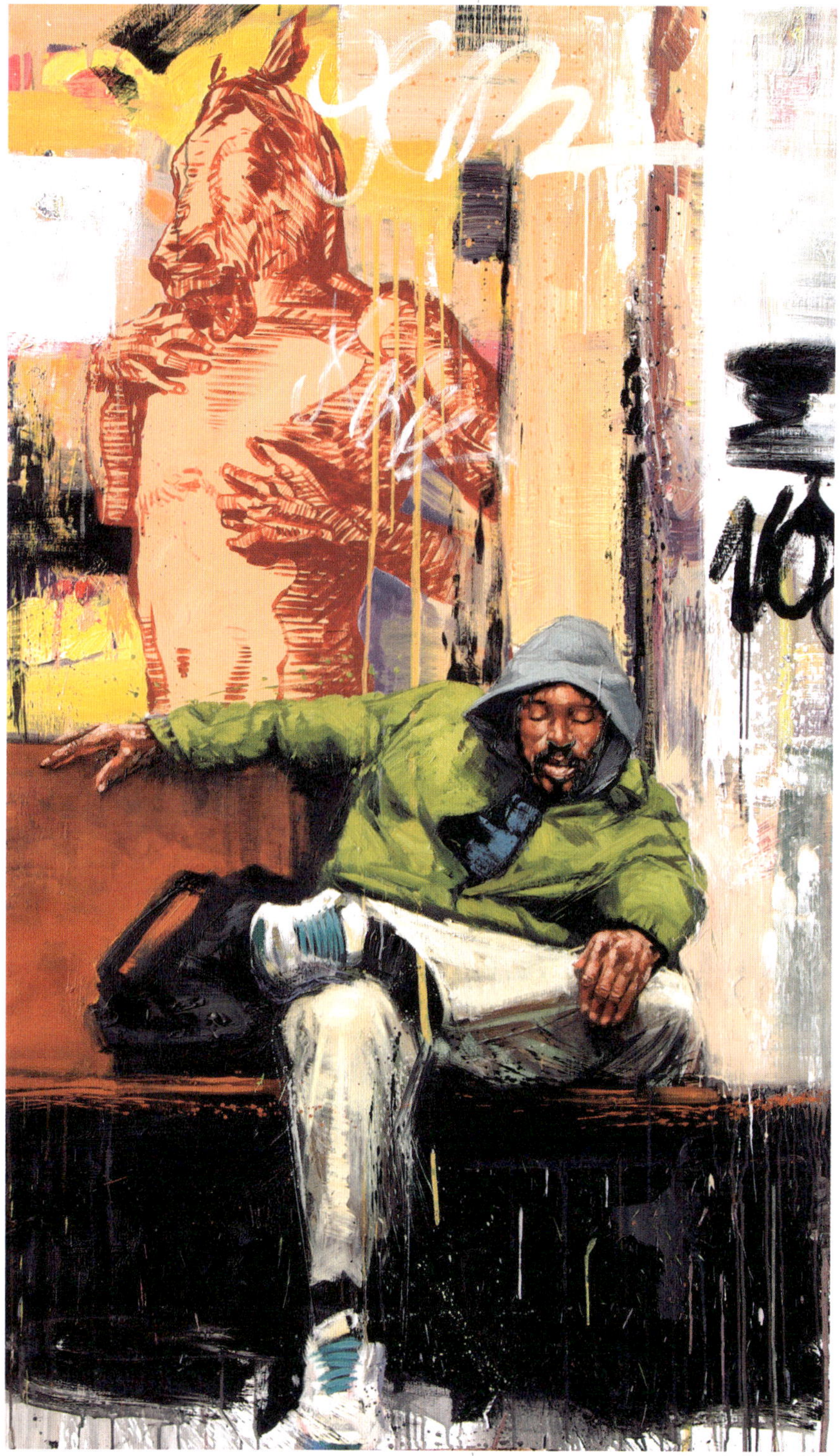

• *"Le ravageur des mers" (above, left) and "Soho"* (Cuba New York, *Elytis, 2013). Emmanuel Michel combines traditional techniques (ink, pencil, oil, acrylic) and collage in his pictorial works.*

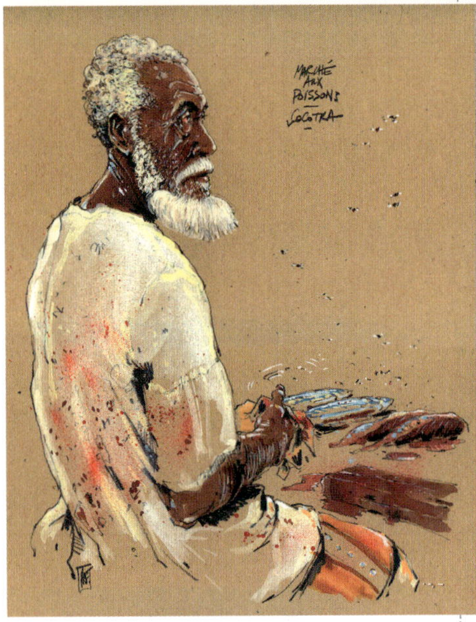

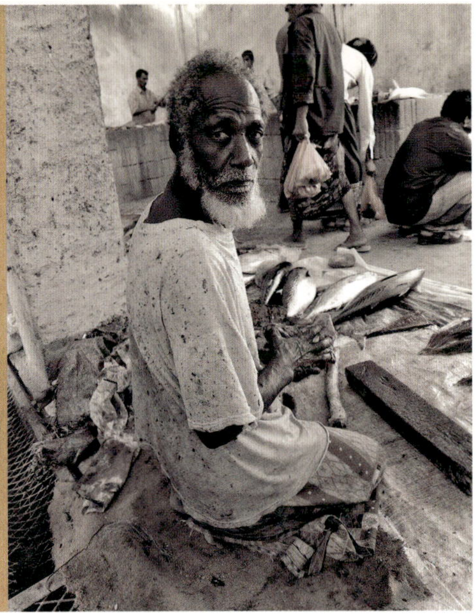

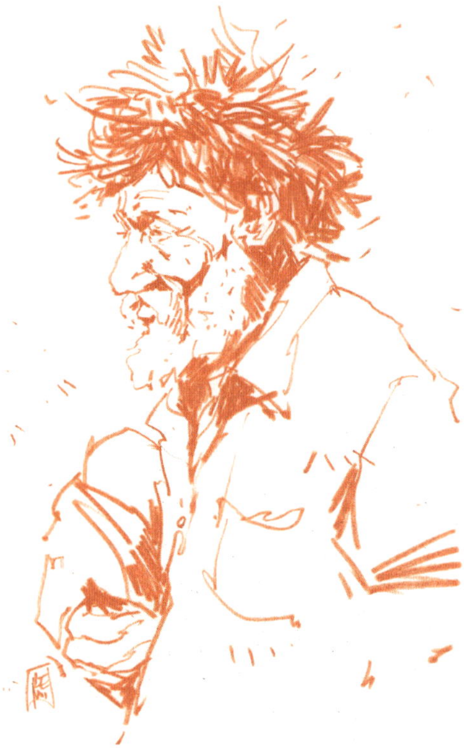

• Journal de la mer d'Arabie, *Éditions de La Martinière, 2012. Above, top, portrait in pencil and watercolour and a photo of a Hadibo fisherman (Socotra, Yemen); below, sanguine portrait of an elderly man in Gujarat (India).*

Claire and Reno Marca

Reno Marca is a passionate illustrator and has been drawing since he was at an age to be filling up exercise books with sketches, a passion that he then complemented with photography. Although he likes to work with the essential traditional tools (pencil, watercolour, inks), he is also enthusiastic about more contemporary ones (graphics tools, video and Photoshop) that allow him to mix genres and seek other forms of graphical expressions to push the sometimes compartmentalized boundaries of the travel diary. Reno does drawing both in the field and in the studio—the quality of artists' strokes and their sincerity are the most important things for him. His pictures revolve around the indispensable presence of the texts written by his partner Claire. Their work is primarily a couple's adventure. Illustrated stories, travel diaries, graphic reportage or cartoons—their work is probably a little of everything at once.

3 ans de voyage, their first book, which was released in 2005 and won many awards, recounts their travels from Africa to the Pacific. It's an illustrated narrative that mixes text, photos and drawings and that breaks with the traditional schema of the travel diary. Spurred on by this success, they then made *Madagascar, 3 mois de voyage sur l'île Rouge* (Grand Prix Michelin, 2008), and then *Algérie, Soyez les bienvenus!* (2009).
Their latest book, the double award winning *Journal de la mer d'Arabie* (Éditions de La Martinière, 2012), was accompanied by a documentary. Having set off to the island of Socotra (Yemen) with a camera, Claire and Reno by chance discovered the dhows, enormous wooden boats that carry trade across the Arabian Sea. Struck by these extraordinary vessels, over six months they traced them back to India, where they are built. Like their books, the 52-minute film combines drawings, photos and video in a unique graphic style and offers a personal and original take on the travelogue.

www.reno-marca.com
Journal de la mer d'Arabie
(Éditions de La Martinière, 2012)
Algérie, soyez les bienvenus!: voyage de la Méditerranée au Sahara **(Éditions de La Martinière, 2009)**
Madagascar: 3 mois de voyage sur l'île Rouge
(Éditions de La Martinière, 2008)
3 ans de voyage: 25 pays par voie terrestre, en histoires et en images **(Éditions de La Martinière, 2005)**

Titouan Lamazou

*I am a "travelling artist." But I've only published one "travel diary," a collection entitled as such for the sake of convenience (*Carnets de voyage*, 1998). It was a real best seller, and it contributed to a frenzy of publications of this sort. My approach to art is shaped by the itinerant nature of my work. It is the chance result of the major encounters over the course of my journeying, which soon became tied to nautical adventure.*

During the year when I was sixteen, the painter Yvon Le Corre was my drawing teacher, and I his most diligent student. That year ended with the departure of this master aboard his cutter and gave rise to the publication of Heureux qui comme Iris *(1978), the first travel diary by Yvon and his then companion, Karin Huet.*

I dreamt of setting out to travel myself. In the footsteps of Saint-Exupéry, London, Conrad, Kessel or Slocum, I saw myself as becoming an artist and traveller. I hitched on boats to the Caribbean, where I made a living from drawing portraits on the terraces of cafés. I also offered my services as a deckhand or ship's boy. And, at one port or another, I soon found myself taken on by Éric Tabarly, my second master. Twenty years of sailing then followed. When I won the solo round-the-world race in 1990, Éric threw a party in my honour and sat me to his right. I had become a sailor; I had gained my legitimacy as a traveller. I then picked up my diaries and my gouaches and the things I had been doing twenty years earlier.

The diaries from when I was sixteen contained the seeds for a more complex method of expression. My eye became more refined, and my art became more engaged. My artistic practice evolved. In the early 2000s, photography took an important place in my approach, particularly with the creation of photo-paintings that required more sophisticated digital technology. My travels are increasingly extended through working in the studio, where I continue to explore new production methods without seeking to follow trends. My work has long been labelled and assigned to the sphere of "travel diary." Yet my books—like those of Delacroix from Morocco, which paved the way for a series of studio works—could more rightly be called "travel notebooks."

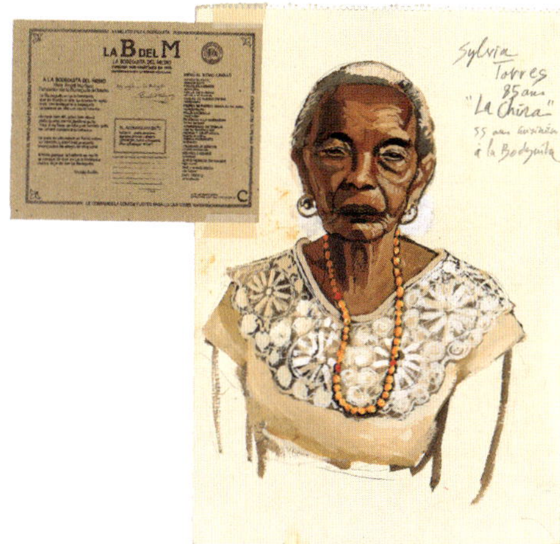

www.titouanlamazou.com

Onze lunes au Maroc (Gallimard, 2012)
Voyage aux pays du rhum (Le Cherche Midi, 2011)
Ténèbres au Paradis (Gallimard, 2011)
Afghanes (Gallimard, 2009)
Zoé Zoé femmes du monde (Gallimard, 2007)
Carnets de voyage (Gallimard, 1998)

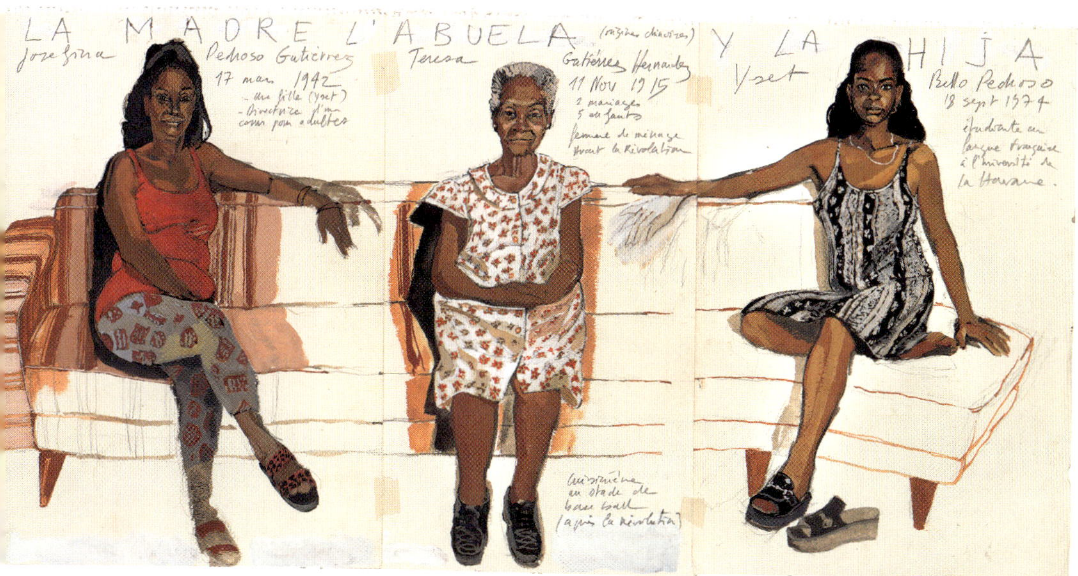

• Carnets de voyage, *Gallimard, 1998. During his stay in Havana in May 1997, Titouan Lamazou met 3 generations of Cuban women within the same family: Josefina, Teresa and Yset (opposite). He also brought back this portrait of "La China," a cook at la Bodeguita del Medio, which, it is said, is where Hemingway went for mojitos (above).*

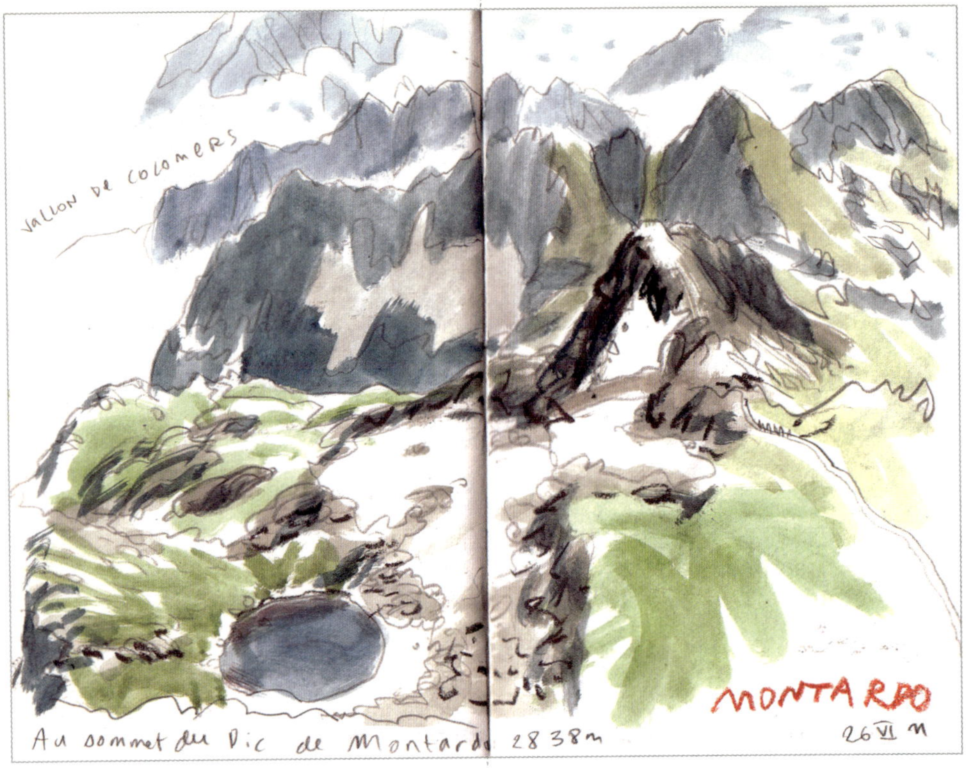

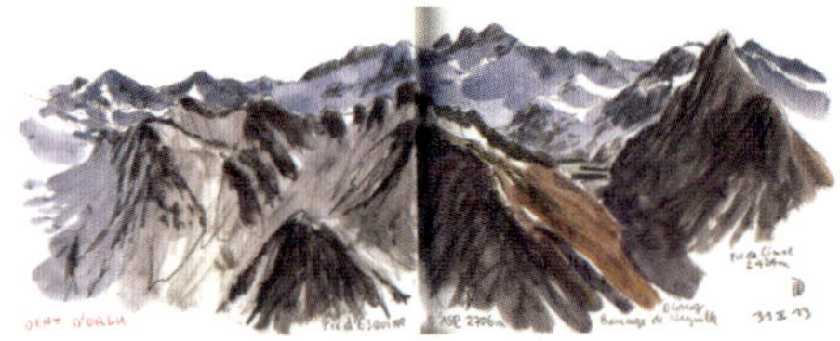

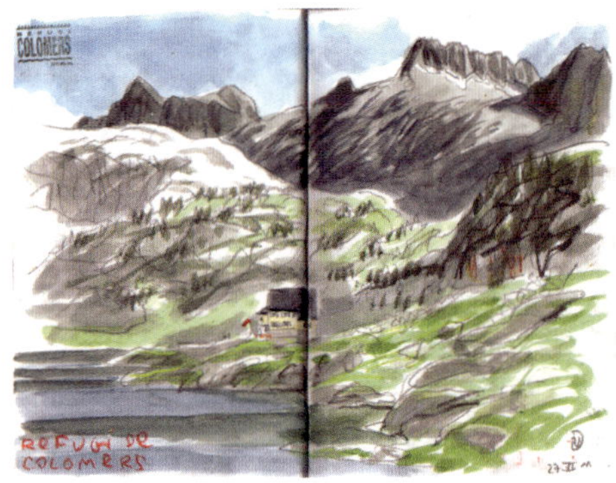

• *"Partage des Eaux." This travel diary project made high up in the sky on crests of the Pyrenees is about one thing: water.*
(Above) At the top of the peak of Montardo, the view plunges down onto a small and round lake, and then onto the val d'Aran (Atlantic slope).
(Opposite, top) The dent d'Orlu is a great lookout point over the watershed between Haute-Ariège and Donnezan (Atlantic slope).
(Opposite, below) the étang majeur collects the waters of the many lakes in the Colomers cirque (Atlantic slope).

Vincent Desplanche

The travel diary is part of my daily life. I take them wherever I go, putting my take on the world that surrounds me in them. The sketch is the gymnastics of the documentary illustrator, but it is also about exploring new spaces of graphic freedom.

Vincent Desplanche started filling in travel diaries during his years at the École supérieure des arts décoratifs de Strasbourg, and ended up making it the topic of his final-year project. He took his first steps in publishing by putting out a book after he graduated. He then had a crucial meeting with Gallimard, and he began drawing the most stunning heritage sites to illustrate guides or to produce watercolour collections—a real plum job!

In addition to this fieldwork, he is also an illustrator of children's documentary books. He particularly enjoys addressing a new topic in each book. Observational drawing occupies a central place in a craft that requires permanent self-documentation and maintaining one's sense of observation. Today he continues to sketch within the Boraldes collective that he founded with his colleagues from Gallimard and leads travel diary workshops for the Randocroquis organization.
He is also France's correspondent for the international movement Urban sketchers.

Le Parc de la Tête-d'Or **(Gallimard, 2007)**
Voyages dans le Tarn **(Éditions De Borée, 2007)**
Au fil du Lot/Along the Lot River **(Gallimard, 2002)**
Les Calanques de Marseille à Cassis **(Gallimard, 1999)**
Québec, barrages au Grand Nord **(Albin Michel Jeunesse, 1994)**

Urban sketchers

Urban Sketchers (Usk) is a nonprofit organization created in 2009 by Gabriel Campanario in Seattle. It promotes the practice and the artistic, narrative and educational value of "on-location drawing," and it creates links between sketchers worldwide, whether they draw where they live or during their travels. Since its founding, the Urban Sketchers movement has spread around the world.

Here's its manifesto:

1. We draw on location, indoors or out, capturing what we see from direct observation.

2. Our drawings tell the story of our surroundings, the places we live and where we travel.

3. Our drawings are a record of time and place.

4. We are truthful to the scenes we witness.

5. We use any kind of media and cherish our individual styles.

6. We support each other and draw together.

7. We share our drawings online.

8. We show the world, one drawing at a time.

Urban sketchers regularly offers different events. The international Usk symposium, a major event held annually in a different country, offers participants the opportunity to follow three days of intense workshops led by experienced instructors from the four corners of the globe. At the annual Usk French gathering, sketchers from France (and elsewhere) meet in a different city over the course of a weekend. They get to know one another, exchange ideas and draw together. And then there is the SketchCrawl, a quarterly event that brings together urban sketchers for a marathon drawing session that takes place on the same day across the planet.

✏ www.flickr.com/groups/urbansketchersfrance
http://france.urbansketchers.org
http://paris.urbansketchers.org
www.sketchcrawl.com/forum
J. Hobbs, *Le Croquis urbain : techniques de dessin sur le vif* (Eyrolles, 2014)
G. Campanario, *Carnets de voyage, l'art du croquis urbain* (Eyrolles, 2013)

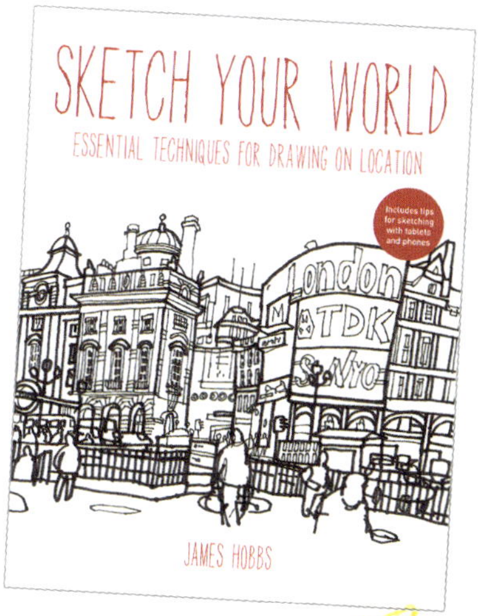

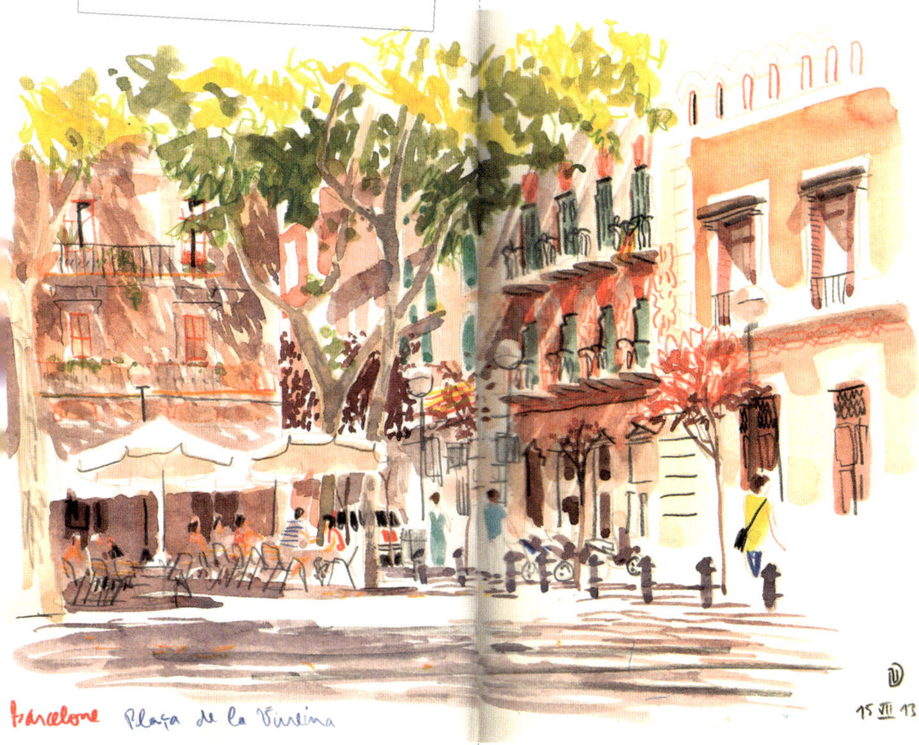

• Carnets de voyage – l'art du croquis urbain, *Eyrolles, 2013. With a presence in more than 50 cities (opposite, Barcelona) around the world, the Urban sketchers are reviving the concept of in situ painting that was so dear to the impressionists.*

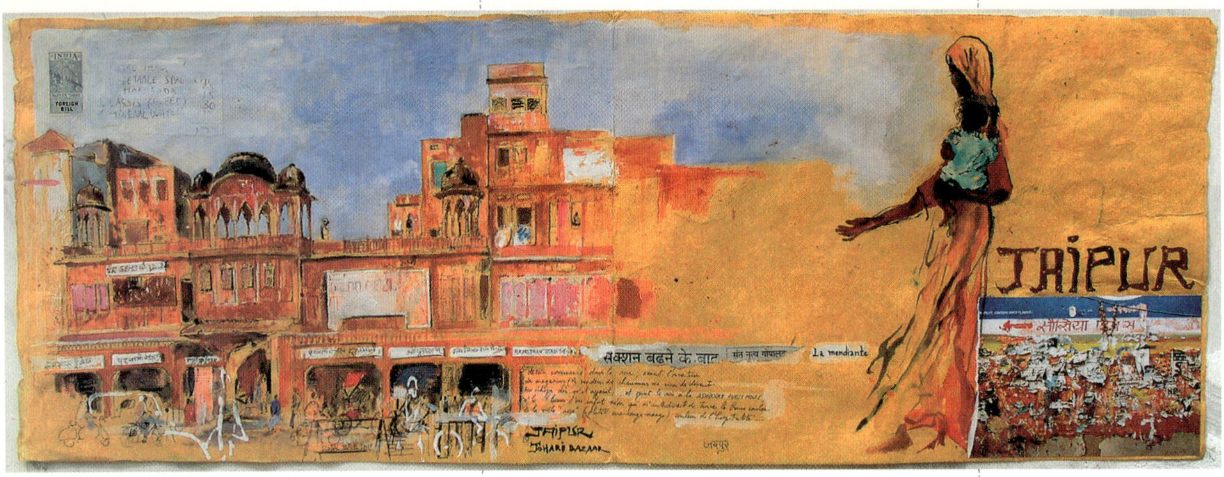

• Dans les mains du soleil, *Alternatives, 2007. According to Simon, this romantic travel diary on Rajasthan is an ode to "India's violent poetry."*

Simon

*I've been dipping into the inkwell since I was a child, and my appetite for travelling did the rest. Wherever the wind leads me, I draw and I write. My first travel diaries date from my twelve years in Algeria. Over time, my trips are transformed into books, where the writing and painting go hand in hand. First there was Europe—England, Italy, France and a long stop in Portugal (*L'Appel du bleu*). Then there was the charm of the desert (*Saharas, Marche avec moi*). Discovering India changed my way of writing, drawing and quite possibly living (*Au corps de l'Inde, Dans les mains du soleil*) ; I picked up the rhythm of the East. It was natural that one day the winds of chance would take me to China, where poetry, painting and calligraphy have never been separate things.*

The travel diary is the freest, most sensual and most open tool that I know of for retelling and for expressing a sense of enthralment with the world. I call them "muddy-boot-wearing travel comments books."

Dans les mains du soleil *is a travel diary ode to Rajasthan. Its ode twofold: it is a love song to India on the one hand, and a love song to beloved woman on the other. I support an idea of the travel diary that is at once poetic, political and erotic—the antithesis of the exotic postcard. The arts of travel and love mix their colours in Nepalese-paper large-format double pages; these interact with the single-sentence texts, which I call my "banyan sentences." In this diary, I explored the richness of collage, using waste paper picked up off the ground, torn cinema posters, cotton, jute and silk as well as all the things accumulated through travelling: stamps, maps, photos, tickets, newspapers, herbs, cigarettes, feathers and camel manure, and some others that I've forgotten. And I revisited them through painting, mixing lots of techniques—ink, gouache, watercolour—in the spirit of India's unique hybridity.*

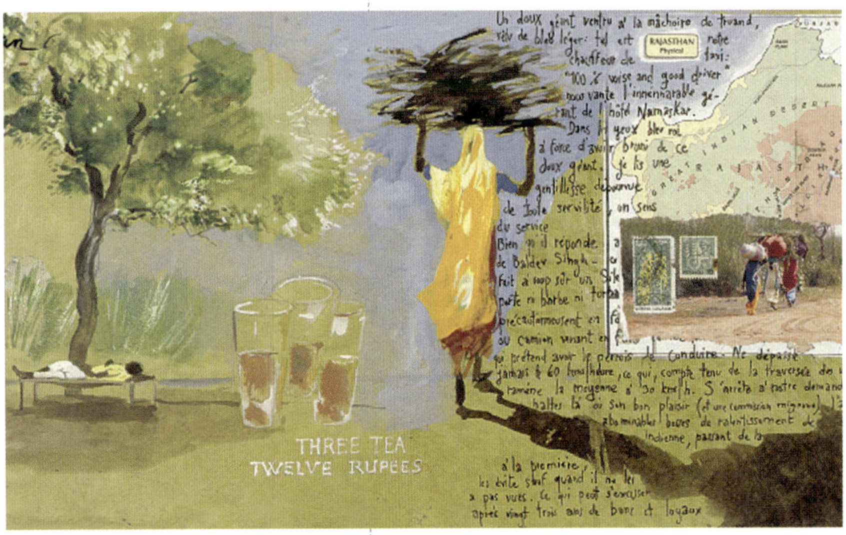

✏ www.simon-artiste-peintre.com

Other titles

Sahara, marche avec moi (Alternatives, 2009)
Carnets de voyage en Chine (Boussole/Libris, 2004)
Saharas, carnets de voyage (Boussole, 2001)
L'Appel du bleu, voyage au Portugal (Boussole, 2000)
Au corps de l'Inde, carnets de voyage (Boussole, 1999)

Les carnettistes tribulants

It's been nearly twelve years since the collective Les Carnettistes tribulants was born. We all had a passion for travel diaries as vehicles for expression and as a testimony to the complexity of this world. We converged around the idea that travel can be done collectively and at home, by taking a fresh look at society and its landscapes, cities and problems.
First we turned our attention to the suburbs of Paris. This disparaged, anarchic, mixed, abandoned or overexploited, poetic or frightening territory became an ideal testing ground for our collective. Éditions Alternatives published Banlieue Nomade *(2006), which came along at the very time where the suburbs were stirring. It offered a different take—an artistic and calm one that didn't talk about cleaning up the streets or burning cars.*
Then Ce que j'aime en toi (Alternatives, 2007) *came out, combining poetry, tenderness, sincerity and eroticism. From 2009, we spent two years in search of individuals who fitted the description of "elderly people." It was a period spent gaining acceptance for the idea of portraits, old age and passion across the ages.* Vivre vieux *was published by Éditions Alternatives, with a foreword by Roger Dadoun.*
And in 2010, we went to China! Ten of us agreed to a one-month trip that was organized by Huang Li and funded by two businessmen and a Chinese painter. During the visit we were given complete freedom and were immersed in the country. In Gratte-ciel & soupe de nouilles, *each author offers a personal journey, his or her own vision of the changing world that we observed in China.*
Finally, as a result of previous projects, we were fortunate to be contacted by CIVAM-PACA, and we then travelled through France to meet women committed to farming. The publisher La Boîte à bulles put out Paysannes, *which has a preface by Coline Serreau.*
They also published Bringuebalés, *an artistic exploration of objects from the donations gallery of the Musée de l'histoire de l'immigration.*
Over twelve years, the collective has published six books, and volunteered many hours for designing, creating, leading and supporting exciting workshops on travel diaries and illustrated reportage. And we have set collective and individual standards for the association.

http://tribulants.canalblog.com/
Bringuebalés (La Boîte à bulles, 2014)
Paysannes (La Boîte à bulles, 2013)
Gratte-ciel & soupe de nouilles (Carnettistes tribulants, 2011)
Vivre vieux! (Alternatives, 2009)
Ce que j'aime en toi (Alternatives, 2007)
Banlieues nomades (Alternatives, 2006)

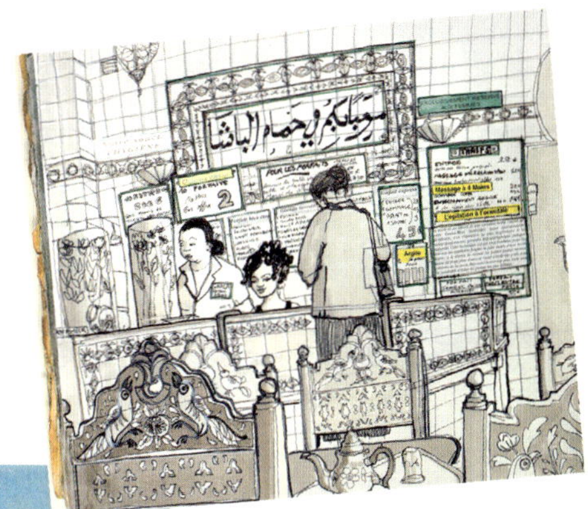

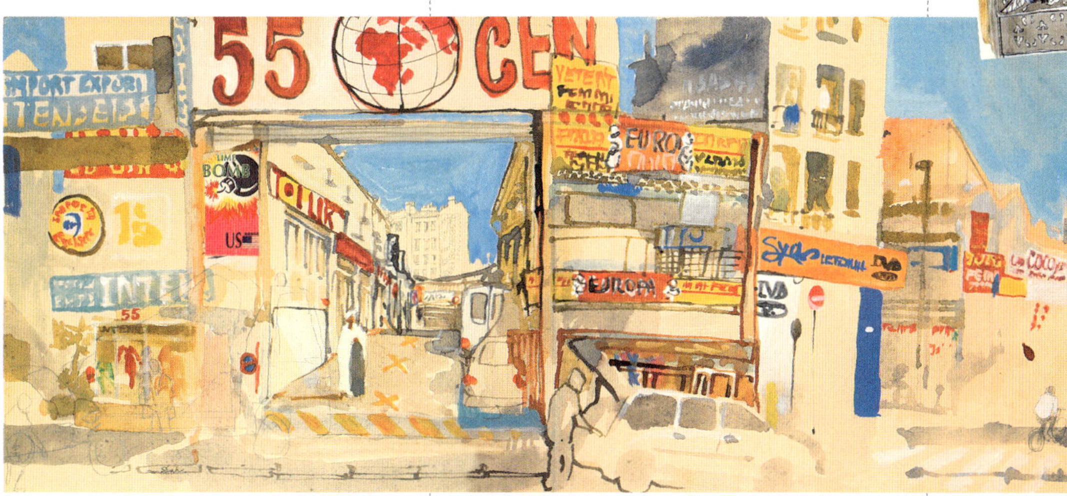

• Banlieues nomades, *Alternatives, 2006. In this diary, Les Carnettistes tribulants offer a vision of the Parisian suburbs that is at odds with media representations.*

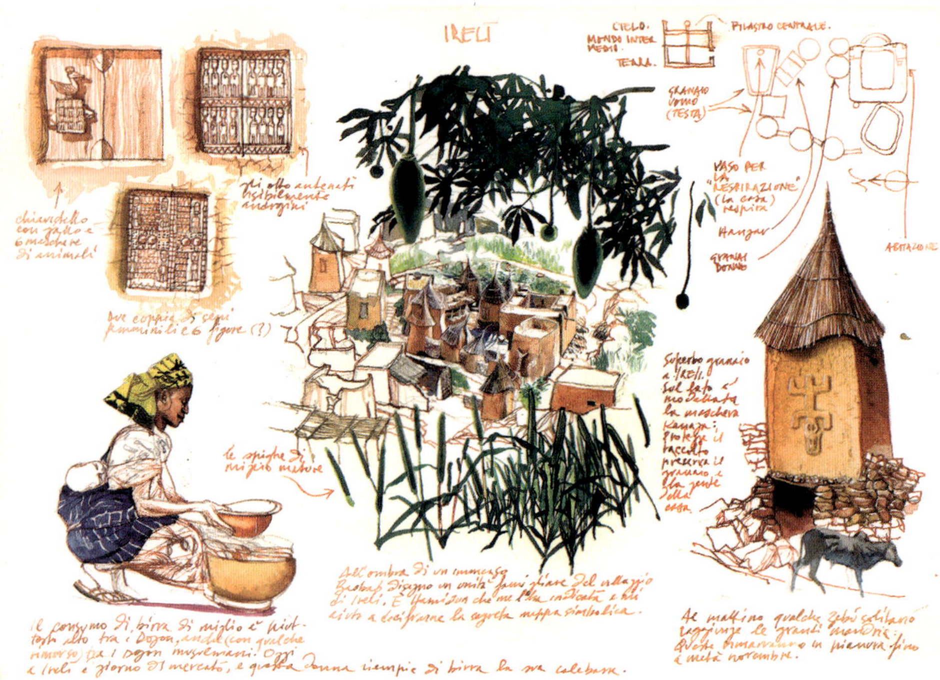

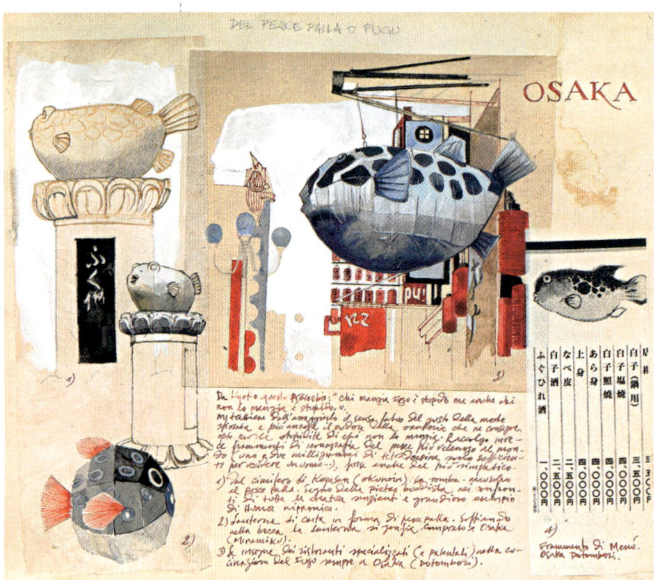

• Mali secret, *Gallimard, 2005 (above) and a take on Osaka (opposite). The engravings of the works of nineteenth-century explorers are what made Stefano Faravelli become an artist.*

Stefano Faravelli

Stefano Faravelli was born on 10 April 1959 in Turin, where he perfected his training as a painter at the Liceo artistico and at the Accademia di belle arti. In tandem with this, he also completed degrees in philosophy and oriental studies. This dual role, combined with his passion for naturalistic illustration, turned him towards the art of the travel diary.

In 1994, he published *Sindh*, a collection of watercolours made in 1989 during a long trip to India that took him to, among other places, the Ranthambore National Park and the Maha Kumbh Mela of Allahabad. He then produced travel diaries in bigger numbers, including ones on North Africa, Turkey, Saudi Arabia, China and Tibet. In the autumn of 2004, he went to Mali, where he made a new book, which won first prize from the public at the Festival du carnet de voyage de Clermont-Ferrand and was then published in France and Italy (*Mali secret*, Gallimard, 2005). Diaries on China, India and Egypt then followed. In 2010, he published *Giappone, taccuini dal mondo fluttuante* with De Agostini. His works have been exhibited in collections and galleries in Italy and abroad. In 2011, he participated in the Venice biennale. His travel diaries have been presented, among other places, in Rome, London, New York, Paris, Istanbul and Jerusalem. He is visiting professor at the Scuola del viaggio and the Scuola Holden in Turin. He is in charge of the travel diary school, in collaboration with the Scuola del viaggio. He also teaches at the European Design Institute (IED). He contributed to the Swiss Italian magazine *Azione*. His latest work is a book made in the Betampona rainforest in Madagascar.

www.stefanofaravelli.it
Carnets des Villes – Tokyo, Delhi, Le Caire, Istanbul, Djenné (Confluencias Editoriales, 2011)
Egitto, cercando l'Aleph (EDT, 2008)
India, per vedere l'elefante (EDT, 2007)
Cina, carnet di viaggio (EDT, 2006)

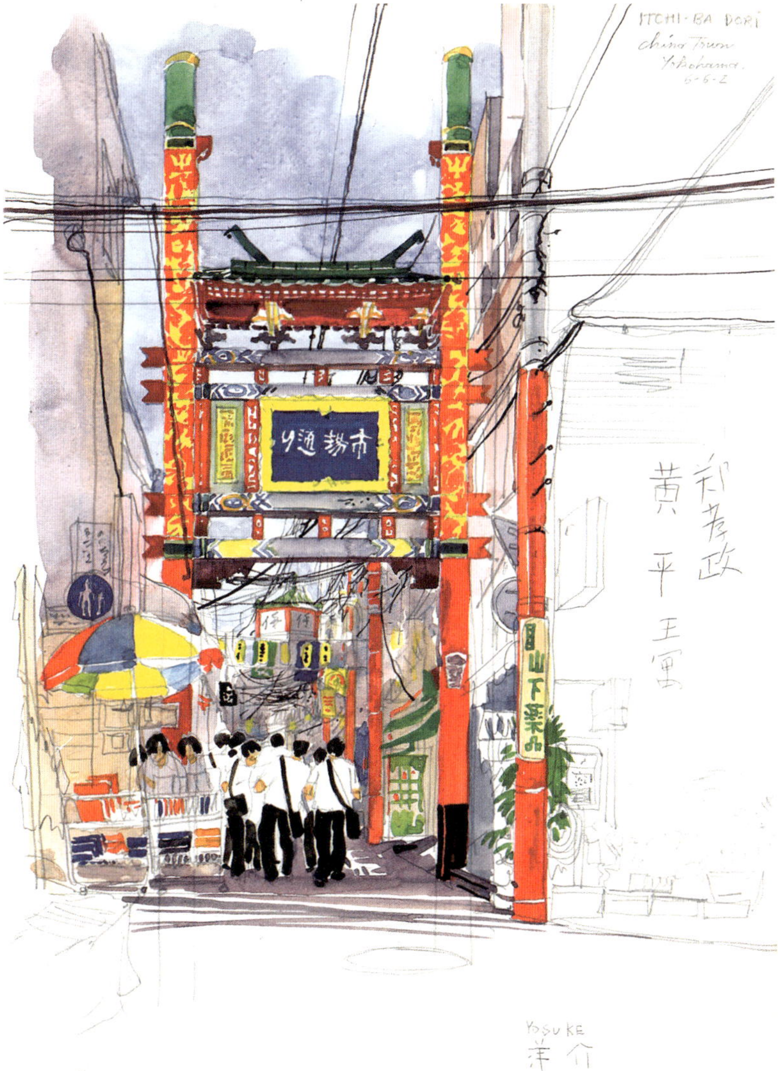

Fabrice Moireau

I've always drawn a lot and very specifically, with a single line and often in great detail. That's just how I do things. I let things go as they come without being able to intervene too much. Studying at the École nationale supérieure des arts appliqués et des métiers d'art in Paris opened up my career to exhibition scenography. In 1987, bound for Czechoslovakia, I threw a brush and some watercolour tubes given to me by a friend in my backpack, without even taking paper. I got some when I was there: A4 school pads... Since then my travel diaries with their practical spiral have come one after another. I began publishing in 1992, and since then I've published at least one work per year.
The myriad attractions of the travel diary, its tics and its many particularities, must not hide what for me is its most essential thing: the rigour of the drawing, whether in its accuracy or expressiveness, the interest of the composition, the feeling of the atmosphere of a place at a given time and the light. Ultimately I feel like a photographer with an impressionist's eye. Although for some people the travel diary is a protean work, for me it is simply a block of sheets on which I transcribe a place with as much subtlety as possible. 4,500 watercolours later I have come to understand why I drew so realistically all the things I saw. It was so I could get the world into my head, appropriate it and keep it warm. Or perhaps it was to dream of it? Or maybe because sometimes it is more beautiful when it is drawn?

Notebook Paris (Éditions du Pacifique, 2012)
Rome : aquarelles (Éditions du Pacifique, 2011)
Les Toits de Paris (Éditions du Pacifique, 2010)
Les Jardins du musée du quai Branly (Gallimard, 2009)
Provence aquarelles (Éditions du Pacifique, 2008)
Jardins de Paris : aquarelles (Éditions du Pacifique, 2006)
Le Jardin de Claude Monet à Giverny (Gallimard, 2006)
New York : aquarelles (Éditions du Pacifique, 2005)
Notre-Dame d'Orsan (Gallimard, 2005)
Venise aquarelles (Éditions du Pacifique, 2004)
Vallée de la Loire : aquarelles (Éditions du Pacifique, 2003)
Paris aquarelles (Éditions du Pacifique, 2001)
L'Île de Tatihou (Gallimard, 1997)

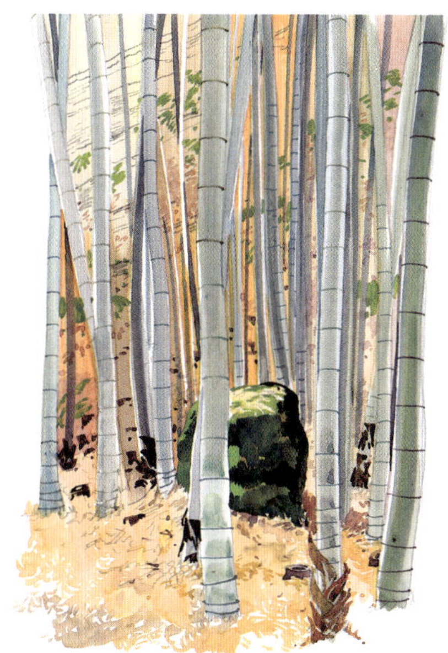

• Passionate about architectural heritage and gardens, as well water and light, Fabrice Moireau was always going to be seduced by Japan!

Lizzie Napoli

Diaries are for not forgetting anything as time goes by, ideas before they take flight, to-do lists, and so on. For me, above all they're for being sure that things exist. For a period of my childhood I totally lost my sight, and I promised myself that if I got better I would draw my room's window and the tree outside it. Later, when I returned to school, most of all I drew, and then I drew even more during the war: I began to illustrate articles in the newspapers of the time and advertising for film studios, where you could rub shoulders with people like Charles Dullin and Jean Cocteau. But, at the end of the war, I went away. I wanted to see—see it all. I went on my first big trip in 1945 alone, all the way to Ukraine without flying. I drew everything in letters to my mother. I talk about these adventures in my next book. One day, in the window of a book store in Paris, I found a blank book. Only its cover had print on it. It was my first travel diary. Now I have 83! I've drawn all my reportage and all my books in them. All my published drawings are taken directly from these diaries. I never use pencil, let alone a rubber; your first stroke is the one that captures your first look, without thinking. Over all these years, I've done a big range of jobs. I've done big factory- and machine-produced pieces, illustrations for three encyclopaedias and children's illustration, and I've worked for Pomme d'Api *for a long time. My first hand-written and illustrated reportage work, which was made like a travel diary, was published in 1965 for the magazine* Partir. *I then worked for about 20 other newspapers, did travel works, made reportage and artwork, and had 40 of my books published. Over all these years, I continued to travel. There are mornings when you wake up with this crazy need to go elsewhere—to take an unknown path, enter a village still full of mystery, leave your name behind, and see what's on the other side of the hill. And even nearby, wherever you are in the world, you can find an image for a painting and the emotion of a landscape. You have to look at everything. Seeing is a gift in itself—just look at Venice, for example (Venise, Équinoxe, 1998).*

✏ http://lizzienapoli.fr

Si j'avais un jardin en Provence (Équinoxe, 2011)
Escapades en France (Équinoxe, 2005)
L'Auvergne et le Massif central (Équinoxe, 2001)
Carnets d'ailleurs de Lizzie Napoli and *En Bretagne avec Lizzie Napoli* (Équinoxe, 2000)
Venise (Équinoxe, 1998)
Ma Provence (Équinoxe, 1997)
Scaloin Corsica and *Escale en Corse: carnet de voyage* (Édisud, 1994)
Provence, carnet de voyage (Édisud, 1993)
Carnets de voyage en Provence (Rivages, 1987)

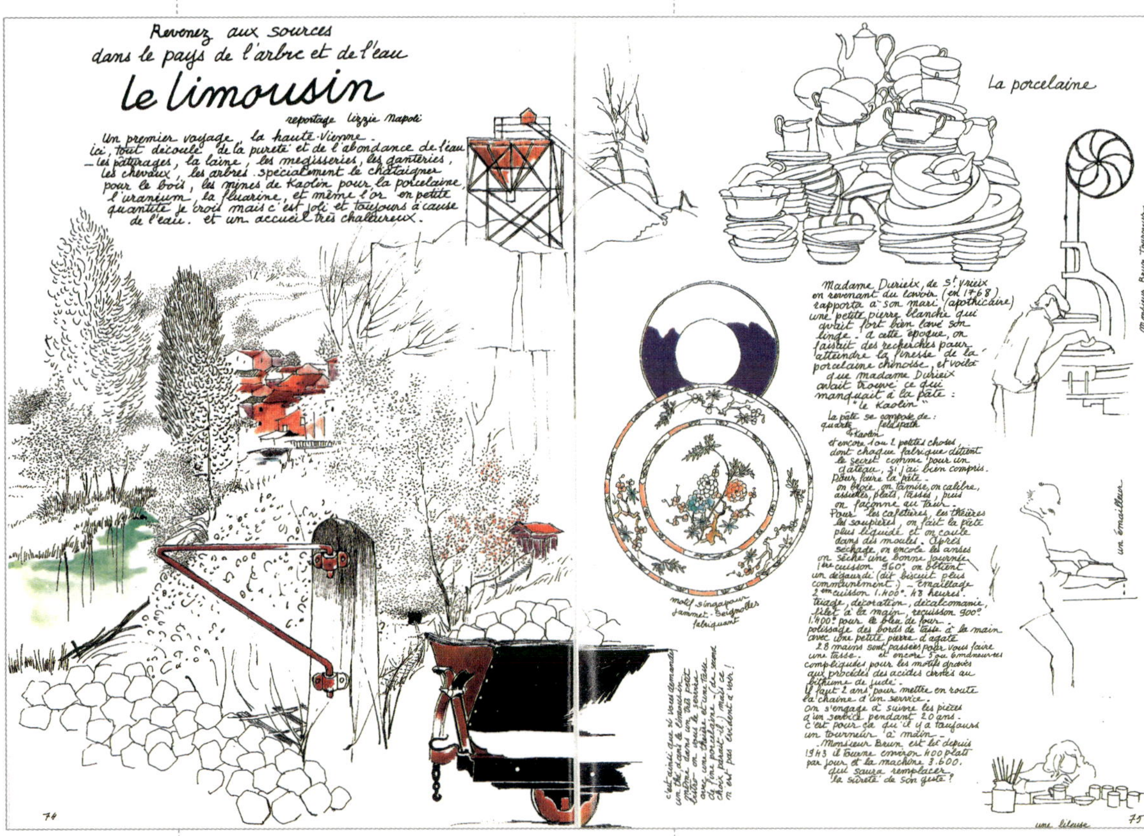

• L'Auvergne et le Massif central, *Équinoxe, 2001. Faithful to her technique (ink and watercolour), Lizzie Napoli reveals to the reader the heritage of Cantal, Creuse, Limousin and Aveyron.*

Damien Roudeau

As an author and illustrator, all my illustrated reportage works are the result of prolonged immersions of several months or years, often within social groups that are apparently self-contained and require an introduction (for example, electronic tribes, Emmaüs communities and groups such as the homeless, squatters and prostitutes). It can seem that this medium of drawing—subjective and therefore necessarily imperfect—is capable of preserving a part of the secrecy of the testimony and of the enigma of the face. October 2001: while studying illustration at the École Estienne, I fled from the usual figures to devote myself to what really inspires me: sketching from life and using it to collect people's own accounts. My final project took the form of a graphic reportage piece ("Portraits cachés, une relecture de la loi contre les exclusions," which won the Grands reportages *jury prize in 2002), and it laid the foundations for the approach that I have focused on since then: drawing to meet people, sharing experiences, observing, and being ready to listen to the people who we've stopped hearing.*

March 2003: I started a period of eighteen months among an Emmaüs community near Chartres, which resulted is the 200-page book De bric et de broc *(Parole et silence, 2006). I did my first drawing on the morning of my arrival in the community—a coffee break. There were some fleeting looks. I used the brown juice in my cup to make a background. This relaxed the atmosphere a little. But I knew it would take a few more weeks before I would be properly accepted. Because illustrated reportage is interactive, it is not limited to conveying a vision of the other. It emphasizes the act of participation. Making portraits, meeting people and negotiating the image that is in the process of being formed allow you to pass questions on to people and to create a voice and an exchange rather than providing responses. There's a potential cross-contamination between the world and the person who sketches it.*

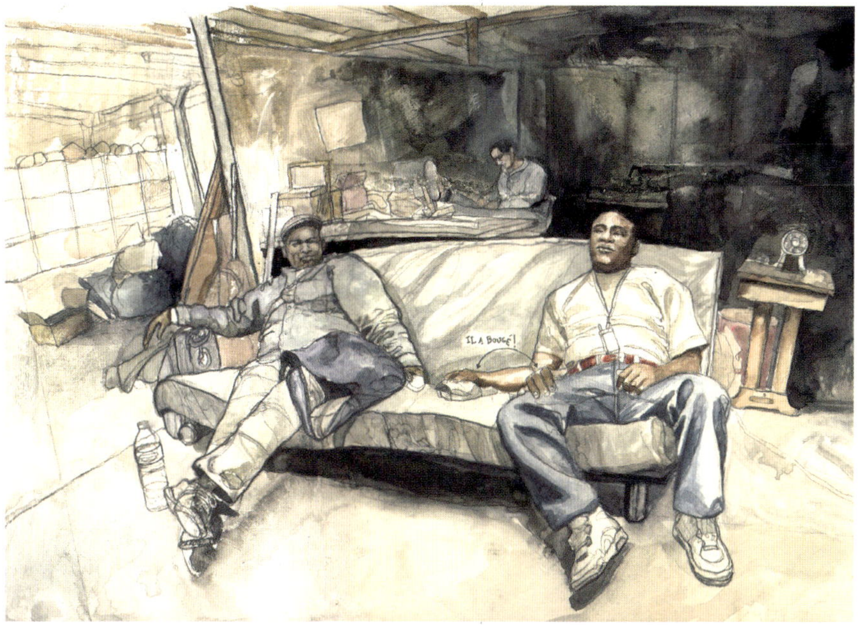

www.lesyeuxdanslemonde.org/membre/damien-roudeau
Rosny, grandeur nature (Folies d'encre, 2011)
Têtes de pioche: la Provence au rythme des chantiers de jeunes (Les Alpes de lumière, 2009)
Villiers rebelle: carnet de rencontres à la Cerisaie (La Boîte à bulles, 2004)

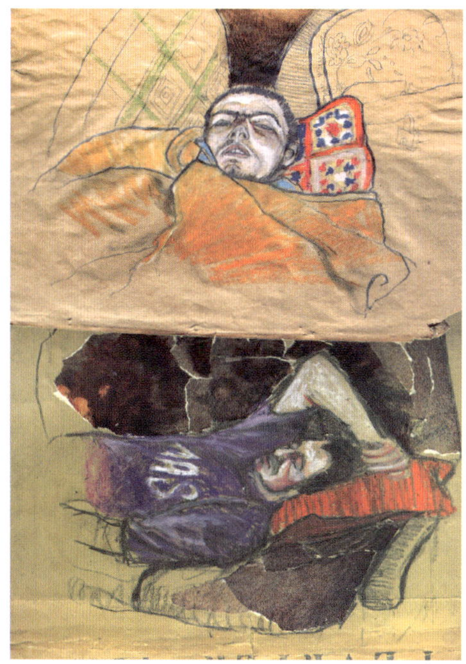

• De bric et de broc, *Parole et silence, 2006. In immersing himself in an Emmaüs ragpicker community , Damien Roudeau sought to use drawing to "listen to the people who we've stopped hearing."*

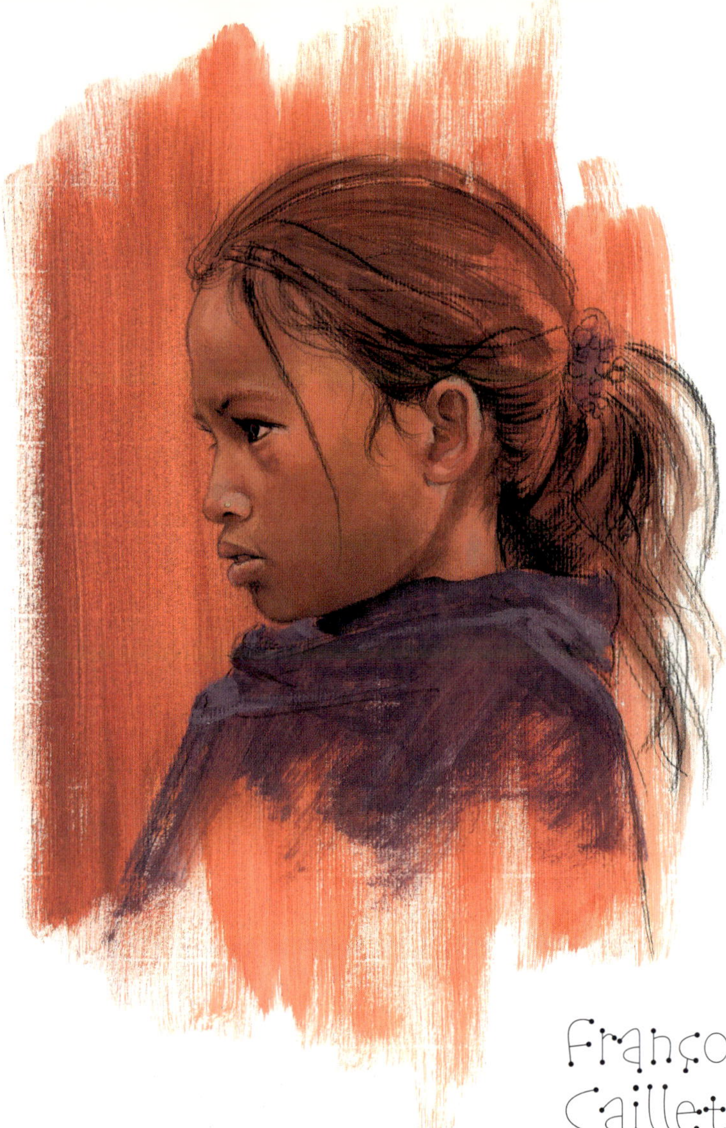

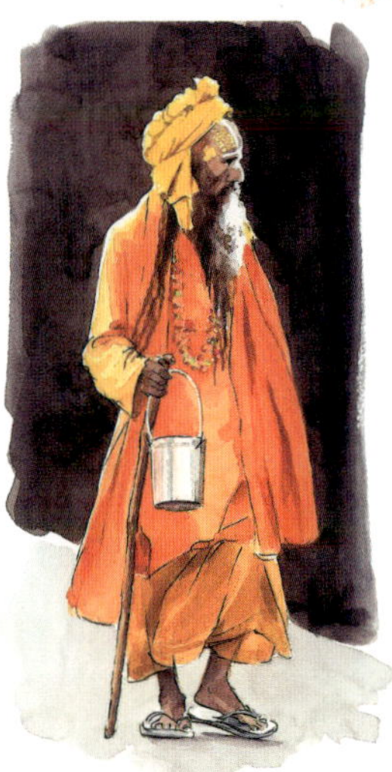

Françoise Caillette-Deneubourg

Born in Paris, Françoise Caillette-Deneubourg discovered drawing through her father, a graphic designer, and through the childhood ritual of visiting on the Louvre on Sunday mornings. After training as a graphic designer under the direction of Pierre Dardel at a school for applied arts, she worked for a decade in advertising and interior design for apartments and offices, before then focusing on painting. She expresses herself through different techniques—gouache, pastel, acrylic and ink—but prefers watercolours for her travel diaries. This rambler brings back many drawings from each place she visits. She has travelled through Morocco, Peru, Yemen, Mali, Namibia, Vietnam and Nepal.

Because it is conducive to reflection and observation, walking allows me to meet the Other, which is my primary motivation for travelling. Drawing gives you the time to feel, observe, see details and capture ephemeral things, simple gestures of everyday life, shapes and faces. And it lets you capture instants and mix two approaches: a contemplative one and a creative one. Drawing can open doors in a unique way. Wherever I am, as soon as I start to draw or paint, children rush up to me, and then adults join them. At first you get laughter and comments, and then silence and respect for the work being done before their eyes. Complicity and trust develops—I'll be offered a seat or a glass of water. I become one of their own. Then I can go into their homes and sketch people in their private environment. Vies du Népal *is a book that is particularly dear to me. The emotions I felt in this endearing country were really vivid and strong. I wanted my take and my drawings to be direct translations of my sensibility and to share these intense moments experienced in this harsh and powerful nature that leaves people feeling naked.*

✏ http://caillettedeneubourg.free.fr/presentation.html
***Vies du Népal* (Magellan & Cie, 2011)**
***Vies berbères* (Magellan & Cie, 2009)**

• Vies du Népal, *Magellan & Cie, 2011.*
For Françoise Caillette-Deneubourg, drawing is the best way to meet others and something that can open doors in a unique way.

Stéphanie Ledoux

Stéphanie Ledoux divides her time between her studio and her long-distance trips, during which she gets people from the other side of the world to pose for sketches. A bond with the model grows during the sitting, in an atmosphere that is sometimes solemn and sometimes casual, and that usually involves a throng of curious people. Above all, she loves observing the reaction of the models as they discover themselves through her hand. The result is portraits that have a striking impact. Stéphanie's fieldwork is above all a pretext to break the ice and spend time with people.

Drawing is the best way I have found to travel and give centre stage to human encounters.

She also uses diaries as the basis for her studio work. Stephanie defines herself more as a painter than as a travel diary maker.

Drawing on the spot with little time or equipment can be frustrating. The model is in a hurry to see the result. So, while there, I finish quickly, and the work that I have in mind takes shape only when I get back and am in the comfort of the studio, with the space and time to work on a bigger scale, nurtured by all my memories of the trip.

Since the age of thirteen, she has accumulated a hundred chatty travel diaries, which are full of portraits, tasty anecdotes and collages of treasures picked up during the journey. These livres-objets have an abundance of colours and a fragrance of mint tea and spices: they are truly memories in concentrate form.

I keep these relics as though they are treasures suffused with good times that were "canned" on the spot. In this respect, travel diaries are treasure troves that hold everything I wanted to keep. Each note and every small object has the power to transport me to the moment when it was collected.

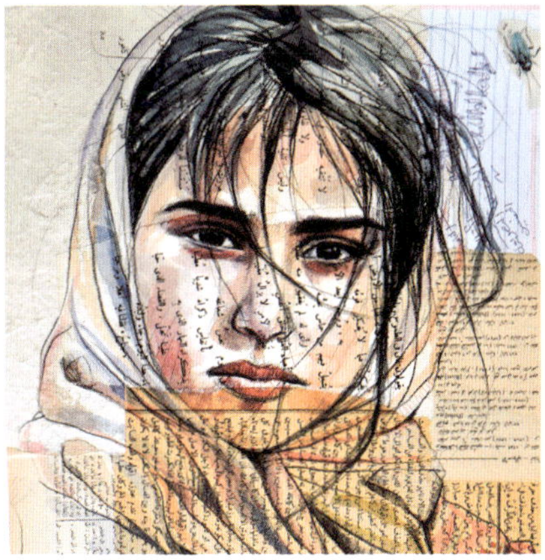

http://stephanie-ledoux.blogspot.fr
Enfant d'éléphants (Elytis, 2014)
Portraits de voyage (Elytis, 2012)

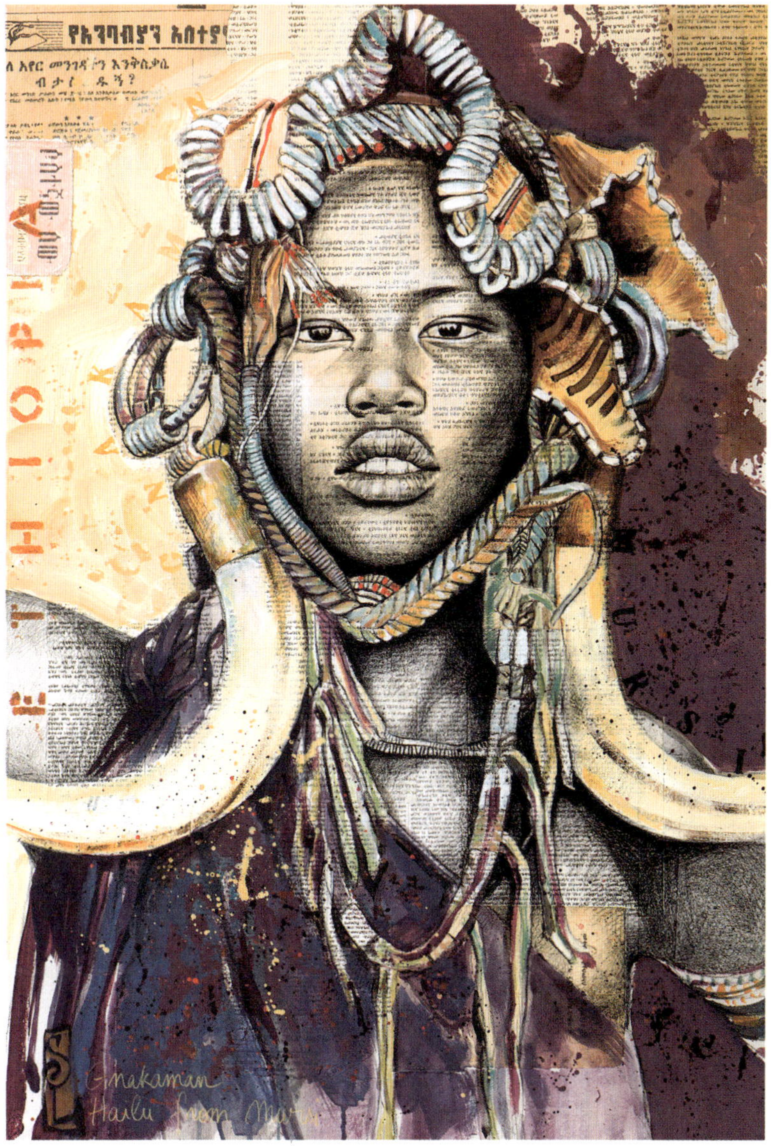

• Portraits de voyage, *Elytis, 2012.*
Even though she has been keeping diaries since she was a teenager, Stéphanie Ledoux appreciates the comfort of the studio to complete drawings made during her travels.

Gwenaëlle Trolez

Born in 1970, Gwenaëlle Trolez grew up in Normandy and Brittany. In 1992, she received a degree in natural sciences and worked as a school teacher from 1994 to 2004, a period during which she wrote numerous pedagogical works for educators. This self-taught artist developed a passion for textiles and photography, and she has also taken evening classes in ceramics and piano. Being a teacher has given her time to travel and discover the world. Her children's books, *Safari* and *Amazonie*, were directly inspired by her travels. In 2004, she opened a ceramics studio, though health problems forced her to stop this activity after three years. In 2005, she created her first collages made from old photographs by Edmond Fortier. In 2008, her stationery publishing house was born.

www.gwenaelle-trolez.fr
***Japon, carnets d'un explorateur au pays du Soleil-Levant* (Magellan & Cie, 2012)**
***Amazonie* (Magellan & Cie, 2009)**
***Algérie, mon amie* (Magellan & Cie, 2008)**
***Safari* (Magellan & Cie, 2008)**
***L'Explorateur, le Photographe et le Missionnaire* (Magellan & Cie, 2007)**

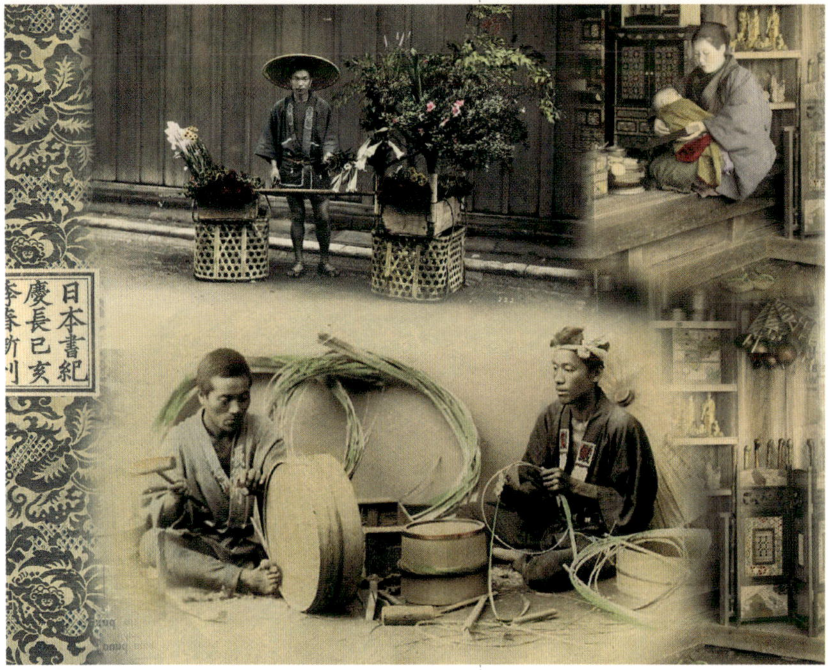

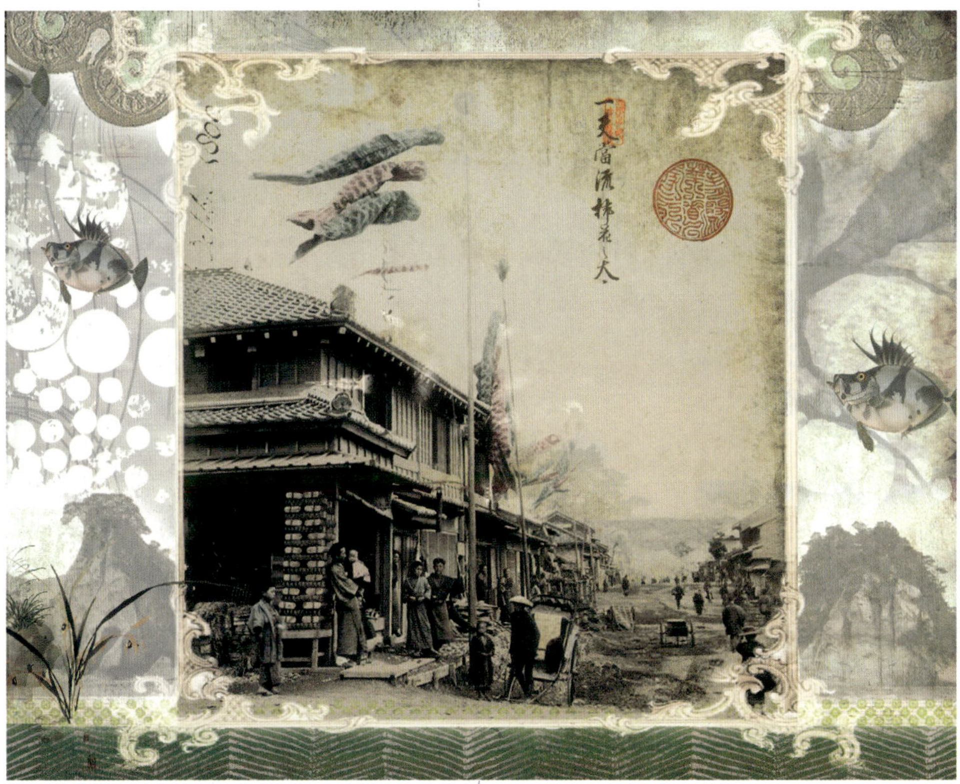

• Japon, carnets d'un explorateur au pays du Soleil-Levant, *Magellan & Cie, 2012*
Gwenaëlle Trolez's collages bring the exotic imagery of the late nineteenth century to life for a trip through time in Japan.

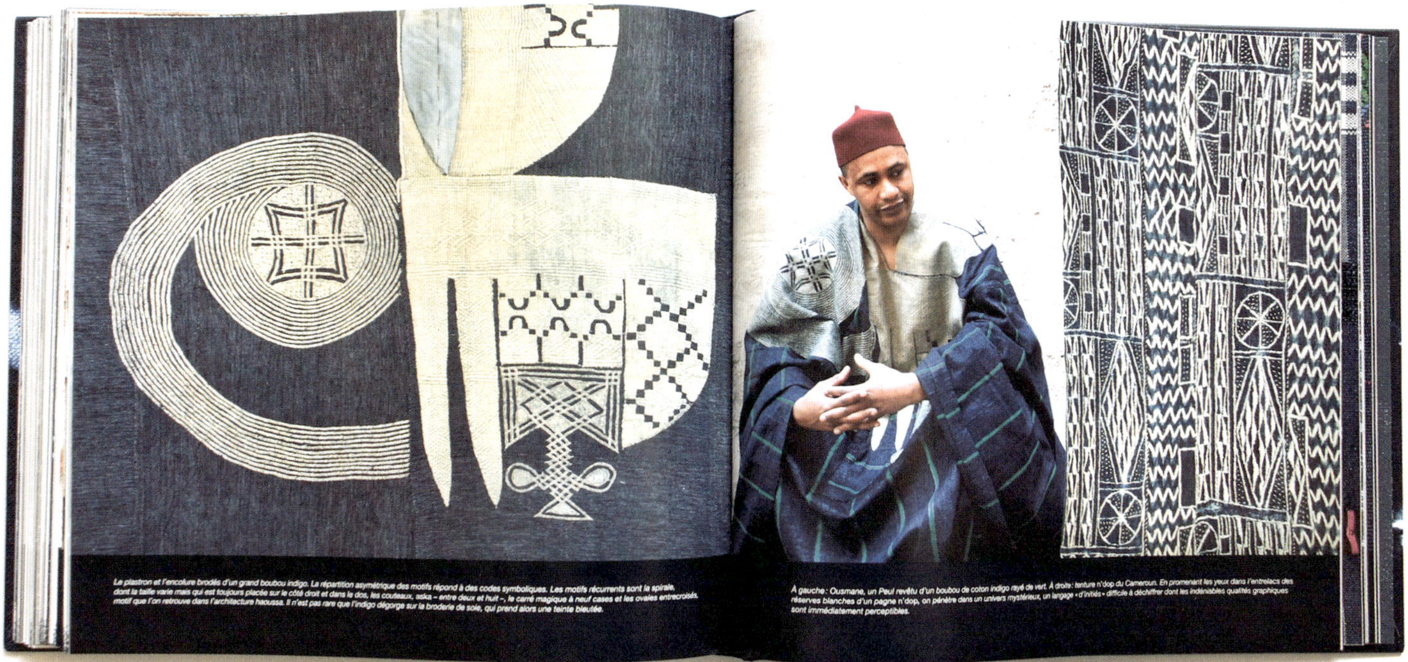

Catherine Legrand

Tailoring journeys like one would tailor an outfit is Catherine Legrand's approach to travel. She plans her trips around her passion for fabrics and ethnic clothing. Pencils, camera and pair of scissors to hand, she travels from fabric workshops to markets, visiting dyers here and embroiderers there. Hers is a "hand-stitched" world tour. Back in Paris, this stylist, fashion designer and avid collector of clothing, fabrics, accessories and trimmings makes beautiful travel books on textiles. These works discuss the following topics: ethnic textiles in the world, clothing traditions and identities, and textile know-how.

✏ www.catherine-legrand.fr
Indigo, le périple bleu d'une créatrice textile (Éditions de La *Martinière, 2012)*
Carnets d'inspirations textiles (Aubanel, 2009)
Textiles et vêtements du monde (Aubanel, 2007)

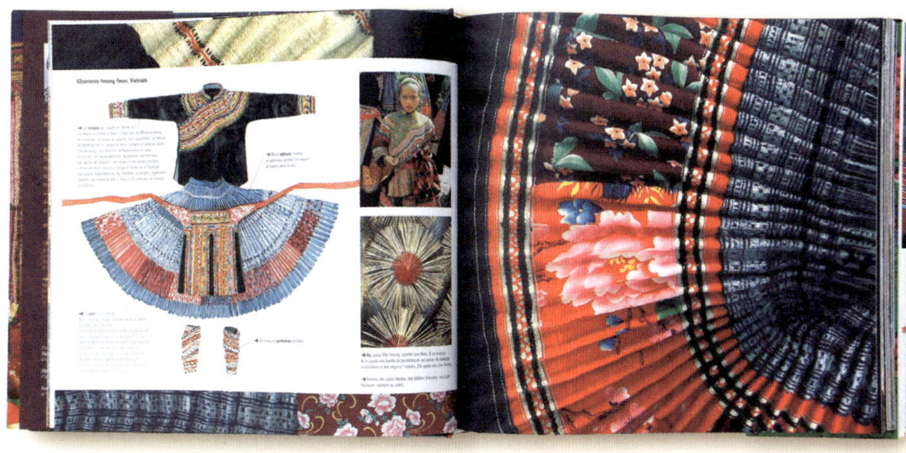

• Indigo, le périple bleu d'une créatrice textile *(above, top; Éditions de La Martinière, 2012) and* Textiles et vêtements du monde *(Aubanel, 2007). A stylist and fashion designer, Catherine Legrand travels in search of textiles.*

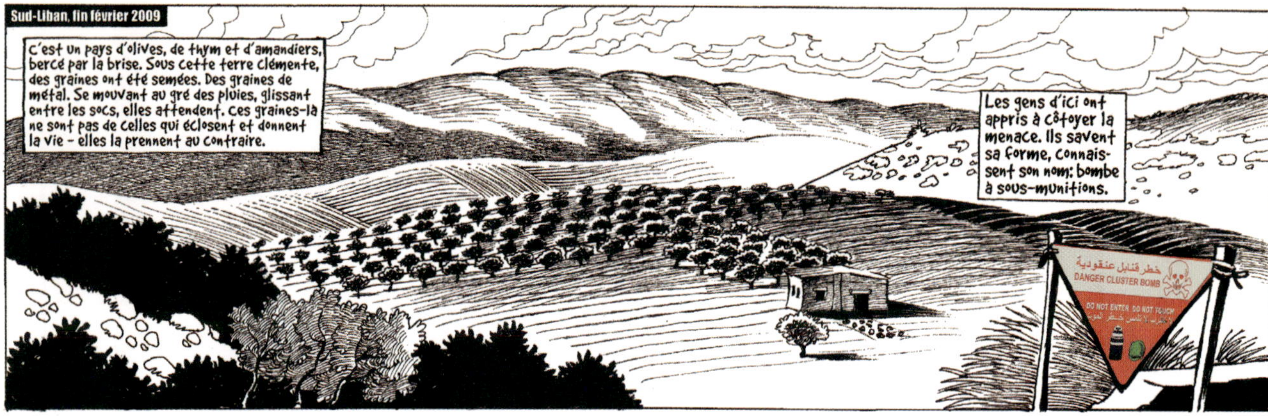

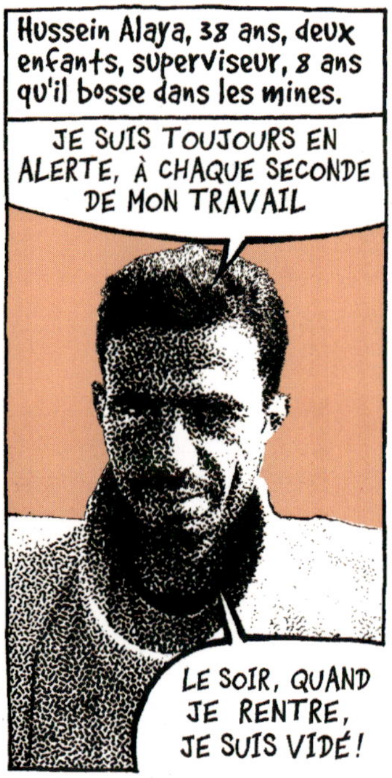

•Because the period after a war ends can still be deadly for civilians, Patrick Chappatte produced a reportage piece in 2009 that shed light on cluster weapons, to "reveal the humanity behind the news."

Patrick Chappatte

I have a great job as a press cartoonist; it requires me to go and see the places and faces from the news. Since 1995, I have also simultaneously been a reporter-illustrator. Thirty of my stories have been published by Geneva's Le Temps *and other newspapers, for example* Courrier International, Internazionale *and* International New York Times. *I like to work with all forms of the graphic journalism genre: short reportage pieces for the press, bigger cartoons the form of books and interactive narratives on the Web. This is why I have created a site entirely dedicated to the genre: bdreportage.com. In 2009, two and a half years after a war between Israel and Hezbollah, I went to South Lebanon with the International Committee of the Red Cross to recount how conflicts continue to kill long after ceasefires have been called. In the last days of the 2009 war, millions of cluster bombs were dropped on the area. Many of them did not explode, transforming the country into a vast minefield. This cluster-bombs story became an experimental subject. With the help of the ICRC, a drawn and animated story,* La Mort est dans le champ, *was released. Broadcast on Swiss channels and Canal+ in France, the film was also shown at twenty or so documentary festivals, and it won an award in Australia. Amid the flow of information and the deluge of images, photos and videos of news, drawing to tell a story allows the reader to strike up a relationship. The simplicity of black lines lends itself to emotion. When I'm out there, I operate as a conventional journalist, but I remember the subjective, anecdotes and doubts—these things say a lot about a reality. Your personal side and your subjective take are what shape graphic journalism. Drawing allows you to take readers by the hand, bring them to a place where they would not have gone, and make them see. I want to show how the most topical issues are reflected in people's everyday lives—to reveal the humanity behind the news.*

✏ www.bdreportage.com
B.D. Reporter, du Printemps arabe aux coulisses de l'Élysée (Glénat, 2011)

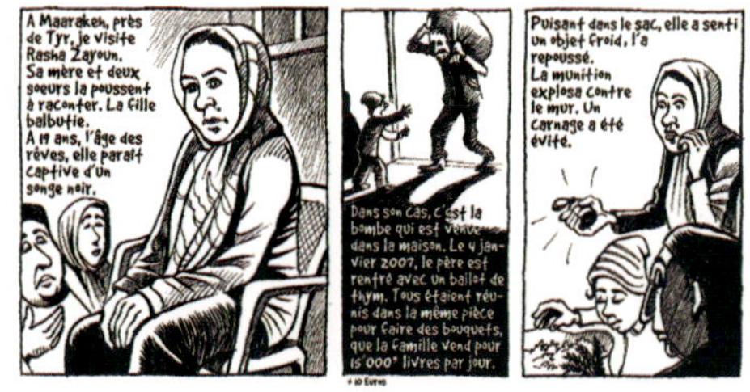

Bastien Dubois

A native of the North of the France, Bastien Dubois was attracted to drawing and computer technology at an early age. At middle school, he tried programming and animation, and he then wanted to work in video games. At senior school, he produced little games, Web sites and Flash animations. During his postsecondary studies in visual communication and his training in 3D animation at Supinfocom, Bastien became passionate about observational drawing and travel diaries. In 2004, he hitch-hiked from Lille to Istanbul, going through Italy and Greece. The journey was both an initiation into the great art cities (for example, Florence and Rome) and the subject of his first travel diary on paper. Supinfocom was where he had the idea for an animated travel diary. Through using 3D software, he was able to allow the viewer to become immersed in his universe, and he then had the idea of creating an animated short-film travel diary. He moved to Madagascar for nearly a year after his studies to make this film. *Madagascar, carnet de voyage* (2009) traces a Western traveller's encounter with this culture. The film received numerous awards in international selections, including the Prix Canal+ at the Annecy Festival and an Oscar nomination in 2011. *Portraits de voyages* is an adaptation of this short film.

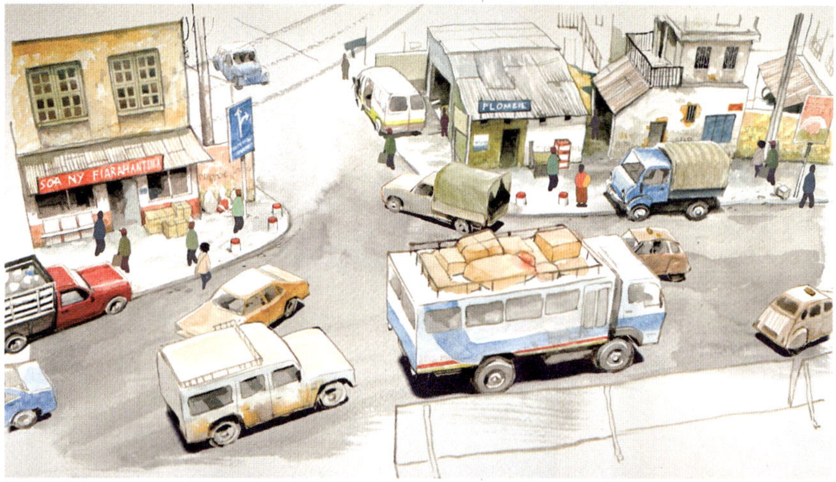

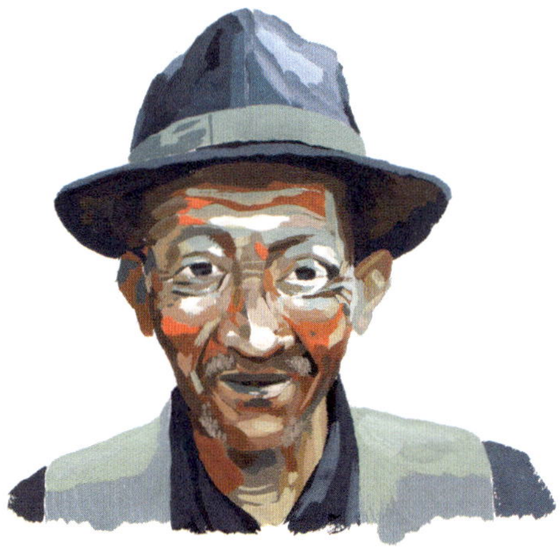

• **Madagascar, carnet de voyage, *2009*.**
In this short animated film and travel diary, Bastien Dubois's drawings come to life thanks to the technique of "camera mapping."

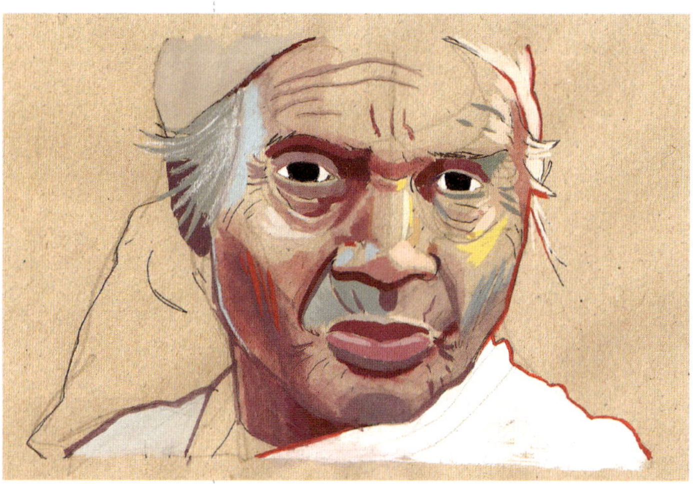

In twenty three-minute episodes, in twenty different locations, this series aired on Arte offers a tour of the world that is subjective, colourful and woven out of original stories. This series is also a technical challenge that mixed motion capture, painting and the aesthetics of travel diaries. Each episode introduces us to an inhabitant of a country who tells the traveller about an aspect of its culture, history or environment. *Cargo Cult* (panorama programme at the festival of Annecy) is Bastien's latest film. This anthropological fable takes place in Papua New Guinea during the Second World War, based on Arthur C. Clarke's statement that "any sufficiently advanced technology is indistinguishable from magic." Today, Bastien is focused on developing new projects: an animated feature film and a short film in collaboration with Antoine Delacharlery. He is also the president of the association Art Brutal, which produces short films and organizes exhibitions on animation and creative workshops.

www.bastiendubois.com
www.artbrutal.com
***Cargo Cult* (2013)**
***Portraits de voyages* (2012)**
***Madagascar, carnet de voyage* (Reflets d'ailleurs, 2011)**
***Madagascar, carnet de voyage* (2009)**
***Ah* (S. Moreau and J. Bacquet, 2006)**

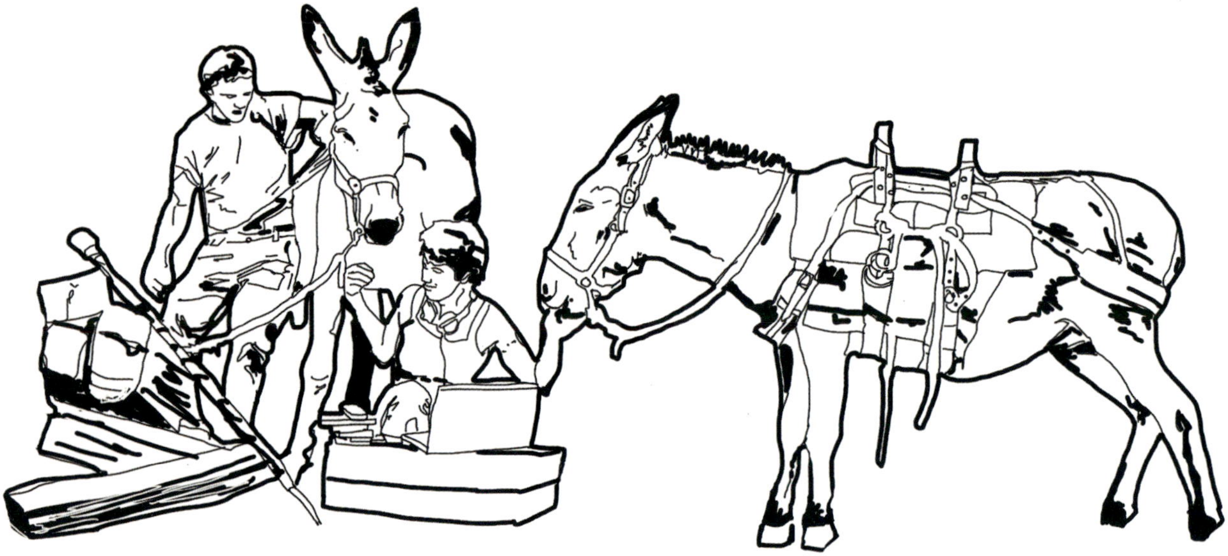

Karen Guillorel

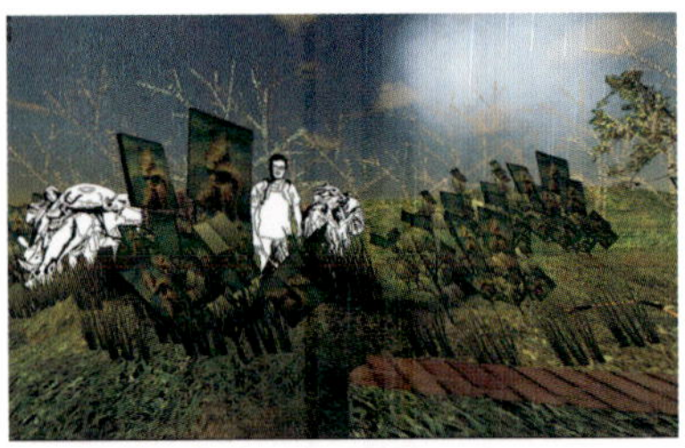

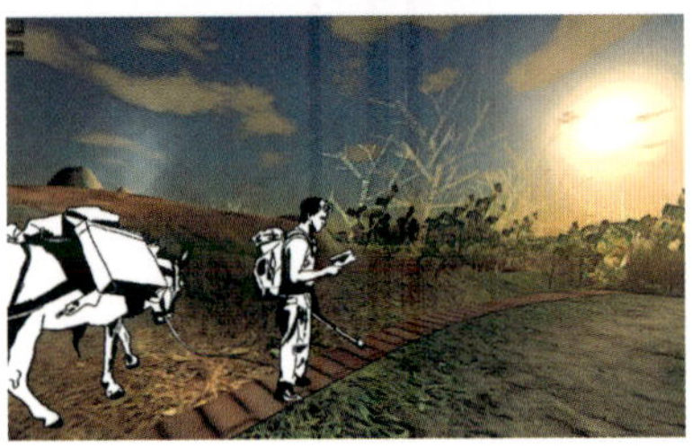

• *"E-migrations," 2014.*
Karen Guillorel carried a library on the back of a donkey on the road between Barcelona and Amsterdam, to swap books with people she encountered along the way.

Born in 1978, Karen Guillorel has been enthusiastically roaming the Earth since 2001, driven on by her thirst for writing and travel. Discovering the world interests her as much as social adventure and exploring virtual worlds created by new technologies. Outside of travelling, she works in video games, audiovisual media and publishing. She cocreated and coedited the magazine *Chasseurs de rêves* and the artbook *Terra Incognita* (Grand Prix de l'imaginaire en 2002). Since 2004, her focus has been on writing new novels and scripts, though she continues to draw. She is a member of Chemins d'étoiles, a group of artists, scientists and explorers created by Gaële de La Brosse and Sylvain Tesson. Upon her return from her latest trip on foot and by bicycle from Paris to Jerusalem, she made a mixed-media documentary, *6000 km du couchant au levant*, wrote a book, *De l'aventure au voyage intérieur* (Presses de la Renaissance, 2009), and then produced a graphic novel, *Je/Sakura*, an excerpt of which was published in the magazine *Bouts du monde*. Moreover, she has created an innovative publishing experiment, *Traverses, livre voyageur*, with her collaborators, which extended to an on-foot journey with donkeys, "E-troubadours," that mixed nature and technology and involved exchanging books with people encountered along the way. To recount this trip, Karen produced an innovative digital installation, "E-migrations," with the support of the Société Civile des Auteurs Multimedia ("Brouillon d'un rêve") and with the involvement of Yann Minh. Currently a script writer and consultant for television, cinema and transmedia, Karen is fully dedicated to telling stories, an art form that she sees as a way to make people happy.

www.karenguillorel.net
http://traverses-lelivre.com
www.e-migrations.net
Films:
***Mon hanami* (2011)**
6000 km du couchant au levant (2009)
Ire (2008)
Digital installations:
***E-migrations* (2014)**
Traverses, livre voyageur (2007)
Illustrations:
Guide spirituel des Chemins de Saint-Jacques (Presses de la Renaissance, 2010)

David Lopez

*A native of Auvergne, I have lived in Paris since 2005. That year, I finished my studies at École Emile Cohl in Lyon, which I left with a diploma in directing animated films. Since then I have directed cartoons, done storyboarding for various series, been in charge of sets (*Le Magasin des suicides* by Patrice Leconte), and done character animation, editing and compositing. I also illustrate works for young people, primarily for the UK market. And when I can, I buy plane tickets, to empty my head by filling my diaries with sketches and stories from everyday life. Travel diaries allow a sort of "awakened" travelling; they help us to observe the small things that surround us a little more keenly. They focus your attention.*

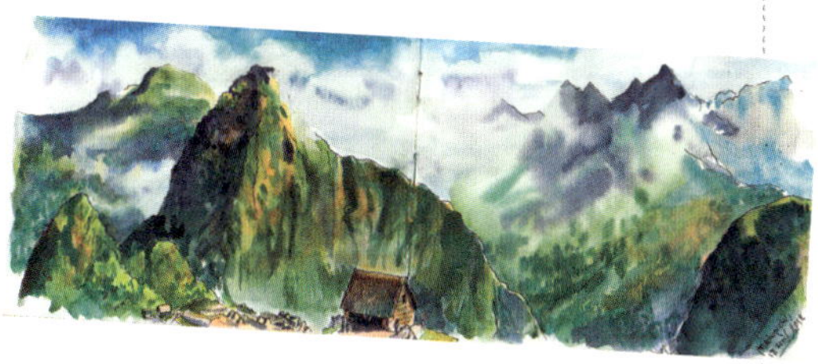

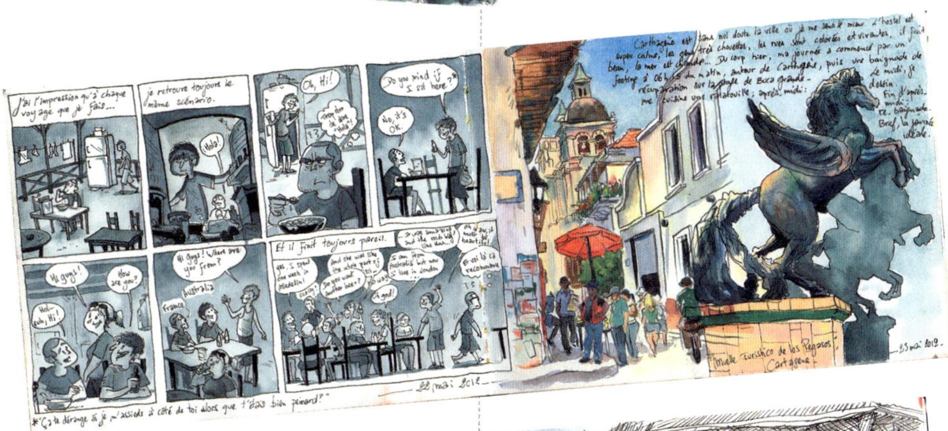

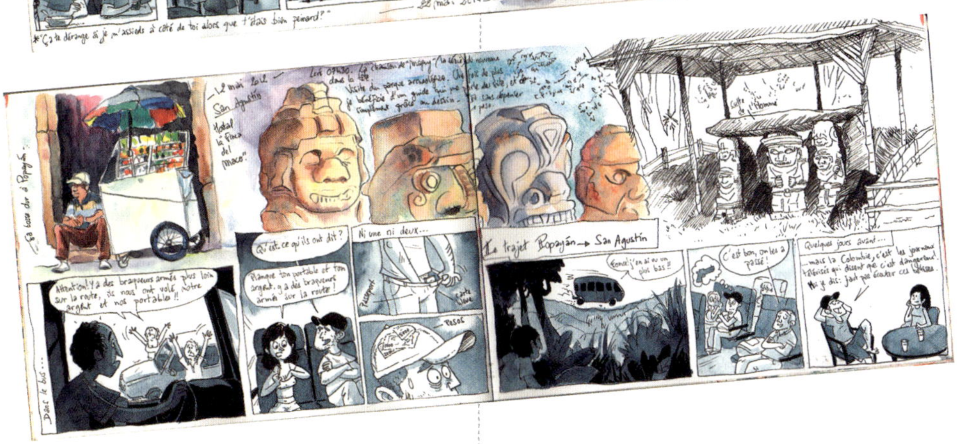

This easy-to-carry medium is used to take notes and to draw and paste in everything that seems to symbolize our trip. For me, it is clearly an art form. It demands observation, as well as a capacity to let yourself be immersed in all the sensations that surround you. Like painters with their canvases, or directors behind their cameras, travel diary makers choose a treatment, a type of narrative and a format, and they retell it throughout the diary. The travel diary is a fun way to retell a travel experience, encounters and anecdotes. And when travelling, it is a good bulwark against loneliness and boredom. From my personal perspective, I have been working in animation for about nine years, and there is always a book of specifications that have to be followed and of the constraints (economic, technical) that need to be juggled in order to be as creative as possible. But the travel diary is a genuine space for freedom. Its only limits are the ones you impose on it. My travel diary Peru-Ecuador-Colombia*, which I made between Peru and Colombia in two and a half months, is a mixture of watercolours, portraits, illustrations and short cartoons. Sometimes I like to be part of everything while also keeping a distance, and the tone I take is, in general, a comedic one.*

http://tidavidtz.blogspot.fr/
***Peru-Ecuador-Colombia* (2012)**
***Mexico-Guatemala* (2011)**
***Argentina* (2010)**

• David Lopez collects his travel memories (Peru-Ecuador-Colombia) in comic diaries that are, for him, "genuine space(s) for freedom."

Julie Sarperi

With the treasures I unearth and collect during my travels (a moment, a meeting, an object), I want to show the world in an optimistic, aesthetic and poetic way. I'm in my element when I'm wandering and just in the moment, so photography—especially instant—and writing are key for me. Polaroids, which are born before our eyes in a somewhat magical way, poetically embody the moment dear to me. On the Web, I also play around with sound, video and very large images for an immersive experience. My digital travel diary, "Japon, Notes de voyage" freely draws on one of the masterpieces of Japanese literature, The Pillow Book (Makura no soshi)*, which was written in the eleventh century by a lady in waiting at the Kyoto court, Sei Shonagon. This surprisingly modern and innovative work lists, night after night, things that spontaneously came to her mind: one night it'll be the season that she prefers, then a list of lakes, fan frames and Buddhist temples. The chapters, which don't try to be exhaustive, are entitled things like "Things that cannot be compared," "Things that just go on" or "Nice things." I found that Japan suited this nonlinear approach well; my Web travel diary "Japon, Notes de voyage" is divided into chapters, and images and facts are mixed together in list form.* Portugal, itinéraires de voyageurs *(Nomades, 2012) is a road trip with a geographic structure. Portuguese poems, reveries, thoughts and historical details punctuate this 144-page book. It is done in the same style as my digital books: handwritten texts and compositions made up of graphical elements and analogue and instant photography. On this occasion I also used a typewriter for texts and worked with an illustrator, Laure Fissore, on the drawings.*

www.carnets-de-traverse.com
Portugal, itinéraires de voyageurs **(Nomades, 2012)**

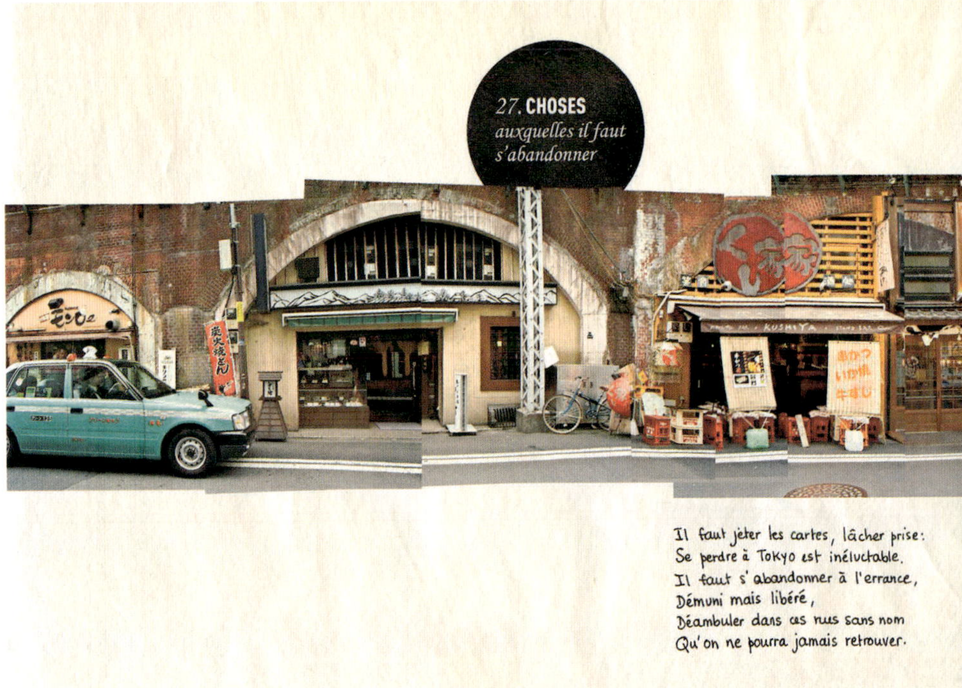

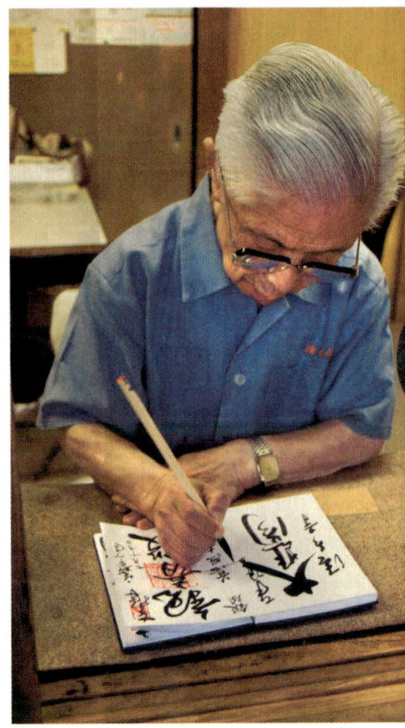

• Japon, Notes de voyage *is an online travel diary in which Julie Sarperi, in a poetic and contemplative spirit, randomly lists the constitutive elements of the country.*

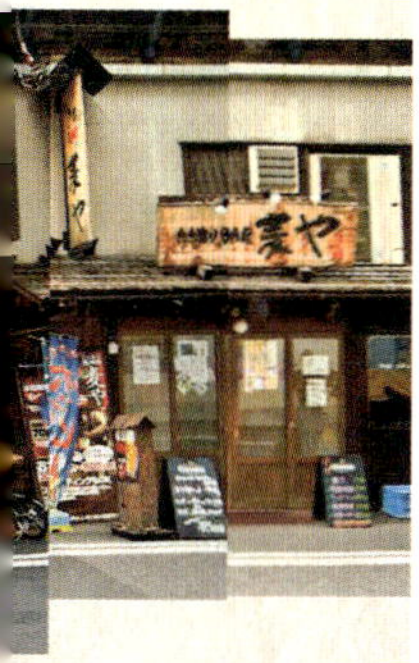

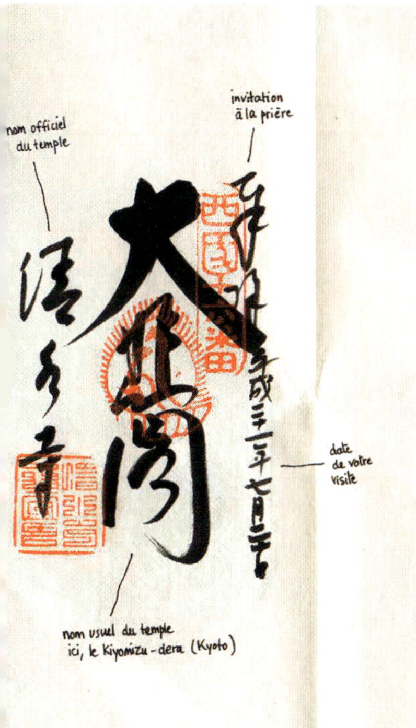

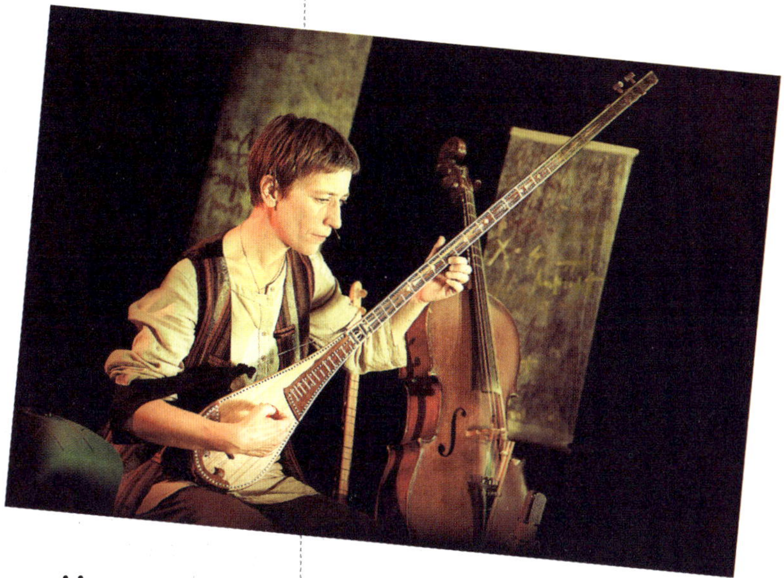

• Trans-Eurasienne, *2013.*
Emmanuelle Troy invites the viewer on a musical and literary journey on the roads of the lands of the East, from Sephardic Spain to Mongolia.

Emmanuelle Troy

For me, the travel diary is a natural extension of travel and the sensations that it conjures. Its multidisciplinarity is the best way to transcribe—better than a book or a movie—that very particular type of porosity that the act of travelling produces within us. It is the most beautiful homage, the most beautiful testimony—precious "traces of reality" and of the lived experience—that can be made to the people we encounter. And it allows you to share and create a bridge and a community of sensations with someone who has not made the trip if he or she wants to delve into the world of the creator of the book, regardless of the media used. Multimedia and personal: these are, in my eyes, the intrinsic characteristics of travel diaries, and the concepts of interdisciplinarity and fragments are essential to them (even if the trip may only be imaginary or largely scripted). This opens many possibilities and serves as a prompt to not be satisfied with a "classic" diary (of writing/drawing/collage) that is produced in the moment or once back home, and to instead exceed this two-dimensional aspect, and extend in time the creation of the book—and therefore the resonance of the trip. I may be a visual artist by training, but above all I am a filmmaker and musician, and so I include cinema and performance (music, dance and staged readings). All the senses awakened, a sense of intensity, and thirsty for encounters: this is the state I want to provoke in the viewer of my resolutely multidisciplinary "transartistic travel diary" shows. They are based on my own travels, on those of my predecessors, and on an imagining that is widespread within the music of the Eastern worlds, which I love and have practiced for a long time.

✏ **http://arkhan-asso.com/**
Performances:
***Trans-Eurasienne* (2013)**
***Carnet(s) de Chine* (2010)**
Films:
***Je rêvais d'aller à Kashgar* (2010)**

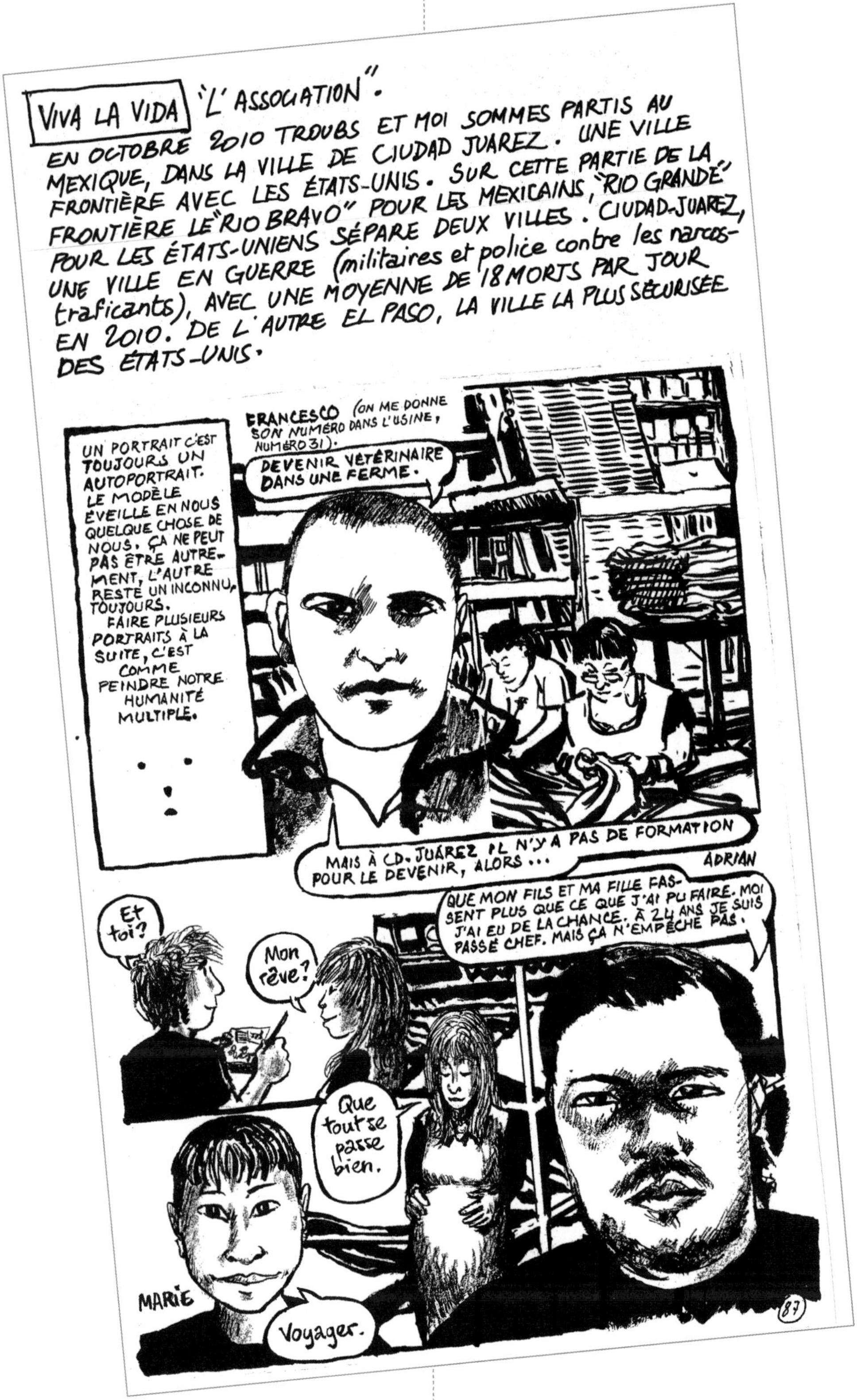

Edmond Baudoin

I was born in Nice in 1942. I started doing comics when I was about forty. I have four children and eight grandchildren.
I've done about sixty books (comic strips and illustrations), and I've travelled a lot. I've been to Mexico, Chile, Venezuela, Cuba, Colombia, the United States, Canada, China, India, Japan, Egypt, Lebanon, Morocco and many other countries to give courses or lectures or to make books. I taught drawing for three years at a university in Quebec. I won the award for best book at Angoulême and also an award for best story for Le Voyage, *and Fred Vargas, with whom I did* Les Quatre Fleuves, *took the prize for best script. I love contemporary dance, and I have worked on choreography. I perform with dancers and musicians. Laetitia Carton made a documentary film on me, which will be released in January 2015.*
It is called Edmond. *Christophe Camoirano and Jacques Samson also did a documentary called* En chemin avec Baudoin. *What else? At the moment I'm working with Cédric Villani, a great mathematician. We're doing a book about the physicists and mathematicians of the Second World War. This summer I'm working with the American author Craig Thomson on a joint book. What else... I think that's too much. Maybe I should just learn to take it easy.*

http://edmondbaudoin.com/edmond_baudoin.html
Travel diaries
***L'Association en Égypte* (L'Association, 1998)**
***Viva la vida: los sueños de Ciudad Juárez* (L'Association, 2011)**

Troub's

After studying at the École supérieure des beaux-arts de Toulouse, and then in Angoulême, Jean-Marc Troubet, known as "Troub's," is passionate about the close or distant elsewhere, unusual travel experiences and sketching on the spot. Based in the Dordogne, he has been making travel diaries since 1994. His first album, *Pour autant que je me souvienne*, recounts the story of wandering between Toulouse, Bordeaux and the shores of Cadaquès. A devotee of the Rendez-vous du carnet de voyage de Clermont-Ferrand, where he has been displaying his originals since the event began, from 2001 he pursued his dreams of adventure in Australia, Madagascar, China, Borneo, Mexico and Laos. The freedom loving Troub's has therefore created many travel diaries. In 2002 he published a reportage diary after eight months spent in the world of Périgord's home distillers: *La Bouille*, a diary of this timeless and yet dying-out activity.

✏ http://troubs.fr/

Le Goût de la terre (L'Association, 2013)
Capitale: Vientiane (Les Requins Marteaux, 2012)
Viva la vida: los sueños de Ciudad Juárez (L'Association, 2011)
Rupestres (Futuropolis, 2011)
Le Paradis... en quelque sorte (Futuropolis, 2008)
Troub's en Chine (Alain Beaulet, 2006)
Penser parallèle (Rackham, 2005)
Walkatju (Alain Beaulet, 2003)
La Bouille (Rackham, 2002)

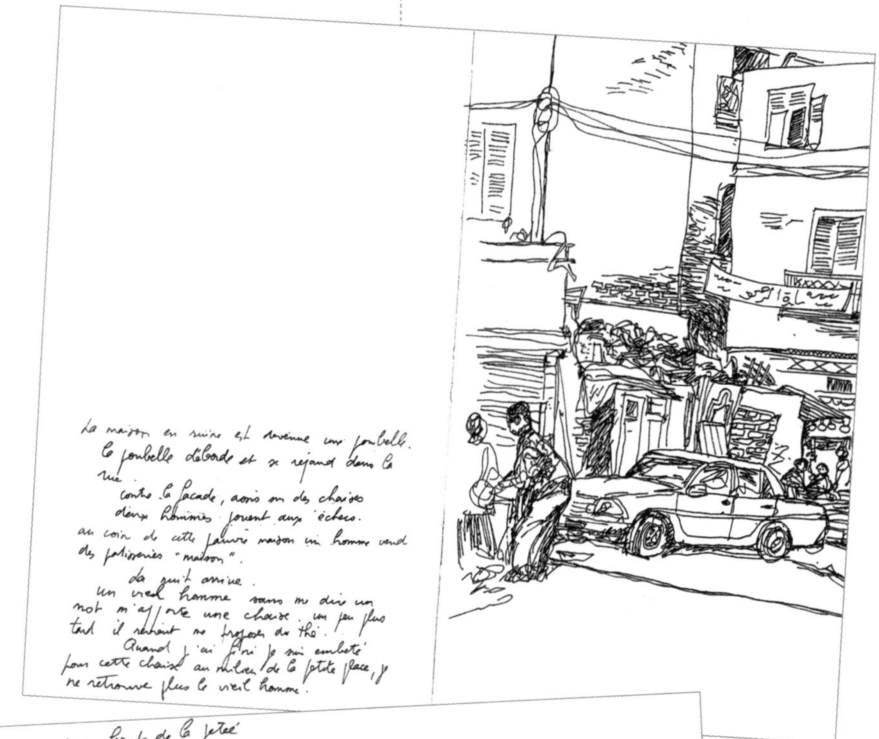

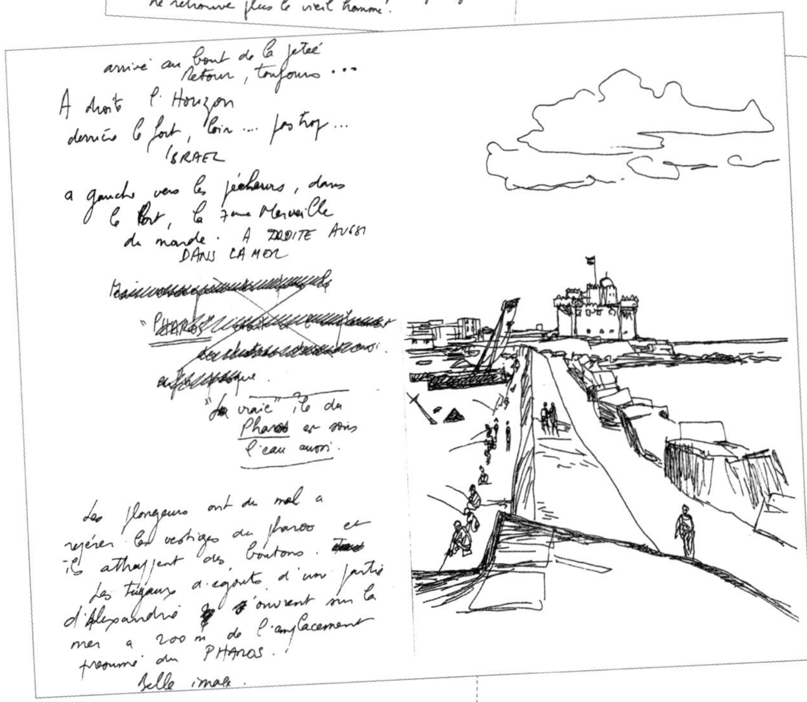

• Viva la vida: los sueños de Ciudad Juárez, *L'Association, 2011. Edmond Baudouin and Troub's turned reporters to meet the inhabitants of Ciudad Juárez. Their diaries were a source of inspiration for future graphic works.*

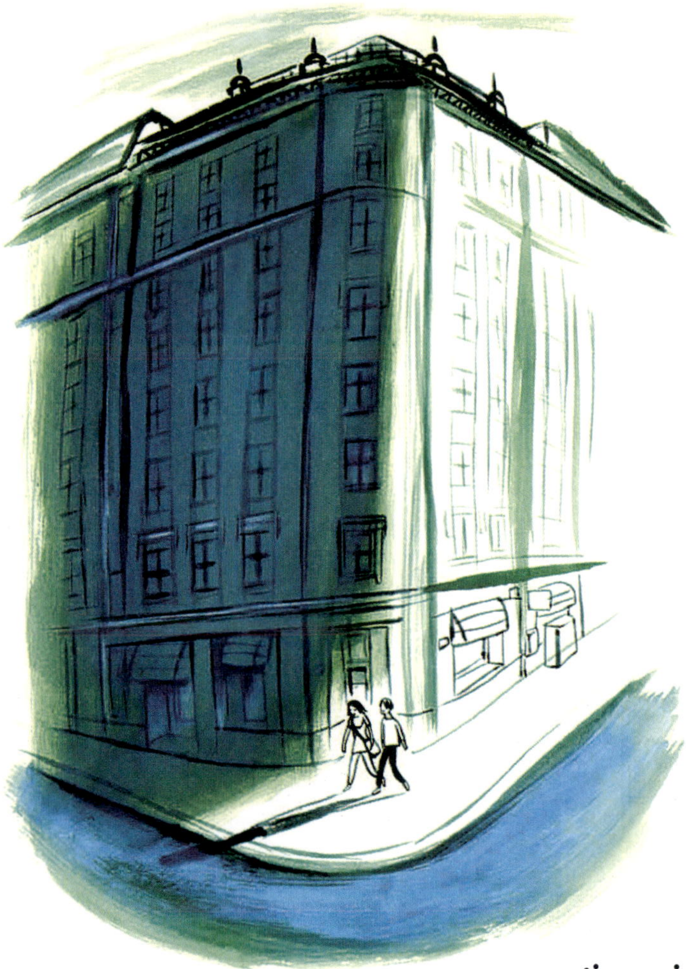

• **Helsinki, visions d'une ville, *SWOY, 2014.*** ***The Finnish capital unfolds through Charles Berberian and Anna Rozen's take on it. It's a declaration of love in over 100 illustrations.***

Charles Berberian

I enjoy walking around with a diary and filling it with drawings to capture a moment, a landscape or a passing shadow. I also like to draw in cafés and out on terraces. Above all I draw when I'm travelling, because I have the most time to do it when I am away from my daily routine. And this is how I've ended up with a collection of travel diaries—though "rambling" diaries might be the better term for them. Actually, the most accurate term would be "graphic journal."

Tanger: carnets **(Cornélius, 2009)**
Bons baisers de Lisbonne **(Cornélius, 2009)**
Istanbul: carnets **(Cornélius, 2009)**
Barcelone: carnets, novembre 97-février 98 **(Cornélius, 1999)**
New York: carnets, avril-octobre 1995 **(Cornélius, 1996)**

Jacques Ferrandez

Born in 1955 in Algiers, Jacques Ferrandez started out by publishing *Arrière-pays*, a collection of short stories about his adopted home of Provence, with Casterman. In 1987 he began his great five-volume epic, *Carnets d'Orient*, on the history of the French presence in Algeria from its conquest to the eve of independence. He then dived back into Provence by adapting *Jean de Florette* and then *Manon des sources* in 1997. The following year, he returned to more contemporary projects with the screenwriter Tonino Benacquista, through which *L'Outremangeur* and *La Boîte noire* (Gallimard/Futuropolis) were born in 1998 and 2000 respectively. From 1998, he expanded his *Carnets d'Orient* with the publication of travel diaries on Syria, Istanbul, Iraq, Lebanon, Sarajevo and Algiers, providing him with a way to strengthen his affinity for the contemporary Mediterranean. In 2008 *Cuba père et fils*, an album that combines fiction and travelogue and that was made jointly with his son Pierre, was published though Casterman. In 2002, he returned to his Algerian saga with a new round of five albums dedicated to the Algerian war, the last volume of which, *Terre fatale,* was published in April 2009. In November of the same year, he adapted *L'Hôte*, a Camus story from *L'Exil et le Royaume*, for Gallimard. In 2012, on the occasion of the fiftieth anniversary of the end of the Algerian war and independence, his drawings served as the connecting thread of the ambitious exhibition "Algérie 1830–1962," presented at the musée de l'Armée, located in Les Invalides in Paris. The anniversary also presented the opportunity to produce a comic-book adaptation of Maurice Bautista's novel *Alger la noire*, marking a return to crime fiction. In 2013, he revisited Camus with the publication of an adapted version of *L'Étranger* through Gallimard.

✏ Other titles

Marrakech: itinéraires (Casterman/Lonely Planet, 2010)
Les Correspondances de Pierre Christin (Dargaud, 2009)
Retours à Alger (Casterman, 2006)
Les Tramways de Sarajevo: voyage en Bosnie-Herzégovine (Casterman, 2005)
Armoriques: balades de Corto Maltese en Bretagne (Casterman, 2004)
Carnets d'Orient: Irak, dix ans d'embargo (Casterman, 2001)
Carnets d'Orient: Liban (Casterman, 2001)
Carnets d'Orient: Istanbul (Casterman, 2000)
Carnets d'Orient: Syrie (Casterman, 1999)

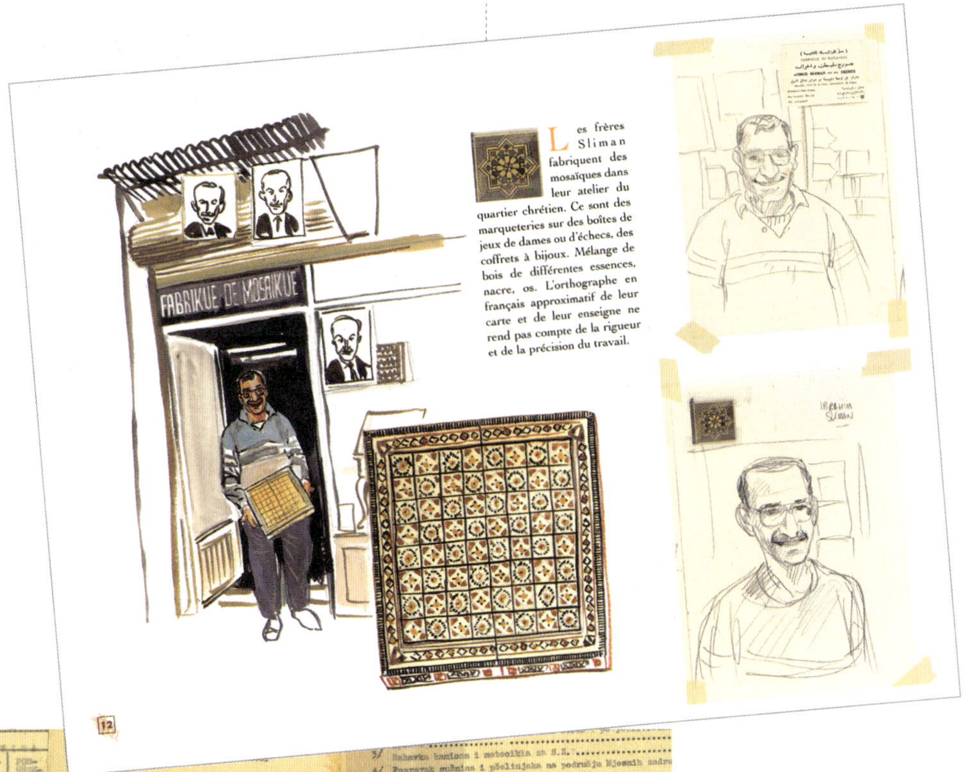

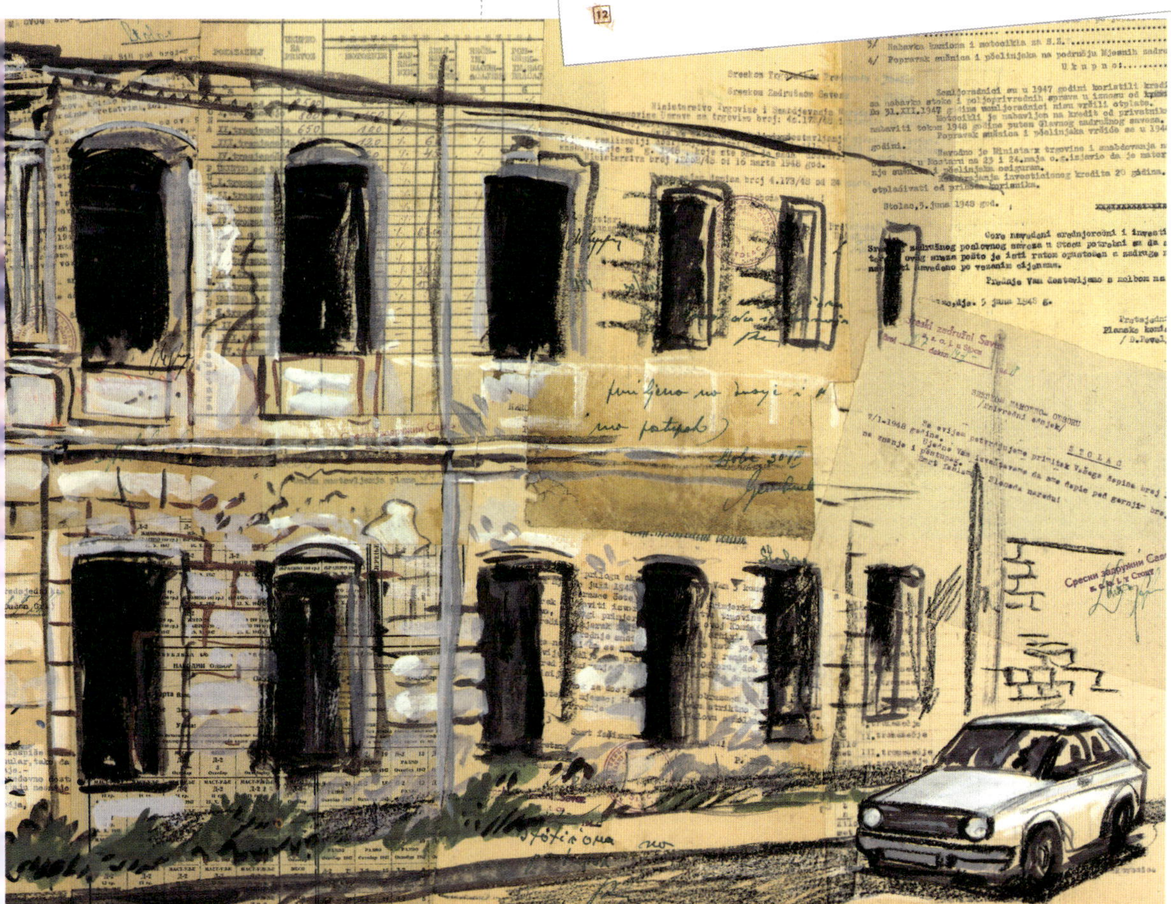

• *In the "Carnets de voyage" collection by Casterman, Jacques Ferrandez provides his impressions on Sarajevo (opposite,* Les Tramways de Sarajevo: voyage en Bosnie-Herzégovine, *2005) and Syria (above,* Carnets d'Orient: Syrie, *1999).*

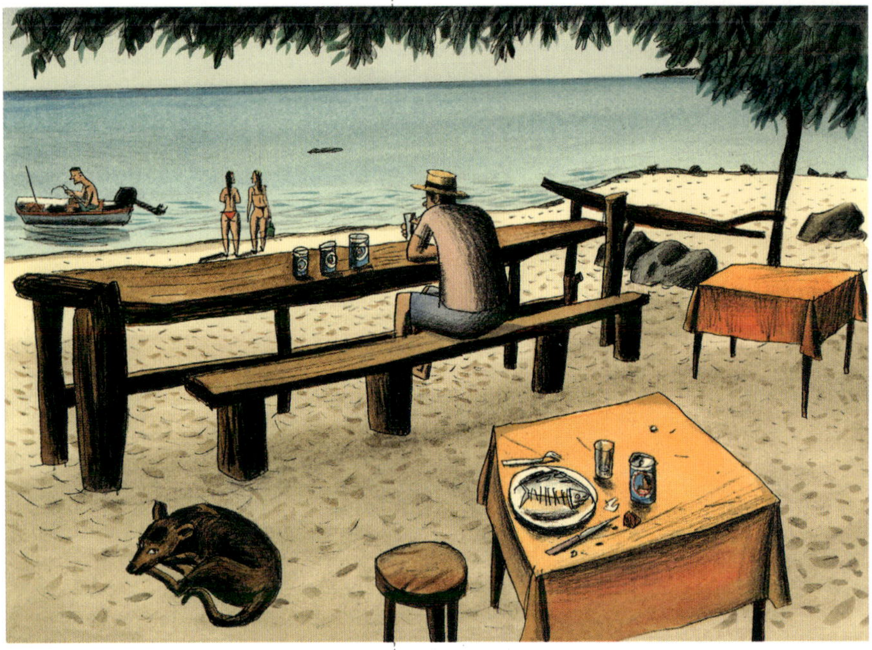

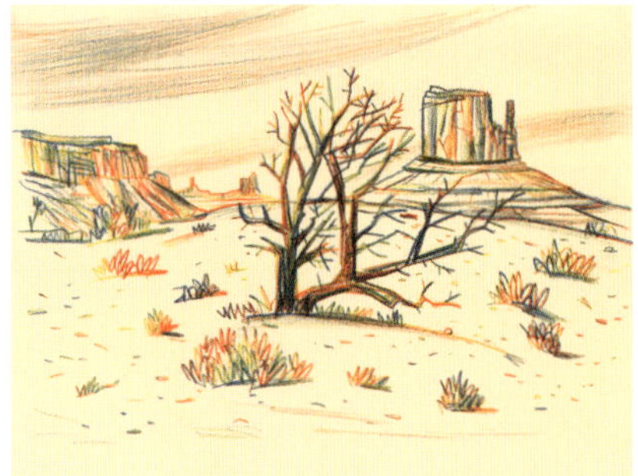

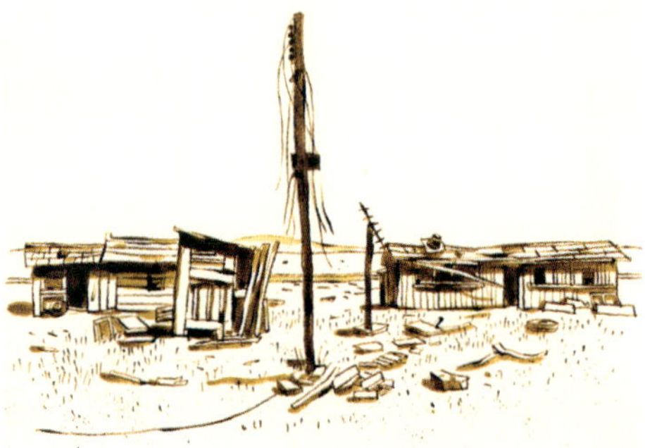

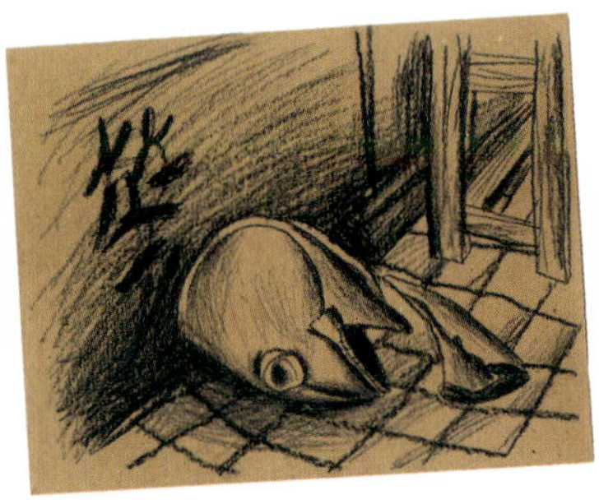

• Esprits d'ailleurs, *La Table ronde, 2014. Loustal used a bigger range of techniques (watercolour over pencil, coloured pencil, sepia ink, charcoal) for a trip to the four corners of the world (including Bora-Bora, the United States and Japan).*

Loustal

An architect by training, I've drawn many cityscapes, using architecture to generate atmospheres, because conveying ambiances is what I try to bring back from my travels. Esprits d'ailleurs, *published in 2014 by* Éditions de La Table Ronde, *is the latest in a series of seven diaries published first by* Seuil *and then by* La Table Ronde *that are more chronological than thematic. And then there has been* Java, à l'ombre du Mérapi *(Christian Desbois, 1996),* Porquerolles *(Nuages, 2008),* 80 % d'humidité *(Alain* Beaulet, *1984) and* South African Road Trip *(Zanpano, 2012). It's a strange way of doing things, but when I've travelled enough and drawn enough to fill a book, I publish it.* Esprits d'ailleurs *covered trips to Japan, Polynesia, Utah, Algeria, Switzerland, Britanny and South Africa. These trips were either personal ones or artistic residences for different overseas French institutes. I abandoned the orthodoxy of a sketch having to be done in situ some time ago. It made me miss arresting images glanced at times when it was impossible to stop. Now, I mix "from life" drawings when the rhythm and the conditions of the journey permit it with work in the studio based on photographic notes that I revisit with more varied and more developed techniques, such as charcoal, ink and watercolour. These results can also be the starting point for larger-format oil paintings. I love the freedom of drawing while travelling and not having constraints. It's the opposite of what an illustrator does, both in terms of the choice of graphical tool and the choice of the subject. These are drawings made in a flash and at a precise moment, ones that I can feel when I come across a landscape or a fleeting scene, for example a decapitated tuna head lying on the ground in the Tsukiji fish market in Tokyo. Charcoal on coloured paper was what I used in that specific case.*

✏ http://www.loustal.com/

Other titles

Zenata 82 **(Alain Beaulet, 2013)**
Dessins d'ailleurs **(La Table Ronde, 2010)**
Les Horizons **(Alain Beaulet, 2008)**
Argentique, USA **(Alain Beaulet, 2007)**
Panoramas. Regards **(Casterman, 2007)**
À travers la ville **(Tricomia, 2007)**
Carnets de voyages: 2003-2005 **(Seuil, 2006)**
Carnets de voyages: 2000–2002 **(Seuil, 2003)**
Carnet de voyages: 1997–1999 **(Seuil, 2000)**
Carnet de voyages: 1981–1989 **(Seuil, 1997)**
Carnet de voyages: 1991–1996 **(Seuil, 1997)**
Zenata plage **(Les Humanoïdes Associés, 1989)**

Marc P.G. Berthier

Marc P.G. Berthier has produced three hundred covers and illustrated sixty works for Gallimard editions; he has written short stories and contributed to twenty art exhibitions. He is a cofounder of the magazine *Voiles et Voiliers* (1971) and the imprint *Voiles-Gallimard*. He edited the series "Le savoir marin" (1977).

My father, an amazing guy with smiling pale blue eyes, was such a good tennis player that it didn't take me long to realize that I'd never beat him in a single set. This turned out to be more than true. And when I was around fifteen I had the unfortunate habit of doing bad sketches instead of working on my Latin, and I've continued on this path for fifty years. That's a roundabout way of admitting that I've hit seventy.
Through a great stroke of luck—something that counts for a lot in this weird occupation—I have had the chance to meet a number of people who not only encouraged me, but also got me working. I owe a great deal to Pierre Marchand, who is now sailing in the clouds over the sea.
Since I was born by the water in North Brittany, where all the kids know how to scull before they learn grammar, quite naturally I started to sail and then to draw and do watercolours of boats, which would take me onto their crew. This must be a compulsive thing, because I don't know how many sketchbooks I have filled and how many boats of all kinds I have painted in watercolours almost everywhere in the maritime world.

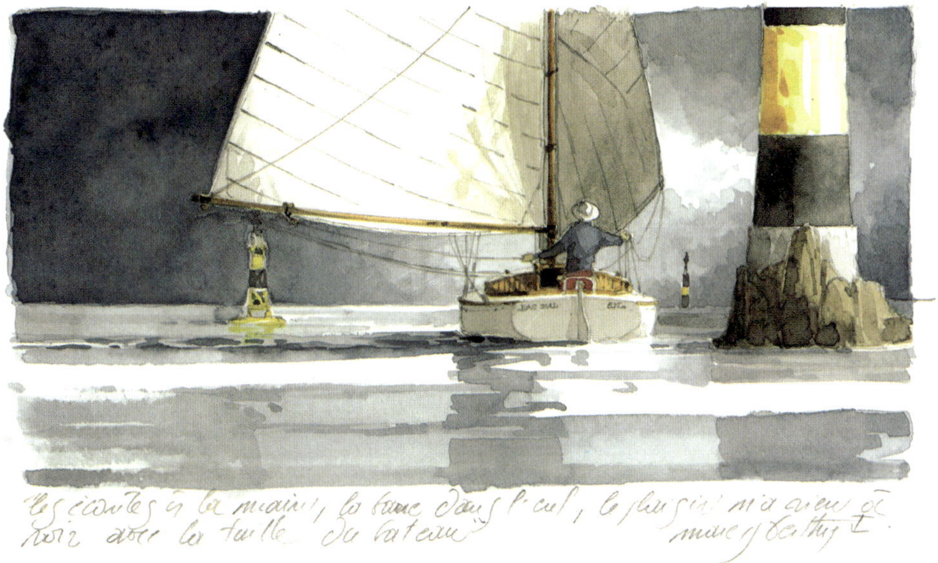

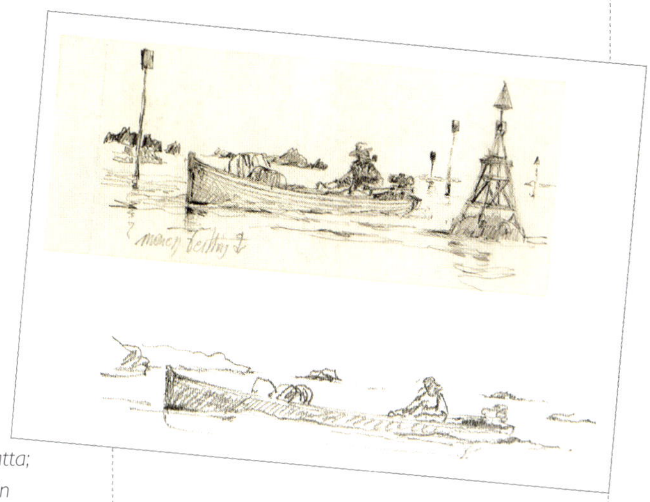

• Pour aller sur l'eau, *Gallimard, 2004.*
"I've been filling diaries for years, a brush in one hand, a sheet in the other," says Marc P.G. Berthier, who heads out to sea for the pleasure of drawing and sailing.

Why watercolour? Because it is like a regatta; right up until the last moment you can ruin everything. Every day, I go to my studio with that same feeling of being "not that far from happiness." I wouldn't claim any "artistic" worries. I'm not gripped by any hesitations. The word "inspiration" makes me laugh. We have ideas and we try to carry them out more or less successfully. That's it. I paint without asking myself questions that I wouldn't be able to provide answers to. In fact, I am just trying to paraphrase my friend Marin-Marie—"do it right," for fun.
I'm still learning to see. May the wind be always at your back.

✏ *Cinquante ans de voile pour le plaisir* (Gallimard, 1992)
La Coupe de l'América (Gallimard, 1992)
Aquarelles inédites sur l'eau et au bord de l'eau (Gallimard, 1988)

Official painters of the armed forces

France's Ministry of Defence awards the title "painter of the armed forces" to forty artists who devote their visual or pictorial activities to military subjects and enhance the reputation of the armed services (navy, air force and army). The official naval painters are elected by the jury of the Salon biennal de la Marine, which is held at the Musée de la Marine in Paris. Inheritors of this military and pictorial tradition, Marin-Marie was made a naval painter in 1934, Jacques Boullaire in 1959, Michel Bez in 1987, Titouan Lamazou in 2002 and Yann Arthus-Bertrand in 2005. Jacques Boullaire published his diaries in 1992, which provide accounts of journeys to French Polynesia in the 1950s: *Carnet de croquis* (Singapour, 1992) and *Tahiti: carnet de croquis* (Le Motu, 2006). Michel Bez produced watercolours of the "Jules Verne" expedition on board the *Belem*, which are collected in *Esquisses d'un voyage Amazonie-Martinique-Açores: une aventure cinématographique et scientifique* (Équinoxe, 2002). John Pendray, meanwhile, produced *Sur les traces de La Pérouse: carnets d'expédition à Vanikoro* (Sillage, 2006). France's geography, for example the Brittany coastline, has inspired Jean-Pierre Alaux, Jean-Pierre Arcile, Alain Bailhache, Michel Bellion, Michel Bez, Michel King, Ronan Olier and John Pendray. Le Télégramme published some of these Breton diaries, beginning in 1998 with *Carnet de bord: Ouessant-Molène* by Jacqueline Duroc. Recently, Jean-Pierre Alaux has continued his hunt for lighthouses in two travel diaries published by Elytis.

In 1931, an air force corps of painters, engravers and sculptors was created. Michel Montigné has been part of it since 1996, and Tiennick Kérével since 2008. Michel Montigné has published three works since 2003: *Carnet de voyage à Djibouti*, *Carnet de Guyane*, *Mauritanie* and *Maroc, Brésil (Salvador De Bahia): carnets de voyages* (Sépia).

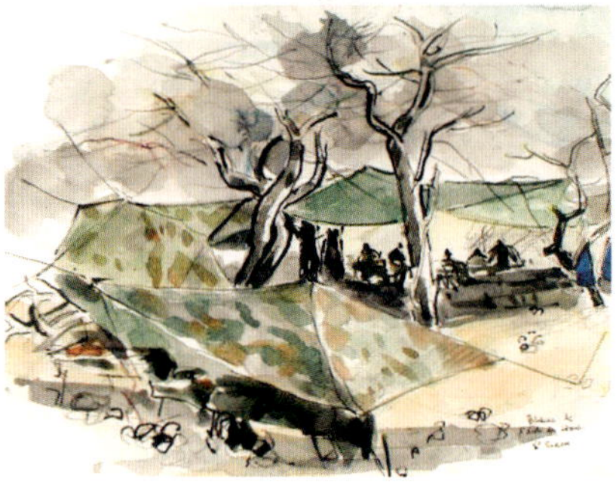

www.peintreofficieldelamarine.fr
www.peintresofficielsdelarmee.odexpo.com
http://peintresairespace.blogspot.fr/
Other titles
En escale en Pays bigouden: les peintres officiels de la Marine **(Le Télégramme, 2014)**
En escale en rade de Brest: les peintres officiels de la Marine **(Le Télégramme, 2013)**
Passeport pour Cordouan: le Versailles des mers **(Elytis, 2011)**
La Baie de Saint-Vaast-La-Hougue: sous le regard des peintres officiels de la Marine **(OREP, 2010)**
Marseille et la côte bleue **(Équinoxe, 2009)**
Carnets de voyages des peintres de la Marine **(Ouest-France/Marine nationale, 2008)**
Voyage au bout des phares **(Elytis, 2006)**
La Presqu'île de Crozon vue par les peintres officiels de la Marine **(Éditions des Équateurs, 2006)**
Tahiti: carnet de croquis **(Le Motu, 2006)**
Dieppe et sa région vues par les peintres officiels de la Marine **(Éditions des Équateurs, 2005)**

Michel Montigné

The self-taught Michel Montigné perfected his skills through sessions and encounters with many talented painters. A watercolourist and author of several travel books, his works can be seen in many art magazines and are part of private and public collections in France and abroad. He has played an important role in the creation and the running of several artists' societies (the French branch of the Institut européen de l'aquarelle, the Société française de l'aquarelle and the Association des peintres de l'armée) and has participated in a number of European watercolour congresses in Italy, Spain and Ireland. His painting is also the testimony and the deeper exploration of the life of a man who has followed an unusual path, one that led him from engineering studies at the École Nationale des Ponts et Chaussées to the army, where he held important responsibilities, and then on to the profession of painter. His taste for inquiring, constantly questioning and taking risks has particularly flourished through watercolour.

Carnet de voyage à Djibouti **(Sépia, 2003)**
Carnet de Guyane **(Sépia, 2004)**
Mauritanie, Maroc, Brésil (Salvador De Bahia): carnets de voyages **(Sépia, 2007)**

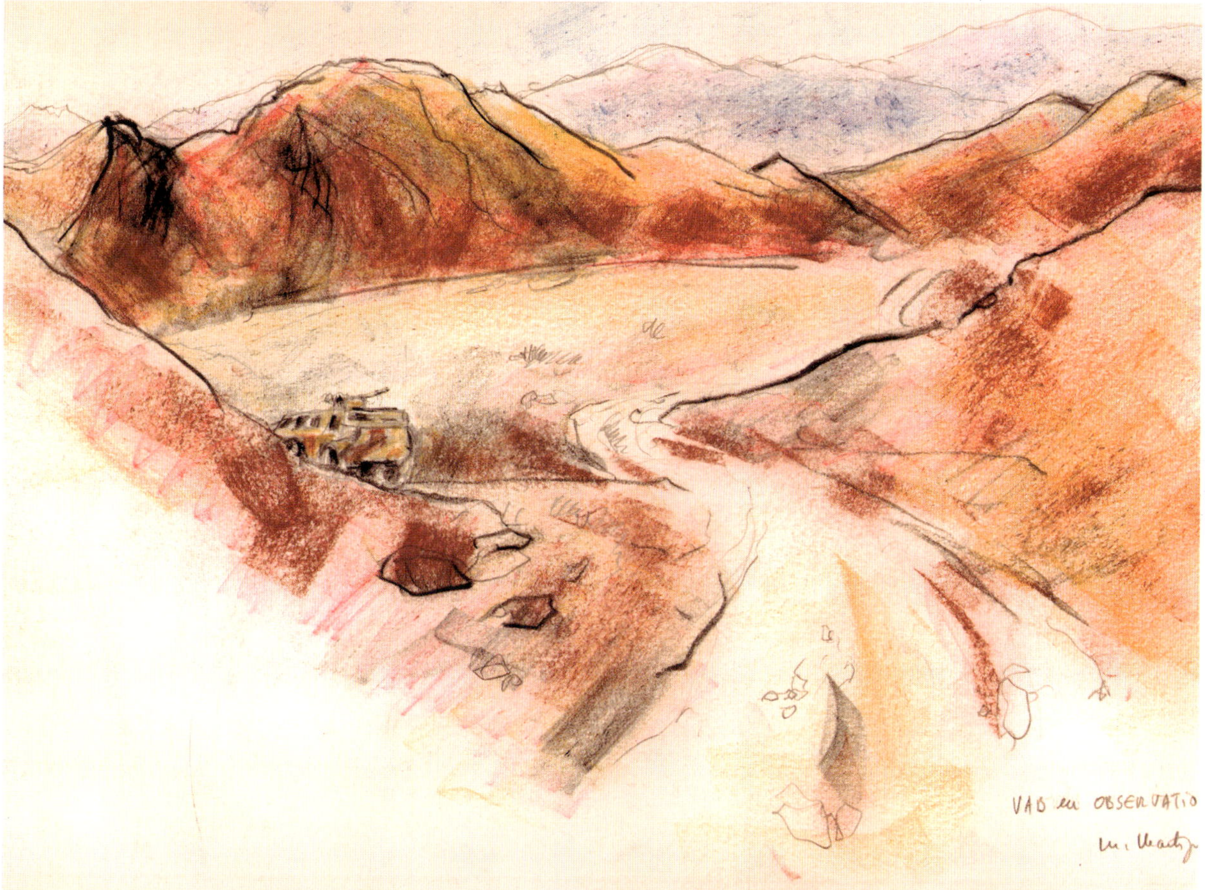

• *An official painter for the armed forces, Michel Montigné is a talented artist who expresses himself through watercolour, painting and photography. One of his latest diaries takes us on a discovery of Uzbekistan.*

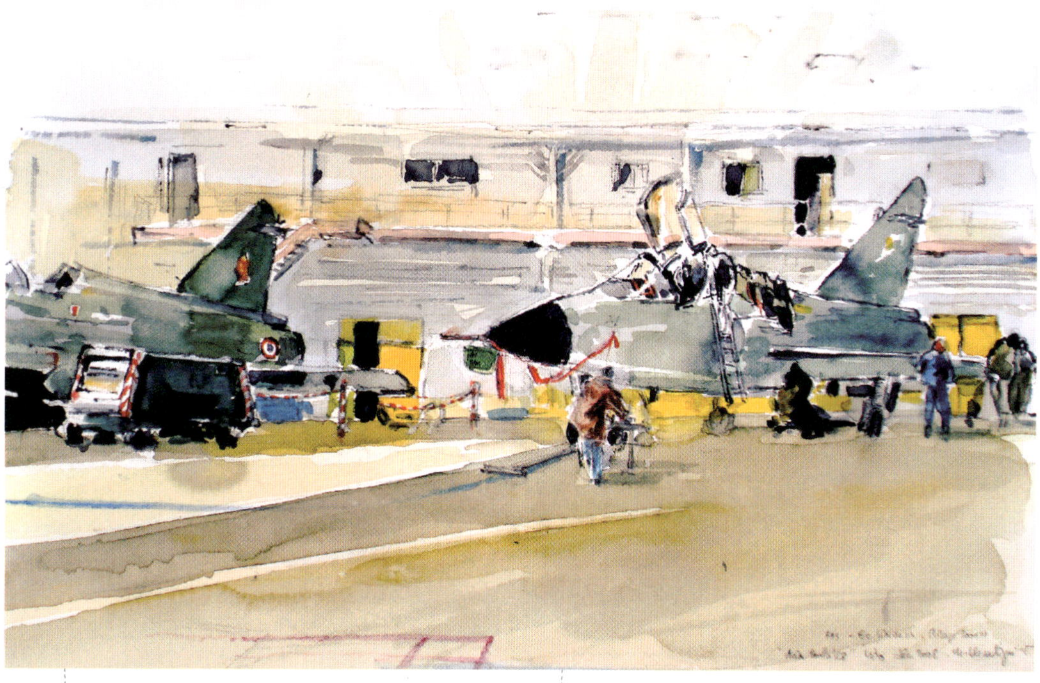

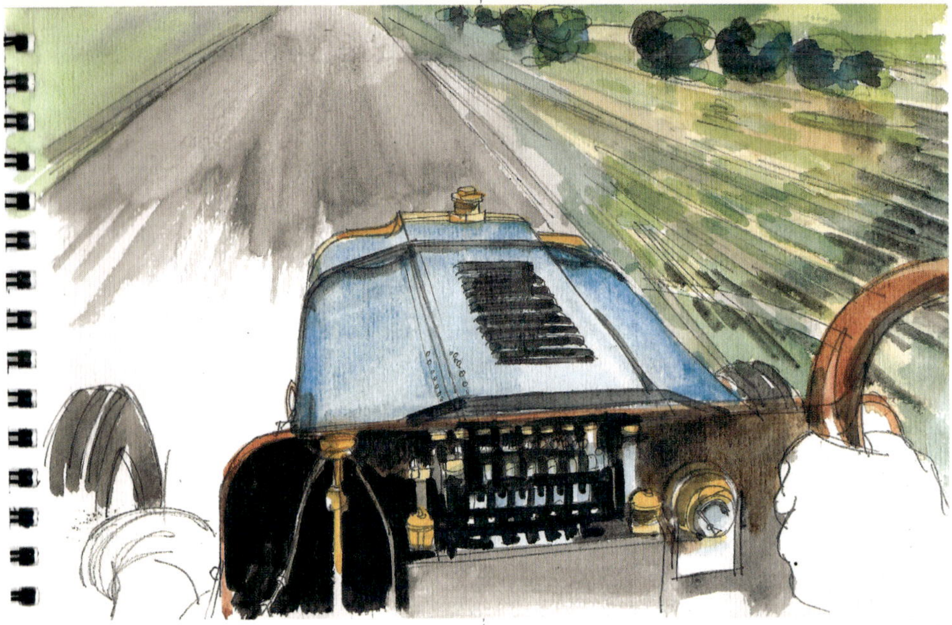

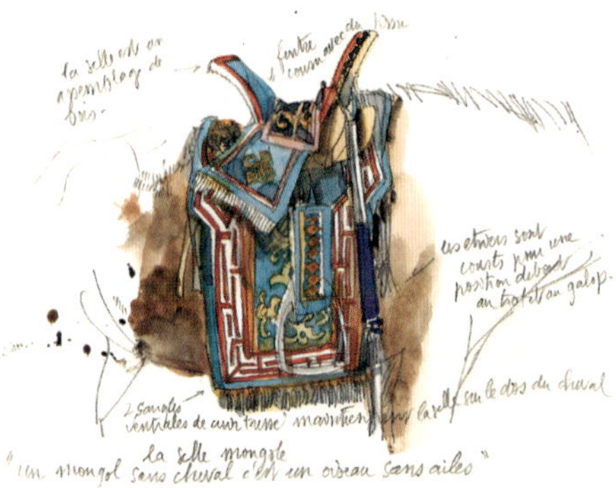

Alain Bouldouyre

For this serial globetrotting illustrator and sketch artist, a pencil, a diary and a box of paint are all he needs to get the most out of life. He illustrated his first travel diary when he was fifteen. He won a prize from the newspaper *Pilote* and set out to discover the world. His drawings of London earned him the drawing prize in France's national schools competition. After winning a Zellidja travel award, he shipped out to New York.

I went further North than the Arctic Circle (Murmansk and Nome), and then further South than Ushuaia (in "Magellania") and further to the East than Boulogne-Billancourt if you keep in mind that I circled the globe several times from East to West. In 1832, Eugène Delacroix was "a young painter with talent, spirit and an excellent character." King Louis-Philippe invited him to accompany the Duc de Mornay to Morocco. The expedition was a diplomatic success and Delacroix discovered the real East. He brought back sketchbooks that nourished and informed his work throughout his life. These notebooks are now kept at Chantilly. They are the "canon" for travel diaries, the essential reference. And that's my inspiration when I make travel diaries: being an (eternally) young man with talent (or at least a little), spirit (?) and an excellent character (something that is indispensable for any traveller!). Having studied the arts and drawing, I like my diaries to be shameless, amused and amusing—and, if possible, well drawn.

Transports peu communs (La Table Ronde, 2013)
Paris XVI (Mercure De France, 2009)
Carnet transcanadien: Toronto-Vancouver à bord du Canadien (Actes Sud, 2009)
Voyages au pays des salles obscures (Hoëbeke, 2006)
Carnets de France – coupe Gordon Bennett (Satcar, 2005)
My Paris sketchbook (Flammarion, 2003)
Mes carnets de Paris (Flammarion, 2002)
Lyon: carnet de chantiers (Horvath, 1993)

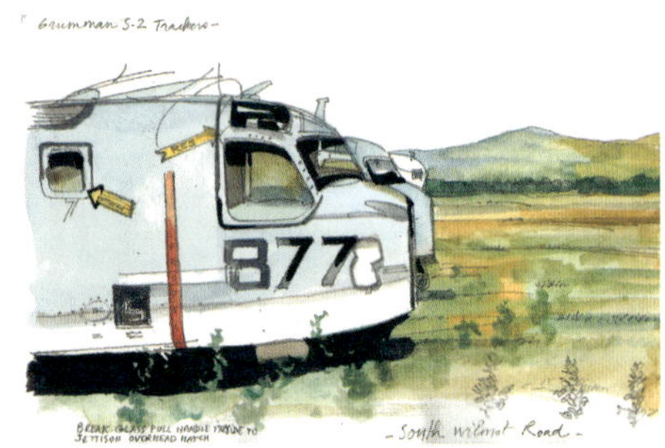

• Alain Bouldouyre criss-crosses the planet to draw the world with his precise pencil lines. "Even in tough countries, illustrations make the most beautiful reality."

Nicolas Vanier

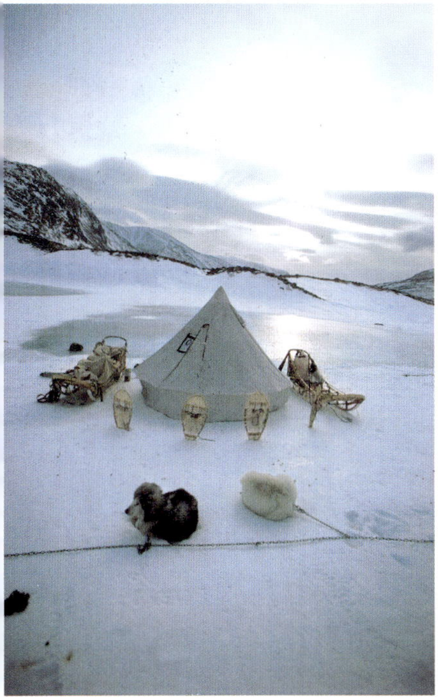

• *Indispensable companions on his adventures through great white landscapes, Nicolas Vanier's dogs are from a breed created especially for these expeditions.*

A writer, photographer and director, Nicolas Vanier been travelling in the regions of the far North for thirty years, sharing his passion for the "countries at the top." From his multiple epic journeys in Canada, Siberia, Alaska and Lapland, this insatiable traveller through cold climes has brought back may beautiful images and exciting accounts. Turning fifty did not make Nicolas hang up his snowshoes.

After a first expedition on foot across Lapland in 1982, and then a crossing of the Quebec-Labrador peninsular on sled, Nicolas and his crew headed in 1986 up the West of the American continent, from the Rockies to the Bering Strait. In 1990, he crossed Siberia from Lake Baikal to the Arctic Ocean over a period of eighteen months. In 1994, he went to live in the heart of the Canadian Rockies with his wife and daughter Montaine, who they nicknamed "the snow child." Two years later, he participated in the most difficult sled dog race, the Yukon Quest, which covers more than 1,600 km of northern Canada. In 1999, his "white odyssey" had him achieve the feat of crossing Canada from Alaska to Quebec—a distance of 8,600 km—with his dogs in less than one hundred days. It was a feat he repeated in 2005 and 2006 with his "Siberian Odyssey," which started on the banks of Lake Baikal and ended, 8,000 kilometres later, in Red Square in Moscow. After the success of *Dernier Trappeur* and *Loup*, Nicolas made *Belle et Sébastien,* a cinema adaptation of the legendary1960s series. For his latest expedition, "Wild Odyssey," he departed with ten dogs from the shores of the Pacific Ocean in Russia to reach Lake Baikal in mid-March 2014, at the end of a journey of 6,000 km through Manchuria, North Mongolia and Siberia's Sayan mountains. The "Wild Odyssey" was a challenge, a human adventure and a great preparation for Nicolas's entry into the two biggest dog-sled races, the Yukon Quest and the Iditarod, in winter 2014.

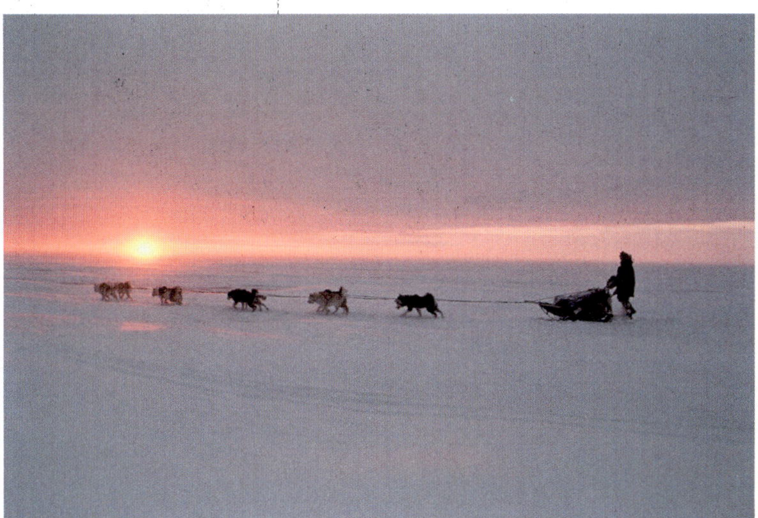

www.nicolasvanier.com
***Belle et Sébastien* (2013)**
***Loup* (2009)**
***Le Dernier Trappeur* (2004)**
***L'Odyssée sauvage* (M6.fr, 2014)**
***L'Odyssée sibérienne* (Fox Pathé Europa, 2006)**
***Chiens des neiges* (Fox Pathé Europa, 2006)**
***L'Odyssée blanche* (Fox Pathé Europa, 1999)**
***L'Enfant des neiges* (Fox Pathé Europa, 1995)**
***Le Voyageur du froid* (Fox Pathé Europa, 1992)**

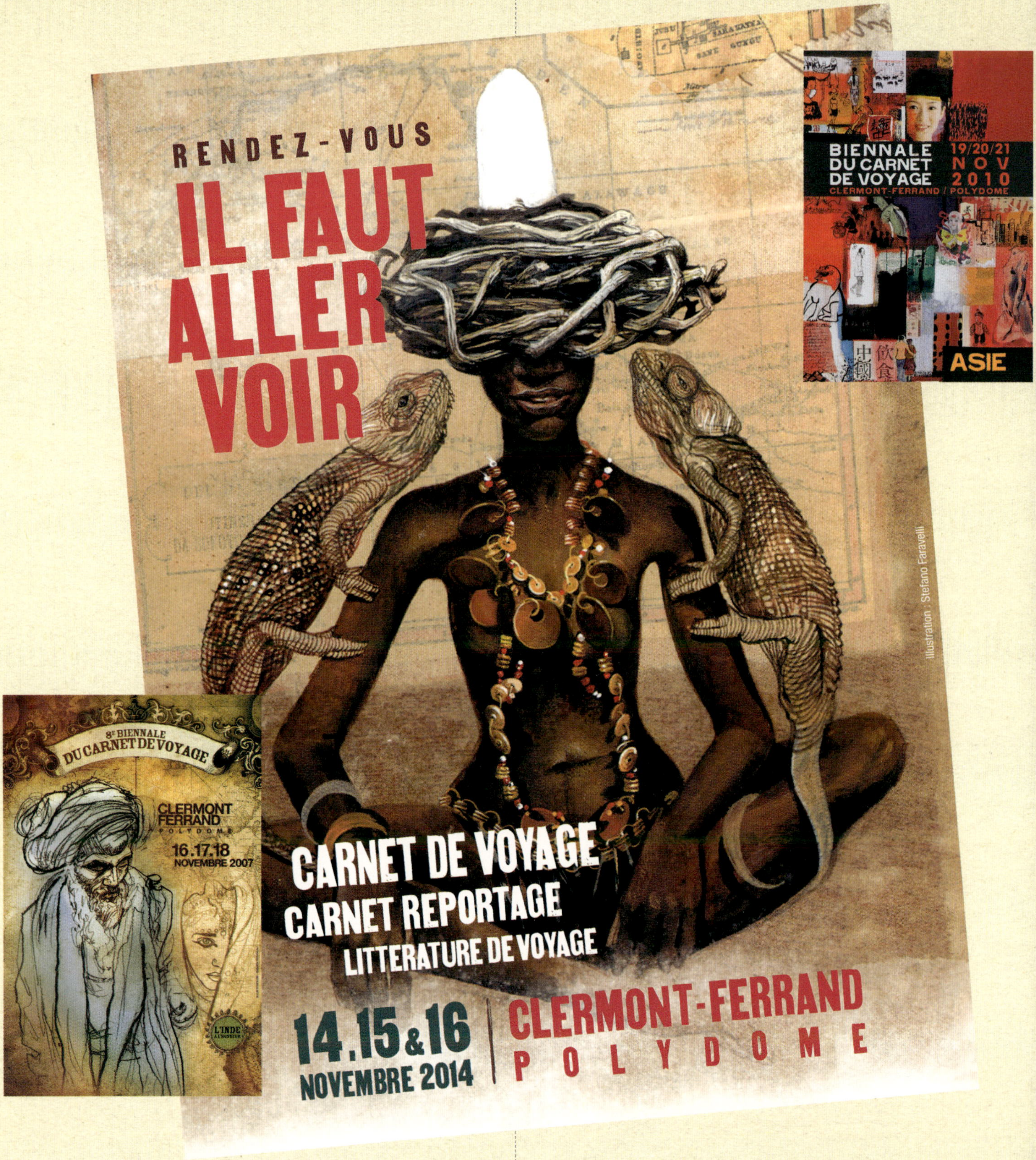
RENDEZ-VOUS
IL FAUT ALLER VOIR
CARNET DE VOYAGE
CARNET REPORTAGE
LITTERATURE DE VOYAGE
14.15&16
NOVEMBRE 2014
CLERMONT-FERRAND
POLYDOME
Illustration : Stefano Faravelli
BIENNALE
DU CARNET
DE VOYAGE
19/20/21
NOV
2010
CLERMONT-FERRAND / POLYDOME
ASIE
8e BIENNALE
DU CARNET DE VOYAGE
CLERMONT
FERRAND
POLYDOME
16.17.18
NOVEMBRE 2007

Clermont-Ferrand's Rendez-vous du carnet de voyage

A NATIONAL, ARTISTIC, AND CULTURAL EVENT SINCE 2000

The Rendez-vous du carnet de voyage, organized by the association Il faut aller voir, takes place every year in mid-November in the Polydome Congress Centre in Clermont-Ferrand. It brings together travel diary makers so that they can exhibit their works, whether they are focused on reportage, first-hand accounts or heritage.
Seasoned travellers also share their adventures with the public through lectures, screenings, debates and meetings, while the diary makers run workshops to inform visitors about the creation of travel diaries. Over a 4,000 m^2 space, there are 100 exhibiting diary makers (including 20 European artists among them), 10 screenings, 13 lectures, 28 workshops, and 10 exhibitions over Clermont-Ferrand and Auvergne.
In addition, international research seminars are organized by the Université Blaise-Pascal, Clermont-Ferrand II (UBP). Another highlight of the event, which is offered by the association with the support of its different partners, is the awarding of eleven prizes, including the Michelin "Cartes et Guides" Grand Prix du carnet de voyage, which is given to a published author, and the Prix du carnet de voyage étudiant, given in partnership with the Université Blaise-Pascal, which is open to any student enrolled in a French or overseas institution of higher learning.

• Created in 2000 by the association Il faut aller voir, the Rendez-vous du carnet de voyage is held annually in Clermont-Ferrand. Posters of the eighth, eleventh and fifteenth editions of the event, respectively by Damien Roudeau, Simon and Stefano Faravelli.

SCHOOLS' DAY

In partnership with the Centre Régional de Documentation Pédagogique of the Académie de Clermont-Ferrand, the Friday of the event is set aside for a programme for young people and, in particular, for students who participated in the national "Prix école-collège-lycée du carnet de voyage" contest (which covers paper and digital formats). More than 2,000 students are welcomed into screenings, workshops and guided tours, and they also have the chance to meet diary makers. The prize turns the travel diary into a teaching tool; 260 travel diaries are submitted to the contest. Arts and cultural education is at the heart of this initiative's approach, which aims to develop the creativity of the students using a transdisciplinary approach to the arts, sciences and humanities and to promote writing and visual or digital creativity. In 2011, the European Language Label (Europe Éducation Formation France) recognized travel diaries (whether in reportage or intermedia forms) as a creative and reflective pedagogical tool due to their ability to encourage the learning of languages and intercultural education, from kindergarten to university, via personal expression and the opportunity that they provide to practice visual arts through exchanges or international trips. This project has been run since 2001 by two organizations, namely the association Il faut aller voir and the Auvergne Centre Régional de Documentation Pédagogique (SCEREN-ministère de l'Éducation nationale), which since 2003 has been organizing a national teacher-training seminar entitled "Enseigner le carnet de voyage" ("Teaching Travel Diaries") as part of a training initiative for experts in the arts and culture that works with a group of forty trainee teachers. It complements the educational activities of the Prix école-collège-lycée du carnet de voyage. In 2013, Il faut aller voir was recognized in the "culture" category of the Fondation EDF's Trophées des associations.

www.rendezvous-carnetdevoyage.com

Bibliography

ABDELOUAHAB (Farid), *Ces merveilleux carnets de voyages*, Sélection du Reader's Digest, 2004.

ABDELOUAHAB (Farid), *Carnets de voyages en France*, Sélection du Reader's Digest, 2005.

ABDELOUAHAB (Farid), *L'Aventure des pôles: carnets de voyages de grands explorateurs*, Sélection du Reader's Digest, 2006.

ABDELOUAHAB (Farid), *Les Carnets de la mer*, Sélection du Reader's Digest, 2007.

ARGOD (Pascale), *Carnet de voyage sans frontières*, Reflets d'ailleurs, 2011.

BELLEC (François), *Carnets de voyage des peintres de la Marine*, Ouest-France/ Marine Nationale, 2002.

GERVEREAU (Laurent), *Inventer l'actualité: la construction imaginaire du monde par les médias internationaux*, La Découverte, 2004

LÉVI-STRAUSS (Claude), *Le Regard éloigné*, Plon, 1983.

MOEGLIN-DELCROIX (Anne), *Esthétique du livre d'artiste - 1960-1980: une introduction à l'art contemporain*, Le mot et le reste/ Bibliothèque nationale, 2012.

ROTH (Marianne), *De l'ailleurs à l'œuvre*, Peter Lang, 2007.

Carnets de voyage, le monde au bout d'un crayon, catalogue for the travel diaries exhibition at Musée de la Poste de Paris, 18 November 2010 to 23 April 2011, Snoeck Publishers, Gand (Belgium), 2010.

Les plus beaux carnets de voyage, *Le Monde 2*, n°20, July–August 2002.

ARGOD (Pascale). "Le carnet de voyage au fil du temps et du trait, un carnet de recherche à la rencontre des sciences et des arts," preface to *Carnets de voyage(s) issue of Revue 303*, Nantes, October 2010, p. 6-11.

ARGOD (Pascale). "Du carnet de voyage et de reportage: hybridité d'un genre album émergent," in *Nous voulons lire*, CRALEJ, June 2012.

ARGOD (Pascale). "Carnets de reportage graphique, de voyage et de société" in the special issue on the "image documentaire" of *InterCDI*, July–August 2008, p. 26-32.

ARGOD (Pascale). "Des carnets de patrimoine" in *ARGOS*, CRDP de Créteil/ SCEREN, June 2010, n°46-47, p. 44-51.

ARGOD (Pascale). "Carnets de voyage: regards et témoignages sur le monde et sur l'Autre," in *Hors Cadre*, n°5, October 2009, p. 6-9.

BOYER (Marc), "Comment étudier le tourisme?" in *Ethnologie française*, vol. 32, 2002–2003.

ARGOD (Pascale). "Le carnet de voyage: approches historique et sémiologique," doctoral thesis supervised by T. Lancien, Université Michel-de-Montaigne Bordeaux III, 10 December 2009.

Acknowledgements

MY WARMEST THANKS

to the creators, artists, travel diary makers, authors, painters, illustrators and directors who are all passionate about this art
Edmond Baudoin, Cathy Beauvallet, Charles Berberian, Marc P.G. Berthier and the Peintres officiels de la Marine, Alain Bouldouyre, Georges Bronner, Françoise Caillette-Deneubourg, Gabriel Campanario and the Urban sketchers, Patrick Chappatte, Damien Chavanat, Denis Clavreul, Arnaud d'Aunay, Philippe Delord, Bertrand de Miollis, Vincent Desplanche, Bastien Dubois, Claire Dupoizat and the Carnettistes tribulants, Stefano Faravelli, Jacques Ferrandez, Karen Guillorel and Yann Minh, Elsie Herberstein, Noelle Herrenschmidt, John Hirvois, Giancarlo Iliprandi, Alan Johnston, Titouan and Zoé Lamazou, Stéphanie Ledoux, Catherine Legrand, Frédérique Le Lous Delpech, Eni Looka, David Lopez, Loustal, Lizzie Napoli, Antonia Neyrins, Julien Malland, Claire and Reno Marca, Emmanuel Michel, Fabrice Moireau, Michel Montigné and the Peintres officiels des Armées, Max Pam, Jean Pattou, Bruno Pilorget, Damien Roudeau, Julie Sarperi, Simon, Jean-Charles Trebbi, Troub's, Gwenaëlle Trolez, Emmanuelle Troy and Nicolas Vanier,

to the publishers, producers and distributors for their kind help and their creative work on travel diaries
Françoise Chabbert (Gallimard/Nouveaux-Loisirs), Michel Francillon and Pascale Fontaine (Reflets d'ailleurs), Xavier Mouginet (Elytis), Marc Wiltz (Magellan & Cie), Sandrine Mercier (Radio France), Fabrice Drouzy (Libération voyages), Zahia Hafs (Jalan Publications), Frédéric Houssin and Anne Bouin (Albin Michel Jeunesse), Sabine Bledniak (Alternatives), Vincent Henry and Coralie Dupont (La Boîte à bulles), Laurence Corre (Gédéon Média Group and Gédéon Programmes), Florence Defos du Rau and Patricia Martine (Passiflore), Olivia Robert and Nicolas Vanier (TAIGA Vanier), Brigitte Gautrand, Christel Masson, Jean-Michel Coblence, Vincent Petit and Charlotte Gallimard (Casterman), Thierry Théault (Éditions du Pacifique), Roger Béracochéa (Zellidja), Franck Bourgeron (*La Revue dessinée*), Jérôme Le Bihan (Édilarge/Ouest-France), Quentin Leeds (*XXI*), Eva Tejédor (Eyrolles), Thierry Dobé (galerie Vue-sur-mer, Alain Beaulet, Atlantica, Cornélius, Équinoxe, Glénat, Ibis rouge, Jeanne Laffitte, Françoise de Maulde (La Table Ronde), L'Association, Nomades, Parole et Silence, Sepia, Fox Pathé Europa and M6.fr, Montparnasse multimédia, Edizioni Nuages (Italy), EDT (Italy), De Agostini (Italy), Les Heures Bleues (Quebec, Canada), Lorraine Vaillancourt (Quebec, Canada),

to Éditions Alternatives and Gallimard for carrying out this project and to Denis Couchaux, without forgetting
The IFAV team of Jean-Pierre Frachon, Michel Renaud, Michel Francillon, Gérard Gaillard and Anaïs Sève, who worked on making our Rendez-vous du carnet de voyage happen, the team at CRDP d'Auvergne – SCEREN – Ministère de l'Éducation nationale and the Académie de Clermont-Ferrand (Delphine Duhamel) for their national teaching initiatives, the CLEMI (Isabelle Martin, Nicole Pavoni and Bruno Rigotard), the Service Culture et Relations Internationales of Université de Bordeaux IV (Bernard Layan and Dominique Vinet), the IUT Tech de Co, the MICA research team at Bordeaux III (Anne Beyaert-Geslin, Thierry Lancien, Didier Paquelin, Alexandre Peraud, Philippe Viallon), the ESPE d'Aquitaine, Université Blaise-Pascal de Clermont-Ferrand II for their academic innovations (Viviane Alary, Catherine Morgan-Proux), the MSH of Clermont-Ferrand (Mauricette Fournier, Stéphane Gomis) and Bordeaux (Alain Bouldoires, Fabien Reix) for their academic innovations, and Agence 2E2F for its European educational projects.

THE ART OF SKETCHING: 400 YEARS OF TRAVEL DIARIES

ORIGINAL TITLE: L'ART DU CARNET DE VOYAGE

AUTHOR: PASCALE ARGOD

TRANSLATOR: TOM CORKETT

ISBN: 978-84-15967-76-7

PROMOPRESS IS A COMMERCIAL BRAND OF:
PROMOTORA DE PRENSA INTERNACIONAL S.A.
124 AUSIAS MARCH STREET
08013 BARCELONA, SPAIN
TEL.: 0034 932451464
FAX: 0034 932654883
EMAIL: INFO@PROMOPRESS.ES
WWW.PROMOPRESSEDITIONS.COM
FACEBOOK: PROMOPRESS EDITIONS
TWITTER: PROMOPRESS EDITIONS @PROMOPRESSED

FIRST PUBLISHED IN ENGLISH: 2016

DESIGN AND LAYOUT: DENIS COUCHAUX
COVER DESIGN: SPREAD: DAVID LORENTE WITH THE COLLABORATION OF BET PUIGBÒ

PRINTED IN CHINA

Photo credits

p. 2 © Loustal (top); p. 2 (middle), p. 41 © Malland-Alternatives/Gallimard; p. 2 (bottom), p. 46-47, p. 80-81, p. 94 (middle and bottom), p. 95, p. 127 © Lamazou-Gallimard; p. 3 (top), p. 125 (right) © Michel-Elytis; p. 3 (middle), p. 93, p. 133 © Moireau; p. 3 (bottom), p. 60 (left, top) © Ledoux; p. 4, p. 61 © Faravelli-EDT; p. 5 (top) © Clavreul-Gallimard; p. 5 (bottom), p. 104-105, p. 114 (top) © Pilorget; p. 9 © De Agostini Picture Library/A. Dagli Orti/Bridgeman Images; p. 10, p. 15, p. 18, p. 26, p. 27 © Bridgeman Images; p. 11 © The Stapleton Collection/Bridgeman Images; p. 13, p. 19 © Giraudon/Bridgeman Images; p. 14 © National Library of Australia, Canberra, Australia/Bridgeman Images; p. 16 © Agnew's, London/Bridgeman Images; p. 17, p. 42 © Christie's Images/Bridgeman Images; p. 21, p. 22, p. 36 © Archives Charmet/Bridgeman Images; p. 24 © RMN-Grand Palais, musée Guimet, Paris; p. 31, p. 38 © Pam; p. 33 Digital image © 2014, The Museum of Modern Art, New York/Photo Scala, Florence; p. 34 © Centre Pompidou, MNAM-CCI, dist. RMN-Grand Palais/A. Rzepka; p. 39 © Centre Pompidou, MNAM-CCI, dist. RMN-Grand Palais/J.-C. Planchet; p. 40 © Pattou; p. 43 © Fonds Ella Maillart, musée de l'Élysée, Lausanne; p. 44 © Dobé-Vue-sur-mer (left); p. 44 (right) © Loustal-Alain Beaulet; p. 45 Bohl Raverdy-Alternatives/Gallimard; p. 46, p. 154 © Bouldouyre; p. 48 © Le Lous Delpech; p. 49 (left) © Looka (left); p. 49 (right, top) © La Revue Dessinée; p. 49 (right, bottom) © XXI; p. 50-51 © Hirvois-Passiflore; p. 52, p. 141 © Dubois-Reflets d'ailleurs; p. 53, p. 111 © Guillorel; p. 56 © Marca-Béliane; p. 57, p. 82-83, p. 86 (bottom) © de Miollis-Gallimard; p. 58 © Delord; p. 59 © Lamazou; p. 60 (right, top) © Neyrins; p. 60 (left, bottom), p. 103 © Johnston-Gallimard; p. 62 (left), p. 136 © Caillette-Deneubourg-Magellan & Cie; p. 62 (right, bottom), p. 137 © Ledoux-Elytis; p. 63 © Michel-Éditions EM (top); p. 63 (bottom), p. 77, p. 79 © Herberstein-Jalan Publications; p. 64, p. 124 © Iliprandi-Nuages; p. 65, p. 88-89 © Beauvallet-Gallimard; p. 66, p. 84, p. 87, p. 126, p. 139 © Éditions de La Martinière, an imprint of EDLM, Paris; p. 67 (top), p. 130 © Simon-Alternatives/Gallimard; p. 67 (bottom), p. 138 © Trolez-Magellan & Cie; p. 68 © McMenemy-Casterman, p. 148-149 © Ferrandez-Casterman, with the kind permission of the authors and Éditions Casterman; p. 68-69, p. 132 (bottom) © Faravelli; p. 73, p. 78 © Paysannes, La Boîte à bulles and les Carnettistes tribulants; p. 74 © Herberstein-Albin Michel Jeunesse; p. 75 © Beauvallet-Jalan Publications; p. 76, p. 135 © Roudeau-Parole et Silence; p. 81 (bottom), p. 114 (bottom) © Salaam Palestine, La Boîte à bulles and Pilorget; p. 85, p. 151 © Berthier-Gallimard; p. 86, p. 94 (top) © Elytis; p. 90, p. 134 © Napoli-Équinoxe; p. 91, p. 92, p. 98-99, p. 122 © d'Aunay-Gallimard; p. 96 © Ouest-France; p. 97 © Les Carnettistes tribulants; p. 100, p. 129 © Urban sketchers-Eyrolles; p. 101, p. 123 © Delord-Gallimard; p. 102 © Éditions Jeanne-Laffitte; p. 104-105, p. 114 (ht) © Pilorget p. 106 © Troy/photo F. Ourth; p. 107 © Troy/photo O. Got (top), © Troy (middle and bottom); p. 108 © Giraudeau-Éditions Montparnasse; p. 108-109 © Herberstein-Gedeon Media Group/Gedeon Programmes/Arte GEIE; p. 110, p. 155 © Vanier-Taiga/Fox Pathé Europa/M6.fr; p. 111, p. 142 © Guillorel and Minh; p. 115 © de Miollis-Gedeon Media Group/Gedeon Programmes/Arte GEIE; p. 116 (top) © Beauvallet-Lorraine Vaillancourt; p. 116 (bottom) © Beauvallet; p. 117 © Herberstein-Seuil; p. 118 © Chavanat-Jalan Publications; p. 119 © Herrenschmidt-Gallimard; p. 120 © Clavreul-Équinoxe; p. 121 © Johnston; p. 125 (left) © Michel; p. 128 © Desplanche; p. 131 © Carnettistes tribulants-Alternatives/Gallimard; p. 132 (top) © Faravelli-Gallimard; p. 139 © "Aubanel," an imprint of Minerva, Geneva; p. 140 © Chappatte; p. 143 © Lopez; p. 144 © Sarperi; p. 145 © Troy/photo C. Amat; p. 146 © Baudoin and Troub's-L'Association, 2011; p. 147 © Baudouin and Troub's; p. 148 © Berberian; p. 150 © Loustal-La Table Ronde; p. 152 © Montigné; p. 156 © Association Il faut aller voir, illustration by Simon (top), S. Faravelli (middle) and D. Roudeau (bottom).

© chapter openings: p. 6 © Giraudon/Bridgeman Images; p. 28 © Malland-Alternatives/Gallimard; p. 54 © Lamazou; p. 70 © Moireau; p. 112 © Faravelli-Gallimard.
© special mentions: p. 34 Schwitters, *Photographie issue d'un carnet légué par Mme Kandinsky*, 1924 © Adagp, Paris 2014; p. 36 Méheut, *Soldats endormis*, 1915 © Adagp, Paris 2014; p. 39 Barceló, *Dessin issu d'un carnet de voyage réalisé en Afrique*, 1995-1996 © Adagp, Paris 2014.